FILMMAKERS SERIES
edited by
ANTHONY SLIDE

WITHDRAWN

Showdown at High Noon

Witch-Hunts, Critics, and the End of the Western

Jeremy Byman

Filmmakers Series, No. 111

The Scarecrow Press, Inc.
Lanham, Maryland • Toronto • Oxford
2004

SCARECROW PRESS, INC.

Published in the United States of America
by Scarecrow Press, Inc.
A wholly owned subsidiary of
The Rowman & Littlefield Publishing Group, Inc.
4501 Forbes Boulevard, Suite 200, Lanham, Maryland 20706
www.scarecrowpress.com

PO Box 317
Oxford
OX2 9RU, UK

Copyright © 2004 by Jeremy Byman

All rights reserved. No part of this publication may be reproduced,
stored in a retrieval system, or transmitted in any form or by any
means, electronic, mechanical, photocopying, recording, or otherwise,
without the prior permission of the publisher.

British Library Cataloguing in Publication Information Available

Library of Congress Cataloging-in-Publication Data

Byman, Jeremy, 1944–
  Showdown at high noon : witch-hunts, critics, and the end of the Western /
Jeremy Byman.
      p. cm.
  Includes bibliographical references and index.
  ISBN 0-8108-4998-4 (pbk. : alk. paper)
  1. High noon (Motion picture) I. Title.
  PN1997.H484B96 2004
  791.43'72—dc22

                                                                    2004000190

∞^{TM} The paper used in this publication meets the minimum requirements
of American National Standard for Information Sciences—Permanence of
Paper for Printed Library Materials, ANSI/NISO Z39.48-1992.
Manufactured in the United States of America.

To Leonard Byman, who loved Westerns—
and who took two small boys to see the new
Gary Cooper picture one late summer day in 1952

Contents

Part V   The Film As Film

Preface

This is a biography of sorts, the story of a film caught between popular admiration and critical dismissal.

To ordinary, nonspecialist audiences, *High Noon* has always been a masterpiece. But to most film theorists, it is both beneath contempt and below the radar. It is never even mentioned, much less analyzed, since it was barred from the "canon" forty years ago—even before the canon was fully formed. The inspiration for a full-length study of a film I had admired since childhood came from discovering this remarkable disconnect while attending the graduate cinema studies program at New York University.

For those caught up in the battle between post-theorists and grand theorists—the adherents of neo-Marxist, psychoanalytic, feminist, structural, and semiotic approaches—a struggle that was essentially over by 1962 must seem like a flashback to prehistoric times. But it was a revealing—if one-sided—dispute, and not only because the winners, those who thought that only the director's vision counts, still control the way films are analyzed and evaluated, judging by the sheer number of books and university courses devoted to directors alone.

These winners, the auteurists, and their successors may have ignored *High Noon*, but others have not. A great many people—typically, academics outside cinema studies departments—have written about *High Noon* in books, journal articles, and essays, and in this book I consider and contrast many of their ideas and offer a few of my own. It is as though dozens of clear-sighted people were examining an elephant so large they could see only one part of it at a time. I like to imagine I have borrowed Fred Zinnemann's crane and pulled back to see the elephant whole—though I hope I'm not like Gary Cooper, finding out at the end of the crane shot that I'm all alone.

For those who still care about the issues raised in this long-ago battle, *High Noon* has always been, as the film studies people say, a "site of contestation"—political, stylistic, and thematic. The traditional view of the film's importance has been that it reflects both the post-World War II ideological battles between the political witch-hunters and the Hollywood Left as well as the struggle for control of the Western genre between the traditionalists and the makers of so-called anti-Westerns.

In film language, the first of these battles is an argument about "context"—the assumption that the social and political conditions under which the film was made determine its meaning. The second is a claim about "intertextualism"—that the evolution of the genre and changes in film practice more generally determine its meaning. This book examines both these disputes but also considers the "text"—the film itself, apart from these alleged influences—on the chance that the filmmakers might have made something new.

There seems to be no agreement on any aspect of the film, especially its "meaning"—as though it must have only one. As George Lipsitz notes of more conventional Hollywood efforts, "successful commercial films often open up wounds and air out social tensions in order to contain them. But they always run the risk that the problems exposed will have more meaning to audiences than the ways in which the film 'resolves' them. . . . The range of positions presented in films allows viewers to experiment with many different points of view."[1] *High Noon* was a successful commercial film, but it was attempting not to "contain" social tensions but to expose them.

Following Noel Carroll's definition, this book is a work of film interpretation rather than film theory. "Film theory," Carroll says, "speaks of the general case, whereas film interpretation deals with problematic or puzzling cases, or with the highly distinctive cases of cinematic masterworks. Film theory tracks the regularity and the norm, while film interpretation find its natural calling in dealing with the deviation, with what violates the norm or with what exceeds it or what re-imagines it."[2]

Nevertheless, though I make no theoretical claims, the book, focusing on a single movie, is, broadly speaking, written in the tradition of the mid-level, research-based work of Carroll and David

Bordwell, who distinguish their "neo-formalist" approach from the nonempirical approach of those who rely on psychoanalytic, Marxist, or other overarching schema.[3] In adopting this stance, I have tried to combine thematic analysis with a consideration of the historical background of the film and of the constraints of filmmaking in Hollywood.

My hope is that I have contributed to film theory by usefully applying several approaches to a single case—something not often done in film studies, where, as Kristin Thompson notes, the usual method in the study of single films is for the analyst to select one approach—perhaps from literary studies, or psychoanalysis, or linguistics, or philosophy—and "then select . . . a film that seems suited to displaying that method." The result is not a test of the method but a confirmation of the method, as well as, often, a reductive approach to the film to get it to fit the "pattern" required by the approach.[4] She urges an approach that "focuses on more of the work's formal subtleties and tackles the work from more than one standpoint."[5] This is what I have tried to do.

High Noon, as I hope to show throughout this book, is a film with many popular interpretations but one dominant "meaning" that fits no one's easy approach. That is so because the creators of the film, Carl Foreman, Fred Zinnemann, Stanley Kramer, and Elmo Williams, played the "defamiliarization" game—they took what was familiar and made it wholly new and disturbing.

NOTES

1. George Lipsitz, *Rainbow at Midnight* (Urbana: University of Illinois Press, 1994), 280.

2. Noel Carroll, "Prospects for Film Theory: A Personal Assessment," in *Post-Theory*, ed. David Bordwell and Noel Carroll (Madison: University of Wisconsin Press, 1996), 42–43.

3. David Bordwell, "Historical Poetics of Cinema," in *The Cinematic Text: Methods and Approaches*, ed. R. Barton Palmer (New York: AMS Press, 1989), 369–98.

4. Kristin Thompson, *Breaking the Glass Armor* (Princeton: Princeton University Press, 1988), 3–4.

5. Thompson, *Breaking the Glass Armor*, 34–35. Ian Jarvie provides a useful set of rules for this kind of analysis in *Philosophy of the Film* (New York: Routledge & Kegan Paul, 1987), 293.

Acknowledgments

This book would have been much harder to write without the help of my wife, Lynn Hamilton, who brought her years of experience as an English instructor to bear on the text through several drafts. She also bore the brunt of my daily inspirations and listened patiently as I developed my ideas.

My thanks go also to Lionel Chetwynd and Shirin Amini of Whidbey Island Films, who helped me obtain access to Carl Foreman's insider's view of the making of *High Noon*, and to the staffs of the Academy of Motion Picture Arts and Sciences Fairbanks Center for Motion Picture Study and of the UCLA Special Collections at Young Library for their assistance. My editor, Anthony Slide, brought his encyclopedic knowledge of Hollywood to bear on numerous questions and helped me obtain still photographs from the making of the film.

I also had help from readers.

My sister, Abigail Byman, is a lawyer who helped not only by reviewing the text in painstaking detail but also by searching out legal opinion on copyright questions. I also received suggestions from two friends and colleagues who teach at East Carolina University in Greenville, North Carolina: Tinsley Yarborough, who analyzes the American legal system by day and thrills to the exploits of movie gunfighters and their more direct approach to law and order at night, and Maurice Simon, with whom I've been talking politics and the movies for three decades. My brother, David Byman, who first saw *High Noon* with me half a century ago, has talked about the movie with me off and on ever since.

Grateful acknowledgment is made to the following for permission to quote from or reprint previously published material:

Eve Williams-Jones, for permission to quote from a letter written by Carl Foreman to Bosley Crowther on August 7, 1952. Copyright © The Carl Foreman Estate.

Robin Wood, for permission to reprint part of his essay on "Rio Bravo" in *Howard Hawks: American Artist,* edited by Jim Hillier and Peter Wollen (London: British Film Institute, 1996).

The *New York Times*, for permission to reprint the review of *High Noon* by Bosley Crowther, July 25, 1952. Copyright © 1952 by The New York Times Company.

The Academy of Motion Picture Arts and Sciences Fairbanks Center for Motion Picture Study, for permission to reprint seven still photographs from the set of *High Noon*.

Part I

THE WORLD OF *HIGH NOON*

Chapter 1

Showdown

In a small, dusty Western town, three gunmen are waiting at the train station for their leader, who is returning to take vengeance on the United States marshal who sent him to prison. The just-retired marshal, married that morning to a Quaker woman who has forsworn violence, decides he must fight the killers and sets out to form a posse. But one by one the townspeople, each for his own reasons, decline to help him and urge him to leave, and he is left to shoot it out with the killers alone.

High Noon stands among the handful of movies that have altered films and filmmaking in fundamental ways. Its production was nearly a victim of the post-World War II "red scare," and it came to be seen as the foremost artistic comment on the period. No Western has ever upset Western lovers so much—partly because a favorite star seemed to be rejecting everything he had done before—and none has so influenced the Westerns that followed. It became the favorite target for a new theory of film that would eventually help to foster university film studies. Because of its notoriety, it would indirectly help build new reputations among directors of Westerns. And it changed the way movies were made, giving heart to the proponents of independent filmmaking.

Few American movies have come to mean so many things to so many people—and few have won so much praise and suffered so much criticism simultaneously.

High Noon is not a documentary, though at times it looks like one. It is set in the West and plays like a Western, but it upsets our preconceived notions about the movie West. It is more about the state of things when it was made, 1951—the politics, the arguments about the way a society should operate and about the way men and women should relate to each other—than it is about the nineteenth-century West. It has endured because it is a remarkably direct and terse statement of a remarkably complex, layered set of themes. From its release a half-century ago, on July 25, 1952, it has become so well-known in America and around the world that it is the "gold standard" when one needs a way to talk about courage in the face of popular hostility and fearful threats.

As Fred Zinnemann, its director, noted in his autobiography forty years after the film's release, "Interestingly, its popularity waxes and wanes; people become very aware of it at times of decision, when a major national or political crisis is threatening."[1]

Not long before President Bill Clinton left office, a reporter asked him what movie he would suggest his successor, George W. Bush, watch before his inauguration. Mr. Clinton recommended his favorite film, *High Noon*.[2] Mr. Bush evidently took the symbolism to heart. He gave Japanese Prime Minister Koizumi, struggling against his country's economic decline and his party's resistance to change, a poster of the film.[3]

Sometimes all that is needed is the picture of a drawn and increasingly desperate Gary Cooper in his dark pinstripe suit, walking alone down that dusty street. Only four years after the film was shown in Britain, Prime Minister Anthony Eden was portrayed as Cooper's Marshal Kane in an editorial cartoon during the 1956 Suez crisis. In March 1978, *Esquire* magazine used the walk down the street to illustrate a cover story on individuals who had single-handedly taken on powerful corporations.[4] Two years later, in 1980, Solidarity, the Polish political party that eventually forced the country's communist government from power, used the picture on its badges and posters—though the party subtly emphasized that its opposition was nonviolent by airbrushing out Cooper's gun and replacing it with a ballot. By the time the country enjoyed its first free election in decades, Cooper's picture was everywhere.[5]

In America, for an elected politician to go against his own party is to invite the comparison. Before New York Republican Congressman Peter King voted against the impeachment of President Clinton, he appeared on ABC's "*Nightline*" to explain his action, comparing himself to Cooper and "expressing no regrets about his decision."[6]

The meaning of the image seemed so self-evident, it never required analysis. You simply used it, and assumed, rightly, that everybody would know what you were trying to convey. Fifty years on, *High Noon*'s place in popular culture seems assured.

The story is deceptively simple. It is told in less than an hour and a half and rarely strays far from that hot, dusty main street in Hadleyville, a small town in post-Civil War New Mexico.

Three gunmen ride into town, past the marshal's office to the train station. They ask the stationmaster about the noon train. Inside the office, just-retired marshal Will Kane (Cooper) is being married to beautiful young Quaker Amy Fowler (Grace Kelly). The clock reads 10:35 A.M. We will see clocks and lonely railroad tracks many more times as noon approaches.

When the wedding party learns that Frank Miller has been pardoned and is returning on the noon train, Will and Amy are hustled out of town. But Will turns around almost immediately, explaining to his pacifist wife that he has to face these killers in town, where he can assemble a posse. She tells him she won't wait to see him killed, that she will leave on the same noon train.

Kane begins a search for help, but none of his friends will stand with him—not the judge (Otto Kruger) who married them, not his friend the town councilman (Harry Morgan), who hides in his bedroom while his wife tells Kane he is at church, not the crippled ex-marshal (Lon Chaney Jr.) who had been Kane's mentor, not Kane's young deputy (Lloyd Bridges), who is angry at Kane because the older man didn't recommend him for the job. Later, the deputy will be so anxious to get rid of Kane, he will try to force him onto a horse and be knocked out in a bruising fistfight. One man volunteers to help, but he backs out when he learns Kane is unable to get anyone else.

As Amy waits for her train at the hotel, she learns that her husband is widely hated; many anticipate good times when Miller (Ian McDonald) and his gang return. Kane is reminded of that fact when no one in the bar will help either. The deputy is the new lover of Helen (Katy Jurado), a sophisticated Mexican businesswoman who owns the general store. She used to be Frank Miller's "woman," and then Kane's, and it is clear she is still torn between love for Kane and anger at him when he comes to warn her about Miller. When the deputy reminds her that Miller is dangerous, she sells her share in the store and prepares to leave on the train.

The ultimate betrayal comes when Kane interrupts the church service in search of support. One by one the men in the congregation give perfectly good reasons why they shouldn't help Kane. Finally, the marshal's good friend, the mayor (Thomas Mitchell), urges Kane to get out because a gunfight will dissuade people "up North" from investing in the town. The marshal leaves, stunned, as the congregants look down at their hands.

Amy visits Helen to find out if she is keeping Will in Hadleyville, but Helen explains that she is leaving on the same train. When the train pulls in, Amy and Helen head for the station, leaving Will to walk toward the gunmen—as the gunmen walk toward him.

In the first few minutes, Kane kills Ben Miller (Sheb Woolley), Frank Miller's brother, in a shootout, then kills another gunman (Lee Van Cleef) in the stable. Hearing the gunfire from her train seat, Amy rushes toward town as the train pulls away and retreats to the marshal's office. When the killers start a fire in the stable, Kane shoos the horses out and, riding low on the last horse, manages to make it up the street to the saddlery across from his office.

Miller and the remaining gunman (Robert Wilke) try to catch Kane in a crossfire, but Amy shoots the gunman in the back. Miller holds her hostage in front of the saddlery and tells Kane to come out. As Kane walks through the door with his gun by his side, Amy reaches up and claws at Miller's face. He pushes her away, leaving himself open, and Kane fires twice, killing him.

As the townspeople gather around silently, Kane helps Amy into their buggy. Looking around contemptuously, he drops his tin badge in the street. As we watch in shock, he and Amy silently ride out of view.[7]

Even before *High Noon* went into wide release, it was being hailed as a masterpiece by newspaper and magazine reviewers. It was, they reported excitedly, an "adult western," a superlative "study of conscience." In his review in the *New York Times*, Bosley Crowther said that it bore favorable comparison with *Stagecoach*, the last word in Westerns until then.[8]

Its theme song, "Do Not Forsake Me, O My Darling," sung by Frankie Laine, became a hit when it was released several months before the film and contributed to the film's success. It was a box-office winner, coming in eighth in earnings among all American films for the year. At the Academy Awards the following March, it won four Oscars, including one for its star.

From the beginning *High Noon* was referred to as a classic, receiving the highest rating in guides to movies on TV, and later videotape and disc. In 1989, in its first annual citation of film treasures, the National Film Preservation Board listed *High Noon* along with such notable films as *Casablanca* (1942), *Citizen Kane* (1941), *Dr. Strangelove* (1963), and *Gone with the Wind* (1939). And in its 1998 listing of the 100 best American movies, the American Film Institute ranked *High Noon* thirty-third of all American films—and highest among the Westerns.

Its masterpiece status has guaranteed that attempts to recapture its unique appeal will not be well-received. A latter-day sequel made for television was evaluated as follows:

> *High Noon, Part II: The Return of Will Kane* (1980). Retired lawman Will Kane steps in to protect a man hounded by a corrupt marshal. Lee Majors takes on the original Gary Cooper role in this TV movie which claims to pick up where the Fred Zinnemann film left off, but fails to explain why.[9]

And a remake in 2000 was widely castigated for its total failure in trying to improve on perfection.[10]

In the world of film-writing outside the popular press, however, the movie was received with a revealing hostility from the beginning, partly because the mainstream critics had been so lavish in their praise. Within a year of its release it was being dismissed as pretentious "social realism" inspired by the screenwriter's victimization by the red-hunting House Un-American Activities Committee. It was, its critics avowed, yet another pack of "liberal homilies" from producer Stanley Kramer and a prime example of filmmaking by "technicians." It was useful, they said, only because it had goaded a great film artist, Howard Hawks, into making his own much-admired Western, *Rio Bravo* (1959). Despite its top ratings in the movie guides, *High Noon* rarely appears on the "best" lists of those who write about Westerns. Some writers who think it violated the conventions of the Western genre also think it was politically subversive; others think it violated the conventions because it was made by a committee; still others find it distressingly "inauthentic."

Political conservatives said its portrait of cowardly townspeople was an "assault on American society." Radicals said it "denigrated the moral and historical claims of popular democracy," and the Soviet government said it celebrated individualism and rejected "the will of the people."

However it is interpreted, *High Noon* is important not just because it is well made, or because its images are so useful to people who don't otherwise care about Westerns. It is important because it turned the Western upside-down at a time when its conventions were more fixed than ever. And it showed, more than any other film, that independent films could make money and be *good*.

High Noon has traditionally been seen as an allegory, though no one can quite agree about what. For those aware of the "red scare" investigations of the late 1940s and the 1950s, its meaning is obvious: It is about political witch-hunting.

It was made at the end of the postwar era, the most disruptive in American film history since the Great Depression. The Supreme Court had broken up the studios' monopoly of production, distribution, and exhibition, even as box-office receipts were falling and television was beginning to be seen as a threat. The censorious, sexually restrictive production code, rigorously enforced for a decade and a half, had begun to be challenged by relatively explicit films. As the studios retrenched, increasing numbers of filmmakers, including *High Noon* producer Stanley Kramer, began to craft films independently for a fraction of the studios' costs.

But overshadowing everything was the communist threat. There were challenges from communist forces everywhere: in Greece, where a civil war raged; in China, which was taken over by the communists the same year the Soviets unexpectedly exploded an atomic bomb; and in South Korea, which was invaded the following year by the North. As the Truman administration searched for spies in the federal government, conservative forces, aided by their friends in Hollywood, began a search for "reds" in the movie industry.

Under threat from the Congress, the studios responded with a blacklist through which hundreds of artists—writers, actors, directors, and producers—lost their careers, sometimes for a few years, sometimes for life. Socially conscious filmmakers like those who made *High Noon* were particular targets of private groups such as the American Legion, of muckraking columnists, and of the House Un-American Activities Committee—HUAC, as it came to be known—which investigated communist influence in the movies.

The finished film has been widely considered an allegory about the witch-hunt because its writer, Kramer associate Carl Foreman, was driven out of the American movie industry by HUAC and Hollywood conservatives even as the film was being edited.

In such a feverish atmosphere, the team producing *High Noon* was nothing less than remarkable. Gary Cooper and the film's composer, Dimitri Tiomkin, were members of the Motion Picture Alliance for the Preservation of American Ideals, the anticommunist Hollywood group that had invited HUAC to investigate the industry. Tex Ritter, who shared their views, sang the title ballad on the soundtrack. Foreman was an ex-communist who was hostile to the friendly witnesses. Cinematographer Floyd Crosby and actor Lloyd Bridges would see their careers temporarily falter when they were "graylisted." And one cast member, Howland Chamberlin, would be blacklisted. Kramer and Zinnemann were the political liberals in the middle, regularly accused of "pink" views.

Foreman was called to testify before HUAC while he was writing *High Noon* and actually did testify while the film was in production. His friends and colleagues knew for several months that he had been subpoenaed, and, he said later, they started avoiding him. When he refused to tell the Committee whether he had ever been a communist, Kramer immediately forced him to sell his share of the company. Hollywood's conservatives did not take kindly to *High Noon*, and its screenwriter was targeted by protesters. John Wayne was a particularly vocal critic, charging that the film was "un-American" because, among other outrages, Marshal Kane drops his badge in the dirt and steps on it. (He doesn't.) To continue in the film business, Foreman was eventually forced to leave for England.

In light of its writer's troubles with his production company and with the government, the allegory of the film is obvious: Foreman is Kane, the villainous Miller gang is HUAC, and the frightened townspeople are "friendly" witnesses and disappearing friends. For many ordinary moviegoers, however, Foreman's interpretation, whether of Hollywood in particular or of HUAC in general, simply did not register. In the Midwest, Cooper was Eisenhower working against the communists. The Soviets attacked the film as "a glorification of the individual." It struck others as an antipacifist tract, and some critics saw it as a statement about the difficulties of the postwar United States as a global law enforcer.

If the political meaning of *High Noon* was unclear, the one interpretation that almost everyone accepted from the start was that it was a drama about responsibility, betrayal, and cowardice in a society ruled by conformism, material selfishness, and complacency—

ideas that were the subjects of influential sociological tracts of the 1950s such as *The Lonely Crowd* (1950).

In Hadleyville there is no leadership—at least, none worthy of the name—just when the town most desperately needs it. The mayor and the town council, who profess to be Kane's friends, desert him and turn the "good," churchgoing people away from him, too. Without the authority of his badge, Kane rejects not only the wishes of the hypocritical townspeople, some of whom care only about future investment from "up North," but also the demands of his wife's religion.

This analysis in terms of conscience and community—the failures of leaders and ordinary people, big business and religion—takes us a step further in understanding the particular complexities of *High Noon*, and in fact leaves us to wonder if there is anything more to be said. In fact, filmmakers and film critics have had a great deal to say.

High Noon is a Western, but it profoundly disturbed lovers of traditional Westerns, who called it an "anti-Western."[11] Westerns are about lone men who must take on a moral responsibility when a corrupted government or business does not. In Westerns, "a man's got to do what a man's got to do." And his women are either virgins or whores.

Westerns enthrone the "little guy." They privilege the rough-and-ready West over the effete East, traditional values over modern institutions, individuals over organizations, small business over big, and violence over legal process when that legal process seems to be rigged against the little guy, as it usually is. Westerns are naturally suspicious of large landowners, bankers, and politicians.

Not only does *High Noon* draw on these conventions to frame its story, its setting is familiar: a Western town, a misguided Easterner, horses, a saloon, a church, gunplay, the honorable marshal fast on the draw. At the center is Gary Cooper, an icon of Westerns since *The Virginian* (1929).

By this definition *High Noon* is nothing if not a Western, yet many writers have felt free to say that it is not. Some assume the allegorical interpretation is correct—and then reject the film because they're certain that a true Western couldn't be an allegory with a real-world reference. Some say it simply doesn't follow the "rules" for being a Western.

In a sense, the critics are right. Before *High Noon*, in the 1930s and 1940s, Westerns set in towns had been nation-building sagas and paeans to community endeavor, such as *Dodge City* (1939) and *My Darling Clementine* (1946),[12] or salutes to a heroic army, such as *She Wore a Yellow Ribbon* (1949).

But *High Noon* was different—it was "realistic." Its women were strong, and they didn't fit the stereotypes. It didn't offer sweeping vistas, galloping horses, and instantly assembled posses. It was set in a confined space, whose claustrophobia was emphasized by the enormous number of shots through the frames of windows and doors.

Its plot was advanced by elliptical dialogue and a structure that tied everything together by observing Aristotle's three unities of time, space, and action.[13] The action in *High Noon* takes place almost entirely in the town, a kind of moral wilderness even if it is not particularly corrupt. The marshal finds it impossible to assemble a posse. Most important, it is about betrayal, not cooperation—thereby implying that those earlier tribute-Westerns, made by masters such as John Ford and Howard Hawks, were sentimental.

This sharp break from tradition made it a natural target for those who defended the "classical" Western. One reason for the venom that Hawks and his star, John Wayne, directed at *High Noon* was their sense that Gary Cooper, symbol of the old form and good friend, had been seduced into betraying it.

Other traditionalists, searching for a handy word with which to dismiss this new type of Western, came up with "psychological" or "adult." But the meanings of these words turned out to be fluid; in the end, they came to refer to a new focus on carefully drawn characters with credible motivations—something that had not always been a strength of the traditional Western.

Perhaps the most disturbing "violation" of the conventions is simply that its hero is openly afraid and his motives are unclear—private conscience or public obligation, fear or pride or shame, or some mixture. The real enemy is the town, not the gunmen, and the shootout, in which the marshal shoots from hiding when he has a choice, is almost an epilogue. In another irony, he is saved by a wife committed to nonviolence.

After *High Noon*, Westerns would be ambiguous and cynical. Ordinary citizens—as against traditionally suspicious characters like bankers—would be undependable, hypocritical, or venal. Even the later classical Westerns, such as Ford's *The Searchers* (1956) and Peckinpah's *The Wild Bunch* (1969), would convey an alienation from society that had not been there before. By the early 1970s, the rule of the cynics and the bitter would be completed with Robert Altman's *McCabe and Mrs. Miller* (1971) and would culminate in Clint Eastwood's vengeance tale *Unforgiven* (1992) and *Dances with Wolves* (1990), Kevin Costner's assault on the post-Civil War-West American army that would have horrified Ford, master spinner of the cavalry tribute.

Even as lovers of the traditional Western were attacking *High Noon*, it was becoming a prime target for those who subscribed to the "auteur" theory, the enormously influential approach to film that spread from France to the United States not long after the film's release. This new group of film theorists admired the traditional Westerns precisely for their ability to inspire film artistry within the constraints of their "rules."

The auteurists insist that films are made by directors, not collaborators, and that the genre they work in is secondary. They search for signs of the director's personal "touch" and despise evidence of slick impersonality. They claim that the "auteur," or "author," explains artistry far better than the screenplay, the genre, or the political and economic circumstances in which the film was made. *High Noon* is at the center of this argument over the "auteur" theory because a hero of the auteurists, Howard Hawks, made a Western, *Rio Bravo* (1959), specifically as a rejection of and answer to it.

The auteurists believe that *High Noon* was made by a committee, that it has no one creator. The question then becomes: If, as so many people feel, *High Noon* is an especially well-written and directed vision of a failing society, how could a "committee," with all the disagreements and compromises that that term implies, come up with a picture that hangs together so well? And that implies a further question: Who did what? What was the relationship between the screenwriter's, the director's, the producer's, and the editor's contributions?

Foreman maintained that the finished film is little different from the screenplay he submitted, but Zinnemann, working with Foreman, made substantial changes to the script, and Kramer and his editor claimed they were able to "save" the film only by making extensive editing changes and adding the famous score and song.

There is a third way to look at *High Noon*, other than the political setting in which it was made and its relationship to other films. What meanings remain—after all talk of "HUAC allegories," "liberal pieties," "failed Western mythology" and "inaccurate history" are set aside as insufficient—to explain its enduring force as metaphor and as art?

High Noon is a Western, true, but it is also a chamber drama and a kind of existential detective story, and it is shot in a style reminiscent of film noir—a style as far removed from the old West as one can imagine. The complicated, stretched-out past hangs heavy over the proceedings. There are no flashbacks, and the dialogue is remarkably concise, but we are never at a loss about who is who and who did what to whom.

It is short, running only eighty-four minutes, and it plays like a thriller, almost (but not quite) in real time. In those few minutes a plot is unveiled, but that plot comes at the end of the elaborate story that precedes and underlies it—the "backstory," as film writers say.

It is an "urban" Western set in the middle of nowhere, a tale of shocking betrayal in which a man desperately tries to escape with both his skin and his conscience. The tone from the beginning is pessimistic, dark, bitter;[14] the style abstract, stylized, and stark; the photography harsh. Nor is there time for the privileging and the sentimental touches so much admired in Ford and Hawks Westerns. Will Kane represents the end of the Western, "represent[s] the confrontation of the older Western hero with the ambiguity and cynicism of postwar America and dramatize[s] the process of his disillusionment."[15]

It is left to the women, the outsiders, to ask why all of this, the threat of death and the self-deception, is going on.[16] Indeed, if there is a central intelligence, or "moral perspective," in *High Noon*, it is not Will Kane but the unstereotyped, un-male, un-Anglo Helen, who speaks "on equal terms with Will Kane, Amy Kane, and others within the narrative."[17] She shocks us by her independence, as Amy shocks us by violating the traditional Western rule that women do not kill.

In fact, there are three protagonists in *High Noon*—Will, Amy, and Helen—in the sense that they drive the plot in scenes without the other two, and in the sense that they are all on a quest. Will must answer to his heroic pride—or whatever it is that drives him—and in the process realize his authentic self. Amy must uncover the meaning of his actions, and so we see things largely through her eyes at the end. Helen must separate herself from a disaster that will destroy her independence.

The drama of failed "family" infuses virtually every scene. "Fathers" deal with "sons"—not just the failed fathers, the mayor, the

judge, the old marshal, and their "son," Kane—but fatherly Kane
and his "son," the deputy. Harve needs to assault Kane and destroy his father figure.[18] That "father figure" is not simply his
mentor but the man he thinks has taken back his ex-lover, Harve's
lover.[19] But there is also the drama of the ex-lovers, Helen and
Kane, and Helen and Frank Miller, and the troubled lovers Helen
and the deputy. It is as though an elaborate sexual dance is being
played out.

Finally, there is the drama of the town's collapse around Will's
search for a posse. But this is seen from Will's and Amy's and Helen's points of view. We don't really know what's going to happen
to this town after Will and Amy and Helen leave. But it's quite possible that it will go on as before, since it no longer appears to be under any threat. If the people up North can be persuaded that the
gunfight was the last act of a personal drama, and all the principals
are either dead or gone, there's every reason to believe that the
hoped-for investment will come.

That is where the structuring anger, the bitterness, of *High Noon* is
most keenly felt—the idea that nothing will change. Except, that is,
for Will Kane, who has been "liberated"[20] by a shocking discovery:
that he is free of the venality that he had unknowingly been surrounded by. He, like the kids and the jailhouse drunk, is free, though
in his case it is from the obligations of manhood, of older Westerns,
of duty, of conscience. He has found his authentic self, which requires a continuing duty to himself and his wife but not to those
who betrayed him. In the end, the bitterest fact of all is that everyone had his reasons; everyone did what he felt he had to do. It is this
bitterness that the design of *High Noon* is most concerned to convey.
It's all so very relative, so very modern—so un-Western. This
modernity would turn out to be, in fact, the end of the traditional
Western, the cause of a beloved genre's evolution into something
very different under the pressures facing the movie industry in the
years immediately after World War II.

It has always been hard to focus on the design, the film style, and
the evolution of the characters—to see, in other words, the playing
out of the film's form—because the red scare and the allegory and
the Western itself were standing in the way. We need to begin, then,
with the brutally contentious world into which *High Noon* was
born.

NOTES

1. Fred Zinnemann, *A Life in the Movies: An Autobiography* (New York: Scribners, 1992), 10.

2. On CBS television's *"60 Minutes II,"* December 19, 2000, at www.cbsnews.com/stories/2000/12/19/60II/main258362.shtml (accessed November 5, 2002).

3. "Bush Gives 'High Noon' Poster to Koizumi," *Japan Today*, September 26, 2001, at www.japantoday.com/gidx/news86548.html (accessed July 16, 2002).

4. Richard Reeves, "The Last Angry Men," *Esquire,* (March 1, 1978): 41; William T. Pilkington and Don Graham, *Western Movies* (Albuquerque: University of New Mexico Press, 1979), 1–2.

5. Zinnemann, *A Life*, 110. The Solidarity poster phrase "w samo poludnie" could mean either "high noon," "moment of truth," or "time of reckoning." My thanks to Dr. Maurice Simon, Department of Political Science, East Carolina University, for his translation.

6. Joe Scotchie, "Peter King's Lonely Vote," *LongIsland.Com,* January 1, 1999, at LongIsland.com (accessed August 13, 2002).

7. Tim Dirks, *"Greatest Films,"* n.d., at www.filmsite.org (accessed July 15, 2002).

8. Bosley Crowther, review of *High Noon*, *New York Times*, July 25, 1952, 14.

9. Edward Buscombe, ed., *The BFI Companion to the Western* (New York: Atheneum, 1988), 408–9.

10. "Even people who have never seen the film probably have an image of Gary Cooper as the heroic marshal striding down Main Street, alone, to face a killer. Few movies have been so inseparable from the star, or so deeply embedded in the popular imagination. . . . The new TBS version is a faithful, pallid, thoroughly wrongheaded echo of the 1952 original." Caryn James, "The Day Gary Cooper Didn't Walk Down Main Street," *New York Times*, August 18, 2000, E 28.

11. This term, supposedly originally coined by Robert Warshow in his seminal essay "Movie Chronicle: The Westerner," in *Focus on the Western,* ed. Jack Nachbar (Englewood Cliffs, N.J.: Prentice-Hall, 1974)—but difficult to find there—was picked up by many writers, including Richard Combs, in "Retrospective: *High Noon*," *Monthly Film Bulletin* (June 1986):, 186–87; and Joan Mellen, in "The Western," in *Political Companion to American Film*, ed. Gary Crowdus (Chicago: Lakeview Press, 1994), 469–75.

12. Michael Coyne, *The Crowded Prairie* (London: I. B. Tauris, 1997), 69.

13. Adam Garbicz and Jacek Klinowski, *Cinema: The Magic Vehicle, Volume Two* (New York: Schocken, 1983), 112; Zinnemann, *A Life*, 110.

14. Peter Biskind, *Seeing Is Believing* (New York: Pantheon, 1983), 45. Stephen Hunter picks up on this urban interpretation: "If you look at 'High Noon' without assumptions, it seems to me that the dichotomy it describes falls along rural vs. urban lines, rather than political lines. It's about the wicked city taking over the pristine rural town, and implicitly returning vices—prostitution, gambling, drinking, the Tenderloin—to a middle-class dream. And in that light, certain things that have made no sense suddenly fit together neatly. I've always been disappointed in Ian MacDonald, who played the evil Frank Miller. When we finally see him, after an hour and a half of buildup, he's a major disappointment. Far from an icon of towering Western evil—think, for example, of Jack Palance's gunslinger in 'Shane'— he's a squirrelly little man in pressed pants and shirt, with a bow tie. He looks about as cowboy as Sonny Corleone. And that's it, exactly. He's not a cowboy, he's a gangster. Look at that face, with its acne, its dark, feral eyes, its quickness. He looks like he should be a hit man, a loan shark enforcer, not a Western outlaw." ("At AFI, 'High Noon" Once More Reaches Its Zenith," *The Washington Post,* May 30, 2001, c. 03)

15. Richard Slotkin, *Gunfighter Nation* (New York: Atheneum, 1992), 43.

16. Gwendolyn Foster, "The Women in *High Noon* (1952): A Metanarrative of Difference," in *The Films of Fred Zinnemann,* ed. Arthur Nolletti Jr. (Albany: State University of New York Press, 1999), 95–96.

17. Foster, "Women in *High Noon,*" 98–99.

18. Lee Clark Mitchell, *Westerns* (Chicago: University of Chicago Press, 1996), 179–80.

19. Mitchell, *Westerns,* 200.

20. Sam B. Girgus, *Hollywood Renaissance* (Cambridge: Cambridge University Press, 1998), 150–51.

Chapter 2

High Noon Enters
Popular Legend

> Real-life fact and filmic fiction remain frighteningly correlated in
> Italy's melodramatic south. Seduced and abandoned by her
> young lover, Antoinetta Pozzello of Giugliano, a town near
> Naples, . . . shot her onetime boy friend six times one recent day
> in the village square, [confessing] afterwards that she was "in-
> spired" by having seen *High Noon* the evening before on televi-
> sion. Time chosen for tragic event: noon.
>
> —*Variety*[1]

High Noon entered American—and international—popular legend in
remarkably short time. When it was released in the summer of 1952,
reviewers searched for superlatives to commend Kramer, Cooper,
Zinnemann, Foreman, cinematographer Floyd Crosby, composer
Dimitri Tiomkin, and editor Elmo Williams.

High Noon was first shown to someone other than preview audiences on April 28, 1952, when it was screened for the trade papers.
Expecting to judge the market value of a standard commodity, the
reviewers weren't quite sure what they were seeing, but they were
impressed.

The *Daily Variety* reviewer praised it but was puzzled that it was
"more of a Western drama than the usual outdoor action feature," and,
oblivious to the film's interlocking structure, thought that it got "a bit
too involved in the development of side characters and their reactions."
But the review stressed the film's "adult appeal."[2] *The Hollywood Reporter* also discovered its cross-over appeal, finding it "offbeat" and "a
gripping, high-tension suspense drama with a western background."[3]

United Artists had shipped prints to London immediately, with the bizarre result that a review appeared in the *Times* of London well before most other reviewers in the United States saw the film. The review praised the film's "atmosphere of terror and suspense" and its "subtleties of character and construction," and it concluded, almost poetically, that "men turn away from him and lose themselves in excuse and argument, and meanwhile the clock moves on, the track of railway lies sleeping yet watchful in the sun, the heat gathers its strength and fear lays hold of the heart of the marshal; the fear of death, the fear of loneliness joining with the desolate sense of being a man abandoned by his fellows."[4]

High Noon opened nationwide in the United States almost three months later, on Friday, July 25, 1952. The influential *New York Times* film critic Bosley Crowther's review appeared that morning:

> Every five years or so, somebody—somebody of talent and taste, with a full appreciation of legend and a strong trace of poetry in their soul—scoops up a handful of clichés from the vast lore of Western films and turns them into a thrilling and inspiring work of art in this genre. Such a rare and exciting achievement is Stanley Kramer's production, *High Noon.* . . . Which one of several individuals is most fully responsible for this job is a difficult matter to determine and nothing about which to quarrel. It could be Mr. Kramer, who got the picture made, and it could be scriptwriter Carl Foreman, who prepared the story for the screen. Certainly director Fred Zinnemann had a great deal to do with it and possibly Gary Cooper, as the star, had a hand in the job. An accurate apportionment of credits is not a matter of critical concern.
>
> What is important is that someone—or all of them together, we would say—has turned out a Western drama that is the best of its kind in several years. Familiar but far from conventional in the fabric of story and theme and marked by a sure illumination of human character, this tale of a brave and stubborn sheriff [sic] in a town full of do-nothings and cowards has the rhythm and roll of a ballad spun in pictorial terms. And, over all, it has a stunning comprehension of that thing we call courage in a man and the thorniness of being courageous in a world of bullies and poltroons.
>
> Like most works of art, it is simple—simple in the structure of its plot and comparatively simple in the layout of its fundamental issues and morals. Plotwise, it is the story of a sheriff in a small Western town, on the day of his scheduled retirement, faced with a terrible ordeal. At ten thirty in the morning, just a few minutes after he has been wed, he learns that a dreaded desperado is arriving in town on the noon train.

The bad man has got a pardon from a rap on which the sheriff sent him up, and the sheriff knows that the killer is coming back to town to get him.

Here is the first important question: shall the sheriff slip away, as his new wife and several decent citizens reasonably urge him to do, or shall he face, here and now, the crisis which he knows he can never escape? And once he has answered this question, the second and greater problem is the maintenance of his resolution as noon approaches and he finds himself alone—one man, without a single sidekick, against a killer and three attendant thugs; one man who has the courage to take on a perilous, righteous job.

How Mr. Foreman has surrounded this simple and forceful tale with tremendous dramatic implications is a thing we can't glibly state in words. It is a matter of skill in movie writing, but, more than that, it is the putting down, in terms of visually simplified images, a pattern of poetic ideas. And how Mr. Zinnemann has transmitted this pattern in pictorial terms is something which we can only urge you to go yourself to see.

One sample worth framing, however, is the brilliant assembly of shots that holds the tale in taut suspension just before the fatal hour of noon. The issues have been established, the townsfolk have fallen away, and the sheriff, alone with his destiny, has sat down at his desk to wait. Over his shoulder, Mr. Zinnemann shows us a white sheet of paper on which is scrawled 'last will and testament' by a slowly moving pen. Then he gives us a shot (oft repeated) of the pendulum of the clock, and then a shot looking off into the distance of the prairie down the empty railroad tracks. In quick succession, then, he shows us the tense faces of men waiting in the church and in the local saloon, the still streets outside, the three thugs waiting at the station, the tracks again, the wife of the sheriff waiting, and the face of the sheriff himself. Then, suddenly, away in the distance, there is the whistle of the train and, looking down the tracks again, he shows us a wisp of smoke from the approaching train. In a style of consummate realism, Mr. Zinnemann has done a splendid job.

And so has the cast, under his direction. Mr. Cooper is at the top of his form in a type of role that has trickled like water off his back for years. And Lloyd Bridges as a vengeful young deputy, Katy Jurado as a Mexican adventuress, Thomas Mitchell as a prudent townsman, Otto Kruger as a craven judge, and Grace Kelly as the new wife of the sheriff are the best of many in key roles.

Meaningful in its implications, as well as loaded with interest and suspense, *High Noon* is a western to challenge *Stagecoach* for the all-time championship.[5]

Aware of the bitter split between Foreman and Kramer, and troubled by the blacklist that had forced Foreman into exile, Crowther was suggesting the significance of collaboration in filmmaking—and hinting at the widely held assumption in Hollywood that *High Noon* was an allegory of Foreman's own experience. But he was also implying that *High Noon* constituted a reworking of the Western genre.

Variety, which backed the blacklist and had had little to say about Foreman's script other than to find it "shallow," acerbically noted the not-so-subtle sentiments of Crowther and his critical brethren, commenting that it appeared the New York critics were boosting the film out of sympathy over blacklisted screenwriter Carl Foreman's ouster from the filmmaking company he had helped to found.[6]

High Noon finally opened in Los Angeles at the end of the month, and the hometown reviews were rapturous,[7] several agreeing with Crowther that it was the equal of the genre's best.[8] *The Daily News* singled out Tiomkin's score for praise.[9]

The Examiner's reviewer, Lynn Bowers, understood why there were so many "side stories" that baffled a few other critics: "The mood of the picture is intelligently and thoughtfully planned to give meaning and purpose to a violent climax. . . . In the hour and half before the train carrying the killer pulls into town, there are more human emotions displayed than you're apt to see in a dozen pictures."[10]

In a way, the most revealing response came in a pair of reviews in the *Hollywood Citizen-News*. On August 14, Lowell Redelings declared *High Noon* "a taut and extremely suspenseful drama."[11] But five days later, Redelings was back with a longer review—and it appeared that he'd heard some disturbing things in the meantime. While *High Noon* came "pretty close to being a classic," there were problems:

> The plot, despite its tightness and sparse use of dialogue, actually is the film's weakest point. . . . Close analysis shows the story is "tired" by mid-telling, and furthermore: Some of the weakness of the "good citizens" of the town, which are underlined repeatedly, are just the kind of thing which brings forth cries of communist propaganda in motion pictures. Not that this means human frailty and extreme self-interest cannot be depicted on screen; it merely means that undue emphasis is going to bring about pointing fingers of suspicion, and with some justification, considering the international crisis.[12]

He had praise for everyone but Foreman, and the plot the latter had created was the only element that came in for criticism.

For the most part, the reviewers in the national magazines were equally enthusiastic. Perhaps reflecting their New York perspective, both Hollis Alpert in the *Saturday Review* and Al Hine in *Holiday* particularly admired the casting, which Hine compared to the best of Broadway.[13]

It was a major box-office hit. Less than a month after it was released, *Variety* was predicting that "*High Noon . . .* appears certain to be producer Stanley Kramer's biggest grosser."[14] A month later the newspaper noted that the "strength being displayed by *Noon* is all the more amazing because some critics were inclined to suspect that Cooper had lost his box-office punch until this came along."[15]

The film had grossed $3.4 million by the end of December and earned $18 million worldwide,[16] and Cooper, who had agreed to an unusually small upfront payment and a percentage of the gross, "was said to have earned $600,000."[17] The film wound up eighth in revenue for the year, well behind the big winner, *The Greatest Show on Earth*, whose $12 million showing put it second on the all-time list after *Gone with the Wind*.[18]

If the critics were largely unstinting in their praise, and ordinary filmgoers loved it, *High Noon* also came in for criticism. *Time's* reviewer felt that "now and then *High Noon* falters, e.g., the moment when the marshal's wife suddenly shows up to help him plug the desperadoes is stronger on gunplay than on screenplay, and Grace Kelly is somewhat over-glamorous as the wife."[19]

Robert L. Hatch, reviewing for *The Reporter*, admired the film's construction: "Zinnemann puts the narrative together from a series of crisp and purposeful scenes that interpret one another like the pins on a strategist's war map. No one bats an eye or rubs an elbow in *High Noon* unless the gesture contributes to the story." But all was not well, especially for a picture with ideas: "The director permits his cameraman a few rather mannered shots of the excellent 1870 frontier-town set, and he is a little too fond of moments so 'pregnant with meaning' that all motion is suspended; otherwise his work is impressively unpretentious. . . . Those . . . excellences . . . are sufficient to make the picture celebrated. But they are all technical. For a movie to be really superior, its content must be taken seriously, and on the level of ideas *High Noon* presents another face."[20]

But it was the early review by *The Nation*'s Manny Farber that best anticipated those of the "auteurists" who would dominate American film reviewing in the next decade: *High Noon*, in Farber's acerbic view, was a "deftly fouled-up Western." Its dramatic action, he said, was limited to Cooper walking. "The contrived result: A movie which does take you into every part of the town and features Cooper's beautiful rolling gait, but which reveals that someone spent too much time over the drawing board conceiving dramatic camera shots to cover up the lack of story. Moral: the Kramer gang *(Champion, The Men)* is making too many films for its own good."[21]

The Marxists were simply disgusted. *The New York Daily Worker* reviewer detected "the usual amount of cynicism and misanthropy. The high point of the film, with Gary Cooper stalking down the street in intense loneliness, is a classic restatement of the anti-human theme of nearly all cowboy and detective yarns: in this world all you can rely on is yourself and the power in a pair of guns; don't trust your neighbors, people are no damn good." And in Moscow, *Pravda* concluded that in *High Noon* "the idea of the insignificance of the people and masses and the grandeur of the individual found its complete incarnation."[22]

But the hostility went beyond pained rejection. There was a real threat to the film, in the form of an attack designed to block its chances for year-end awards. It came from the best known and most powerful entertainment columnist in the country. Hedda Hopper for years had been using her bully pulpit—a six-day-a-week, nationally syndicated column in *The Los Angeles Times*—to attack Communists, ex-Communists, and "pinkos." Foreman, who had left the party a decade earlier, was now one of her chief targets because he had refused to "name names" of other Communists when he had appeared before the House Un-American Activities Committee a year earlier during the filming of *High Noon*. She and John Wayne had driven Foreman from the film business, but it was not enough. *High Noon* was tainted, and she committed herself to preventing her worst fear—that it would win the Academy Award for best picture—from being realized.

From early December 1952, when the film began to be mentioned as a major contender for the industry's top prize, until the day of the ceremony in mid-March 1953, Hopper kept up a steady drumbeat, attacking the Hollywood left in general and *High Noon* and its makers in particular. She regularly reiterated her support for the black-

list[23] and fretted that not enough was being done to block the distribution of downbeat films[24]—especially if they were made by blacklistees like Foreman.[25]

She began the new year by plumping in earnest for her Oscar favorite. "*The Greatest Show On Earth* . . . deserves an Oscar . . . but
there seems to be a natural antagonism toward the man [Cecil B. De
Mille] who has been making good pictures and giving employment
to thousands of people for the past forty-odd years." She noted that
"*My Son John*, an anti-commie film helmed by that master craftsman
Leo McCarey, was almost annihilated by an unfriendly press." She
concluded that the best picture Oscar should go to either *The Greatest Show on Earth* or John Ford's *The Quiet Man*.[26]

Her mail, she reported, was now running ten to one in favor of *The
Quiet Man* or *The Greatest Show on Earth* for best picture,[27] and "The
Federation of Women's Clubs, with some six million members, . . .
voted *The Quiet Man* as Best Picture."[28]

At the end of January the Director's Guild picked John Ford as
best director for *The Quiet Man.* She proudly noted that De Mille was
"the first director to receive the D. W. Griffith Award at our Screen
Directors Guild dinner . . . , and many believe *The Greatest Show On
Earth* will receive the Academy Award."[29] In a follow-up a few days
later, she added that

> when . . . De Mille received the . . . Griffith Award for his 40 years ser-
> vice at the directors' dinner, there was a standing ovation and cheers—
> except for the occupants of one table, who sat on their hands. . . . I'd
> like to point out to those ungrateful ten . . . , including three directors,
> one of whom was [Fred] Zinnemann, . . . that but for men like De Mille
> and Griffith not one of them would be in Hollywood today.[30]

She omitted mention of a possible explanation for such discourtesy:
a showdown in the fall of 1950, two and a half years earlier, between
De Mille, then head of the guild, and some of the people at that table
over De Mille's insistence that all directors take loyalty oaths.

Hopper continued boosting her favorites to the end: "[John] Ford
says the British are talking of nothing but our Academy Awards. The
British hope *The Quiet Man* gets the Oscar, but the Fords are rooting
for *The Greatest Show On Earth*."[31]

By way of contrast, on February 14 she helpfully reported a comment by a director at Columbia's annual board meeting: "'We have
had very poor success with Stanley Kramer. His films are highly

acclaimed but unfortunately the public hasn't bought them.' Then a stockholder spoke up: 'We're interested in dividends, not awards.'"[32] By this time there had also been good news to report about an old friend. Gary Cooper, who had been separated from his wife and carrying on a highly publicized affair with the actress Patricia Neal, was now back in the bosom of his family.[33]

If she was increasingly confident that Ford and Cooper would win, Hopper was sufficiently worried about the best picture award to invent some movie history: *High Noon*, she allowed, was "excellent. However, this is about the fourth time the story of *High Noon* has been filmed. Cecil B. De Mille made it twice—as *The Virginian* [the 1914 version] and *The Plainsman*, and John Ford screened it again in *Stagecoach*."[34]

What had clearly made her nervous was that *High Noon* was enjoying a virtual sweep of awards handed out beyond the gates of Hollywood. Although the National Board of Review had picked *The Quiet Man*,[35] Stanley Kramer's little film had won top honors from the New York Film Critics, who also preferred Zinnemann's direction.[36] It was the favorite of the *New York Herald Tribune*'s Otis L. Guernsey Jr., who called it "an American movie achievement which can stand beside the tallest from anywhere and look most of them in the eye."[37]

Over the next month it won top honors from *Film Daily* and the Associated Press,[38] *Photoplay* and *Look*, and "a Golden Globe award, and Foreman won the Screenwriters Guild award for best screenplay."[39] *Variety* headlined its "straw poll" prediction "*High Noon* Looks to Sweep Oscars." The newspaper said the movie would win four or five of the top eight awards, including best picture (it was a "cinch"), best actor, best screenplay and best song. Foreman's "victory looks virtually certain."[40]

Meanwhile, *The Greatest Show on Earth* was showing up in top ten listings but never quite making it to number one. That is, until the night of the Oscars, when Hopper's hard work paid off. The 25th Academy Awards, on March 19, 1953, was the first to be telecast,[41] with Ronald Reagan as a commentator.[42]

High Noon had been nominated in seven categories. It would win in four: Elmo Williams and Harry Gerstad for editing, Dimitri Tiomkin and Ned Washington for the ballad, Tiomkin for the score, and Cooper for best actor. Neither Floyd Crosby's cinematography nor Rudolph Sternad's set decoration had been nominated, nor had any other cast members.

The Academy bowed to Hopper, awarding best picture to *The Greatest Show on Earth,* which defeated not only *High Noon* but also *The Quiet Man, Moulin Rouge,* and *Ivanhoe.* "The shock of the evening," noted a film historian, "was a best picture win for . . . an undistinguished movie that had won no acting nominations and had little but box-office success to recommend it for a supposedly artistic award."[43] The combination of Hopper's tub-thumping and *Greatest Show*'s box office had been too much.

When Janet Gaynor announced Gary Cooper's name, an old friend accepted for him. Cooper "had bumped into John Wayne shortly before the awards and [knowing he would be on location in Mexico] asked Wayne to pick up the Oscar for him if he won. He had no doubt that he wouldn't win."[44]

"In his acceptance speech for Cooper," noted a Cooper biographer,

> Wayne said: "Ladies and gentlemen, I'm glad to see that they're giving this to a man who is not only most deserving, but has conducted himself throughout his years in our business in a manner that we can all be proud of. Coop and I have been friends hunting and fishing for more years than I like to remember. He's one of the nicest fellows I know; I don't know anybody nicer. And our kinship goes further than that friendship because we both fell off of horses in pictures together. Now that I'm through being such a good sport spouting all this good-sportsmanship, I'm going back and find my business manager and agent, producer and three name writers and find out why I didn't get *High Noon* instead of Cooper."[45]

The speech was a particularly breathtaking bit of hypocrisy, because Wayne had been attacking the movie as un-American and scolding Cooper for appearing in it. In her column, Hopper emphasized the political aspect: "Also pointed was Wayne's remark upon Gary Cooper's standing as a good American as well as actor." [46]

Foreman would not be so lucky. And as a target of the right-wing activists he was not alone. *Hollywood Reporter* columnist Mike Connolly, a fellow traveler of Hopper's in the anti-communist crusade, noted that original screenplay nominee Michael Wilson (for *Five Fingers*), an Oscar winner the previous year for *A Place in the Sun,* had taken the Fifth Amendment before HUAC two years earlier. He warned Academy voters, "If you give unfriendly witness Michael Wilson another Oscar this year, you'll be giving the Academy a body blow from which it may never recover."[47] Perhaps because of these rumblings, in the end neither Foreman nor Wilson would win; the award went to Charles Schnee for the Hollywood backstage tale *The Bad and the Beautiful*. Zinnemann's and Foreman's losses were of particular concern to Bosley Crowther.

He complained that Zinnemann's "extraordinarily artful direction . . . was passed over in favor of the robust but stock direction" of Ford and that *High Noon*'s "excellent script [from] the (Sshh!) controversial Carl Foreman" lost to *The Bad and the Beautiful*'s "'craftsman's model.'" His New York colleague, Otis Guernsey, joined in the complaint. "A staple, workmanlike job like *The Bad and the Beautiful* (wins out over) . . . one of the tightest, soundest, technically most perfect American movie scripts on the record."[48]

The Greatest Show on Earth, Crowther concluded, was "spectacular but old-fashioned" compared to the "intelligence, imagination, dynamism and moral fibre" of *High Noon*. He thought the entire telecast looked backward nostalgically with its awards to ancients like De Mille.[49]

The ever-gracious Zinnemann congratulated the winners. A note to Ford said, "Dear Jack, I'm sorry I lost, but very proud indeed to lose to John Ford. Please accept my warmest congratulations." And he told Cooper: "Dear Marshal—We're so happy you got it."[50]

Despite its Oscar loss, *High Noon* was firmly established in American popular culture almost immediately. While it was still in the theaters, presidential candidate Dwight Eisenhower was heard "whistling the song . . ., which he could not get out of his head." Eisenhower and Clinton weren't the only presidents who liked it: *High Noon* has been shown in the White House screening room more often than any other film.[51] Six years after its release, its showing on New York television station WRCA drew the "biggest feature film audience in New York TV history. . . . [It] gathered a larger audience than any other show—network or local—on any other station all month."[52]

It was also beginning its long career as a target of cineastes and film historians, who received it with a revealing hostility from the beginning. Assessments by film writers have been, at best, grudging in their praise. In one recent survey of thirty-nine American, British, and French film writers, only two listed *High Noon* on their ten-best Western lists.[53]

New Yorker reviewer Pauline Kael famously dismissed the film's "insights" as "primer sociology passing for dramatic motive, . . . the town's cowardice is Q.E.D . . . and . . . the Western form is being used for a sneak civics lesson." She concluded that people now saw the film as dated because they realized they had "over-responded to its public-ity and reputation, or to its attempt to deal with a social problem or an idea, and may have ignored the banalities surrounding the attempt; now that the idea doesn't seem so daring, they notice the rest."[54]

High Noon's remarkable history had made it a target too big to ig-nore. But the Western films and the directors who would follow would owe it an enormous debt of gratitude because it had been central to a revolution in film production that would eventually free everyone from the constraints of the past.

NOTES

1. December 8, 1965, 2. Reviews from Hollywood trade papers are archived in the Academy of Motion Picture Arts and Sciences Fairbanks Center for Motion Picture Study in Beverly Hills (hereinafter Fairbanks Center).

2. *Variety*, April 30, 1952, 6.

3. *The Hollywood Reporter*, April 30, 1952.

4. *The Times* of London, May 5, 1952.

5. *New York Times*, July 25, 1952, 14. Copyright © 1952 by The New York Times Company. Reprinted with permission.

6. *Variety*, July 30, 1952, 15.

7. Richard Griffith, "'High Noon' Wins Praise from Eastern Critics," *Los Angeles Times*, August 5, 1952, III-6; Philip K. Scheuer, "Gary Hits Target on Stroke of Noon," *Los Angeles Times*, August 14, 1952, III-8.

8. Harrison Carroll, "'High Noon' Is Top Suspense," *Los Angeles Herald Express* , August 14, 1952 (located in Fairbanks Center).

9. Howard McClay, "High Noon," *Los Angeles Daily News*, July 29, 1952 (located in Fairbanks Center).

10. *Los Angeles Examiner*, "'High Noon' Superb Film," August 14, 1952 (located in Fairbanks Center).

11. Lowell K. Redelings, "'High Noon' A Suspenseful Western Film," *Hollywood Citizen-News*, August 14, 1952 (located in Fairbanks Center).

12. Lowell K. Redelings, "The Hollywood Scene," *Hollywood Citizen-News*, August 19, 1952 (located in Fairbanks Center).

13. *Saturday Review*, July 5, 1952, 29; *Holiday* 12 (September 1952): 26.

14. *Variety*, August 20, 1952, 10.

15. *Variety,* September 3, 1952, 4.

16. Jon Tuska, *The Filming of the West* (New York: Doubleday, 1976), 542; Jef-frey Meyers, *Gary Cooper* (New York: Morrow, 1998), 249–50; Ed Andreychuk, *The Golden Corral* (Jefferson, N.C.: McFarland, 1997), 35; William R. Meyer, *The Making of the Great Westerns* (New Rochelle, N.Y.: Arlington House, 1979), 216.

17. Meyers, *Cooper*, 249–50.

18. *Variety*, January 7, 1953, 61.

19. Unsigned review, *Time*, July 14, 1952, 92–94.

20. "Gary Cooper A Tragic Hero," 38, September 16, 1952, in Stanley Hochman, *American Film Directors* (New York: Frederick Ungar, 1974), 524.

21. *The Nation* 174 (April 26, 1952): 410.

22. Meyer, *Great Westerns*, 216.

23. *Los Angeles Times*, March 16, 1953, III-8.

24. *Los Angeles Times*, March 11, 1953, III-6.

25. *Los Angeles Times*, January 14, 1953, III-6.

26. *Los Angeles Times*, January 1, 1953, I-20.

27. *Los Angeles Times*, January 12, 1953, I-20.

28. *Los Angeles Times*, January 14, 1953, III-6.

29. *Los Angeles Times*, January 30, 1953, III-6.

30. *Los Angeles Times*, February 4, 1953, III-8.

31. *Los Angeles Times*, March 4, 1953, II-6.

32. *Los Angeles Times*, February 14, 1953, I-8.

33. *Los Angeles Times*, December 4, 1952, III-10.

34. *Los Angeles Times*, February 7, 1953, I-12.

35. *New York Times*, December 19, 1952, 34.

36. *New York Times*, December 30, 1952, 23.

37. *New York Herald Tribune*, December 28, 1952 (located in Fairbanks Center).

38. *New York Times*, March 9, 1953, 25.

39. John H. Lenihan, *Showdown* (Urbana: University of Illinois Press, 1985),120.

40. *Variety*, March 18, 1953, 1.

41. *Variety*, February 25, 1953, 2.

42. *Variety*, March 11, 1953, 4.

43. Anthony Holden, *Behind the Oscar* (New York: Plume, 1993), 199.

44. Stuart M. Kaminsky, *Coop* (New York: St. Martin's Press, 1980), 173.

45. Kaminsky, *Coop*, 173.

46. *Los Angeles Times*, March 23, 1953, II-12.

47. Mason Wiley and Damien Bona, *Inside Oscar* (New York: Ballantine, 1986), 225.

48. Otis L. Guernsey Jr., "Oscar's Getting Stodgy," *New York Herald Tribune*, March 29, 1953 (located in Fairbanks Center).

49. *New York Times*, March 29, 1953, II-1.

50. Both located in Fairbanks Center.

51. Michael Coyne, *The Crowded Prairie* (London: I. B. Tauris, 1997), 1. The screening room results were reported in the documentary *All the President's Movies*, shown on the Bravo channel on August 7, 2003.

52. Double full-page ad in *Variety*, February 5, 1958, 34–35.

53. Phil Hardy, *The Western* (New York: Morrow, 1983), 367–69. The members of the Western Writers of America, however, rank it among the ten best Westerns. See www.westernwriters.org.

54. Pauline Kael, *Kiss Kiss Bang Bang* (New York: Bantam, 1969), 281.

Chapter 3

Independent Production and the Rise of Stanley Kramer

High Noon was produced near the end of the greatest period of transformation the American movie industry had experienced in two decades. During the Great Depression the industry had been upended by the advent of sound, near-bankruptcy, and the imposition of a highly restrictive censorship regime. Now the studios were in turmoil again. *High Noon*'s production would come about as a result of this second, postwar transformation, which occurred in the five years from 1947 to 1952 and forever changed the way in which American films were made.

The studios must have thought they were entering a golden age after World War II. In 1946, they sold so many tickets they set a record that still stands. But within a year they had fallen into a financial abyss. In the next seven years ticket sales sank 75 percent as returning servicemen married, started families, moved to suburbia, and found other things to occupy their time.[1]

The studios' economic distress was dramatically magnified in 1948, when the United States Supreme Court, in the *Paramount* case, ordered an end to their monopoly of production, distribution, and exhibition. The Court outlawed "blind-booking," that is, forcing theaters to take whatever films were available, and "block-booking," requiring theaters to take the less desirable films if they wanted the more desirable ones. As a result, the studios were no longer guaranteed a return on their investment because the theaters could book any films they wanted. Each film would now have to be sold on its own merits, something that hadn't happened since before the rise of the studio monopolies in the years during and after World War I. With the pipeline disrupted, production declined, and studio after studio laid off workers and allowed long-term contracts with major stars to lapse.[2]

New cost constraints, and to a lesser extent the impact of Italian "neo-realism," which made American studio-bound films look increasingly artificial, encouraged producers of straight dramas to begin a decades-long national and international search for settings that were both more realistic and less costly in which to film.

Foreign governments, desperate to stem an outflow of cash after the near-bankruptcy caused by the war, severely restricted the studios' "repatriation" of their foreign earnings—while trying to hold down, under the guise of protecting domestic culture, the number of American films being shown. The U.S. government stepped in with subsidies to encourage foreign distribution, but only on the condition that the films were "positive" reflections of American life.[3]

The censorious, sexually restrictive production code, rigorously enforced for a decade and a half, began to be challenged by explicit films such as *The Miracle*. An Italian film released in 1952, it became the center of another Supreme Court decision that year,[4] which granted film the same First Amendment rights as other forms of expression.

At the invitation of a group of writers, actors, and directors called the Motion Picture Alliance for the Preservation of American Ideals, Congress, in 1944, renewed its prewar investigation of communist influence in the film business, setting off a witch hunt that resulted in the devastation of hundreds of Hollywood careers. Pressured from all sides, economically, politically, and artistically, the studios, when they did make films, relied more than ever on the genre pictures that had been their bread and butter.[5]

Though they would continue to make their own films, the studios had no future as theatrical feature production companies. To Carl Foreman, partner in a new independent, the big studios were dinosaurs who jettisoned virtually everything in a desperate gamble to survive: "The whole surge of independent production came about because the major film companies, the studios, were shocked by the onrush of television," he told an interviewer. "In an almost suicidal action they sold off their stocks of old pictures to television. By favoring relatively few of the big stars, they created Frankensteinian monsters who all but devoured their masters. They blundered by failing to develop cadres of younger creative talent."[6] What they did have were huge, largely unused production facilities, which could be rented out to independent production.

The plight of the studios created new opportunities for increasing numbers of directors and producers to create independent production companies that could make films for a fraction of the studios' costs, without studio control—and, frequently, on subjects the studios would not consider. It was not the first time in American film history that producers and directors who chafed under studio policies would try to do things their own way, but it would be by far the most important because of its long-term impact.

As two film historians have summarized the process, the independent producer

> selected the property, the stars and the director, raised the money, and supervised the selling of the finished film. Perhaps the production company rented space on a studio lot; perhaps it used the studio's distribution offices to help sell the film. But the producer, not the studio, made the picture. Without a lot, no long-term contracts with stars, no staffs of writers and technicians, the producer assembled a production company for a particular film, disbanded it when the film was finished, and assembled another for the next film. . . . For major productions . . . both studio and independent producers bought established, already written properties that simply required an artful, professional translation into film form. . . . It was easier for a producer to raise money for a film that was considered "pre-sold;" it was easier to sell one of these familiar properties back to the public after the film had been finished.[7]

In this new world of film production, in which studios couldn't rely on box-office receipts to fund new movies, and independents had no money, each film had to be individually financed. With banks central to financing[8] and studios still the major distributors of movies, the true independence the new companies sought was threatened.[9]

One studio, though, stood out from the rest in its willingness to work with this new wave of independent companies. "United Artists . . . offered independent producers complete production financing, creative control over their own work and a share of the profits, in exchange for distribution rights. Other companies expected to approve shooting and the final cut as well as the basic property and cast."[10]

The trick for a new production company, then, would be either to work with a company like United Artists or on its own to find independent financing, make the films it wanted to make, and control their distribution, despite the considerable pressure from the distributors and banks to produce conservative genre pieces.

In 1947, it must have seemed that everyone was nevertheless taking that gamble, despite these not-inconsiderable constraints and the fall-off at the box office from the 1946 high.[11] When Stanley Kramer and Carl Foreman created their production company in 1947 and began making movies, there were no fewer than ninety-six rival independents fighting for financing and distribution.[12] That number, which had increased fifteenfold since 1940, included some of the biggest names in Hollywood: Frank Capra, John Ford, William Wyler, Howard Hawks, Leo McCarey, and George Stevens.[13]

Anyone contemplating a career as an independent could now follow the experiences of these film notables in the trade papers and learn some hard lessons at a distance. Star directors might, like John Ford, have to buy their own properties with no guarantee of recovering their investment, or make films for a major studio to fund their own projects, or go in with an existing independent, as Ford did on *Stagecoach*. They might have to endure unpleasant breakups with partners over financial arrangements, lawsuits over notorious studio bookkeeping, or ego battles.[14] Their films might fail instantly, as Hitchcock's independently made *Rope* (1948) and *Under Capricorn* (1949) did. They might, like Frank Capra, who partnered with William Wyler and George Stevens after the war, discover that one partner (Wyler) was contractually obligated to another studio (Goldwyn) for a final film—and that that film (*The Best Years of Our Lives*) would be so successful it would steal the box office from the partnership's first project (Capra's *It's a Wonderful Life*), forcing the company to sell itself early to a big studio (Paramount), which would then, of course, demand script approval.[15] Ford, Hitchcock, Capra, and the others were interested in controlling their filmmaking, but if their films were critical of society, it would be left to the auteurist critics of the 1960s and 1970s to uncover their subtextual critiques.

Situated on the left, Kramer and Foreman would be far more influenced by their observation of the struggles of Hollywood's Left to produce films independently. These were the filmmakers, many soon to be blacklisted, who wanted to control their productions less for the money than to make statements.

Producer David Loew, with whom Kramer had worked on the independently-made *The Moon and Sixpence* in 1942, created Enterprise Productions in 1947 to produce and distribute films made by Communists, ex-Communists, and liberals, including actor John Garfield, producers Bob Roberts and Abraham Polonsky, directors Robert Rossen, Robert Aldrich, Cy Endfield, John Berry, and others.[16] Garfield, who like most of these artists would soon be blacklisted, was the most important "name" willing to appear in these dramas. Attracted by the chance to combine a larger take of the profits with a message, he and his former business manager Bob Roberts "began by providing Enterprise with [the noir boxing expose] *Body and Soul*, which cost $1.8 and grossed $4.7 million, becoming the studio's one major commercial success from its nine productions released between 1947 and 1949."[17]

Polonsky, who had written *Body and Soul*, was then given the chance to direct *Force of Evil* for Garfield and Roberts. It was completed only with an emergency loan from the Bank of America,[18] but it failed at the box office—though it was one of only two Enterprise Pictures, along with *Body and Soul*, to receive critical acclaim. With no serious financial controls in place and an otherwise weak slate of films, Enterprise, like most other independents, was forced to ally with MGM, but it went bankrupt the next year anyway.[19] To Polonsky, Enterprise was a grand new idea; the problem was that "they didn't make very good pictures."[20] The producers, directors, writers, and actors who had hoped to make films with Enterprise were now left on their own, but most had little time left before the blacklist clamped down.

By far the most successful "graduate" of Enterprise was Stanley Kramer, whose production company, Screenplays, Incorporated, would make its first film, *So This Is New York* (1948), for the studio in return for a completion loan.[21] Kramer, whose career as a producer of "liberal" films would last thirty years, would now make several films that would pave the way, both thematically and financially, for *High Noon*. He would experience a success almost from the start that would separate him from the independent production pack, not so much because he made good films, though the critics generally praised them, but because he enjoyed a degree of creative independence for much longer than the rest.

Most important, Kramer would devise a new method of financing and distributing films that would permanently change the way films were made and distributed. As the screenplay for *High Noon* was being written, Kramer was entering into an unprecedented arrangement with a major studio—Columbia—in which the studio would provide most of the financing for a series of films, Kramer would have the sole responsibility for production, and the two would split the profits. Ironically, Columbia production chief Harry Cohn would consider making an offer for *High Noon* but then reject an early cut of the film that would in effect become the ultimate proof of the effectiveness of Kramer's approach. Kramer would then use the film, as initially agreed, to close out his previous distribution arrangement with United Artists. When his arrangement with Columbia eventually failed after three years, he would survive because, unlike the deals many other independents had made with the major studios, his company preexisted its agreement with Columbia and had enough financial "angels" to survive its collapse.

Kramer operated according to three ironclad rules:

1. a Spartan budget financed by non-Hollywood investors such as a Midwestern department store owner and a California lettuce grower,
2. a long preproduction period to eliminate as many production glitches as possible without a crew on standby, and
3. intensive one- or two-week rehearsals. The films were typically shot in a breathtaking three to six weeks.[22]

By way of describing his role in the arcane art of raising money, Kramer once told an interviewer, "I'm a bit of a shill artist."[23] He demonstrated how the process worked in an article that appeared just as he was signing on with Columbia. The independent producer, he wrote,

> starts with an idea—the notion that a certain story would make a great picture and that he is just the man to produce it—provided he can raise the money to buy the story and can then convince a bank or a gimlet-eyed financier to lend him several hundred thousand dollars. . . . If he succeeded in pretending to have the story in order to raise the money to buy it, he must now dangle a star and director whom he has not yet [put] under contract as part of the bait for the investor whose money will make production possible. Before he is through, the independent producer may have a dozen or more such balloons floating in the air.[24]

But beyond the grubby details of the fund-raising, said Kramer, was the commitment to a difficult project. A major studio producer's

> financing is assured and automatic. He has a roster of contract players, directors and writers to choose from, as well as a stockpile of story properties. A major studio can afford to take an occasional gamble on an offbeat theme. If it loses money, they chalk it up to "prestige," and more than make up the loss with a couple of in-the-groove musicals. The independent producer can't afford what department stores call a loss leader. One of these will put him out of business. Nor can he, or should he, start out with a lush, safe musical. The economies he has to practice make it impossible for him to compete with the major studios in this form of entertainment. To make a place for himself the independent producer has to add something to the industry's output. He cannot be a small scale echo of what the majors are doing—much better than he can hope to.[25]

"In our case," Kramer observed,

> instead of relying on star names, we pinned our faith in stories that had something to say. If it happened to be something that other movies hadn't said before, so much the better. The only basis of choice was personal taste. It was a case of saying, "If I like this story, there must be enough people in this country who will also like it." So far, that simple formula has worked. The independent producer's budgets have definitely defined limits. Therefore he must be very discriminating in his choice of the people who are to carry out the production methods he has outlined. For every nickel he spends must show on the screen. On all of our pictures we have had a small team which operates as a perfectly integrated machine. Two of my partners—George Glass, who is associate producer and vice president in charge of advertising and publicity, and Carl Foreman, our screenwriter—also have a say in shaping overall policy and methods. . . . Clem Beauchamp, as production manager, controls technical and physical departments; Rudolph Sternad is both production designer and art director; Harry Gerstad is our film [editing] director; and Dimitri Tiomkin is musical director.[26]

Kramer had begun working his way up in Hollywood in 1933, in the classic fashion—as a story intern, a stagehand, an assistant editor, and an assistant director.[27] In 1947, after several failed attempts to start his own company and a stint in Frank Capra's wartime Signal Corps unit making propaganda films, he formed Screen Plays, Inc., with his army buddies Herb Baker and Carl Foreman, and an old friend from his studio days, George Glass.[28] Screen Play's early experiences revealed some of the complexities of independent production at the time—and how nimble the company was in getting around them.

The company's first production was *So This Is New York*, directed by Richard Fleischer and adapted by Foreman from a Ring Lardner satire about a small town family enduring endless nonsense in the big city. British critic Penelope Houston praised its star, radio comedian Henry Morgan, and allowed that it "was written and directed . . . with pace, invention and a pleasantly dry humor."[29]

It barely got made, as money problems of the sort that had sunk more famous independents plagued the operation from the start. Kramer had to sell a half-interest to Enterprise and never expected to make any money, but it did eventually show a profit, and, more important, attracted the attention of prospective investors to its producer.[30]

For the company's second film, the first of five to be distributed through United Artists, Foreman adapted, and Mark Robson directed, another Lardner story, *Champion*, in which Kirk Douglas played a boxer who was thoroughly corrupted by his success. It would give Foreman, by now an ex-Communist but still on the Left, a chance to try his hand at the political allegory he would perfect with *High Noon*. In *Champion*, prize fighting would stand in, not completely successfully, for capitalism. Comments Brian Neve,

> Foreman clearly attempts to provide an environmental rationale for [Kirk Douglas's character's] ruthless rise—orphanage, cold and hunger, etc.—and there is the same emphasis on an alienated world of money and sex that is prevalent in *films noir* . . . While the film is relentlessly powerful, with fast montages and fight scenes, it lacks the darker tone of *film noir*—apart from the opening and closing scenes—that might broaden the critique beyond boxing. No social alternative to the fight game melodrama . . . is available, as it is in *Body and Soul*.[31]

Shot in twenty days at a cost of $500,000, the picture made Douglas a star; earned 400 percent on its investment; received six Oscar nominations, including Best Picture, Best Actor, and Best Screenplay; and won an Oscar for Harry Gerstad's editing. Kramer had avoided using stars, so he didn't have to pay his actors much.[32]

The film was also a classic example of Kramer's financing technique. It got made because he exaggerated how far along he was in tying up actors and distribution. Ultimately he needed a loan from retired Florida dry goods manufacturer John Stillman to add to a bank loan to complete production.[33] Stillman would invest a substantial sum, $347,000 in *Champion* and the next film, *Home of the Brave.*

Adapted by Foreman from Arthur Laurents's play and once again directed by Mark Robson, *Brave* was shot in a mere twenty-four days. Laurents's play had been about anti-Semitism in the army, but Kramer decided to change the victim to a black soldier so affected by the bigotry of his fellow soldiers that he has a mental breakdown. It would be the first sound film about antiblack racism.

Kramer, wanting to shock the film world with a controversial picture that would make money, had Foreman produce a screenplay that was unexpectedly blunt about race relations for its time.[34] This was, not surprisingly, an approach the studios avoided. "The subject matter was so touchy that Kramer shot the film in total secrecy [under the cover title, *High Noon*] to avoid protests by antiblack organizations. . . . Robson, the cast and crew entered and left the studio inconspicuously by a rear gate and ate on the set instead of in the commissary."[35]

The plot was a twist on the standard small-group camaraderie of soldiers in battle, in which a squad on a dangerous mission behind enemy lines includes a black man, James Edwards, and his white high school buddy, Lloyd Bridges. "One of the other squad members is an open racist. When the Bridges character utters a racial epithet at a desperate moment and subsequently dies in his old friend's arms, [Edwards] cracks up. The story is told in flashback in conversations between a psychiatrist and the black soldier."[36]

The critics liked the film, and it was another hit for the newly renamed Stanley Kramer Company.[37] Noted Foreman: "We budgeted [it] for $215,000 and got into trouble and were able to get another $25,000 with which to finish the film. We thought at that price we could beat the system. . . . We thought we could sneak it by and if we got by with it it would be marvelous—and we did get by with it."[38]

In terms that would be heard repeatedly about Kramer's films, the producer and the screenwriter were accused by reviewers at the time and later of pulling their punches, as they had in *Champion*. The performances were said to be too broad, the plot was contrived, the psychoanalyst treated the problem all too easily, and the film was inconsistent in its explanations.[39]

By way of perspective, though, Nora Sayre notes that it is "easy to mock the naiveté of some of the racial movies of [the late 1940s and early 1950s]. But what perturbs us now had a flavoring of courage then—despite the paternalism that seeps through the spongy liberalism."[40]

Even as he was reorganizing his company in August 1949, the successes of *Champion* and *Home of the Brave* were winning Kramer new financing, from Salinas lettuce grower Bruce Church.[41] After the Stillmans departed—over, as Kramer put it, "creative interference"—his company was reorganized as Stanley Kramer Productions, Inc. Church, unlike almost every other financier of independents, was willing to take a percentage of the profits instead of stock, and he provided the money early enough so that the company could rehearse ahead of shooting.[42]

The Kramer Company's next film, *The Men*, marked the first collaboration between Kramer, Foreman, and Fred Zinnemann, an MGM contract director who had just gone independent. Zinnemann contracted to make three pictures for Kramer.[43] He was impressed with Kramer's setup:

> They struck me as being enormously efficient. Kramer was very inventive in finding quite unlikely sources of finance. . . . This method of outside financing . . . was truly original and far ahead of its time. Another of Kramer's talents was to organize very tight but feasible shooting schedules. His crews were always promised a small percentage of hoped-for profits—a strong incentive for speed in production. I was enthusiastic about this independent setup and the energy it created. Working in a small rental studio near Cahuenga Boulevard, we were our own front office, responsible to no one for our decisions on screenplay, casting or production. There were no luxurious offices, no major-studio bureaucracy, no small internal empires to be dealt with, no waste of time or effort.[44]

The subject of the new picture had come about fortuitously. "Kramer . . . had screened *Champion* for World War II paraplegics at the Birmingham VA hospital in Los Angeles and Kramer was fascinated, talking to the vets. He had Foreman write a . . . screenplay and signed Marlon Brando, fresh from his Broadway triumph in *A Streetcar Named Desire*, for his screen debut."[45] Foreman would write yet another treatment of his favorite theme: "How the . . . character faced life in an impossible situation."[46]

Zinnemann had had success working with nonprofessionals in *The Search* (1948), so he decided to use the patients who had fascinated Kramer. "Because they had undergone the experience in real life, Zinnemann felt that they were able to give authenticity to the film. Explaining this aspect of his directing to a reporter, Zinnemann said: 'I wanted people who would be behaving rather than acting. . . . The real paraplegics made jokes about their condition that sounded genuine; they'd have sounded horrible coming from actors.'"[47] It was the method actor at work. "Brando went to live for a month with paralyzed soldiers, staying in a wheel chair and hooking himself up to a catheter."[48]

The Men opened in July 1950[49]—on the same day, as it happened, that America entered the Korean War. . . .[50] But once again they had a success.[51]

The daily critics by and large liked what they saw. Bosley Crowther wrote that "nothing yet demonstrated has so fully realized and portrayed . . . the inner torments, the despairs, the loneliness and the possible triumphs of a paraplegic as this picture does. . . . A striking and authentic documentary quality has been imported to the whole film in every detail, attitude and word."[52]

The British critic Penelope Houston, writing two years later, had a few reservations.

> This story of paralyzed ex-servicemen, of the efforts of the irreconcilable patient (played with great force and perception by Marlon Brando . . .) to adjust himself again to the world, had some of the faults inherent in the convention of the problem picture. But the courage, resolution and compassion of the approach were never in question. Zinnemann's handling of the professional and non-professional players, the balance maintained between the central story and the hospital background, the grasp of the human implications . . . and the vitality of Carl Foreman's script, made this a film of unusual honesty.[53]

Zinnemann left temporarily to make *Teresa*, about an Italian war bride, and Kramer, with the redoubtable lettuce-growing financier Church behind him, decided to proceed with an adaptation of Edmond De Rostand's nineteenth-century stage success, *Cyrano de Bergerac*. Kramer knew it was risky: "Our only assurance that it could become a box-office attraction was the fact that it had always been a financial success on the stage, and that we could get Jose Ferrer to play it."[54] Church's money once again guaranteed rehearsal time, and production went ahead without significant snags at the team's usual breathtaking pace of under a month and at a cost far below studio rates.[55] Set designer Rudolph Sternad created the sets for only $50,000, "having devised ingenious methods for cutting costs and yet maintaining a sense of historical accuracy."[56]

Not everyone, though, would be impressed with the film itself.

Foreman, who had wanted to get on with the long-planned *High Noon*, had been disappointed with the decision to proceed with *Cyrano*, "a project I had great reservations about; . . . I felt we were not equipped to do a good job on it. And I don't think we did," he told Crowther in a letter a year after *High Noon* was released.[57] But, ever the reliable partner, he dutifully wrote the screenplay.

Foreman wasn't the only one with doubts. To Ferrer, who would win an Oscar for his performance, "*Cyrano* was one of those films that nobody had any faith in. It was done for $400,000 and shot in four weeks."[58]

Ironically, given his misgivings, Foreman treated *Cyrano* as something of a dry run for *High Noon,* according to Maurice Yacowar. As in the Western, Foreman uses "a remote time and setting and a remote set of conventions, to dramatize the McCarthy paralysis of Hollywood. . . . Not for Foreman the confections that Kramer could churn out, nor for Foreman the frequent shallowness one finds in the lead-footed liberalism of a Kramer film."[59]

Foreman liked to say that he didn't employ villains so much as people who feel compelled to do what they do, and that was how he portrayed the ostensible villain, Cardinal Richelieu. "There are no villains in the Foreman *Cyrano*, just a larger-than-life hero against a backdrop of small, ordinary, scampering humanity, in a social situation of great anxiety, fright, panic. It is a situation of censorship, so Cyrano is finally assassinated by forces embarrassed at his satires."[60]

Rostand's Cyrano speaks for Foreman when he refuses to rewrite his plays to satisfy the Cardinal:

> The film is very much concerned with the artist's relation to his art. . . . Often the film Cyrano aims his insults—and his sword—directly at the audience. This is particularly important in the death scene, where he draws his sword to fight off Death and the phantoms of his old enemies: Falsehood, Prejudice, Compromise, Cowardice and his most dangerous opponent, Vanity.[61]

Writing a year after the film's release in November 1950, Houston found both the movie, and the fact that Kramer had produced it, "curious": "That a company which had achieved some reputation for realistic treatment of the contemporary scene should trot out this old theatrical warhorse was in itself surprising. . . . Ferrer (another actor new to the screen) gave a performance which, though it strikingly lacked pathos and substituted a brief show of fireworks in the early scenes for the authentic *panache,* had a style and intelligence." Otherwise the film offered only weak supporting performances and direction: "One might have expected *Cyrano* to attract largely through grace and elegance of setting; the drab, unimaginative sets and rather somber photography indicated that what may, perhaps, be called repertory technicians share some of the limitations of repertory actors."[62]

With United Artists in financial trouble, Kramer booked the film himself: "Under the preexisting contract, United Artists nevertheless was to receive 10 per cent of the gross, in lieu of its regular distributing fee."[63] After *Cyrano,* "we held off production for several months," Foreman told Crowther, in his August 1952 letter, "because of United Artists' shaky condition."[64]

But the situation at Kramer Productions was about to change dramatically.

In the winter of 1951, Kramer began negotiations with Harry Cohn, production head at Columbia, to make movies in collaboration with the studio. The idea was that Kramer would use his now-celebrated efficiencies to make thirty films over five years for under $980,000 apiece. Kramer, whose company would move to the Columbia lot, would have a free choice of what movies he made and Columbia would finance and release them. Cohn would have to approve any cost overruns but otherwise had no say over the films made. Kramer would use the Columbia lot, but he would own the negatives, split the profits evenly with Columbia after all costs, including distribution, were paid, and would remain independent and self-operating.[65] Kramer would say later that he had to be seduced into a partnership that might compromise his independence. His partners, he told a biographer, "were encouraged into this deal by a film executive named Sam Katz, who had been fired at MGM and was looking for a way back into the business."[66]

Cohn called the deal, announced March 18, 1951, "the most important deal we have ever made. . . . Never before has an arrangement of this kind been concluded between a major corporation and a completely self-operating independent organization."[67]

As the deal was being announced, Foreman was in the middle of writing *High Noon*. He would be associate producer on this last film to fulfill the United Artists contract, a development he relished, given his reservations about what was happening. He would stay at Motion Picture Center in Hollywood while Kramer and the rest of the company moved to the Columbia lot.[68]

As Foreman told Crowther, he

> had strong reservations against both these developments [that is, the Columbia deal and the hiring of Katz], but I was outvoted by Stanley and George. Finally, both deals were made. Obviously, great changes would now come into being, and only time would tell if they were to be beneficial to the people involved and their work. On a personal level, it became apparent at once that I would not now be able to direct our next picture, as had been the plan. I would now have to become a full producer as well as an executive of a large company. And our great need now was product. We had to make seven pictures in our first year, six for Columbia and one for UA, still owed by contract. We needed stories, lots of them.
>
> To meet this need, and for the benefit of the Columbia program, Stanley devised the stratagem of purchasing New York plays and published novels. This would give the new company not only important, prestige product, but would enable us to get going in a hurry. . . . For the last remaining UA picture he was not too concerned. I would produce it, as well as two more on the Columbia slate, and the choice of subject was left to me.[69]

Seven months later, with Foreman's "choice of subject," *High Noon*, being edited, and a few days after *Variety* reported that Kramer had forced Foreman out of the company over the blacklist, the paper noted that Kramer had signed repentant blacklistee Edward Dmytryk to direct *The Sniper*, one of the Columbia pictures. *Death of a Salesman, My Six Convicts, The Member of the Wedding*, and *The Fourposter* had been completed. Still to be made were *The Happy Time, Eight Iron Men, The 5,000 Fingers of Dr. T.* (from a script by Foreman's wartime buddy, Ted Geisel, a.k.a. Dr. Seuss), *The Juggler, The Wild One, The Caine Mutiny, Ethan Frome*, and *The Sound of Hunting*.[70]

It was a fatally overambitious schedule. *Ethan Frome* and *The Sound of Hunting* would never be made. "After the first six were unsuccessful, Columbia limited the number to three a year, resulting in a reduction of staff. Finally, after eleven failures, Columbia terminated the agreement on 24 November 1954, even before *The Caine Mutiny*, Kramer's one hit, had a chance to prove itself."[71] The success of *Caine*—its huge box office paid for the losses on all the others—had come too late to save the relationship.[72]

Some of the films that failed—in particular *The Member of the Wedding, The 5,000 Fingers of Dr. T.*, and *The Wild One*, in which Marlon Brando created an indelible image of a rebellious biker—would earn later critical respect or develop second lives as cult films.

Though the relationship had proved too ambitious, the mold had been set: From now on, independents would be looking for partnerships with the majors like Kramer's.

Kramer was on his own again. By the next year, he was back with United Artists, where he immediately had another success with the apolitical melodrama *Not As a Stranger*—the first film he directed as well as produced.

Kramer's politics, as he readily reminded anyone, were New Deal liberal, not Marxist. His films, both those he produced and those he later produced and directed, dealt with social problems. He would always argue, to no avail, that he was merely telling a story with a point, not preaching.

Kramer would go on to make more than a dozen films after the blacklist ended, many of them critical as well as commercial successes, in which he reverted to telling tales with morals on a grander and more explicit scale. Among them would be *The Defiant Ones* (1958), another film on race relations; *On the Beach* (1959), about the aftermath of a nuclear war; *Inherit the Wind* (1960), about the Scopes "Monkey Trial"; *Judgment at Nuremberg* (1961), on Nazi war crimes; and *Guess Who's Coming to Dinner* (1967), another antiracism drama.

Kramer would eventually be dismissed by most film historians as a relic, a message-monger who traded film craft for preachy statement. Indeed, he would become the poster boy for what was wrong with a certain kind of American film—the kind that would inflame auteurist commentators. Even though the venom would be aimed primarily at the later, more expensive films, the ones he directed as well as produced, the shadow of irrelevancy would fall on all his films. It wouldn't help that the movie industry "certified" his importance with so many Academy awards: sixteen Oscars and eighty nominations.[73]

Pauline Kael put it this way; Kramer's movies

> were melodramas with—to use legalese—redeeming social importance;
> and if their messages were often irritatingly self-righteous, the situations
> and settings were, nevertheless, excitingly modern, relevant. There was
> talent in these [early] productions [though not necessarily his] . . . The
> producer, like an editor, needs only the talent to buy talent—then all too
> frequently he attempts to shape it in his own image. The shaping in Stan-
> ley Kramer productions was harsh, shallow, opportunistic. . . . Despite
> his reputation as a courageous director, and a serious thinker, the subject
> matter when it isn't already pulp is turned into pulp.[74]

Perhaps the most devastating criticism, though, came much earlier, when Kramer was impressing Hollywood with his success and
High Noon had just been released in Britain. Penelope Houston, in an
otherwise admiring essay, claimed that "his most fitting territory is
that range of material sufficiently unusual to attract public notice,
without being so daring or so novel as to frighten it away."[75] She was
saying, almost as an afterthought, that he was less a crusader than a
commercially calculating provocateur, and it was this, more than the
sentiments expressed, that would incite a range of critics over the
decades to attack him bitterly.

Many who dismissed Kramer's films nevertheless learned his production methods: Find reliable sources of independent financing willing to take payment as interest or profits rather than shares; use the financing to pay for construction and rehearsal before large crews show
up; pay stars a percentage of the gross against straight salary; use the
same reliable crew over and over and pay them partly in profit par-
ticipation to encourage speed; avoid work-for-hire at the major studios unless that is the only way to pay for your own films; keep tight
budgetary control over the entire project; minimize the ability of distributors to influence casting, script, or final cut; retain ownership of
the film negatives; and take chances on offbeat subjects. Not everyone
followed this prescription, but everyone in the film industry has been
operating on some combination of these principles ever since.

Kramer lost his way when he attempted a much too ambitious
production schedule. And he lost Foreman, his ace screenwriter—
and Foreman's political themes—just when he needed him, and
them, most. The production rules he had devised made sense; it was
ambition and the blacklist that undercut his groundbreaking contract with Columbia.

Perhaps the greatest irony was that *High Noon*, made on a shoestring even by Kramer's inexpensive standards, would become by far the most important film of his early career—not only for what it was, but for how it was made, in the shadow of what seemed, at the time, brilliant deal making. Kramer's diminished reputation would come back to haunt *High Noon*—the film in whose production he had been the least involved of any of his films, the film that had been made almost independently of his independent company, the film that of all his films resisted categorizing as a simple didactic story.

By its very nature, *High Noon*, the film Stanley Kramer cared about least, celebrated independent filmmaking—a process that, like Will Kane and the victims of the blacklist, was subject to manipulation and betrayal on all sides.

NOTES

1. Robert Sklar, *Movie-Made America* (New York: Vintage, 1975), 272; Gerald Mast and Bruce Kawin, *A Short History of the Movies* (Boston: Allyn & Bacon, 1996), 295.

2. The implications of *United States v. Paramount Pictures* are reviewed in Richard Maltby, *Harmless Entertainment* (Metuchen, N.J.: Scarecrow Press, 1983), 63–64. Mast and Kawin, *Short History*, 298–99, recount the devastation that hit the studios.

3. Sklar, *Movie-Made America*, 276; Brian Neve, *Film and Politics in America: A Social Tradition* (London: Routledge, 1992), 88; Richard Pells, *Not Like Us* (New York: Basic, 1997): 214–15; Richard Maltby, "Film Noir: The Politics of the Maladjusted Text," *Journal of American Studies* 18 (1984): 64–65.

4. *Burstyn v. Wilson*, 72 S. Ct. 777 (1952).

5. Sklar, *Movie-Made America*, 282.

6. Quoted in Hollis Alpert, "Something Worth Fighting For," *Saturday Review*, December 28, 1963, 16.

7. Mast and Kawin, *Short History*, 309.

8. "Perhaps more than the Red Scare, the demise of the studio production line and the individual marketing of pictures meant a far greater reliance on bank financing—and the banks were conservative about everything." Sklar, *Movie-Made America*, 287. Thus it is all the more intriguing that Kramer apparently had no trouble getting financing from the Bank of America.

9. Maltby, *Harmless Entertainment*, 77–78.

10. Tino Balio, *United Artists: The Company That Changed the Film Industry* (Madison: University of Wisconsin Press, 1987), 46–47.

11. Neve, *Film and Politics*, 114.

12. Philip Drummond, *High Noon* (London: British Film Institute, 1997), 15–17.

13. Neve, *Film and Politics*, 87; Robert Sklar, "Empire to the West: Red River," in *Howard Hawks: American Artist,* ed. Jim Hillier and Peter Wollen (London: BFI Publishing, 1996), 154.

14. J. A. Aberdeen, *Hollywood Renegades: The Society of Independent Motion Picture Producers* (Los Angeles: Cobblestone Entertainment, 2000), quoted at www.cobbles.com/simpp_archive (accessed November 12, 2002).

15. Neve, *Film and Politics*, 38; Aberdeen, *Renegades.*

16. Maltby, *Harmless Entertainment*, 278; Neve, *Film and Politics*, 126.

17. Neve, *Film and Politics*, 126.

18. Neve, *Film and Politics,* 126.

19. Maltby, *Harmless Entertainment*, 278.

20. Quoted from Neve, *Film and Politics*, 126.

21. Neve, *Film and Politics*, 126.

22. Drummond, *High Noon*, 15–17; Hollis Alpert, "The Postwar Generation: Movies," *Saturday Review* 36 (March 14, 1953): 62; Penelope Houston, "Kramer and Company," *Sight and Sound* 21 (July–September 1952): 20.

23. Rick Lyman, "Stanley Kramer, Filmmaker with Social Bent, Dies at 87," *New York Times,* February 21, 2001 [Web site archive].

24. Stanley Kramer, "The Independent Producer," *Films in Review* 2 (March 1951): 2.

25. Kramer, "Independent Producer," 3–4.

26. Kramer, "Independent Producer," 4.

27. Bruce Eder, *All Movie Guide,* n.d., at movies.yahoo.com (accessed March 13, 2002).

28. Adapted from "Stanley Kramer," in *Current Biography*, Vol. 12 (New York: H. W. Wilson, 1983), 356–58.

29. Houston, "Kramer and Company," 20.

30. "Stanley Kramer," *Current Biography,* 357.

31. Neve, *Film and Politics*, 115.

32. "Stanley Kramer," *Current Biography,* 357.

33. Adapted from Donald Spoto, *Stanley Kramer: Filmmaker* (New York: Putnam, 1978): 27–42; also Neve, *Film and Politics,*115; Balio, *United Artists,* 46–47; Houston, "Kramer and Company," 20.

34. Spoto, *Kramer*, 22.

35. Charles Champlin, "It's Been a Life of Pride, Passion—and Defiance," *Los Angeles Times,* September 20, 1997, F:13. Archived in the Academy of Motion Picture Arts and Sciences Fairbanks Center for Motion Picture Study in Beverly Hills.

36. Walsh, David, "Why Was Stanley Kramer So Unfashionable at the Time of His Death?," *World Socialist Web Site,* February 26, 2001, at www.wsws.org/articles/2001/feb2001/kram-f26.shtml (accessed February 28, 2002).

37. Balio, *United Artists,* 47.

38. Foreman, in Terry Sanders and Freida Lee Mock, *Word into Image: Portraits of American Screenwriters: Carl Foreman,* (video) (Santa Monica: American Film Foundation, 1981).

39. Houston, "Kramer and Company," 20; Nora Sayre, *Running Time* (New York: Dial Press,1982), 45, 47.

40. Sayre, *Running Time,* 48.

41. Kramer, "Independent Producer," 2–3.

42. "Stanley Kramer," *Current Biography,* 357.

43. Stephen Prince, "Historical Perspective and the Realist Aesthetic in *High Noon* (1952)," in *The Films of Fred Zinnemann,* ed. Arthur Nolletti Jr. (Albany: State University of New York Press, 1999). 81.

44. Fred Zinnemann, *A Life in the Movies: An Autobiography* (New York: Scribner, 1992), 80–81.

45. Champlin, "Pride, Passion," F13.

46. "Dialogue on Film: Carl Foreman," *American Film* 4 (April 1979): 36.

47. "Fred Zinnemann," in *Current Biography,* Vol. 14 (New York: H. W. Wilson, 1983), 673.

48. Walsh, "Why Was Kramer Unfashionable."

49. "Stanley Kramer," *Current Biography,* 358.

50. Eder, *All Movie Guide.*

51. Spoto, *Kramer,* 65–68.

52. Quoted in "Stanley Kramer," *Current Biography,* 358.

53. Houston, "Kramer and Company," 22.

54. Kramer, "Independent Producer," 2–3.

55. Kramer, "Independent Producer," 4.

56. Spoto, *Kramer,* 69.

57. Letter from Carl Foreman to Bosley Crowther, August 7, 1952, 1–2. Copyright © The Carl Foreman Estate. Loaned by Eve Williams-Jones, Foreman's widow.

58. Jose Ferrer (interview), "Cyrano and Others," *Films and Filming* 8 (July 1962): 45.

59. Maurice Yacowar, "Cyrano de H.U.A.C.," *Journal of Popular Film* 5 (January 1976): 74.

60. Yacowar, "Cyrano," 73.

61. Yacowar, "Cyrano," 74.

62. Houston, "Kramer and Company," 22.

63. "Stanley Kramer," *Current Biography,* 358.

64. Foreman to Crowther, August 7, 1952, 3.

65. *New York Times,* March 19, 1951, 23; *Variety,* June 25, 1952, 18 (Columbia, like everyone else in Hollywood, would turn to the banks: "Bulk of cash outlay for production comes from Bankers Trust and Guarantee Trust, both in New York, on a joint basis. They advance 50% of the budget for each pic and are well-satisfied with results, since the loans are cross-collateralized on

the various films, and there's no danger whatsoever of the banks not coming out."); Eder, *All Movie Guide*; David Caute, *The Great Fear* (New York: Simon & Schuster, 1978), 104–5.

66. Quoted in Spoto, *Kramer*, 73–76.

67. Quoted in Victor Navasky, *Naming Names* (New York: Viking, 1980), 156.

68. Rudy Behlmer, *Behind the Scenes* (Hollywood, Calif.: Samuel French, 1990), 27; Neve, *Film and Politics*, 185.

69. Foreman to Crowther, August 7, 1952, 3.

70. From "Dmytryk Signs for Another Kramer Pic," *Variety*, October 31, 1951, 5.

71. Bernard F. Dick, *The Merchant Prince of Poverty Row* (Lexington: University Press of Kentucky, 1993), 182.

72. Bob Thomas, *King Cohn* (New York: Putnam, 1967), 319–20.

73. Champlin, "Pride, Passion," F13.

74. Pauline Kael, *Kiss Kiss Bang Bang* (New York: Bantam, 1969), 204.

75. Houston, "Kramer and Company," 23.

Chapter 4

The Red Scare
and the Blacklist

What was going on was a hysteria of a shameful nature. Old friends wouldn't talk to each other. Someone would call up and say, "How are you? Remember the hammer you borrowed? Can I come by and get it back?" And that guy was going to testify the next day, and give your name. That was the atmosphere.

—John Berry[1]

If there was a single moment that inspired the Hollywood anti-"red" crusade that would damage so many lives connected with *High Noon* and inspire its political interpretation, it came at the Oscar ceremony on February 29, 1940, when the winners for 1939 were announced. With only the Marx Brothers comedies *A Night at the Opera* (1935) and *A Day at the Races* (1937) to show for two decades at Paramount and MGM, Sam Wood had directed his first "prestige" film, *Goodbye, Mr. Chips,* and expected to win the prize for best director. So he was profoundly shocked when his friend Victor Fleming took the statuette for *Gone with the Wind* instead. Making the situation worse was that Wood had directed several scenes in Fleming's movie without credit. Why he should have been surprised is a mystery: *Gone with the Wind* was the movie of the year. It had been nominated in twelve categories and would win in eight, including best picture. In losing for best director that night, Wood found himself in distinguished company: Frank Capra for *Mr. Smith Goes to Washington,* John Ford for *Stagecoach,* and William Wyler for *Wuthering Heights.* But according to Wood's daughter, Jean, "the defeat galled and disappointed him beyond measure."[2]

Wood was a friend and admirer of William Randolph Hearst, whose anticommunist feelings he shared. The combination of this perceived slight on Oscar night and his friendship with Hearst would prove highly combustible. "When Hearst turned on Roosevelt during the war, Wood's own frustration suddenly curdled into a hatred of the New Deal and a conflation of liberalism and communism. He began carrying a little black book in which he jotted the names of those radicals, often no more than supporters of the New Deal, he hoped someday to purge from Hollywood."[3]

During the war, Wood and his friends were incensed not only by the film community's endless meetings, rallies, and speeches in favor of the "Second Front," a U.S. invasion of Nazi-occupied Europe that would relieve the pressure on the Soviets, but also by what they saw as communist influence in films that the studios, acting at the suggestion of President Franklin D. Roosevelt, made during the war to promote the alliance with the Soviet Union. Particularly galling was Warner's *Mission to Moscow*, which justified the purge trials, the Nazi–Soviet pact, and the Red Army invasion of Finland. As irritating was *The North Star*, with its naïve vision of a collective farm in an unnamed country fighting the Nazis, and *Song of Russia*, with Robert Taylor as an American conductor marrying a Russian peasant girl.[4]

"Possessed by his mission . . . Wood decided to organize like-minded film people into a new group," says Neal Gabler.[5] Wood's organization, called, rather grandly, the Motion Picture Alliance for the Preservation of American Ideals, "began informally with a small group of anti-Communists who would meet regularly at the home of James Kevin McGuinness, an executive producer at MGM."[6] On February 7, 1944, after weeks of secret meetings, "the MPAPAI (known afterward as the *MPA* or the *Alliance*) was organized at a mass meeting in the grand ballroom of the Beverly–Wilshire Hotel. About fifteen hundred persons, from every craft union and economic stratum of the industry, were present."[7]

Wood had himself elected president before a who's-who of Hollywood conservatives. Among the new group's officers were two well-known anti-Semites—McGuinness, who had been fighting leftist screenwriters for a decade, and Walt Disney, who refused to hire Jews and had threatened to shut his studio rather than pay his striking cartoonists any more money.[8]

Wood was able to attract a constellation of stars to his new group in its first year, among them Clark Gable, just returned from the war;

John Wayne; Adolphe Menjou; Ginger Rogers; and Gary Cooper, who had appeared in Wood's *The Pride of the Yankees* and *For Whom the Bell Tolls*.[9] Others among the leadership, most of them Wood's friends and colleagues from MGM, were directors Victor Fleming, John Ford, and Cecil B. De Mille, and composer Dmitri Tiomkin.[10]

The MPA had many grievances. "The founders," notes Garry Wills,

> were opposing not only communism, but the New Deal, labor unions, and civil rights organizations at a time when others connected with those causes were pulling together for the war effort, postponing their differences for the duration. . . . Some, like Walt Disney and Cecil B. De Mille, resisted unions in general. Others had opposed the forming of their respective talent guilds. A large bloc of Alliance founders . . . were involved in [MGM production chief Irving] Thalberg's attempt to undo the Screen Writers Guild. Others went back to Louis B. Mayer's use of the Academy as an anti-union force. But all were sincere anti-Communists whatever their other political sympathies.[11]

"In our special field of motion pictures," said the statement with which the MPA introduced itself, "we resent the growing impression that this industry is made up of, and dominated by, Communists, radicals and crackpots. . . . We pledge to fight, with every means at our organized command, any effort of any group or individual to divert the loyalty of the screen from the free America that gave it birth."[12]

Outside the movie industry, only the Hearst press, which was backing the Alliance financially, took it seriously. Wood told the Hearst papers that

> the organization was assembling because "those highly indoctrinated shock units of the totalitarian wrecking crew have shrewdly led the people of the United States to believe that Hollywood is a hotbed of sedition and subversion, and that our industry is a battleground over which communism is locked in death grips with fascism. . . . We intend to correct that erroneous impression immediately and to assure the people of the United States that . . . Hollywood is a reservoir of Americanism and that those forces which have presumed to speak in the names of our industry and under the geographical identity of Hollywood, have been acting under false pretenses and that we repudiate them entirely."[13]

The formation of the MPA came as something of a bombshell in the feverish political world of the movie industry. "For many weeks," reports Maurice Zolotow, "Hollywood seethed with rumors that a gang of 'Fascists and anti-Semites' were plotting to start a company union. In an industry in which many Jews were studio heads and producers, the anti-Semitic innuendos threatened the Alliance."[14] The liberals—joined by some fellow travelers and Communists—organized the Hollywood Independent Citizens Committed to the Arts, Sciences and Professions, or HICCASP. "A galaxy of stars joined—Humphrey Bogart, John Garfield, . . . Danny Kaye, Edward G. Robinson and numerous others."[15] Prominent by their absence were the politically reactionary Jewish studio executives, who sympathized with the MPA even as they suspected them of trying to realign power in Hollywood.[16] They "wanted nothing to do with it—especially after it called on Congress to investigate the movie industry."[17]

The new Hollywood anticommunist organization wasted no time. A month after its formation, in March 1944, the MPA wrote to Red-hunting Senator Robert Reynolds of North Carolina, "about the dangers of subversion in the movie industry . . .,"[18] in effect inviting him to investigate communism in Hollywood.[19] The letter had an immediate effect. In April, investigators from the House Un-American Activities Committee showed up in the studios and began asking questions.

But these initial investigations by the HUAC staff came to nothing. It would take three years—after Roosevelt's death, the end of the war and the emergence of the Cold War, a spate of Hollywood labor disputes, and an election in which the Republicans would take control of Congress—for the Alliance's efforts to pay off.[20]

The Alliance had had good reason to think they would be taken seriously in Washington. There had always been a significant number of Communists in the motion picture business in the decades before the War, and they and their fellow Leftists were highly politicized. They supported Roosevelt and unions, hated fascism, and attacked "reactionaries" ranging from California produce growers and studio management to conservative politicians and congressional committees.[21] "They had raised money to fight the fascists in prewar Spain; they had written for the Communist press and recruited members of the Party; they had helped to organize the screenwriters', actors' and directors' guilds, they had participated in strikes against the studios in the mid-1940s, and they supported Henry Wallace for president."[22]

The Hollywood Communists' relationship to the Party was complicated and, frequently, troubled. The movie people tended to be more idealistic than Marxist, and the films they admired "illustrated American radical and progressive themes in the tradition of Thomas Paine, Thomas Jefferson and Abraham Lincoln: *I Am a Fugitive from a Chain Gang* (1932), *Juarez* (1939), *The Story of Louis Pasteur* (1935), *The Life of Emile Zola* (1937), and *The Grapes of Wrath* (1940)."[23]

The Communists ran writers' clinics in Hollywood that taught newcomers like Carl Foreman and argued about whether movies should be focused on the social conditions in which people found themselves or on more conventional dramas. "The party was helpful," recalled Foreman. "I don't know if it was at the [League of American Writers] schools or in the Party discussions, but I was learning about form and content."[24]

The Hollywood Communists made a great deal of money, which could be useful to the Party, but many failed to follow the party line scrupulously.[25] When they did follow the line, they got into trouble: They promoted the Non-Aggression Pact the Soviets signed with the Nazis in 1939 and urged the United States to stay out of Europe— only to change their tune instantly and call for a Second Front when the Nazis invaded the Soviet Union.

Despite the efforts of their enemies to depict them as all-powerful, the Communists' influence in any of the guilds was limited, partly because of their dogmatic defense of every Soviet excess.[26] "As defenders of the Soviet regime the screen-artist Reds became apologists for crimes of monstrous dimension, though they claimed to have known nothing about such crimes, and indeed shouted down or ignored those who did."[27]

Their influence on movies, the subject of so much hysteria at the time, was far more limited. They tried, more than other screenwriters, to emphasize social justice and eliminate racial stereotypes, but relatively little could get past their producers, and for the most part their films are hard to distinguish from those by non-Communists.[28]

Various congressional committees had been investigating the movie industry since 1937, when chairman Martin Dies of the House Un-American Activities Committee had searched for Jewish plots in the industry. He had come back three years later and had taken testimony from stars like Humphrey Bogart and James Cagney, but that investigation, too, had come to nothing.[29]

At the beginning of the war, President Roosevelt drafted the industry for the duration, freeing movies from censorship and arranging for Hollywood talent to make propaganda films[30] to build support for the

war, such as *Mission to Moscow* (1943) and the *Why We Fight* series produced by Frank Capra. The Office of War Information, sounding very
much like Hollywood progressives, described the war as a struggle
between fascism and democracy and said it would mean the end of
colonialism, militarism, and racial prejudice.[31]

During the war the studios turned out hundreds of patriotic feature films, and many of the industry's leading artists made them, including—along with Capra—John Huston, John Ford, William
Wyler, Walt Disney, Edward Dmytryk, Michael Curtiz, Alfred Hitchcock, and Howard Hawks. Hollywood's most successful war propaganda films, including *Action in the North Atlantic* (1943), *Destination Tokyo* (1943), *Tender Comrade* (1943), *Thirty Seconds over Tokyo*
(1944), and *The Pride of the Marines* (1945), were mostly written by
Communists and featured collective rather than individual heroes.[32]
The industry's enthusiastic selling of features as propaganda would
come back to haunt it after the war when its enemies would claim
that it proved what they—the enemies—were saying: that movies
could be used to mold ideas for evil as well as for good.[33]

There was not much for the Red-hunters to work with; once they
had roundly condemned *Mission to Moscow, The North Star,* and *Song
of Russia,* the films that explicitly supported the alliance with the Soviets and sugarcoated the evils of the Soviet system, they would
have to stretch interpretations or search for odd snippets of conversation to make their case.

During the three years from the MPA's initial request for help until HUAC finally stepped in, various members of the committee issued hair-raising warnings—one said he was "on the trail of the
tarantula"—but were unable to follow up until the Republicans took
over in January 1947.[34]

There was no mystery about the congressional obsession with the
movie industry. "Hollywood's overwhelming attraction for the
Committee," notes Nora Sayre, "was its celebrities: the investigators
had a fixation on the famous. Although the public hardly knew the
names of writers or directors, the word 'Hollywood' conferred a
kind of royalty—which meant dazzling exposure and banner headlines for the Committee."[35]

All of this congressional activity as the war ended was taking
place against the backdrop of a concerted conservative campaign
against "un-Americanism." From the 1944 presidential campaign
on, the right wing in America developed a three-step plan to roll

back the New Deal by linking Joseph Stalin to American communists, liberals, and social critics generally.[36] Communism was said to be the ideology of atheistic, collectivistic internationalists—in contrast with an Americanism of organized religion, private property, and nationalism. "Rightwing spokespeople hammered away at the theme that reformist activists and critics weakened America; they therefore had to be Communistic in identity or sympathy, and, in the national interest, had to be exposed and quarantined."[37]

The Right was angry at the movie industry for supporting a war they—the Right—"saw . . . as a sacrifice of American lives to save the Jews and Europe and help the Soviets defend the Eastern front."[38] The Jewish movie executives, right-wing anticommunists themselves, were caught in the middle of this attempt to link Jews, communists, unions, and the New Deal with which they were so closely associated[39]—and thus would consider any way to escape the assault that didn't involve giving up control of filmmaking.

The studios tried to blunt the influence of businessmen in this attack by hiring as their spokesman Eric Johnston, the president of the United States Chamber of Commerce, which was producing a series of pamphlets linking unions and communism and recommending "the institution of a strict federal loyalty program and an investigation of Communist influence in the cultural media, notably the motion picture industry."[40]

Though they represented only a tiny fraction of the membership, the Communists since the mid-1930s had led the effort by the Screen Writers Guild and the Screen Actors Guild to organize the studio workers into unions. By 1945, the industry was totally unionized.[41] "There was a fierce jurisdictional strike in 1945 between the AFL's craft union, the International Alliance of Theatrical Stage Employees . . . and the leftwing Conference of Studio Unions."[42] In March 1945, "the CSU affiliate in the dispute went out on strike, and nearly all the craft unions refused to cross its picket lines." The newly arrived leader of IATSE, Roy Brewer, "decided that his best tactic against CSU was to attack it as Communist-dominated." Brewer quickly aligned himself with the MPA, despite its antiunion stance. He would make connections at the studios through the Alliance and the Alliance would win "labor support for its assertion that Communists were trying to dominate the industry."[43]

Brewer, who would briefly become the president of the MPA, would later tell HUAC that "the one potent force that stood between complete control of the industry by the Communists and their defeat at the crucial point in 1945 were the A. F. of L. unions."[44] Brewer insisted that the Communists were trying to control the unions so that they could force the producers to accept communist scripts.[45] He had also allied with the newly chosen Screen Actors Guild president, Ronald Reagan, who denounced the CSU strike as a communist plot to create one giant union "with everyone in it from producers to grips."[46]

"The strike, especially at Warner Brothers," report Ceplair and Englund, "witnessed picket line scenes reminiscent of the worst labor–management confrontations of the thirties in Detroit, Chicago or Oakland. Warners (and their IATSE allies) employed scabs, thugs, tear gas, fire hoses and the studio's private police and fire departments to disrupt picket lines and break the strike."[47]

Jack Warner's "anger against the strikers spilled over into a determination to fight the Communists who Brewer and the MPA claimed were behind the disorders, and he became the first major convert from the top of the industry's hierarchy to the anti-Communist front."[48]

It was in the midst of this political hothouse that HUAC began its newest investigation in Los Angeles in May 1947. The congressmen were welcomed by the principal voice of the Red-baiters in the press, Hedda Hopper, who was an MPA board member. In April she had written to FBI director J. Edgar Hoover, "I loved what you said about the commies in the motion picture industry. But I would like it even more if you could name names and print more facts."[49] From 1946 to 1948, she traveled the country lecturing on the Hollywood Red problem. In a 1947 speech to American Legion women, she attacked *Mr. Smith Goes to Washington* (1939) because it implied that there were no honest men in the Senate, and *Meet John Doe* (1941) because it portrayed an American industrialist unsympathetically. "*The Farmer's Daughter*," she said, "ridiculed free elections." And "she urged all Americans to boycott pictures with actors who had Communist connections or any film made at Metro Goldwyn 'Moscow.'"[50]

The Committee's general justification for its investigation was fluid; at various times it was investigating communist control of studio unions, communist propaganda in films, and the subsidy by Hollywood's Communists of subversive activities nationwide. But the primary concern of the Republican-controlled Committee was to tie film workers to the Communist Party and the Roosevelt administration. The implication was that the Hollywood Communists were subversive, though insiders knew the Communists had never actually controlled any union or movie and were hardly in a position to spy or commit sabotage for the Russians.[51] It hardly mattered what the Committee's official charge was. Attacking the movie industry guaranteed publicity.[52]

Because movies were not constitutionally protected forms of speech, there was little to restrain a search for propaganda.[53] The committee ignored the union battles and focused on the Screen Writer's Guild, which, though numerically tiny, had a significant percentage of Communists in its ranks and had been the most politically active of all Hollywood groups. The Committee's focus served the interest of the Alliance witnesses, whose primary target was the writers' guild and its preeminent Communist members, who would come to be known as the Hollywood Ten.[54]

Chairman Thomas and Pennsylvania Republican committee member John McDowell opened their Hollywood investigation working from lists of Communists supplied by the Alliance, the FBI, and the Los Angeles Police Department Intelligence Squad. The idea was to frighten the studio heads into helping the Committee.[55] The witnesses they called in executive session, other than Jack Warner, were almost all members of MPA, including the novelist and screenwriter Ayn Rand, Lela Rogers (mother of Ginger), and Robert Taylor,[56] who complained that he had been forced to make *Song of Russia*. The witnesses were anxious to denounce several films. Along with the usual targets—*Mission to Moscow, Song of Russia,* and *The North Star*—*The Best Years of Our Lives* (for its scene of returning veteran Dana Andrews punching a man who says, "It looks like we fought the wrong people"), *The Strange Love of Martha Ivers*, and *The Pride of the Marines* were said to contain "sizeable doses of Communist propaganda."[57]

Angry about the strikes, and increasingly fearful of damage to his studio, Warner told the committee he had blocked communist propaganda, named several well-known non-Communists as Communists, and insisted he had fired fifteen Communist writers. He would later deny employing Communists and insist that "*Mission to Moscow* . . . was 'made only to help a desperate war effort and was not for posterity.'"[58]

That summer Committee investigators, most of them FBI agents, threatened studio executives in their offices with the wrath of Congress or the public if they didn't suspend the employees named by the

Alliance.[59] The studio executives now faced a difficult choice—aiding HUAC's anti-Semitic, anti-studio agenda, or risking charges of un-Americanism. They tried to finesse the issue by cooperating with the Committee "while refusing to acknowledge subversive content in their own films. . . . There was nothing noble or civil libertarian about the executives' resistance to demands that they fire communists. They didn't like being told what to do by outsiders, they feared suits by those fired, and they didn't want to do what had always been done to Jews."[60]

When HUAC moved its investigation of the film industry to Washington in October, it began with twenty-four "friendly" witnesses who would help it lay out the conspiracy in Hollywood. Jack Warner, Walt Disney, and Louis B. Mayer represented the studio heads; Gary Cooper, Robert Taylor, Robert Montgomery, and Ronald Reagan represented actors. The MPA's resident intellectual, Ayn Rand, denounced a favorite target, *The Best Years of Our Lives*—this time for showing a banker turning down a loan to a veteran.[61]

Sam Wood, one of the first witnesses, was finally able to get national attention for his view that American Party members were Soviet agents. Fellow MPA member Adolphe Menjou assured the Committee that American Communists were "engaged in treasonable activities."[62]

The biggest star among the "friendly witnesses" was Gary Cooper, who had been a highly visible member of Hollywood's right wing since the middle 1930s. He was an "extremely outspoken anti-Communist,"[63] though that had apparently not kept him from appearing in *The General Died at Dawn* (1936), written by communist screenwriter Clifford Odets, in which Cooper plays the suspiciously egalitarian opponent of a Chinese warlord much like Chiang Kai-Shek, the leader of the anticommunist forces.[64]

But despite his long political activism, when Cooper appeared before the Committee on October 23, his testimony was so vague and noncommittal that historians can't agree about just what he was doing that day. He said his present occupation was "actor," and then looked around with a smile, as if in acknowledgment of its obviousness. Asked if he'd seen communist influence at work, he allowed that he'd heard talk at social gatherings. "I have heard tossed around such statements as, 'Don't you think the Constitution of the United States is about 150 years out of date?' and . . . 'Perhaps this would be a more efficient government without a Congress'"—and then looked around the room, waiting for the inevitable laugh.[65]

He said he'd "turned down quite a few scripts because I thought they were tinged with communistic ideas," but he couldn't name any because he read most of the scripts at night, "and if they don't look good to me, I don't finish them."[66]

Asked whether he considered Communists agents of a foreign government, he replied, "I am not in nearly as good a position to know as some of the witnesses that have been ahead of me, because I am not a very active member in our guild. They, therefore, know much more about the politics and the workings of what communists there are in the guild than I. From the general, overall things that you hear in Hollywood, I would assume that there is such a close parallel."[67]

And when he was asked if he thought communism was increasing or decreasing in Hollywood, he answered, ambiguously, "It is very difficult to say right now, within these last few months, because it has become unpopular and a little risky to say too much. You notice the difference. People who were quite easy to express their thoughts before are beginning to clam up more than they used to."[68]

When he was asked if it would be a good idea to outlaw the Communist Party, Cooper responded, "I think it would be a good idea, although I have never read Karl Marx and I don't know the basis of communism, beyond what I have picked up from hearsay. From what I hear, I don't like it because it isn't on the level. So I couldn't possibly answer that question."[69]

His appearance has troubled historians. Said one, "The most pointless testimony came from Gary Cooper, who had been invited to Washington for show, and whose appearance in double-breasted suit, light blue silk necktie, and white shirt brought sighs from the spectators."[70] Another thought "Cooper's political behavior suggests more confusion than commitment. . . . He espoused a rather simplistic 'my country right or wrong' patriotism. He opposed Communism without knowing anything about it and seemed rather proud of his ignorance. . . . He allowed himself to be manipulated. . . . Just as he hurt his own reputation by lending his enormous prestige to paramilitary organizations in 1935, so [he] . . . hurt the film industry [in 1947]."[71]

One observer, though, suspected guile rather than innocence. "He never gave that committee a single name it could follow up on, nor did he cite a single script he had ever seen that could get anyone into difficulty with the committee. In fact, his testimony before that committee is so amazingly true to his screen persona that it is difficult to tell if Cooper was acting or really unable to remember scripts and names."[72] Said another,

> The spectacle of him trying to demonstrate concern for what he thought (or was trying to make himself think) were the committee's laudable general aims while at the same time avoiding the specific mention of people he vaguely suspected might be of the undemocratic left was really rather touching. He was a fair-minded and tolerant man, and never did he resort more broadly to his shit-kicker's image than he did in this appearance. Innocence, naiveté—this was the loophole through which he successfully squirmed.[73]

Whatever Cooper actually intended, Sam Wood was angry after his testimony: "He came across badly. Stupidly. He emphasized hearsay and couldn't remember the names of scripts he turned down because of an anti-American theme. He was just as opposed as the others, but could not get himself to label anyone."[74]

Perhaps the truth emerged later: "Cooper would eventually make a show of repudiating what he had done [in testifying]. He never recanted his testimony, or said he regretted having been a friendly witness. He became conciliatory, however, during the subsequent . . . blacklist. As an independent producer, he eventually hired players and technicians who had been blacklisted. He did say he had never wanted to see any actor lose the right to work, regardless of what he had done."[75]

After hearing from Cooper and the other "friendlies," the committee got down to its main business: identifying supposed subversives and forcing them to testify against others. HUAC had targeted some of the most prominent names in Hollywood: screenwriters, directors, and producers who had worked on wartime propaganda films, as well as postwar "social realist" films such as *Crossfire* (1947), *Cornered* (1945), and *Body and Soul* (1947)—films that exposed anti-Semitism and secret Nazism or implied criticism of capitalism. The ten "unfriendlies" who were eventually called denounced the committee and refused to cooperate, citing the First Amendment. All ten were held in contempt of Congress.

HUAC suspended its hearings for three years while the Hollywood Ten appealed their convictions for contempt and then, when they lost, went to prison for a year. But the effect of the hearings on Hollywood was just beginning. A month after they ended, the studio heads, at a meeting with their financiers in a New York hotel, instituted a blacklist at the suggestion of their front man, Eric Johnston, the president of the Motion Picture Producers Association, beginning with the Hollywood Ten. This, he suggested, would keep Congress from further involvement in movie production. The studios announced they would not "knowingly employ a Communist," and invited "the Hollywood talent guilds to work with us to eliminate any subversives, to protect the innocent, and to safeguard free speech and a free screen wherever threatened."[76]

In retrospect, the blacklist appears inevitable. The Supreme Court was about to hand down its antimonopoly ruling; television was suddenly a threat; the Left had lost the studio union wars; and the winner of those wars, Roy Brewer's militantly anti-communist IATSE, had allied with the MPA in encouraging government intervention. And the studios themselves were increasingly owned by Eastern business conglomerates such as J. P. Morgan, General Foods, and United Fruit, which had no particular interest in the freedom of the screen.[77]

Over and above all of this, the movie industry, along with the rest of the country, was facing what seemed a vast, monolithic threat both abroad and at home. Challenges from communist forces seemed to be coming in rapid succession everywhere: in Greece, where a civil war raged; in China, which "fell" to the communists the same year the Soviets unexpectedly exploded an atomic bomb; in England, where atomic spy Klaus Fuchs was arrested; and in South Korea, which was invaded in 1950 by the North.

At home, State Department official Alger Hiss was convicted of perjury for lying about his contacts with Soviet agents; Senator Joseph McCarthy's campaign against alleged communists in government began; the McCarran Internal Security Act required the registration of communists and provided for the detention of suspected "subversives"; the Supreme Court found constitutional the Smith Act prohibiting attempts to organize the overthrow of the government; and Julius and Ethel Rosenberg were arrested for passing atomic secrets to the Soviets.[78]

The Screenwriters Guild was torn apart by the hearings and by the continuing pressures over the next few years from HUAC, the studios, and the FBI. Carl Foreman, a member of the guild, would be caught up in a battle in 1950 over whether the members of the guild's executive board should take a loyalty oath:

> The fights were so bitter and I stood out against that loyalty oath. And [Leonard] Spigelgass, who had been my commander when I was in his regiment during the war, begged me, crying, not to vote against the

loyalty oath. "It'll ruin you," he said to me; "you're throwing your career away." There was a special bond between the writers who had served together in the army, which added tension to the political splits that began in 1947.[79]

Said one writer several years later about the events of 1947, one

must remember the conjunction of events in that period. Television was a reality, and the Consent Decree [that is, the Supreme Court decision in the government monopoly suit against the studios] severely changed the economics of the industry. On both sides there was unemployment, bitterness, frustration. Your bread-and-butter writers . . . on the extreme right, being out of work and not quite understanding what had happened, vented their spleen in hostile acts and often blamed the communists for what had happened to them and to the industry.[80]

These were the MPA's glory days. Working with Screen Actor's Guild president Ronald Reagan, the studios, HUAC, the FBI, the unions, and the American Legion, the Alliance's Roy Brewer oversaw "a systematic procedure to deal with the many unsubstantiated charges pouring in from free-lance Red hunters. Gradually a system of 'clearance' evolved. . . . For non-Communists, 'clearance' required repudiating all liberal opinions and associations; former Communists were required to perform a humiliating public ritual of expiation by naming names of other Hollywood Communists."[81]

Once Brewer was satisfied that the recanter was sincere, he would advise him to talk to the FBI; seek to recant, with names, before HUAC; and, if he were a celebrity, write a newspaper or magazine article renouncing past activism. The MPA, recanters were then told, would help them get their jobs back.[82]

The Alliance was, in effect, a full-service agency. When one executive committee member, Hedda Hopper, would target a suspect, such as Jose Ferrer, star of Kramer's just-released *Cyrano de Bergerac*, her colleague, Roy Brewer, would arrange for Ferrer and others to repent, confess, and seek "clearance" so they could continue working.

The accused had no help. "The guilds refrained from even token support of those witnesses who refused to cooperate, while" nearly sixty former communists or "fellow travelers" agreed to name names.[83]

Meanwhile, as Eric Johnston put it, "We'll have no more *Grapes of Wrath*, we'll have no more *Tobacco Road*s. We'll have no more films that show the seamy side of American life. We'll have no pictures that deal with labor strikes. We'll have no pictures that deal with the banker as villain."[84]

Johnston, Brewer, and Reagan "helped distribute a new film code written by . . . Ayn Rand, *Screen Guide for Americans*," notes historian Lary May. "Under broad headlines, it preached 'Don't Smear the Free Enterprise System,' 'Don't Deify the Common Man,' 'Don't Show That Poverty is a Virtue . . . and Failure is Noble.' The 'nobility' of the 'little people' was now labeled the 'drooling of weaklings.' In this atmosphere, dramatists of the commoners' former hostility to monopoly, even the militantly anti-communist director Frank Capra, found their security clearances taken away."[85]

"Widely reprinted and blessed with the MPA imprimatur," James Lorence notes in his history of the suppression of the film *Salt of the Earth* (1954),[86] "*Screen Guide for Americans* influenced the political and economic content of 1950s feature films, as well as HUAC's definition of appropriate film messages." Its influence was clear in HUAC's 1951 report, in which the congressional investigators claimed they were less interested in little-seen leftist art films than in the popular commercial films that slipped in the dollops of "progressive" thought that so concerned Rand.[87]

The HUAC hearings began again on March 8, 1951. The Committee's decision to focus on individuals rather than studios meant the executives, no longer concerned about attacks on them or their films, could now freely cut embarrassing employees loose.

The limited naming of names from the first round would be dramatically expanded, as hundreds of people were now named on television. "Friendly" witnesses were "coached on how to testify. 'Sincerity' was important" for the new television audience. A witness demonstrated his or her 'sincerity' by affecting a cooperative attitude during the questioning and congratulating HUAC for its good work. . . . The key to a successful appearance, i.e., one that guaranteed continued employment, was the prompt recital of the names of a few dozen Hollywood Reds."[88]

The witnesses in the spring of 1951, including Sterling Hayden, Edward Dmytryk, and Jose Ferrer, would be "friendly."[89]After this first round, though, the Committee would begin hearing from people like Carl Foreman, who would not cooperate in the drama it had devised.

NOTES

1. Quoted in Patrick McGilligan, "John Berry, Man of Principle," *Film Comment* 31 (May–June 1995): 50.

2. Larry Ceplair and Steven Englund, *The Inquisition in Hollywood* (Berkeley: University of California Press, 1983), 209–10.

3. Stephen J. Whitfield, *The Culture of the Cold War* (Baltimore: Johns Hopkins University Press, 1996), 127–28.

4. Ceplair and Englund, *Inquisition*, 211; Whitfield, *Culture*, 127–28.

5. Neal Gabler, *An Empire of Their Own* (New York: Doubleday Anchor, 1988), 362–64.

6. Maurice Zolotow, *Shooting Star* (New York: Simon & Schuster, 1974), 250–51.

7. Zolotow, *Shooting Star*, 248.

8. Nancy Lynn Schwartz, *The Hollywood Writers' War* (New York: Alfred A. Knopf, 1982), 204–5; Gabler, *Empire*, 364.

9. Gabler, *Empire*, 364; Zolotow, *Shooting Star*, 248.

10. Ceplair and Englund, *Inquisition*, 211; Whitfield, *Culture*, 127–28; Zolotow, *Shooting Star*, 248.

11. Garry Wills, *Reagan's America* (Garden City, N.Y.: Doubleday, 1987), 250.

12. Quoted in Ceplair and Englund, *Inquisition*, 211.

13. Quoted in Schwartz, *Writers' War*, 207.

14. Zolotow, *Shooting Star*, 249.

15. Zolotow, *Shooting Star*, 252.

16. Gabler, *Empire*, 364.

17. Ceplair and Englund, *Inquisition*, 211.

18. Eyman, Scott, "The Blacklist in Hollywood: A Look Back—50 Years Later," *Palm Beach Post*, October 19, 1997, 1J.

19. Ceplair and Englund, *Inquisition*, 213.

20. Gabler, *Empire*, 364–65.

21. Ceplair and Englund, *Inquisition*, 242–4; Michael Paul Rogin, *Ronald Reagan: The Movie* (Berkeley: University of California Press, 1987), 27–28.

22. Richard Pells, *The Liberal Mind in a Conservative Age* (New York: Harper & Row, 1985), 304.

23. Ceplair and Englund, *Inquisition*, 72–73.

24. Quoted in Schwartz, *Writers' War*, 193–94.

25. Larry Ceplair, "The Communist Party in Hollywood," in *Political Companion to American Film*, ed. Gary Crowdus (Chicago: Lakeview Press, 1994), 68.

26. Ceplair and Englund, *Inquisition*, 241.

27. Ceplair and Englund, *Inquisition*, 239.

28. William L. O'Neill, *A Better World* (New York: Simon & Schuster, 1982), 241–42; Ceplair, "Communist Party," 69.

29. Gabler, *Empire*, 353–54; Robert Sklar, *Movie-Made America* (New York: Vintage, 1975): 256–57.

30. Richard Maltby, "Made for Each Other: The Melodrama of Hollywood and the House Committee on Un-American Activities, 1947," in *Politics and Society in America*, ed. Philip Davies and Brian Neve (New York: St. Martin's Press, 1981), 86–87.

31. O'Neill, *Better World*, 242–43.

32. Brian Neve provides one such compilation in *Film and Politics in America: A Social Tradition* (London: Routledge, 1992), 72, 73, 78, 79.

33. Sklar, *Movie-Made America*, 256.

34. Gabler, *Empire*, 356–58. Also, Nora Sayre, *Running Time* (New York: Dial Press, 1982), 17.

35. Sayre, *Running Time*, 17 .

36. Ceplair and Englund, *Inquisition*, 208.

37. Ceplair and Englund, *Inquisition*, 202–3.

38. Gerald Mast and Bruce Kawin, *A Short History of the Movies* (Boston: Allyn & Bacon, 1996), 297.

39. Gabler, *Empire*, 362–64; Ceplair and Englund, *Inquisition*, 207.

40. Ceplair and Englund, *Inquisition*, 215–16.

41. "Somewhere between 250 and 300 movie employees (or about one percent of the studio worker population) joined the party at one time or another. Screenwriters predominated, 145 joining between 1936 and 1946. There were approximately sixty actors, twenty directors and producers, and fifty back lot, sound stage, and front office workers enrolled in party ranks for varying lengths of time." Ceplair, "Communist Party," 66–67.

42. O'Neill, *Better World*, 218–19.

43. Sklar, *Movie-Made America*, 257–58.

44. Rogin, *Reagan*, 28–9.

45. Sayre, *Running Time*, 152.

46. Quoted in Schwartz, *Writers' War*, 251–52.

47. Ceplair and Englund, *Inquisition*, 216–17.

48. Sklar, *Movie-Made America*, 259–60.

49. From the website of Gordon Williams, who identifies himself as the stepson of Hopper's son William: *The Queen Bee and the Stork Club, or Hedda Hopper's Hollywood*, n.d., at www. sonic. net/~doretk/ArchiveARCHIVE/ 1's%20of%20a%20Kind/ HeddaHopper.html (accessed August 17, 2002).

50. George Eells, *Hedda and Louella* (New York: Putnam, 1972), 267; Williams, *Queen Bee*.

51. The Party itself was legal until 1954. The Committee was relying on the Smith Act, which prohibited attempts to overthrow the government. Peter Roffman, and Jim Purdy, *The Hollywood Social Problem Film* (Bloomington: Indiana University Press, 1981), 284–85. Later, the McCarran-Walter Act required party members to register as subversive until the Supreme Court acknowledged the obvious element of self-incrimination.

52. This was so obvious to reporters at the time that *Newsweek*, in its issue of September 15, 1947 ("HUAC Communist Probe for Publicity, Not Correction," 13) said of HUAC: "Don't look for any so-called corrective legislation to result from the forthcoming Un-American Activities Committee investigation of Communism in Hollywood. Primarily the committee is fishing for headlines."

53. Sklar, *Movie-Made America*, 256–57.

54. Maltby, "Made for Each Other," 86.

55. Ceplair and Englund, *Inquisition*, 256–57.

56. Gabler, *Empire*, 364–65; Walter Goodman, *The Committee* (New York: Farrar Straus & Giroux, 1968), 202–3.

57. Neve, *Film and Politics*, 92–93.

58. Adapted from Neve, *Film and Politics*, 108; Sklar, *Movie-Made America*, 261; Ceplair and Englund, *Inquisition*, 259.

59. Goodman, *Committee*, 202–3; Gabler, *Empire*, 365.

60. Gabler, *Empire*, 365, 367, 368.

61. Whitfield, *Culture*, 129.

62. Menjou testimony, October 21, 1947, in Eric Bentley, *Thirty Years of Treason* (New York: Viking, 1971), 127.

63. John Cogley, ed., *Report on Blacklisting I : The Movies* (New York: Fund for the Republic, 1956), 33.

64. Dorothy Jones, "Communism and the Movies: A Study of Film Content," in *Report on Blacklisting I : The Movies,* ed. John Cogley (New York: Fund for the Republic, 1956), 229.

65. Gary Cooper testimony, October 23, 1947, in Bentley, *Treason*, 148–53.

66. Cooper testimony, in Bentley, *Treason*, 148–53.

67. Cooper testimony, in Bentley, *Treason*, 148–53.

68. Cooper testimony, in Bentley, *Treason*, 148–53.

69. Cooper testimony, in Bentley, *Treason*, 148–53.

70. Goodman, *Committee*, 209.

71. Jeffrey Meyers, *Gary Cooper* (New York: Morrow, 1998), 212–13.

72. Stuart M. Kaminsky, *Coop* (New York: St. Martin's Press, 1980), 5.

73. Richard Schickel, *Gary Cooper* (London: Pavilion Books, 1985), unpaginated.

74. Quoted in Meyers, *Cooper*, 210–11.

75. Larry Swindell, *The Last Hero* (Garden City: Doubleday, 1980), 274–76.

76. Wills, *Reagan's America*, 255–56.

77. Schwartz, *Writers' War*, 285; Maltby, "Made for Each Other," 94–95.

78. From Ceplair and Englund, *Inquisition*, 362–63.

79. Schwartz, *Writers' War*, 265.

80. Quoted in Schwartz, *Writers' War*, 266.

81. Sklar, *Movie-Made America*, 267; Wills, *Reagan's America*, 253.

82. Ceplair and Englund, *Inquisition*, 390–91.

83. Larry Ceplair, "The Hollywood Blacklist," in *Political Companion to American Film*, ed. Gary Crowdus (Chicago: Lakeview Press, 1994), 195–97.

84. Quoted in Lary May, "Movie Star Politics: The Screen Actors' Guild, Cultural Conversion, and the Hollywood Red Scare," in *Recasting America*, ed. Lary May (Chicago: University of Chicago Press, 1989), 152, footnote.

85. May, "Movie Star Politics," 152, footnote. Capra's clearance was restored after John Ford publicly pilloried the decision.

86. James Lorence, "Cold War Hollywood: Militant Labor and the Rise of Anticommunism," in *The Suppression of* Salt of the Earth (Albuquerque: University of New Mexico Press, 1999), at www.unmpress.com/book/suppression.html (accessed November 9, 2001).

87. Whitfield, *Culture*, 130–31.

88. Ceplair and Englund, *Inquisition*, 371.

89. Bentley, *Treason*, 295.

Part II

COMMUNISM AND CONFORMITY

Chapter 5

Writing *High Noon*, Facing the Blacklist

I am currently engaged in writing, and I am an associate producer of a picture called *High Noon*, starring Gary Cooper. . . . It is the story of a town that died because it lacked the moral fiber to withstand aggression. It is a suspense story.

—*Testimony of Carl Foreman*[1]

HENDERSON: Mind you, you know how I feel about this man. He's a mighty brave man, a good man. He didn't have to come back today . . . and for his sake and the town's sake I wish he hadn't. Because if he's not here when Miller comes in, my hunch is there won't be any trouble, not one bit. Tomorrow we'll have a new marshal and if we all agree here to offer our services to him, I think we can handle anything that comes along. To me, that makes sense. To me, that's the only way out of this. (Turning to Will) Will, I think you ought to go while there's still time. It's better for you—and better for us.

—*High Noon* screenplay[2]

In March 1951, Stanley Kramer was preparing to join Columbia in their historic production deal and leave behind his relationship with the financially troubled United Artists. There was only the matter of the one picture he owed the studio. . . . "For the last remaining UA picture [Kramer] was not too concerned," Carl Foreman would tell the *New York Times* critic Bosley Crowther after the film was released, in a remarkably revealing ten-page letter that has only recently come to light:

I would produce it, as well as two more on the Columbia slate, and the choice of subject was left to me. . . . At this time Fred Zinnemann returned

71

from making *Teresa* and rejoined the group for two pictures. We took it for granted that we would work together. I told him the story of *High Noon*, and another one of my own, *The Children*. . . . [To] my surprise, he went wild about *High Noon*. That he had to do. Of course, by now I had lived with *High Noon* so long that I finally felt equipped to direct it myself, but I sighed inwardly and said okay. Naturally, I've never regretted it. . . . Well, Stanley didn't particularly care which picture I made for UA, so I turned the Cunningham story over to the company and got my money back. And it was finally getting made.[3]

But just as Foreman began to turn the notes he had assembled over the previous three years into a shooting script, he was targeted by Redhunters in Hollywood and Washington, with Gary Cooper's old friend and fellow film legend John Wayne leading the charge against him.

On March 23, four days after he completed a first, rough draft of the script, the Motion Picture Alliance arranged for an ominous press release to appear in the *Los Angeles Evening Herald and Express*, headlined "Loyal Actors Call for Film Industry Purge of All Subversives." "Hollywood has treated the Communist menace in its midst too lightly," it read,

and the time has come for the film industry to purge itself of subversive elements, according to actor John Wayne, who today started his third term as president of the Anti-Red Motion Picture Alliance for the Preservation of American Ideals. . . . "Let no one say that Communists can be tolerated in American society and particularly in our industry," Wayne declared. "We do not want to associate with traitors. . . . We hope that those who have changed their view will cooperate to the fullest extent. By that I mean names and places, so that they can come back to the fellowship of loyal Americans."[4]

The press release, obviously timed to underscore the new round of HUAC hearings that had begun March 8, appeared six days before the 1951 Oscar ceremonies. Jose Ferrer, the star of the Kramer–Foreman production *Cyrano de Bergerac*, and Judy Holliday, who was starring in *Born Yesterday*, were being attacked as communist sympathizers as the Oscars approached, but each somehow managed to win the best actor Oscar at the March 29 ceremonies.[5]

Foreman has said of that time:

The fact was that from the time of the Congressional investigations, from the time that it became obvious in Hollywood that this industry would in fact begin a blacklist, . . . certainly by 1950 and very early 1951, when the Committee . . . had forced Larry Parks and Sterling Hayden to become informers, now was when the community began to fall away, now was when the terror began here. . . . I . . . felt it would be marvelous but unlikely if I escaped being named. . . . Sooner or later someone would have to say that they remembered me being in the Party.[6]

Foreman was subpoenaed in April 1951, for a June hearing at the Federal Building in downtown Los Angeles, "so in a way it was almost a relief, because the waiting for it was very unpleasant. . . . I had no intention of being what was called a cooperative witness."[7]

"I was in the middle of the screenplay when I was subpoenaed," Foreman told Crowther in the August 1952 letter:

It came as somewhat of a shock, altho [sic] I suppose I must have been expecting it all along. . . . By now the Hollywood brainwashing had gone on for so long that one was becoming almost used to the sorry spectacle of people striving to save their careers by recanting and informing on their friends, or those who had become their enemies. I had no enemies, at least any I knew about, so I suppose I had become lulled.[8]

Anyway, I remember that day well. I called my wife, went home early. We talked about it. My little girl ran into the room, surprised and happy to see me home before dark, prattled a bit, and ran out. I looked at my wife, and said, "Who do you suppose the son of a bitch was who did this to us?" And in that moment, if there ever was a shadow of a chance that I would buy my career or our security at the price of someone else's it was gone forever. No hero me, and no saint, believe me, but way too much to pay.[9]

Next day I told my partners about the subpoena, and how I felt about it. They took it well, even Mr. Katz [Columbia's man at the company]. Stanley was fine. We had overcome some pretty horrible things in the past, and we could lick this, too. After all, the hearings were two months off. I was to go back to work, and somehow we'd figure out something. So I went back to work. It was hard, and even if we partners were sticking together I felt, indeed I knew, that *High Noon* would be the last picture I would ever make—in Hollywood anyway—for a long time to come, and maybe forever. Of course, we were keeping it secret, and I didn't tell Fred for the time being, knowing how it would upset him.[10]

Foreman had made no secret of his plan to be an "uncooperative witness," meaning he would not tell the Committee whether he had ever been a member of the Communist Party and would refuse to name names. As he recalled in 1952, "I joined the Communist Party in 1942, left it when I went into the Army, rejoined it for a while afterwards, then dropped out. I don't think it's necessary for me to go into my motives for either entering or leaving it."[11] Other writers cite a longer period, from 1938.[12] This disagreement about the actual period of Foreman's membership in the Party may reflect the amorphousness of membership: One could be active in Party activities without actually acquiring a Party card. Nor did the Party automatically drop you from its roster if you resigned. Not that such niceties mattered, either to Foreman or to the Committee.

Struggling to break into the movie business just before the beginning of World War II, Foreman had signed up with the Federal Writers' Project and used his $85 a month stipend to study screenwriting at the League of American Writers with future blacklistees Lester Cole and Robert Rossen and future MGM production chief Dore Schary, who paid his tuition when the government money ran out.[13] By 1940, the contacts he had made at the L.A.W., if not the writing instruction, got him his first movie work, on two films for the East Side Kids, *Spooks Run Wild* and *Bowery Blitzkrieg*, and a Mills Brothers musical, *Rhythm Parade*.

After a wartime stint in the Army Signal Corps, where he met Kramer and George Glass and coauthored scripts for several of Frank Capra's celebrated propaganda films, he and Kramer formed the Screen Plays Company and began work on *So This Is New York* (1948). During 1950, the year that *Cyrano* was released, Foreman became active in a battle in the Screen Writers Guild over a loyalty oath that would later be recalled in his HUAC testimony.[14]

Now his past activism was catching up with him, and it wouldn't matter that, as his children Amanda and Jonathan would say, he "had briefly flirted with communism in his youth" and that "the vast majority of the hundreds of thousands of Americans who passed through the American Communist Party in the thirties and forties had no contact with Soviet agents and could not in any valid sense be said to be members of a vast conspiracy. . . . There was no reason for even the most paranoid red hunter to assume that movie folk—of all people—were the shock troops of the Revolution."[15]

"My problem," Foreman told a film class later, "was that I felt very alone. I wasn't on anybody's side. I was not a member of the

Communist Party at that time, so I didn't want to stand with them, but obviously it was unthinkable for me to be an informer. I knew I was dead. I just wanted to die well. . . . I suppose that has permeated my work." One of the students in the class suggested that his movies reflected his situation—they were about characters "caught in a futile situation but still sticking to a code."[16]

The subpoenas were widely publicized, and Foreman quickly discovered that frightened friends and acquaintances were anxious to avoid him. He had the strange experience of walking down the street and watching people he knew cross the street or turn the other way when they saw him. It was an experience—one of many he would have in the next few months—that he would write into the *High Noon* script, in the scene in which two men scurry off the street when they see Marshal Kane approaching.

For the rest of his life he would insist that the loyalty oath battle and the subpoena had had a profound effect on his approach to the script: Art would be made to parallel life:

> At this point the ideas and the story took on a different image, and it was then that I began to write it as a parable of what was happening in Hollywood. . . . I really began serious work on the screenplay, as opposed to the outline, in early 1951 at the time of the Parks and Hayden hearings. So that I quite consciously knew what I was doing at that point, although I saw no point in discussing it, even with Fred, because I felt that it would be in a way dangerous knowledge for him. It would make him a kind of conspirator, when this was my thing.[17]
>
> My associates were afraid for themselves—I don't blame them—and tried to get me off the film, unsuccessfully. . . . There are scenes in the film that are taken from life. The scene in the church is a distillation of meetings I had with partners, associates, and lawyers. And there's the scene with the man who offers to help and comes back with his gun and asks, where are the others? Cooper says there are no others. . . . I became the Gary Cooper character.[18]

The allegory was complete: The villainous Miller gang is HUAC, the frightened townspeople are "friendly" witnesses, and Kramer is the greatest betrayer of all, town mayor Jonas Henderson.

Even as he was working on the script and, later that summer, revising it in a series of discussions with Fred Zinnemann, Foreman was trying to minimize the damage his testimony might cause. He met with a New York lawyer named Sidney Cohn, who had devised a variant on the Fifth Amendment protection against self-incrimination he called the "qualified" or "diminished Fifth." Testifying under the "diminished Fifth" would theoretically allow Foreman to make clear that he had not been a member of the Communist Party for a long time—nearly a decade—without forcing him to name names.[19]

As the spring and summer wore on, the HUAC hearings continued and so did the Motion Picture Alliance assault on Hollywood Communists. On July 30, the day Foreman submitted his shooting script, and a month before *High Noon* was to go into production, Ronald Reagan summarized the MPA version of the Hollywood political wars in an article for the *Hollywood Citizen News* under the title, "Reds Beaten in Hollywood." Reagan trumpeted the success of the anti-communist forces he had led as president of the Screen Actors Guild in defeating the elaborate Red plot to take over the movie industry, indoctrinate eighty million moviegoers, and "prepare the way for Russian conquest of the world."[20]

Foreman's testimony would later be postponed until September 24, a delay that prolonged his personal agony but contributed much to making *High Noon* what it would eventually become, because he would be available to work on the screenplay with Zinnemann and produce the film (under an "associate producer" credit that was eventually removed).

"In the meantime, the subpoena situation had drifted along and had deteriorated," he told Crowther. "Gradually, each time I saw Stanley and George [Glass] and Mr. Katz, the atmosphere became increasingly pessimistic. Then, to make matters worse, George was subpoenaed."[21] When George decided to become an informer,

> my position was seen as untenable. I tried to explain, but Stanley wouldn't listen. He said to me, "What are you going to do when you go before HUAC? Are you going to take the Fifth?" I said, "Yes, Stanley, but I am going to take the qualified Fifth." He said, "Don't tell me about the qualified Fifth. They'll say, 'Do you know Stanley Kramer?' and you'll take the Fifth and then I'll be in trouble." Stanley wouldn't listen. He was scared.[22]
>
> My partners began to wonder why I couldn't be reasonable, too, and they began to point out what very likely lay ahead for me as an individual and for them as a group. They began to ask who I was being loyal to—them or a bunch of guys I never saw or had anything to do with anymore. And as time went by they began to hint that if I persisted, I might well have to take a long leave of absence from the company, and perhaps leave it entirely. I told them that I accepted this possibility, that I had no desire to embarrass or hurt them. I tried to explain

my position: my belief in the dangers of the situation as it affected not only Hollywood but the nation, of the cruel, almost farcically demagogic nature of the whole operation. I told them I had nothing to hide from the Committee about myself, or from the world for that matter, if such things had become the business of the Committee and the world. Over-simplifying, I told them truthfully, that I knew no-one anywhere [who] I could say was a Communist; that insofar as the past was concerned, some of the Hollywood Communists I had known were very nice people and some were not, but that none had ever contemplated treason; that I couldn't buy my career by being just a little bit of an informer and just name those who had already been named; that if we fought we would be making a good fight, that we had a chance, that— but why go on? It all sounds and reads somewhat fantastic now.[23]

Foreman's children, Amanda and Jonathan, would later put their father's position on being a "friendly witness" somewhat more prosaically: "For a working class boy from Chicago, becoming a 'rat' was not an option."[24]

"So, we drifted along," the letter to Crowther continues:

Naturally, the staff at Columbia got wind of something, and it increased their disdain for the western. Interestingly enough, the growing storm clouds began to be reflected in Stanley's attitude during the few times we met on *High Noon*. We seemed to buck each other on practically everything. I was in no mood to compromise any more, and I fought for everything I thought necessary all the way. Finally, he washed his hands of the whole picture, his attitude [implying] that he was giving me enough rope.[25]

Naturally, all of this affected the content of the picture. Or maybe the content of the picture affected me. I really don't know, now. It was easy for me to draw parallels at the time, of course. Anyway, by the time we reached rehearsals, it was obvious that I was going to have to go before the Committee, and the future thereafter was uncertain. I thought the time had certainly come when certain people had to know, so that they could protect themselves in any way they saw fit. These were Fred— very insecure these days because of his foreign birth and name— Cooper—considering his political background and point of view—and Bruce Church—our angel and not only a Republican but a businessman with money invested. All of them had the right to back out of the picture if they felt that my association with it or them could hurt them. I met them individually and told them about the subpoena and what I intended to do. I held nothing back. Well, you know that they didn't get out. And, each in his own way, they were quite wonderful. They were, if you will forgive me, real Americans.[26]

Foreman had not told his colleagues that he intended *High Noon* as a *roman à clef*, and it's not clear that Cooper knew.[27] But Foreman's talk with Cooper was the beginning of a brief but remarkable alliance between the movie star long associated with right-wing causes and the ex-communist screenwriter. When Foreman told Cooper his plans, Cooper, who had only recently been signed for the part, told him that he would back him. According to Foreman, Cooper, despite his politics and membership on the board of the MPA, was not part of the anti-communist assault: His "attitude was more complex than that. The actor had considered himself generally on the left during his youth, Foreman insisted, but felt . . . he had been exploited by [it] and abandoned it."[28]

As Foreman told a Cooper biographer, "Cooper put his whole career on the block in the face of the McCarthyite witch-hunters. . . . [In April, after Foreman's subpoena became public knowledge,] Cooper was immediately subjected to a violent underground pressure campaign aimed at getting him to leave the film, and he was told that unless he agreed to do so, he, too, would be black-listed. . . . But Cooper believed in me. He saw it through." Cooper would later explain that both Foreman and the actress Patricia Neal, Cooper's lover, had explained HUAC's destructiveness.[29]

Neal put it a little differently: "He [Cooper] was always very secure and avoided fights, but I think his doing *High Noon* in spite of the House Un-American pressure on Carl Foreman had something to do with me [after failing to push her for the female lead in *Bright Leaf* that went to Lauren Bacall]. That time he had the courage to go out and say, 'I'll stick with him.'"[30]

Only a week after production started, the lines were drawn. "I was summoned to a meeting at Columbia," Foreman told an interviewer:

> I came over from the *High Noon* set and my lawyer, Sidney Cohn, came along. They had their lawyer there, or two. . . . Something had happened since the last time. . . . Sidney said he was going to represent me. He was quite confident that everything would be done to protect my interests. That upset Stanley. He said something about not having a New York shyster to dictate what was going to happen, and that he had formed the company, perhaps even molded this company with his own hands. And he [Foreman] was prepared to wreck it on the basis of principle. It was *that* Stanley that he had now become—the Hitlerian carpet-eater. By now, Stanley was calling me "Foreman."[31]

"I was to hand in my resignation from all my posts and offices in the various companies," he told Crowther:

> This was so the group could disassociate itself from me either before or during my appearance before the Committee. I was also to turn over my stockholdings to him. At a later date, some settlement would be made. And, until further notice, I was to stop work of any kind, including the production of *High Noon*.[32]
>
> I refused, (a) to turn my stock over to the tender mercies of Mr. Katz, (b) to appear before the Committee as a man already tried, judged and found guilty by his own friends and associates, and (c) to leave *High Noon*. I told them I would not leave the picture under any circumstances: that it was a difficult picture with a stringent schedule complicated by half a dozen widely separated locations; that under these conditions Fred needed me; I reminded them of his sensitivity and his limited physical resources, and that we had worked so closely that my departure would add to his problems, and so on. I said that it was widely known in Hollywood that I had written and was producing the picture, so . . . if it was being contaminated by me, the disease was too far advanced.[33]
>
> Stanley said that he would take over the picture. I pointed out that he had had little contact with it, and that in addition he was burdened by many other duties and responsibilities at Columbia. I was told that if I didn't stay away voluntarily, I would be barred physically. The meeting ended unhappily and abruptly for all concerned. I went back to the set. I said nothing to anyone, and continued as before. However, the next two days were somewhat of an ordeal, because I was afraid that I would be met by a policeman or two at the gate each morning, or that I might be escorted off the set at any time during the day. Meanwhile, my Committee appearance was only a week off, and I was using my nights to prepare myself for it. I desperately didn't want to make a fool of myself. I knew I couldn't win, but I didn't want to crawl. I wanted to come off with some kind of dignity.[34]
>
> A few days later, they decided they'd better take action. I was on the set at the ranch again. George Glass came out with an envelope for me. It contained a copy of a letter from Stanley to me. In fact, Stanley wrote me two letters, which also came to the house in Brentwood, registered. In one letter, as president of the Stanley Kramer Company at Columbia, he told me I was discharged from all my positions at the company, as a member of the board of directors, and as a company officer, that I was not to come around anymore, and not to come around Columbia. In the other letter, he wrote to me as head of Stanley Kramer Productions, which was producing *High Noon*, and told me I was no longer to serve as a producer on *High Noon* and not to come around that picture, either.[35]

Stanley was shocked when Fred, Cooper and Church—individually and on their own—each pleaded and, in fact, insisted, that I remain with the picture. None was concerned with the political aspects of the situation but only with the welfare of the picture. Naturally, he was annoyed, too, for he was offering to take over himself. At any rate, he had gone too far to back down.

Then I got a lucky break. It developed that I hadn't yet signed my deferment papers for the Bank of America, and without my signature the loan could not go through [because the bank would be forced to make payments to him up front, instead of waiting for profits]. And I was in the driver's seat. I got a new letter from the Company, signed by Stanley, George and Katz, that I was to return to my duties with special emphasis on *High Noon*, that the question as to whether my name on it as producer would harm the picture at the box-office would be decided by Cooper and Church at the time of release, and that no public statements of any kind would be issued by any of us until sixty days after my appearance before the Committee. I had still never left the set.[36]

Stanley asked me to see him. He was still stunned, almost shattered, puzzled by the attitudes of Fred, Cooper and Church, bewildered by my rather new intransigence. We had a long and really rather intimate talk, and altho [sic] it was obvious that we could never be the kind of friends we had been, and that most likely my days with the company were numbered, we reached what I thought was sympathy and understanding. I had never wanted to fight him. I had loved him, and even now I hated to see him feel humiliated by defeat, as I knew he did. He confessed his own personal fears, and the dangers to his own career he felt inherent in my Committee appearance. I assured him that if his name came up I would insist on informing the Committee that he had always been a liberal and, indeed, an anti-communist—which, of course, was true. He begged me to rescind the power of decision I had given Cooper and Church as to my producer credit, and to give it to him, as head of the Company. He explained that without it he was in an untenable and humiliating position. I agreed.[37]

We were together for two hours. He told me that if it became necessary for me to leave the company that we should try to avoid bringing in lawyers, that he would protect my interests. And he reiterated the promise that there would be no statements made for sixty days. When we parted, it seemed as if we were as close as we had ever been in the last year. We shook hands, put our arms around each other. I went back to the set. We have never spoken to each other since.[38]

I was tired that night, and I overslept. Just before leaving for the studio [on September 19], I switched on the television to catch a bit of the hearings, and I heard myself named. Ironically . . ., the man who named me [screenwriter Martin Berkeley] was a perjurer; my name had been given to him by the Committee investigators, with about ten others, on a might-as-well basis.[39]

At the studio, I informed Fred, and told him I thought the cast and crew should know about it, from me and at ease, rather than read about it in the morning papers, with a consequent disorganization of the next day's work. He agreed. At the completion of the next scene, we called the company together.[40]

I told them I couldn't foretell the future, or what would happen, but I didn't want this to affect the film in any way. Because I was afraid that it might. The film meant a great deal—we'd all worked very hard. . . . I said Fred and I had worked closely together. I might have to be away from the film for some time, so I wanted them to all give Fred their complete support. . . . Since the papers had not yet come out, many of them were shocked. The vast majority were very moved and very supportive. I concluded by saying what was true—that I was now going to see my lawyer and get ready for the hearings and my appearance which was in a few days from now. Then I went to the parking lot. . . . I was almost at the car when I heard Coop yelling after me. He'd followed me from the set and he'd been very moved by it. He said, "Uncle, that's the best speech I ever heard. Listen, you do what you feel you have to do, but don't let them put you in jail." Those were Coop's exact words. He didn't want me to go to jail. And he wasn't sure about the legal position. He thought if you didn't cooperate, then you would go to jail.[41]

I had been right about telling the cast and crew. The work went on without a hitch. As a matter of fact, the company was wonderful all the way through. If anything, they all worked harder thereafter. Nobody talked about it, except to come on me when I was alone and to wish me well; after a day or so, when the grips and the prop and wardrobe guys began to rib me about going to jail and being a spy, I knew I was still at home, that the sickness hadn't infected everybody in the country, and that in Hollywood the hysteria and terror were still only at the so-called top levels.[42]

Two days later it was time for me to go downtown. The night before, very late, I had received an urgent telephone call from a writer who had become a "co-operative" witness. He had to see me. I stopped and met him on the way to the hearing. He wanted to tell me, for whatever motives, that the Committee investigators had worked on him for hours the night before to get him to name me, that he had told them he couldn't, and had refused, even after they had told him he might as well since they could get others who would. I thanked him for the information, and went on. It was getting crazier and crazier.[43]

That night he "was desperately afraid," Foreman told an interviewer, but "my wife and I made love—it was the best we had had in some time."[44]

With two weeks left of filming, Foreman appeared before the House Un-American Activities Committee in the Federal Building in Los Angeles on September 24, 1951. "I wore a very sincere tie and a nice blue suit," he told the interviewer.[45] What had struck him about the experience was its sheer theatricality. "[Testifying] was just like a film itself—a film within a film. The Committee knew in advance whether you were going to cooperate."[46]

"I [had] waited for my turn," he told Crowther,

> listening and watching the ridiculous, cynically stage-managed parade: the "co-operative" witnesses beating their breasts or posturing with new-found patriotism, parroting their carefully rehearsed answers to the rehearsed questions, some of them blushing when the ceremony reached the point of the naming of the names: the "uncooperative" witnesses going up, getting their heads bashed in, and walking off like somnambulists.[47]
>
> Finally, it was my turn. I faced the television cameras, did my best, and it was over in an hour. It didn't hurt too much.[48]

Following his "diminished Fifth" strategy, in which he would testify only about the years he had not been in the Party, he began his testimony. "I am currently engaged in writing and I am an associate producer of a picture called *High Noon*, starring Gary Cooper. . . . It is the story of a town that died because it lacked the moral fiber to withstand aggression. It is a suspense story." If he understood Foreman's implication, the Committee's chief interrogator, Frank Tavenner, ignored it. Getting right to the point, he noted that Martin Berkeley had told the committee, "There is in the [Screen Writers] Guild today only one man I know who was ever a Communist. This man has never, to my knowledge, disavowed his communism. His name is Carl Foreman." Tavenner asked Foreman if he was "at one time" a member of the party. Foreman declined to answer, invoking both the First and the Fifth Amendments. But he noted that "on September 11, 1950, I voluntarily signed an oath as a member of the executive board of the Screen Writers' Guild that I was not a member of the Communist Party, or of any party dedicated to the overthrow of the United States Government by force and violence. That statement was true at that time, sir, and is true today."[49]

Variety, which along with the other trade papers showed no sympathy to "commies," reported:

> Foreman . . . declined . . . to answer questions as to his possible affiliation at any other time, and also declined repeated invitations to talk of party activities or name names. Foreman's testimony brought the Committee face to face with the problem of legality vs. morality. Writer unequivocably [sic] stated his loyalty to the U.S. but declined to answer questions, stating his belief that "this committee knows far more about Communist activities than I do. If I knew anyone who now or ever had an intention to overthrow our form of government, I would consider it not only my duty but a privilege to report that person." Foreman's mention of [Screen Writers Guild] loyalty oath brought a series of questions from Representative Donald Jackson (R., Cal.), who sought to establish that Foreman had fought against the loyalty oath, motivated by some Communist ties. Foreman readily admitted he had not accepted the first draft of the loyalty oath proposition, but made the point that he had been willing to sign as a member of the Board but wanted to be sure that such an oath was not mandatory on the part of the rank and file members. Jackson opined he personally would "not place any credibility" on the testimony of the witness, who declined to name names and places of activity.[50]

"I took the diminished Fifth," Foreman summed up later, "and when it was over I was finished in Hollywood."[51]

"I called home," he told Crowther,

> but the line was busy. It remained busy for more than an hour. When I reached my wife, she said that she was proud of me—she watched it on television. I felt good about it. She said that people were calling constantly and saying nice things. I went home and packed, because the company was moving to the Sonora country for location. Telegrams began coming, and continued to come for several days afterward, and letters, too. All nice. Nothing, however, from Stanley or George or Katz.[52]

The next day, as Foreman was returning to the set and Kramer was trying to contain the damage, the Red-hunters were lining up to proclaim their anger over his testimony. The two most visible leaders of the MPA, John Wayne and Hedda Hopper, "demanded publicly that Foreman be fired" and that, as Hedda wrote, "'he never be hired here again.'"[53]

"I joined the company [the next day at the northern California location] in time for the first shot," Foreman told Crowther.

The work went well. But that night my wife called. There were big stories in the press that Stanley was disassociating himself from me. AP and UP had called her: what should she say? I told her to say nothing. Next day I flew into Los Angeles, and went to Columbia. Stanley had just left for New York. I left word for him to call me, either from New York or when he returned. He never did. Anyway, I went back on location. The cast and crew, particularly the crew—most of whom had worked on all our independent films—were bewildered and upset, but morale remained high. Of the entire company, only one man—drunk one night—made some remarks linking me with the Korean situation. The fellows with him shut him up quickly. They kept it from me, and I heard about it accidentally only a week later. Everyone was very nice; everyone worked hard; everyone was excited about the picture. I heard nothing from the front office, saw no-one except for one or two shame-faced visits from George, and finally it was in the can. We had a party for the cast and crew. One or two secretaries and a few of the production staff at the Columbia offices dropped in, but no-one else. It was a nice party.[54]

Next day I was called by the Company lawyers, and advised to get a lawyer of my own for settlement discussions. I did.[55]

On Monday, October 21, two weeks after production on the film wrapped, Foreman and Cohn showed up at Stanley Kramer Productions for "discussions," as Foreman said, that "were held in an unpleasant atmosphere."[56] Three days later, *Variety*'s story was headlined "Kramer Buyout of Foreman Ends 4-Year Team-up."[57] Cohn had managed to push the settlement figure up from the original offer of $55,000 to $285,000.[58]

A surreal day needed a suitably surreal ending—and got one:

> The night I signed the papers, I stopped at the Vine Street Derby for a drink, and ran into the Committee investigator who had handed me my subpoena, a real Hollywood coincidence. We kidded around a while. I said something about his perjured witness, the fellow who had named me. He laughed, and said, "Oh, it doesn't matter. We've got some legitimate ones on you now." And so I went home.[59]

The nightmare of the summer, after he had been subpoenaed, was back:

> It's no fun to walk down Wilshire Boulevard and have people cross the street, just like in the movie, so as not to have to speak to you. It's no fun to be told by John Wayne and people like that that if you don't

come through, if you don't come back and hit the sawdust trail and ask for another hearing, you'll never work in the films again, as long as you live, anywhere in the world. . . .[60]

Now I was through with the company I'd helped form and build. I was too tired to feel really badly about it, altho [sic] I did regret leaving behind projects like *The Four Poster*, which I'd brought in, *Cyclists' Raid* and *Full of Life*, which I'd been responsible for buying, *Happy Time* and *Member of the Wedding*. I had also been responsible for hiring Ted Geisel to write his fantasy, *The 5000 Fingers of Dr. T*, and I was curious as to how it would turn out. And so on. But it was over. By terms of my settlement, I was now finished with *High Noon*, too.[61]

Years later, Foreman saw no reason to change his view that the Committee could have been beaten back:

We had a contract with Columbia. As a group there was no way our films could have been attacked for being subversive. . . . Instead, [Columbia] said the pressures were too great. I'm not talking only about the right-wingers, who told Kramer and Katz to get me to cooperate [with HUAC]. If Stanley had had the guts to ride it out we might have won. . . . But Stanley was scared. In the crunch he said he was not prepared to have his career destroyed by my misguided liberalism.[62]

Though Kramer has offered several different reasons over the years for ousting Foreman, what seems clear is that he was pressured by Harry Cohn and other executives at Columbia and frightened by the assaults from the MPA and other Red-hunters.

The pressures on Kramer were undeniable. As Foreman was being forced out, the company was being targeted by demonstrators denouncing "Reds" appearing in his plays and movies. A corporate-funded, anti–collective-bargaining front group called "The Wage Earners Committee" was picketing the film version of *Death of a Salesman* that October.[63] Five days after the fateful meeting, on October 26, the *Los Angeles Times* reported that the "Wage Earners" were picketing five local theaters that were showing the soon-to-be-blacklisted Kramer associate Joseph Losey's remake of the Fritz Lang classic, *M*.[64]

Kramer recalled that at the time he didn't know anything about the politics of his colleagues who were subpoenaed, and that he had proposed a buy-out figure to Foreman that was appropriate for their kind of company. He assured Columbia that he disagreed with what Foreman was doing—not because he was refusing to name names, but because he hadn't been straight with Kramer, and, in fact, had almost sounded as though he was threatening to tell the Committee about Kramer's past, possibly suspicious associations. "I never heard the phrase 'qualified Fifth.' All I got from Foreman was the threat, 'I could name other names besides these.' I don't want to get into that business because it's . . . not true, because I never was a part of it [the Communist Party]." He was cooperating with Columbia out of anger at Foreman, not because he liked Columbia. In fact, he hadn't really wanted the coproduction deal; the others in the company had talked him into it.[65]

The battle over who did what has never ended. A half-century after the event, Kramer's widow, Karen, insisted that *Darkness at High Noon*, a documentary broadcast by PBS on September 17, 2002, which took Foreman's side in the dispute, was maligning her husband's name: "Carl Foreman was a very paranoid man. I would be paranoid, too, I suppose, if this happened to me. But you have to understand that this was his free choice to become a communist. It wasn't Stanley's choice. Stanley didn't believe in the blacklist." As for Foreman, she says, "[Kramer productions] had just moved their offices to Columbia Pictures and he had just signed a deal with Harry Cohn to have autonomy in his choice of material, but they were still under contract to Harry Cohn. This documentary skirts the role the studio played in this. Harry Cohn said, 'If Carl Foreman takes the 5th Amendment, I'm firing him.'"[66]

By October 1951, John Wayne, Cooper's good friend and rival Western star, was in his third term as president of the MPA.[67] Wayne had joined the MPA soon after its founding at the urging of his friend and frequent costar, Ward Bond, because, as Wayne would later say, he was in favor of "alerting Hollywood to the danger that a small group of Communists, under party discipline, would take over the unions and control American movies."[68]

It was with the goal of "cleaning house" that Wayne now confronted Carl Foreman and *High Noon*. He later summarized his concerns about the film this way: "Four guys come in to gun down the sheriff. He goes to the church and asks for help and the guys go, 'Oh well, oh gee.' And the women stand up and say, 'You're rats. . . .' So Cooper goes out alone. It's the most un-American thing I've ever seen in my whole life. The last thing in the picture is old Coop putting the United States marshal's badge under his foot and stepping on it."[69] Concerned about Cooper's good name, he called Foreman and tried to get the associate producer and writer to remove his name from the credits.[70]

Foreman refused—and Wayne set in motion the process that would make it impossible for Foreman to find work. Later, Wayne would have trouble acknowledging the existence of a blacklist, and he always denied that the MPA during his tenure had provided names to HUAC.[71] That led him to this remarkable explanation: "There was no blacklist at that time as some people said. . . . The only thing our side did that was anywhere near blacklisting was just running a lot of people out of the business. . . . I'll never regret having helped run Foreman out of this country."[72]

Only two days after his ouster from the company,[73] Foreman had announced that he and Gary Cooper were forming a production company with Cooper's business partner,[74] "B"-picture filmmaker Robert L. Lippert, to make three films that would be distributed by Lippert's company. The films would be budgeted even more cheaply than Kramer's, at $300,000 each, which meant that Cooper wouldn't be in them.

It turned out that Cooper had called Foreman the night of the ouster. Foreman told Cooper he was going to form his own company. "Count me in—now. Use my name," Cooper had said. "I mean it." On the advice of Henry Rogers, a friendly publicist, Foreman had held a press conference announcing the deal. The announcement had made page one of *Daily Variety* and the *Hollywood Reporter*.[75]

Hedda Hopper immediately called Rogers at home. "Now I know why I got mad at you years ago," she said. "You're just no good. You've got yourself mixed up with that commie bastard Carl Foreman. That washes you up in this town. I'm going to see to it that you're driven out of business." Rogers' phone was tied up for six hours with calls from Wayne, Ginger Rogers, Ward Bond, and dozens of others, and he realized he was being targeted. "It was," he said later, "a calculated plan of terror."[76]

On her radio show and in her newspaper column, Hopper "expressed amazement that Gary Cooper would associate himself with Carl Foreman productions, since Foreman had refused to answer 'the $64 question' about whether he still was or ever had been a communist when he appeared before the Un-American Activities Committee."[77]

Within days *Variety* was anticipating bad news. Under the head-line "Report Pressure on Cooper May Force Break with Foreman" it noted that the

> greatest eyebrow-raiser in years in an industry of strange bedfellows was the disclosure last week that Gary Cooper would be a partner in the new Carl Foreman unit to release through Robert L. Lippert. . . . Reports in Hollywood yesterday were that such pressure is being brought to bear on Cooper that he may decide to pull out of the Fore-man tie-up when he returns to the Coast Friday [November 2]. If he withdraws, other of Foreman's new partners may follow suit and then the question is whether Lippert will continue the association."[78]

Cooper had no idea of the hornet's nest he had helped stir up be-cause he had gone fishing with his old friend Ernest Hemingway in Montana. "Cooper and . . . Hemingway were casting for trout when a Western Union man showed up at the stream with a fistful of telegrams." One was from Wayne. "One was from Warner Bros—they wanted to break Cooper's contract, using an outdated 'morals clause.' And there were threats from Louis B. Mayer and producer Walter Wanger warning Cooper he might never get a decent role if he didn't back off." Cooper called Foreman, but before he could ex-plain, "Foreman stopped him. 'I know. Nobody can hold up against this . . . not even you.'" Foreman would later note that "he [Cooper] was the only big one who tried, the only one."[79]

With the other investors pulling out, Cooper was left to put out a euphemistic press release: "I have received notice of considerable re-action, and now I feel it best for all concerned that I should not pur-chase this stock." But he added, "I had indicated a willingness to purchase stock because I was convinced of Foreman's loyalty and Americanism and of his ability as a filmmaker. My opinion of Fore-man has not changed."[80] Foreman responded in kind: "Gary Cooper is the finest kind of American and one of the most decent men I have ever met. . . . I regret to lose him as a business associate, but I hope to keep him always as a friend."[81]

In November, John Wayne tried to get Foreman to recant and tes-tify. He told Foreman at a private meeting between the two of them, "'You're the kind of man we need. You can't turn your back on us. Who are you? Who do you think you are?' He was furious. He was on his feet at that point. He went around hitting the wall with his fist—the largest fist I'd ever seen. . . . He was very angry with Cooper, because Cooper betrayed his movement and all that."[82]

All through the fall and early winter of 1951, Hopper kept up her assault on Foreman—and on the "pink" Kramer. On November 14, she wondered why Cooper would "take to the road in behalf of Carl Foreman's picture *High Noon*, which will have every studio furious. To my knowledge he's never gone barnstorming on behalf of any other picture. Why for Carl Foreman?"[83]

On November 28, she urged that "the December issue of *American Legion* magazine . . . be read by everyone in Hollywood. J. B. Mathews' story about Commie infiltration in Hollywood, titled 'Did the Movies Really Clean House?,' is sickeningly accurate. His answer is no. He points out names of stars, writers, directors and titles of pictures they're working on. You'd be amazed to know how many are still working."[84]

On December 12, she issued a barely veiled threat: "Mary Pickford tells me she has not yet signed a contract with Stanley Kramer to appear in *The Library* [an assault on censorship that would be made six years later as *Storm Center* (1956)]. Deal still is in the talking stage. I've said it before and I'd like to repeat, I don't think she'll make it."[85]

And she continued her sympathetic coverage of Cooper, now that his contractual obligation to *High Noon* was over. He was battling various ailments[86] and his wife wanted him back. On December 29, she reported that "Gary Cooper's in Sun Valley with wife Rocky and daughter Maria. Pat Neal has issued an ultimatum to Coop: He must choose between her and Rocky. Gary looks awful; has to eat baby food every two hours for that ulcer."[87]

While Hopper was keeping up her attack on Carl, the Foremans were in New York arranging for a passport. He also tried to make a deal with the British film producer Sir Alexander Korda.[88] Meanwhile, he was keeping "in close touch with [*High Noon*] through Fred, Dmitri Tiomkin and Elmo Williams, my editor. Fred's version followed the script throughout. Stanley didn't like it, and took over. He cut it brutally, almost it seemed with venom. Everyone agreed the version was bad. He gave in, finally, and Elmo Williams took over and returned the cut to Fred's original version."[89]

If the months-long struggle over the film was turning in Foreman's favor, everything else started going wrong. In January, Lippert withdrew from his production deal.[90] By the spring every production office was closed to Foreman. Roy Brewer of IATSE told his union men they would be blacklisted if they worked with Foreman.[91] Eric Johnston, the studio organization president who had instituted the blacklist, met with the American Legion to discuss ways "to eliminate the 'menace' of communism from movies."[92] The owner of RKO, Howard Hughes, took the draconian step of shutting down his studio to weed out Communists.[93] And the major studios instituted a new round of loyalty tests.[94]

"When the film came down to release time," Foreman said later, "United Artists seemed to feel that my name on the film would result in the American Legion picketing us from coast to coast, . . . so they removed my name from the credit titles on the production credit. But much to their chagrin the Screenwriters Guild refused to allow them to take my screen credit off. So that the picture was only half-tainted. . . . I was only the writer, it didn't really matter."[95]

Thwarted at every turn in his months-long effort to revive his career, there was nothing left for Foreman to do but leave the country if he wished to continue in the movie business. "I finally got tired of watching the darkness settle in on Hollywood, tired of watching people being hammered and pressured until they crumbled, tired of being offered black market deals.[96]

"I had my passport and the possibility of England loomed so large. Estelle and I discussed it and it was determined that I should leave and try to rebuild a life, and she'd join me as soon as things were settled."[97]

Foreman sailed alone for England in May—two months before *High Noon* was released nationally.[98] As his British-born children would later note, "He was allowed to stay in England by a [conservative] Tory government that remained completely untouched by the paranoia that gripped the United States."[99] His wife, Estelle, and his five-year-old daughter joined him several months later.

Only three months into his exile, Foreman was putting the best face on things, proudly telling Crowther how pleased he was at the success of *High Noon* and offering his inside account of its troubled production. But the generally upbeat tone of the Crowther letter disguised his real despair. His marriage soon fell apart, and his passport was confiscated. Although he eventually found work, he had to write under a pseudonym for films being distributed in the United States.

Foreman's intended political allegory, it turned out, was clear to those who followed Hollywood politics. "In England," he said, "I was very pleased to get letters from people here who were impressed by the film [and who] believed it was about Hollywood. I'd never said it to anyone. I couldn't even say it to my associates because then the film would not have been made."[100]

After four years of working anonymously on a dozen films made by others, he bought the rights to Pierre Boulle's World War II drama *The Bridge on the River Kwai*. Even before he and his lawyer were able to persuade the State Department to return his passport and the new chairman of HUAC to let him testify in secret without naming names, he entered into a secret collaboration with Columbia, of all studios, to write and produce the film—though neither his name nor that of his cowriter, fellow blacklistee Michael Wilson, would be used on the final credits.

If Washington no longer cared about Foreman, it would take a bit longer for him to separate himself entirely from the blacklist in Hollywood. *Bridge* won an Oscar for Boulle, who received sole writing credit though he spoke no English and had had nothing to do with the script. It would be twenty-eight years before Foreman would receive his Oscar for the film—posthumously.

He stayed on in England for another seventeen years, writing and producing films,[101] remarrying, and fathering two more children. With the worldwide success of *Kwai*, Columbia now felt free to defy the blacklist and openly hire Foreman to write and produce films, the best known of which was *The Guns of Navarone*.[102]

Although by the early 1970s he was once again living in the United States with his young second family and working on films, it seemed to some that Foreman had never recovered from the blacklist, at least professionally. "After he left the United States," commented screenwriter Malvin Wald, "there was a subtle change in theme throughout his screenplays. Without totally abandoning his examination of the human condition, he was more inclined to refrain from controversy and the artistic exploration that marks his earlier films."[103]

Foreman died of a brain tumor in Los Angeles on June 26, 1984—the day after it was announced that the Academy of Motion Picture Arts and Sciences, trying to make amends for the blacklist, would award Oscars for *Bridge on the River Kwai* to Foreman and Wilson. Their widows picked up their statuettes at a special ceremony.[104]

Though *Bridge on the River Kwai* is widely considered his other masterpiece, and he had other financial successes as a producer, Foreman always said that *High Noon* was "his proudest professional accomplishment."[105]

Foreman was the most visible blacklist victim among those associated with *High Noon* or the Kramer Company, but he was not alone. Lloyd Bridges, who played deputy Harve Pell, had been a member of the Actor's Lab, a radical theater group.[106] By the time he began shooting his scenes, he had been subpoenaed to testify at the Los Angeles hearings of the Committee. On October 22, the day after Foreman was forced out of the Kramer Company, Bridges arranged to testify in secret about his former Communist Party membership. Though he named names, he was still "graylisted" for several years until the *Sea Hunt* television series revived his career.[107]

Howland Chamberlin, who played the snide desk clerk, was not so fortunate. On September 18, 1951, five days after he filmed his scenes and six days before Foreman's testimony, he refused to affirm or deny membership in the Communist Party.[108] Under the following day's headline, "Howland Chamberlin Takes Fifth Before HUAC," *Variety* reported that "Chamberlin told the committee that he found it 'deeply repugnant and profoundly un-American to be smeared, black-listed and strangled economically' by his appearance before the committee."[109] He was immediately blacklisted and did not work again in Hollywood until 1979.

Two years earlier Fred Zinnemann, also confronting the blacklist, had found himself forced to acquiesce in one of the most obnoxious rituals of the Red Scare in order to win a larger battle. In the fall of 1950, Cecil B. De Mille and his friends on the board of the Directors' Guild had passed a resolution requiring the members to take loyalty oaths. Those, like Zinnemann, who failed to respond to the first letter received a telegram and then nighttime visits by motorcycle riders. Zinnemann and a few others called for a mass meeting and a vote. To get that referendum, he had to sign the oath, ironically, under the new rules. At the meeting, on October 22, 1950, the De Mille group was shocked, and the loyalty oath opponents pleasantly surprised, when John Ford, thought to be extremely conservative, attacked the oath.[110] It was defeated.[111]

Stanley Kramer would eventually confront the now-weakened blacklist head-on, but not until 1958, seven years after the breakup with Foreman and three years after he had started directing his own company's films.

At first he had been careful about his choice of politically themed movies—and directors. One of his greatest post-*High Noon* successes, *The Caine Mutiny* (1954), had been directed by Edward Dmytryk, who had returned to the industry's good graces after serving several months in prison as a member of the Hollywood Ten and then naming names for HUAC. The first of his two allegorical treatments of the blacklist (the other is *Warlock* [1959]), *Caine* "is an *apologia* for the witch hunt, chastising an insidious, plotting left-winger for fomenting a shipboard revolt against an obviously incompetent Captain."[112]

In 1958, the year after *Bridge on the River Kwai* credited Boulle with the screenplay, the blacklist was weakening, and Kramer could thumb his nose at it with an inside joke in the credits of his new film about race relations. In "the opening shots of a prison truck in *The Defiant Ones*, . . . the credits 'Written by Nathan E. Douglas, Harold Jacob Smith' were superimposed on the faces in the front seat, seen through the windshield. 'Douglas' himself was on the left, a nom de plume for (the blacklisted Nedrick) Young."[113]

The Defiant Ones won the Academy Award for original screenplay. "As Young and Smith went onstage (on April 6, 1959) to pick up their Oscars, the man who had disowned Carl Foreman seven years before was at last able to say, 'Well, at least we beat the blacklist.'"[114]

Kramer remained proud of his gesture. Two years later, during a televised debate with the American Legion commander over "Red" movies, the moderator asked him if he stood by a previous statement that he would hire any writer he pleased, regardless of his past affiliations or suspected affiliations. Kramer replied, "I stand by that statement on the basis of conscience, on the basis of not withholding income and support to a man who I feel is worthy for a job, and on the basis that I feel there are plenty of law enforcement agencies— and plenty of opportunities to change an existing law or put one on the books to cover a situation." He went on to say that a writer's views could be completely divorced from political subjects, and that many Leftists were doing nonpolitical pictures.[115]

Kramer would go on to great popular success over the next few years directing *On the Beach* (1959), *Inherit the Wind* (1960), *Judgment at Nuremberg* (1961), and *Guess Who's Coming to Dinner* (1967). Unlike Foreman in 1951, he wouldn't need to rely on allegory. In any case, allegory was not his style. All his films would be criticized for wearing their liberal politics on their sleeves.

There is no reason to doubt that Carl Foreman spent that fraught summer of 1951 intentionally turning *High Noon* into a coded metaphor for the evils of the House Un-American Activities Committee and its effect on the Hollywood community in general and himself in particular. As he notes, many of his friends saw it that way, too, without prompting from him. And at least one magazine, *The Nation*, had picked up on that interpretation.

It's an appealing notion, that the *roman à clef* is *the* important fact about *High Noon*. The assumption was perhaps unavoidable. With the Committee hearings at their height, *High Noon*, like all Left-inspired political commentary in the early 1950s, had to avoid naming, or even implying, names to escape assault by the Red-hunters and their allies.

But for most ordinary moviegoers in 1952, Foreman's interpretation, whether of Hollywood or of HUAC, simply did not register. For one thing Gary Cooper's screen persona, developed in the sentimental-traditionalist films of Frank Capra, confused the issue of conventional social criticism, especially because he was still the heroic individual standing up to betrayal. For another, the film's abstractness permitted many interpretations. In the Midwest, for instance, Cooper was seen as a symbol of Eisenhower working against the communist threat,[116] a view Eisenhower himself presumably adopted with his numerous White House screenings of the film.

Foreman's enemies could as easily identify their hero, Senator Joseph McCarthy, with Will Kane: "Kane's unpopularity for choosing to fight rather than abide with Hadleyville's do-nothing policy is akin to McCarthy's self-image of a crusader risking 'smear and abuse' from those upset by his forthright approach." [117] At the other end of the political spectrum, the Soviet Union's Communist Party newspaper *Pravda* attacked the film as "a glorification of the individual." Still others saw it as an antipacifist tract, and later, as an inspiration for Clint Eastwood's supposedly anti–civil-libertarian *Dirty Harry*, which also ends with a badge being thrown away.

There was even a foreign policy interpretation: Cooper's marshal (like America itself) had wanted peace after clearing up the town five years before (that is, World War II), and reluctantly must buckle on his gunbelt again in the face of new aggression (the Korean War); eventually his pacifist wife (American isolationists) must see where her true duty lies and support him.[118]

Conservative political commentary was something altogether different. Some forty anti-communist films, most of them low-budget, were made by the studios between 1951 and 1953 to show the Committee their good faith in the fight against communism. Wayne made one; in *Big Jim McLain* (1952), he was a HUAC investigator who exposed communist plotters in Hawaii. The anti-communist allegories, such as *The Thing from Another World* (1950), privileged government investigators and taught viewers to be wary of intellectuals and scientists.[119] Sometimes, though, the science fiction allegories, as in *Invasion of the Body Snatchers* (1956), remained so abstract that any group could infer the message they felt most comfortable with.

Even B-Westerns of the period had a message beneath the gunplay. In one film, Roy Rogers uncovered a conspiracy to smuggle uranium to a foreign power. The heroes of another Western learned that a police state was turning Texas into a "Siberia." In yet another, federal agents discovered that gold was being smuggled to Peking by supposedly respectable citizens. And in a fourth, Randolph Scott discovered a nest of separatist conspirators in Los Angeles. He comments, "It is hard to believe that the City of the Angels had its share of unholy activities."[120]

At a far more sophisticated level, the Committee's friendliest witness, Elia Kazan, was making a series of films—*Panic in the Streets, Viva Zapata, Man on a Tightrope,* and *On the Waterfront*—that stressed the importance of cooperating with government investigators and exposed the dangers of totalitarian societies and revolutionary action. In *On the Waterfront* (1954) Kazan and his fellow "friendly witness," screenwriter Budd Schulberg, were widely believed to have expressed their mea culpas by making a hero of Marlon Brando's informer.

Perhaps the greatest irony of the allegorical filmmaking of this tortured period, though, was that one of Foreman's tormentors, Ronald Reagan, made a film at about the same time that proved to be the mirror image of *High Noon*. In *Storm Warning* (1951) Reagan is a Southern district attorney who exposes the Ku Klux Klan. Although ostensibly about the nation's most notorious racist organization, it makes no mention of race, because it is really about "subversives"—the Klan stands in for the Communist Party. Reagan's D.A. "is determined that the local community should clean up 'our own nests,' rather than wait for 'New York or Washington to start poking their noses in.'"[121]

In other words, Reagan is playing himself in his public role as president of the Screen Actors Guild: His character

> is asked at the outset of the film if he plans to "name names" and expose the respected members of his community who secretly belong to the Klan. He responds that he stands for "law and order." Later a committee of prominent citizens asks him to leave the Klan alone and not encourage outsiders to divide the community. The actors playing the

prominent citizens speak the lines of the Hollywood Committee for the First Amendment, which had tried to protect the Hollywood Ten. . . . Thus, *Storm Warning's* committee members are actually fellow travelers of the Klan—that is, the Communist Party.[122]

If *High Noon's* allegorical intent was far from clear, Nicholas Ray's 1954 *Johnny Guitar* was much clearer as a *roman à clef* Western. "Each faction in the story can be associated with the various actors in the wider drama—friendly witnesses, communists, fellow travelers, witch-hunters, government and business. For those in the know, it even offered the amusing sight of Ward Bond, one of Hollywood's most militant anti-communists, and Sterling Hayden, one of the actors who had 'named names' to the Committee, as enemies in the drama."[123]

And *Storm Center* (1956), whose production by Kramer six years earlier Hedda Hopper and the MPA had worked so hard to block, was a far more literal attack on the right-wing assault. Bette Davis plays a librarian who is "denounced not only for refusing to ban a book—*The Communist Dream*—but for her wartime memberships [in] groups such as the 'Council for Better Relations with the Soviet Union.' She is hounded [by a library board that closely resembles HUAC] despite the fact that she resigned when she discovered that such groups were communist fronts; as in other liberal films . . ., there could be no question of supporting the civil liberties of a communist."[124]

The end of the decade brought the most elaborate Western allegory yet, *Warlock* (1959), directed by Edward Dmytryk and feeling much like an apology. Henry Fonda plays a gunman hired to clean up the town who eventually earns the enmity of the resentful and fearful townspeople. If Fonda is the witch-hunter stand-in, Richard Widmark, who is with him at first and then opposes him, represents the director. At the beginning of the picture, "Widmark is alone in the frame as Dmytryk's screen credit appears. Thus, even before one word of dialogue is uttered producer-director Dmytryk has established [Widmark] as a man of conscience, accompanying but apart from his confreres—literally, a reluctant fellow traveler. *Warlock* is, like *On the Waterfront*, its director's rationalization of his cooperation with HUAC."[125]

In the end, the *roman à clef* of *High Noon* was revealing, but it was only the outermost layer of a complex, interlocking set of ideas. A more comprehensive way of viewing the film, assimilating the social criticism of the time without tying the film to a specific set of events, would broaden the allegory to consider the relationship of individual conscience to the pressures of social relationships. And that would permit a closer look at one of the most remarkable aspects of *High Noon*—that it is the law enforcer who is the rebel.[126]

NOTES

1. September 24, 1951, Los Angeles Federal Building, Congressman Francis Walter presiding. Reported in "Hearings Before the Committee on Un-American Activities, 82nd Congress, 1st Session, 'Communist Infiltration of Hollywood Motion Picture Industry—Part 5,'" 1753–71.

2. July 30, 1951. Reprinted in George P. Garrett, O. B. Harrison Jr., and Jane R. Gelfman, *Film Scripts Two* (New York: Meredith Corporation, 1971), 34–155.

3. Letter from Carl Foreman to Bosley Crowther, August 7, 1952, 3. Use of Carl Foreman's letter made possible by the kind permission of the Carl Foreman Estate. Copyright © The Carl Foreman Estate.

4. Quoted in Eric Bentley, *Thirty Years of Treason* (New York: Viking, 1971), 299–300.

5. Bentley, *Treason*, 306.

6. Foreman interviews, January 20–25, 1978, tapes 25–30, quoted in Lionel Chetwynd and Norman S. Powell, prods., *Darkness at* High Noon (PBS documentary, broadcast September 17, 2002).

7. Quoted in Rudy Behlmer, *Behind the Scenes* (Hollywood, Calif.: Samuel French, 1990), 272–73.

8. Foreman to Crowther, 4.

9. Foreman to Crowther, 4.

10. Foreman to Crowther, 4.

11. Foreman to Crowther, 4.

12. Brian Neve, *Film and Politics in America: A Social Tradition* (London: Routledge, 1992), 115; Nancy Lynn Schwartz, *The Hollywood Writers' War* (New York: Alfred A Knopf, 1982), 163–64; Victor Navasky, *Naming Names* (New York: Viking, 1980,), 156–57.

13. Schwartz, *Writers' War*, 163–64.

14. Neve, *Film and Politics*, 185.

15. Amanda Foreman and Jonathan Foreman, "Our Dad Was No Commie," *New Statesman* 128 (March 26, 1999): 20–22.

16. "Dialogue on Film: Carl Foreman," *American Film* 4 (April 1979): 36.

17. Foreman interviews.

18. Quoted in Behlmer, *Behind the Scenes*, 269. One historian who hadn't bothered to check the film's production schedule actually had Foreman

rewriting a script after testifying rather than before—which would have meant changes to a script being shot totally out-of-sequence with only two weeks of shooting left. Anthony Holden, *Behind the Oscar* (New York: Plume, 1993), 201.

19. Navasky, *Naming Names*, 156–57.

20. Bentley, *Treason*, 293–95.

21. Foreman to Crowther, 5.

22. Quoted in Navasky, *Naming Names*, 157–58.

23. Foreman to Crowther, 5.

24. Foreman and Foreman, "No Commie," 20–22.

25. Foreman to Crowther, 5.

26. Foreman to Crowther, 6.

27. Some believe he did. See Tom Stempel, *FrameWork* (New York: Continuum, 1991), 167. Also David Walsh, "Why Was Stanley Kramer So Unfashionable at the Time of His Death?," *World Socialist* Web site, at www.wsws.org/articles/2001/feb2001/kram-f26.shtml, 26 February, 2001 (accessed February 28, 2002).

28. Walsh, "Why Was Kramer Unfashionable."

29. Jeffrey Meyers, *Gary Cooper* (New York: Morrow, 1998), 248.

30. Quoted in Stuart M. Kaminsky, *Coop* (New York: St. Martin's Press, 1980), 167.

31. Foreman interviews.

32. Foreman to Crowther, 6.

33. Foreman to Crowther, 6

34. Foreman to Crowther, 7

35. Foreman interviews.

36. Foreman to Crowther, 7.

37. Foreman to Crowther, 7.

38. Foreman to Crowther, 8.

39. Foreman to Crowther, 8.

40. Foreman to Crowther, 8.

41. Foreman interviews.

42. Foreman to Crowther, 8.

43. Foreman to Crowther, 8.

44. Foreman in Terry Sanders and Freida Lee Mock, *Word into Image: Portraits of American Screenwriters: Carl Foreman,* video interview (Santa Monica, Calif.: American Film Foundation, 1981).

45. Foreman in Sanders and Mock, *Word into Image.*

46. Foreman in Sanders and Mock, *Word into Image.*

47. Foreman to Crowther, 8.

48. Foreman to Crowther, 9.

49. HUAC testimony of Carl Foreman, September 24, 1951, 1753–71.

50. *Variety*, September 26, 1951, 20.

51. Foreman in Sanders and Mock, *Word into Image.*

52. Foreman to Crowther, 9.

53. Peter H. Brown and Jim Pinkston, *Oscar Dearest* (New York: Harper & Row, 1987), 246.

54. Foreman to Crowther, 9.

55. Foreman to Crowther, 9.

56. Foreman to Crowther, 9.

57. *Variety*, October 24, 1951, 3 .

58. David Caute, *The Great Fear* (New York: Simon & Schuster, 1978), 104–5; William R. Meyer, *The Making of the Great Westerns* (New Rochelle, N.Y.: Arlington House, 1979), 218.

59. Foreman to Crowther, 9.

60. Foreman in Sanders and Mock, *Word into Image.*

61. Foreman to Crowther, 9–10.

62. Quoted in Navasky, *Naming Names*, 157–58.

63. John Cogley, *Report on Blacklisting I : The Movies* (New York: Fund for the Republic, 1956), 113.

64. Caute, *Great Fear*, 104–5.

65. Quoted in Navasky, *Naming Names*, 158–60.

66. Quoted in Susan King, "High Noon Showdown," *Los Angeles Times*, April 11, 2002, F58. The documentary, *Darkness at* High Noon, was produced for PBS by Lionel Chetwynd and broadcast on September 17, 2002. Karen Kramer said that she doubted "the authenticity of the Crowther letter, explaining that the critic was a lifelong friend and admirer of her husband and never mentioned the letter to him." The Crowther letter, copyright by the Foreman estate, was supplied to me by Foreman's widow, Eve Williams-Jones, who cooperated with Chetwynd in the making of the documentary, and I have quoted liberally from it throughout this chapter with her permission.

67. Meyers, *Cooper,* 212–13.

68. Maurice Zolotow, *Shooting Star* (New York: Simon & Schuster, 1974), 250–51.

69. Quoted in Stephen J. Whitfield, *The Culture of the Cold War* (Baltimore: Johns Hopkins University Press, 1996), 148–49.

70. Zolotow, *Shooting Star*, 257; Whitfield, *Culture*, 148–49.

71. Richard F. Shepard, "'Duke,' an American Hero," *New York Times*, June 12, 1979: B8.

72. Interview in *Playboy* 18 (May 1971): 78; Garry Wills, *Reagan's America* (Garden City, N.Y.: Doubleday, 1987), 254.

73. *New York Times*, October 25, 1951, 36.

74. *Variety*, October 31, 1951, 4.

75. Brown and Pinkston, *Oscar Dearest*, 246.

76. Quoted in Brown and Pinkston, *Oscar Dearest*, 246.

77. Quoted in George Eells, *Hedda and Louella* (New York: Putnam, 1972), 273; Hector Arce, *Gary Cooper* (New York: Morrow, 1979), 245; *Los Angeles Times*, October 30, 1951, Part II-6.

78. *Variety*, October 31, 1951, 4.

79. Peter Brown, "Blacklist: The Black Tale of Turmoil in Filmdom," *Los Angeles Times*, Sunday Calendar Section, February 1, 1981, 5; Brown and Pinkston, *Oscar Dearest*, 245–46.

80. Stefan Kanfer, *A Journal of the Plague Years* (New York: Atheneum, 1973), 131–33, quoted in Richard Schickel, *Gary Cooper* (London: Pavilion Books, 1985), unpaginated.

81. Quoted in Arce, *Cooper*, 245.

82. Foreman interviews

83. *Los Angeles Times*, November 14, 1951, II-10. In the Fairbanks Center there is a draft of a letter to Hedda from Zinnemann dated November 16, apparently responding to this attack: "Dear Miss Hopper: Regarding your paragraph on *High Noon*, I wish to say that in addition to Carl Foreman, a number of other people including myself were associated in the making of the picture. It is vitally important to all of us that *High Noon* be judged by the public on its own merits and demerits. It seems only fair not to condemn a piece of work and then to destroy the hopes and perhaps to damage the careers of many people whose honest efforts have gone into this movie, and who had nothing whatsoever to do with the political issue, until the picture has had its day in court." It is not clear if the letter was ever mailed.

84. *Los Angeles Times*, November 28, 1951, II-8.

85. *Los Angeles Times*, December 12, 1951, III-10.

86. "Cooper had an ulcer on top of his back ailment, hernia, and assorted pains." Kaminsky, *Coop*, 168.

87. *Los Angeles Times*, December 29, 1951, I-8.

88. *Variety*, December 19, 1951, 5.

89. Foreman to Crowther, 10.

90. *New York Times*, January 13, 1952, II-5. The article quoted Lippert as saying that Foreman would not be affected because he had his own financing. He didn't.

91. Foreman interviews

92. *New York Times*, April 1, 1952, 35.

93. *New York Times*, April 8, 1952, 35.

94. *New York Times*, May 23, 1952, 17.

95. Foreman in Sanders and Mock, *Word into Image*.

96. Foreman to Crowther, 10.

97. Foreman interviews

98. He was preceded by the film itself, which was favorably reviewed by *The Times* of London on May 5. Meyers, *Cooper*, 248; Malvin Wald, "Carl Foreman," in *Dictionary of Literary Biography*, vol. 26, *American Screenwriters*. (Detroit: Gale, 1984), 107.

99. Foreman and Foreman, "No Commie," 20–22.

100. Foreman in Sanders and Mock, *Word into Image.*

101. "Dialogue on Film: Carl Foreman," 35.

102. Wald, "Foreman," 107.

103. Wald, "Foreman," 106.

104. Mason Wiley and Damien Bona, *Inside Oscar* (New York: Ballantine, 1986), 291.

105. Burt A. Folkart, "*High Noon* Writer Carl Foreman, Ex-film Exile, Dies," *Los Angeles Times,* June 27, 1984, Part 2, 3.

106. Gloria Hilliard, "Variety a Hallmark of Lloyd Bridges' Career," *CNN.com,* March 11, 1998.

107. At www.obits.com/bridgeslloyd.html (accessed March 3, 2002).

108. United States Congress, *The Annual Report of the Committee on Un-American Activities for the Year 1952,* excerpted in *Film Culture* (Fall–Winter 1970): 77–78.

109. *Variety,* September 19, 1951, 2.

110. Ford's politics are much harder to pin down than Zinnemann's remark would suggest. According to one of his numerous biographers, Ford liked to call himself a liberal Democrat. "The blacklisting of the McCarthy era disgusted [Ford]. . . . He made fun of the Defense Department's accusation that Capra was Communist-involved and called the hearings a 'publicity stunt.'" Tag Gallagher, *John Ford* (Berkeley: University of California Press, 1986), 341–42.

111. Brian Neve, "A Past Master of His Craft: An Interview with Fred Zinnemann," *Cineaste* 29 (Winter 1997): 15–19.

112. Peter Roffman and Beverly Simpson. "Stanley Kramer," in *Political Companion to American Film,* ed. Gary Crowdus (Chicago: Lakeview Press, 1994), 235–36.

113. Whitfield, *Culture,* 150.

114. Holden, *Oscar,* 215.

115. "F. Y. I.," CBS television broadcast, February 14, 1960, from the Stanley Kramer collection, Young Special Collections, UCLA.

116. Tom Stempel, *FrameWork* (New York: Continuum, 1991), 167. Stempel adds in a footnote: "I was living in Indiana when *High Noon* was released and remember people talking about the film in those terms."

117. John H. Lenihan, *Showdown* (Urbana: University of Illinois Press, 1985), 120–21.

118. Harry Schein, "The Olympian Cowboy"(trans. from Swedish by Ida M. Alcock), *American Scholar* (Summer, 1955): 309–20. Quoted in Philip French, *Westerns* (London: Secker & Warburg, 1977), 35.

119. Neve, *Film and Politics,* 187–88.

120. John H. Lenihan, "Classics and Social Commentary: Post-war Westerns, 1946–60," *Journal of the West* 21 (October 1983): 37.

121. Neve, *Film and Politics,* 183.

122. Michael Paul Rogin, *Ronald Reagan: The Movie* (Berkeley: University of California Press, 1987), 261.

123. Neve, *Film and Politics*, 186.

124. Neve, *Film and Politics*, 186.

125. Michael Coyne, *The Crowded Prairie* (London: I.B. Tauris, 1997), 100–1.

126. Whitfield, *Culture*, 147.

Chapter 6

The Failed Community

Critics who detected a political message in *High Noon* were right in the most general sense, but misguided in trying to assign too specific allegorical equivalencies. *High Noon* is political in the way that the genre is political, for it is about leadership, the community, the very idea of what a city is. Unlike many Westerns that depict the founding of a city, *High Noon* probes the question of the survival of a city.

—Don Graham[1]

Cineaste: When you made *High Noon* were you aware that Carl Foreman intended it as a comment on Hollywood in the McCarthy period?
    Zinnemann: No. I read much later that Carl saw the piece as an allegory of his own personal experience. I did not think of it in political terms. To me the film was about conscience and degrees of compromise. Most people, when they encounter such a situation, will rationalize their way out of it, they will always have a reason why they can't help.

—Brian Neve[2]

Carl Foreman's Red Scare parable was doubly disguised—it came wrapped in a broader political allegory about a community disintegrating into atomized, self-interested individuals. And it reflected a unique convergence—of a star icon whose screen image could be employed in unexpected ways, a political movement that was being reinterpreted by its enemies, and a classic Hollywood fable inspired by that movement.

Even as Foreman was dealing with the four-year-old Red Scare, the nation's intellectuals were trying to understand a phenomenon that had not only ripped Hollywood apart but was terrorizing government officials, academics, and others who dealt in political ideas. By the 1950s, a group of widely read social scientists known variously as "vital center" liberals and "mass society theorists"[3] were interpreting "McCarthyism"—the name by which the Red Scare had come to be known by the time Foreman was being interrogated by HUAC—as an irrational response by ordinary people outside of party politics, a lashing out at established authority out of anxiety over their diminishing status.

These theorists put their faith in elites and interest groups as checks on destructive mass movements[4] and supported the goals, if not the methods, of the internal security programs. Their assumptions about the sources of support for the Red Scare would eventually be shown to be unjustified: McCarthy and the HUAC were widely supported not by ordinary people but by leaders in the Republican Party who also supported the Red Scare and the blacklist. But at the time these ideas provided important intellectual support for the attack by congressional committees on civil liberties.[5] Thus, the threat of a community disintegrating into a mob and threatening people of principle was very much in the air—and available to producers and screenwriters.

The historical, turn-of-the-century populism that the social scientists thought had been revived in a sour, antidemocratic form was a real movement of desperate people who had despised "bigness"— industrialization and its bosses and unions, government bureaucracies and political machines, cities and urban elites, and intellectuals. The Populists wanted to reform America by "replacing corrupt and conspiratorial elites with representatives of the truer, agricultural America."[6] They were nostalgic for a life on the land that was purer and simpler, and their watchwords were "common sense," "biblical morality, and leaders who can represent—or sometimes personify— these values."[7]

This earlier, idealistic populism had inspired a traditional Hollywood narrative—the fable about the man of the people who fights "them," the forces grinding the people down. This attenuated version of populism was perfect for the movies, as the film historians Roffman and Purdy note, because its combination of progressive idealism and sentimental conservatism was just vague enough to appeal to everyone. Instead of calling for socialist revolution, populist films offered a solution:

> free enterprise, the work ethic, a return to the land—that reflected the
> concerns of an increasingly threatened small-town middle class. . . .
> Capitalism is attacked by arguing on behalf of laissez-faire; social dis-
> content is vocalized by reasserting traditional values. Populism al-
> lowed the movies to combine innovativeness with wish fulfillment,
> Depression cynicism with the American Dream.[8]

The director who effectively created the Hollywood version of populism was Frank Capra. In his classic films of the mid-1930s to the mid-1940s—*It Happened One Night* (1934), *Mr. Deeds Goes to Town* (1936), *Lost Horizon* (1937), *You Can't Take It with You* (1938), *Mr. Smith Goes to Washington* (1939), *Meet John Doe* (1941), and *It's a Wonderful Life* (1946)—he told stories about a troubled America rescued by unassuming men who were stronger than they appeared. Each of his films was darker than the one before, as the accumulation of disasters—the obvious ones of Depression, fascism, and world war, and the associated ones he deplored, such as the growth of big business, big government, and big labor and the decline of small towns and their values—dimmed his optimistic view of American capabilities.

A lifelong Republican who declared himself the enemy of dictatorship but admired Mussolini and Franco, Capra spun middle-class "fables of success, humiliation and last-minute redemption"[9] in which the heroes were not elected representatives but decent fellows chosen by the dispossessed to return America to its mythical "Golden Age"[10] when good neighbors helped each other, people failed because of their own inadequacies, and sometimes all that was needed was "a little push up the hill."

Capra's film populism, much like American "political" movies generally, threatened no one, least of all the studios, because in place of a political movement he offered, against all these ills, the apolitical notions of "good neighborliness," equality of opportunity, and the pursuit of individual happiness free "from the oppressive hand of the forces of Organization."[11]

The classic Capra heroes combined an almost Christ-like innocence, determination, innate goodness, boyishness, and common sense. Along with James Stewart, Gary Cooper personified this man of the people who was a natural leader, who rose above the mass. The Cooper character in *Mr. Deeds Goes to Town* triumphed in the end over tremendous odds: the opposition of the wealthy and the powerful. The Cooper character of *Meet John Doe*, released only five years later with America about to enter World War II, is virtually destroyed at the end; indeed, in one, unreleased ending, he actually commits suicide as he had threatened. The wealthy and the powerful are very nearly victorious, and there is no sense that they will go away. The Stewart characters experience the same darkening world: *Mr. Smith* triumphs only because a corrupt man has an improbable last-minute change of heart. In *It's a Wonderful Life*, Stewart's character survives—though he can be saved only by an angel—but the villain is unpunished and undiminished, and he—that is, big business—will soon control everything.[12]

Surprisingly, considering his acceptance of capitalism and his condescension toward the average citizen, who always needed rescuing not by a revolution but by an extraordinary man, Capra's films were admired by the Left because they agreed with him that large-scale capitalism was a threat to individual freedom.[13] To the Left, Capra's stories about differences melting away and the little guy triumphing seemed not all that different from their own films, in which, under the thumb of the studios, "they attacked obvious wrongs, racism and anti-Semitism especially, while promoting tolerance and the like."[14]

Unlike most people in the movie industry, who knew Capra only from his films, Carl Foreman and Stanley Kramer knew the man himself, because they had worked for him. Their feelings about that less-than-pleasant experience might go some way to explaining why they turned his fable inside out.

Foreman and Kramer had originally met in 1944, while working in Capra's War Department propaganda unit, the group that produced the famed *Why We Fight* series. Foreman cowrote two of the unit's films, *Know Your Enemy—Japan*, with Irving Wallace, and *Our Job in Japan*, with Ted Geisel (already the author of children's books as "Dr. Seuss").[15] Foreman's and his colleagues' experience working under Capra was depressing. According to a Capra biographer,

> Wallace felt that he and his collaborators were "writing in a vacuum without instructions," because the American high command "did not know how we should treat the Japanese except to beat them in the field." But he was convinced that "the real problem was our boss, Frank Capra himself. . . . He was totally unsophisticated when it came to political thought. He knew only one thing, America had been good to him, America was beautiful. . . . For Capra it was not difficult. He

came up with a simple foreign policy toward Japan. It added up to this: The only good Jap was a dead Jap. He did not say it in those words, but that was what his words added up to. . . . Foreman and I fought this terribly, persistently, because it was all wrong. Foreman and I used to leave those meetings with Capra and say to each other, 'We can't allow Capra's attitude toward the enemy to be our government's policy in this picture for our troops, because while Capra doesn't understand it, the direction the film is taking is utterly racist.' How could we indict an entire people in our film?"

In fact, says biographer Joseph McBride, Capra was only following orders—though if he was, he was incapable of conveying that fact, judging by his writers' disgust.[16]

There is no evidence that Kramer and Foreman intentionally turned that experience with Capra against his favorite narrative, or that Cooper's hiring was influenced by some desire to get even in such a roundabout way. But the result was the same: In an important sense, *High Noon* became the darkest inversion of Capra and his standard Cooper character through its rejection of Capra's conservative populist perspective on the innate decency of the little people and the moral small-town life.

It's important to note, though, that Foreman and Kramer were not actually "reversing" the Capra narrative, because the "happy endings" of his films were clearly not happy: They failed to eradicate the sourness left by the near-triumphs of the big business-politics-media-intellectual complex that he despised but was too honest to think could really be beaten. In *It's a Wonderful Life*, Capra's darkest fantasy, a small entrepreneur wins no more than a temporary victory, and corporate capitalism is clearly lurking in the wings. In *High Noon*, six years later, an offstage corporate capitalism will win as the Mexican businesswoman, the exemplar of entrepreneurialism, and the marshal, the defender of law and order, both leave town. Now, the people could not be rallied, the hero's heroism was not celebrated, there could be no happy ending—because Capra's nineteenth-century populism had been replaced by a 1950s vision of elite betrayal and popular weakness. The Capra-esque natural leader—still Gary Cooper—is a failure as a leader, and the popular leader, town mayor Jonas Henderson, the man to whom everyone defers, is the true villain. In that sense, *High Noon* simply takes the familiar Capra tale to its logical conclusion.[17] Capra's hopefulness has not so much been inverted as simply rejected as the ultimate naiveté.

What had happened in the six years between *It's a Wonderful Life* and *High Noon* to make such a rethinking of "the people" salable was, of course, the start of the Cold War and the wholesale government assault through the Red Scare and blacklist on public officials and on intellectuals who thought they were protected by the First Amendment guarantee of free speech. "One of the objectives of the House Committee was to associate the popular culture of the Popular Front, and of anti-fascism, with the apparent threat of communism," notes Brian Neve. "In early 1948 William Wyler commented that a film such as *The Grapes of Wrath* could no longer be made, and a writer talked of the difficulty of making Westerns given that staple elements of their plots, including foreclosing bankers, were no longer acceptable. Capra's analysis of corrupt elites, however disguised by happy endings, seemed less welcome in the emerging age of the military industrial complex."[18] In the feverish atmosphere of 1952, *High Noon's* enemies would see it as an assault on them and on the ordinary people they claimed were backing their effort to "clean house."[19]

Later critics, particularly Pauline Kael, would dismiss *High Noon* as "primer sociology"[20] in which "the high-minded (like Grace Kelly's Quaker) . . . are there only to violate their convictions."[21] Kael was assuming a parallel between Kane and the townspeople on the one hand, and on the other sociologist David Riesman's comparison in *The Lonely Crowd* (a best-seller the year before *High Noon* went into production) between the "inner-directed," or principled American who was supposedly disappearing, and the "other-directed," or conformist American who was said to be becoming dominant.[22]

In fact, *High Noon's* treatment of the idea of community has always been considered open to a wide variety of interpretations. And there is no doubt that the starkness of its storytelling and clipped nature of its dialogue lends itself to many uses. Some critics have always been troubled by the fact that the "rebel" is the symbol of law and order. "Liberal films tend to be about empowerment and reform, while conservative films tend to be about authority and the restoration of order. Liberal films tend to celebrate a pluralistic culture . . . and conservative films tend to celebrate the institutions of society—the police and the military, for example."[23] Others have been bothered by the ease with which the film spoke to the prejudices of people all over the political spectrum. Foreman's liberal polemic, argues one, closely resembles the arguments of those he attacked. McCarthy viewed liberals as responsible for selling out the nation; opponents viewed him as the threat to fundamental freedoms. But pro- and anti-McCarthyites shared a conviction as deep as anything dividing them: that the true enemy was civic complacency. And this capacity to provoke a common assessment of America's current malaise explains much of the film's appeal. No matter one's political stripe, all agree that the citizens of Hadleyville have regressed to a state of infantile dependency, requiring a paternal figure to protect them. And the very elaboration of Will Kane's self-restraint, moral authority, and masculine skills suggest by contrast what calm maturity might actually entail.[24]

As flexible as *High Noon*'s allegory appears, though, it is not really true that all interpretations are equally supported, and in fact it is possible to show—by considering the traditional interpretations and the evidence in their support—that the film moves in one general direction.

The most popular interpretation has always been that *High Noon* is an attack on "the people." The residents of Hadleyville are shown to be hypocritical, and it is this vision of individual conscience challenging an inherently corrupt society that is supposed to have upset John Wayne and the other MPA critics. This is the generalized version of the Foreman Red Scare allegory, and it has been reinforced by the large number of Western "clones" of the film that portray townspeople in the same hostile light.

In *High Noon* the marshal, the agent of civilization who is moral, strong, and secular but is resigned to the confrontation rather than relentless in seeking it, is deserted by organized religion and the formally religious. In Hadleyville, religion is exclusively an institution, an organized church that is socially significant but not a moral force. The minister appears only briefly during the crucial meeting in which the church-people suppress their few good instincts out of fear and material interest and rationalize their abject cowardice and desertion of the hero. When Kane appears at the door, the preacher has just launched into Malachi 4:1 from the Old Testament: "For behold, the day cometh that shall burn as an oven; and all the proud, yea, and all that do wickedly, shall be. . . ." He stops at the interruption; the passage continues "stubble: and the day that cometh shall burn them up, saith the Lord of hosts, that it will leave them neither root nor branch." Later, when he is asked his opinion, the preacher finds biblical support for a position against taking part in violence.[25]

More than one commentator has noted the similarity between "Hadleyville"—a name featured prominently at the depot and on the bank near where the gunfight takes place[26]—and the "Hadley-burg" of Mark Twain's short story,[27] where the most prominent members of the community are revealed to be greedy, fearful, and corrupt.[28] Foreman himself said that "Hadleyville" was a variant on "Hollywood"—the target, he insisted, of his cautionary tale.

Another, related allegorical reading inspired by Foreman's troubles insists that the film is about resisting the pressures to conform. Ironically, it is this particular reading that lends itself so readily to anti-communist interpretations, as when critics lump *High Noon* with other films of the period such as *On the Waterfront* (1954) and *Invasion of the Body Snatchers* (1956).

In this view, "*High Noon* raised the question of how strongly the private sense of right and wrong—and of personal honor—can resist 'the tyranny of the majority.' Everyone in Hadleyville but Marshal Will Kane seems to agree that the town will be more secure if he leaves, yet his arguments for remaining are as principled as they are practical. Though fearing for his life, he holds one truth to be self-evident—that dangerous evil must be faced and routed rather than evaded or denied."[29]

A third variant is that the town is not worth saving because its citizens will not protect it. "Authority without support of those it defends, says *High Noon*, is meaningless."[30] Kane becomes heroic by default when no one else will do what needs to be done. "Kane discredits the community, which proves itself unworthy of the sacrifices he has made for it. At the end, Kane contemptuously drops his badge in the dust at the mayor's feet and rides out of town. The people have been saved, but they have less value than the man who saved them."[31] And after all, when Cooper drops his badge in the dust, it's after he's saved the town for the *second* time.[32]

Even as critics across the political spectrum were ignoring the politically "timely" in *High Noon* and lauding its criticism of conformity and hypocrisy, Marxists in Hollywood and elsewhere, while sympathetic with Foreman's travails, were unhappy with the movie for reasons similar to those of the Right—its apparent attack on ordinary people. In the Left's version of "mass theory," the people of the United States were being manipulated by elites,[33] and *High Noon* was nothing more than an assault that reflected the contempt of the elite for the people they were manipulating.

"In fact," argues Stephen Whitfield,

> no film could be more remote from the cultural sensibility of the Party
> than this Western, which repudiated the populism integral to the Com-
> munist faith in the "masses." Whether during the popular Front period
> (when Foreman had joined the Party), or the Second Front period of
> the war (when Foreman quit the Party), or the sentimentality of "pro-
> gressivism" . . . thereafter, Communism asserted that it alone truly rep-
> resented those who were worthy of inheriting the earth. But no film
> was more disenchanted with "the people" than *High Noon* or examined
> more unsparingly the frailties of those whom Marxism exalted as the
> agents of historical progress.[34]

It was taken for granted by critics on both the Left and the Right
that the film thought the enemy was the entire town—"a mass of
people indistinguishable from one another"—and rejected popular
democracy in favor "of the man of superior knowledge, courage,
and capability."[35] Kane is, in effect, a vigilante ignoring the wishes of
both the people[36] and the judge and old marshal, who have nothing
but contempt for the town's complacency.[37] As the judge relates to
Kane the history of Athens and of his own narrow escape from a
similar threat, "he takes down the American flag from his office and
packs up his scales of justice and law books, emblematic of the collapse of democracy. . . . 'Nothing [he says] that happens here is really important.'"[38] The church-people and the bar-people are the
same; they are equally hostile or fearful or defensive in the end. The
only difference is that the bar-people, who had ties to the Millers,
make their hostility clear immediately; the church people reveal
their concerns more slowly.

Judging by MPA ideologue Ayn Rand's *Screen Guide for Americans*
(1950)—that other political "theory" then circulating in Hollywood—
High Noon was a mixed bag as democratic propaganda. Clearly Kane
met two of her standards: "America is based on the ideal of man's
dignity and self-respect. Dignity and self-respect are impossible
without a sense of personal achievement." Filmmakers should not
"preach that all mass action is good, and all individual action is
evil."[39]

But clearly the picture of the good burghers of Hadleyville—at
least as presented by those who thought the movie undemocratic—
was not helpful: "Communism preaches the reign of mediocrity,"
Rand continues, "the destruction of all individuality and all personal

distinction, the turning of men into 'masses', which means an undivided, undifferentiated, impersonal, average, common herd." She adds,

> The Communist's chief purpose is to destroy every form of independence. . . . Conformity, alikeness, servility, submission and obedience are necessary to establish a Communist slave-state. . . . Don't preach that everything done for others is good, while everything done for one's own sake is evil. Don't preach that everything "public-spirited" is good, while everything personal and private is evil.[40]

In fact, despite the overwhelming sense that Kane was all alone, the town had not quite united against him. Family man Herb Baker volunteers, but he backs out when Kane can get no one else, in the process summarizing the fearful citizen's position. Sam, Helen's assistant, asks her if he should help Kane—and offers no objection when she says no. A teenage boy and a drunk beg to be allowed to help—and Kane regretfully turns them away. Several men in the church scene offer to help—until they're talked out of it by Mayor Henderson. Even Harve Pell, the one experienced gun, offers his help—as part of a quid pro quo that Kane rejects. They all have their reasons, though only one, Baker's, is truly public-spirited. It is as if to say, as Kane is deserted by most of his fellow townsmen, that "the moral order [must] not rest on one unwilling hero."[41]

The critics who see *High Noon* as the story of a lone man who saves a town must answer a troubling question: In what sense does he save it? What would have happened if he and Amy had kept going the first time they left town? Were the townspeople actually in danger? We know Kane fears for the safety of the town's women, but Miller sought revenge on no one except Kane—and possibly Ramirez. A lot of people wanted Kane to lose, because he stood in the way of progress, or of fun—or, most important, of the fearful citizenry's self-image.

And what if those financiers up North get a different picture?

> If the North hears that Hadleyville is still overrun by violence, it may not send needed financial support, as Jonas feared, and the town may decay. Of course, what the North does depends on what it hears. And if it hears that violence has been put to rest in this last gunfight, the desired money may come, and statehood will follow.[42]

It was quite possible to interpret *High Noon* from the other direction—that it was against an elite presumed to be leading—or misleading—the people. Critics on the right wing, for instance, had no problem seeing the film not only as antidemocratic but as anticapitalist. In her *Screen Guide*, Rand warned against a sly communist assault on the free market. "All too often," she suggested, "industrialists, bankers and businessmen are presented on the screen as villains, crooks, chiselers or exploiters." The solution was to "make it clear that what you denounce is dishonesty, not moneymaking. Make it clear that you are denouncing evildoers, not capitalists."[43] Pauline Kael might have been speaking for Rand when she declared that Hadleyville "was used as a microcosm of the evils of capitalist society."[44]

The primary evidence for this interpretation is Mayor Henderson's elegant, almost poetic speech in church in which he at first seems to be speaking on Kane's behalf, and then abruptly reverses direction and worries aloud about the town's future if the moneymen "up North" hear about shoot-outs. As film historians Paul Buhle and Dave Wagner put it,

> As an example of the standard American political speech conflating the interests of finance capital with the public interest, the mayor's speech . . . approaches the quality of verse, with delicate internal echoes and long and short rhythms that alternate from one line to the next:
> "People up North are thinking about this town,
> Thinking mighty hard,
> Thinking about sending down money,
> Money to put up stores and to build factories.
> That would mean a lot to this town, an awful lot.
> But if they're going to be reading about shooting and killing in the streets—
> What are they going to think, then?
> I'll tell you.
> They're going to think this is just another town.
> And everything we worked for will be wiped out in one day,
> Everything we worked for in five years will be wiped out."[45]

The problem with the general "evils of capitalism" argument, as Buhle and Wagner's reference to "finance capitalism" suggests, is that Helen is presented as an admirable small businesswoman, and the only man in town clearly identified as a businessman is "a decent and fair silent partner of Helen . . ., who is a victim of racial prejudice—not economic exploitation. The villains are not capitalists but outlaws, and the cowards include a judge but no bosses. In Mark Twain's 'The Man That Corrupted Hadleyburg' the sin is greed, but in Hadleyville the problem is fear."[46] It is not capitalism as such that is a problem, but a large-scale capitalism looming in the town's future. After all, Will plans to run a store in retirement. In that sense, Foreman and his screenplay are direct descendants of Capra and *It's a Wonderful Life*.

Perhaps the most elaborate of these "anti-elite" interpretations is that of Peter Biskind, who argues that *High Noon* is a "radical" assault on the values of the "mass society" or "vital center" theorists. "Consensus," in this view,

> is bankrupt, the refuge of fools, knaves and cowards. . . . Whereas pluralists applauded themselves for their 'idealistic' pragmatism and ridiculed extremists for their preoccupation with fundamental questions of right and wrong, which they considered irrelevant and even obstacles to the smooth operation of democracy, *High Noon* does the opposite. The center is ridiculed for its obsession with mean, trivial, business-as-usual affairs, whereas Kane is applauded for his life-and-death confrontation with the Millers. . . . Both corporate liberals and conservatives are bad. *High Noon*, therefore, attacks both centrist models of the community: the federal focused, top-down model favored by the corporate liberals and the more bottom-up, populist model favored by the conservatives. . . . It is because of the federal government that Frank Miller is free in the first place . . . The corporate liberals have stabbed [Kane] in the back.[47]

High Noon thus becomes the opposite of Ford's (and Capra's) celebration of the people, but it does not share their celebratory view of traditional institutions. Biskind assumes that *High Noon*'s leftist filmmakers implied the language—"individualism," "corruption," "immorality," "coddling of criminals"—of conservatives hostile to a manipulative elite to cover their real class-warfare purposes.[48] In the end, he says, *High Noon* is difficult to tell apart from a right-wing film like *Dirty Harry*.

What Biskind's reading ignores is that the hero of *Dirty Harry* never thought his police bosses were his friends, though he feels betrayed anyway. Harry is the voice of a traditional morality as Kane is, but the difference is that Kane is part of the society, and Harry lives apart from it. Harry is a lone wolf, protecting his own vision of the right by his own, dubious means; Kane is a good citizen—and so suffers all the more.

As initially persuasive as they are, the "anti-people" and the "anti-elite" interpretations are incomplete, both because they don't fit all the facts and because they insist on "global" explanations; that is, "the town" or "the people" are hypocritical, or they "desert" Kane. The "left populist" view underlying Foreman's perspective was hostile neither to "the people" nor to "the elite," as such. Growing out of his own experience, it was both more specific and more personal than such broad-brush views. It is in that specific, personal way that his allegory about one Western town must be understood: The leadership failed, everyone had his reasons, and it was necessary for the central characters—Will, Amy, and Helen—to escape these people and their way of looking at the world.

Because *High Noon* is told almost exclusively from the point of view of these three, who are ultimately seen as outsiders, the film discourages any other way of understanding the actions of the people who fail them. But if we focus on what the others actually say and do, it's possible to see their actions as rational—at least by their own lights.[49]

Some of the characters won't help Will because they don't want him to get hurt; some because they want him to get hurt; some because they're afraid for the town's "image." From the mayor's point of view, the main thing is that the town be prosperous, that there be no bad publicity, that people get along, and that "troublemakers" (however unintentional) like Will and Amy get out of town, as they were planning to do anyway.

This is the dark side of what Thomas Schatz, in speaking of the Western genre, calls "the community's demand for order through cooperation and compromise."[50] Schatz, of course, is not talking about betrayal but about the struggle to wrest civilization from the wilderness. But to Jonas Henderson, his own version of cooperation and compromise is crucial. If those unfathomable politicians "up North" choose to pardon a man who was supposed to be hanged, that is just a fact of life. "There's a sharply critical attitude toward the supposedly simple folk of a century ago: they're shown to be just like people of any era, capable of a pathetic cowardice and of abandoning their loyalties as quickly as their Sunday go-to-meeting clothes," says Donald Spoto. "The Hadleyville of *High Noon* is thus no romanticized refuge from the evils of encroaching civilization, which is part of the structure of the Western. The saloon here is not the community meeting place, but an area where petty jealousies and prejudices and cowardices stand out clearly."[51]

As the mayor and everyone else in church knows and one man actually says, Will was connected to Frank Miller through Helen; the coming shoot-out has an unavoidable personal element even if Will denies it. Will's ties to the church and its people were always ephemeral, as is suggested by the minister's querulous complaint: "You don't come to this church very often, Marshal. And when you got married today, you didn't see fit to be married here." The church-people rationalize that since Kane is the villain's target, Kane's departure and perhaps some further accommodation of Miller will vent his wrath. Besides, Kane is no longer marshal, making the situation completely different. And, as the mayor had noted earlier, the new marshal would be arriving the next day. As Stephen Prince notes, "Each of [the] speeches offered in the church denies the close connection of personal behavior with the social and political health of a community, which Kane has intuitively grasped."[52]

So the townspeople talk themselves into a corner. In the words of Sam Girgus, "The town's collective intelligence and rationality ultimately succumbs to fear. The townspeople begin to analyze their situation and choices rationally, but they yield to inner, unconscious, collective doubts."[53]

Meanwhile the bar-people, who were friends of the Millers and have nothing to fear from them, use this same fact—Kane's connection to Miller through Helen—as a reason to enjoy watching him squirm. As the hotel clerk explains to Kane's new bride, he will not be sorry to see Kane killed, because the lawman has been too zealous in clamping down on free-spending freebooters like the Millers.[54]

In a situation where everyone "has his reasons," strong leadership is needed to overcome fear and unite people for the common good. Thus *High Noon* is as much about a failure of leadership as it is about individual withdrawal. "*High Noon* does have a political dimension. It is a movie about the relationship between a community and its leaders and thus political as an Elizabethan play about kingship is political."[55]

The "message" is the importance of leadership, but the message is muddled, because there is more than one leadership and more than one goal. Henderson is a false leader, Kane a real leader who is being rejected, and the returned killers are also "leaders," in a way. The people in the bar are anxiously awaiting their return to power, as is the hotel desk clerk, who speaks for "lots of people" who await the return of good times. As in *It's a Wonderful Life*, with its presumably opposed viewpoint, *High Noon* holds open the distinct possibility that Jonas Henderson is ultimately right; the town may not survive the shoot-out, but more important, had there been no shoot-out, the town, even with Frank Miller, would have blossomed: Why can't industry and corruption coexist?

In the end, leadership fails; most people retreat into themselves; and Kane, Amy, and Helen do what they have to do and then leave. Helen is, in her own way, at home in the modern world, but Kane and Amy leave what is to them simply a dangerous place, in which politicians can't be trusted and killers and railroads bring not just prosperity but the threat of death. "Civilization and community," as Mike Selig puts it, "are split apart" for the first time.[56] Kane remembers simpler frontier days when, the film implies, people stuck together and he had "six top guns" to enforce law and order. He rejects this dangerous modern "civilization" by dropping his star in the dust and heading out of town with Amy to form a new community of two on "the prairie."[57]

The feeling we get at the end is more complicated than the traditional interpretations would have it.

> Kane . . . seems to repudiate the town . . . when he throws his star in the dirt," says Prince, "but it would be wrong to conclude that he has been driven to [the judge's and the old marshal's] nihilism and disillusionment. Instead, he repudiates this community, as the film's conclusion sounds a note of warning, but not of cynicism. A delicate balance is maintained throughout the film between political bitterness and cynicism (Foreman's perhaps) and an urgent but more balanced and hopeful understanding of history as a dialectic incorporating . . . opportunism and disillusionment, on the one hand, and, on the other, courage and commitment."[58]

Kane can arrive at this point because he has come to realize that he has freed himself from illusion. The movie that tells his story has been, says Spoto, "about interiority, and about that quiet point deep inside the soul where the act of heroism is the logical and perhaps sometimes the only possible outcome of the habit of being true to oneself."[59]

Perhaps, as this comment suggests, it would be easier to understand *High Noon* not as an allegory about community with immediate real-world references but as a revision of the Western so deliberate it could allow its hero to come to such a realization.

NOTES

1. *"High Noon* (1952)," in *Western Movies,* ed. William T. Pilkington and Don Graham (Albuquerque: University of New Mexico Press, 1979), 59.

2. "A Past Master of His Craft: An Interview with Fred Zinnemann," *Cineaste* (Winter 1997): 16.

3. Among the leaders of this school of thought were David Truman, *The Governmental Process* (New York: Alfred A. Knopf, 1951); Arthur Schlesinger Jr., *The Vital Center* (Boston: Houghton Mifflin, 1949); and David Riesman, *The Lonely Crowd* (New Haven, Conn.: Yale University Press, 1950).

4. Brian Neve, *Film and Politics in America* (London: Routledge, 1992), 54.

5. See the famous rebuttal of the "mass society" theorists in Michael Paul Rogin, *The Intellectuals and McCarthy: The Radical Specter* (Cambridge: MIT Press, 1967).

6. Neve, *Film and Politics,* 29.

7. Neve, *Film and Politics,* 33.

8. Peter Roffman and Jim Purdy, *The Hollywood Social Problem Film* (Bloomington: Indiana University Press, 1981), 64.

9. Richard Corliss, "Still Talking," *Film Comment* 28 (November–December 1992): 17; Jeffrey Richards, "Frank Capra and the Cinema of Populism," in *Movies and Methods,* ed. Bill Nichols (Berkeley: University of California Press, 1976), 65.

10. Neve, *Film and Politics,* 31.

11. Richards, "Capra," 74.

12. Richards, "Capra," 70.

13. Neve, *Film and Politics,* 44.

14. William L. O'Neill, *A Better World* (New York: Simon & Schuster, 1982), 241–42.

15. Capra lists Foreman, but not Kramer, as a staffer on the Army films. Frank Capra, *The Name Above the Title* (New York: Macmillan, 1971), 340.

16. The film itself wasn't released until 1977. Joseph McBride, *Frank Capra: The Catastrophe of Success* (New York: Simon & Schuster, 1992), 498–99.

17. See Neve, *Film and Politics,* 44.

18. Neve, *Film and Politics,* 54.

19. Neve, *Film and Politics,* 188.

20. Pauline Kael, *Kiss Kiss Bang Bang* (New York: Bantam, 1969), 281.

21. Kael, *Kiss,* 281.

22. Neve, *Film and Politics,* 154.

23. Stephen Hunter, "No Escaping Politics in Movies," *Baltimore Sun,* August 23, 1992, 1L.

24. Lee Clark Mitchell, *Westerns* (Chicago: University of Chicago Press, 1996), 192.

25. Jeremy Byman, "Religion and Respectability in the Western: *Hell's Hinges* and *High Noon,*" unpublished paper New York University Department of Cinema Studies, January 1982, 8.

26. Graham, "*High Noon* (1952)," 55.

27. "The Man That Corrupted Hadleyburg," in *The Man That Corrupted Hadleyburg: And Other Essays and Stories*, by Mark Twain (New York: Harper, 1903).

28. Graham, "*High Noon* (1952)," 55–59. Also Cheyney Ryan, "Print the Legend," in *Legal Reeling*, ed. John Denvir. (Urbana: University of Illinois Press, 1996), 42.

29. Stephen J. Whitfield, *The Culture of the Cold War* (Baltimore: Johns Hopkins University Press, 1996), 148.

30. Donald Spoto, *Stanley Kramer: Filmmaker* (New York: Putnam, 1978), 105–6.

31. Richard Slotkin, *Gunfighter Nation* (New York: Atheneum, 1992), 395; also Ryan, "Print the Legend," 29.

32. Graham, "*High Noon* (1952)," 55–59.

33. See C. Wright Mills, *White Collar* (New York: Oxford University Press, 1951) and *The Power Elite* (New York: Oxford University Press, 1956).

34. Whitfield, *Culture*, 147–48.

35. Quotes from John A. Barsness, "A Question of Standards," *Film Quarterly* (Fall 1967): 34; and Slotkin, *Gunfighter Nation*, 396, respectively.

36. Slotkin, *Gunfighter Nation*, 392–93.

37. John H. Lenihan, *Showdown* (Urbana: University of Illinois Press, 1985): 117–19.

38. Stephen Prince, "Historical Perspective and the Realist Aesthetic in *High Noon* (1952)," in *The Films of Fred Zinnemann*, ed. Arthur Nolletti (Albany: State University of New York Press, 1999), 89–90.

39. Ayn Rand, *Film Guide for Americans*. (Los Angeles: Motion Picture Alliance for the Preservation of American Ideals, 1950), 5.

40. Rand, *Film Guide*, 7–11.

41. Pacific Film Archives, at www.bampfa.berkeley.edu/cgi-bin/ifetch? PFA_Filmnotes +74565919630+F (accessed December 15, 2002).

42. Mary P. Nichols, "Law and the American Western: *High Noon*," *The Legal Studies Forum* 22, no. 4 (1998): 604.

43. Rand, *Film Guide*, 1–3.

44. Kael, *Kiss*, 150.

45. Paul Buhle and Dave Wagner, *Radical Hollywood* (New York: New Press, 2002), 419–20.

46. Whitfield, *Culture*, 147–48.

47. Peter Biskind, *Seeing Is Believing* (New York: Pantheon, 1983), 45–47.

48. Biskind, *Seeing Is Believing*, 47–48

49. Richard Combs, "Retrospective: *High Noon*," *Monthly Film Bulletin* (June 1986): 187.

50. Thomas Shatz, *Hollywood Genres* (Philadelphia: Temple University Press, 1981), 50.

51. Spoto, *Kramer*, 101–2.

52. Prince, "Realist Aesthetic," 88–89.

53. Sam B. Girgus, *Hollywood Renaissance* (Cambridge: Cambridge University Press, 1998), 149.

54. Byman, "Religion and Respectability," 7.

55. Graham, "*High Noon* (1952)," 55–59.

56. Mike Selig, *Cinema Texas Program Notes* (Department of Radio/Television/Film, University of Texas at Austin, February 28, 1979), 4–5.

57. Selig, *Cinema*, 5–6.

58. Prince, "Realist Aesthetic," 90.

59. Spoto, *Kramer*, 101–2.

Part III

WESTERNS AND ANTI-WESTERNS

Chapter 7

Formula and Subversion

High Noon is well handled and forms a good companion piece to *The Virginian*, showing in both conception and technique the way in which the Western movie has naturally developed.

—Robert Warshow[1]

The marshal's [throwing down of the star] was simply a gesture of contempt for the craven community. The nervousness about subversion was perhaps . . . a subconscious worry that the classic myth of the fearless Western hero . . . was in danger of being subverted. The Marshal was not fearless, he was scared; he was not a mythical figure—he was human.

—Fred Zinnemann[2]

The ending . . . was arrived at not for purely commercial reasons. By far the most important reason for the gunfight and the happy ending was the fact that we wanted to do a Western in the strict, time-honored tradition. We wanted to see whether we could take the rigid classic form of the Western and give it new meaning.

—Fred Zinnemann[3]

High Noon had the bad luck to be released just before the first wave of a seemingly endless flood of essays and books from French and American critics about the "meaning" of the Western.[4] What mattered to these critics, beyond simple evaluation, was, almost without exception, not formal readings—analyses of the films' style or visual art—but interpretations of the films' themes, and the tools necessary for classifying films and themes. Some of these interpretations were psychological, which quickly became reductionist, but most sought to devise an intellectual armature from which to hang hundreds of Westerns and thereby understand them.

These "armatures" were heavily influenced by literary-critical analysis: mythology, "oppositions" or "antinomies," allegory, genre evolution, literary adaptation, historical recreation. Westerns, as with film in general, were to be understood as the product of social change, or shifts in artistic fashion, or a stylistic "dialectic" among filmmakers. The results were often fascinating and revealing, but they were inevitably limited by their very nature. The rule was, apply the tool you have, and if that meant that the films all fell into the preconceived categories, so much the better—even if elements were being taken out of context, or the underlying themes were obviously in conflict.[5]

The most common idea was that the Western illustrated a "myth" that summarized the nation's most deeply held values and that people turned to for reassurance. This "myth" that the critics invoked with near-religious devotion was an interlocking set of themes that existed apart from and preceded any movie, rigidly controlled the way the movie played out, supplied all of its meaning, and must never be violated except to point up the futility of deviating from the Westerner's code. The myth was all, the merits of individual films nothing. To ignore genre requirements was foolhardy at best—and at worst represented a horrifying fall into the trap of the "liberal anti-Western," as it would come to be known.

The irony is that beneath the proliferation of analytical schema and the arguments about the elements of the "myth" there has always been a great deal of agreement about the conventions, and even the meaning, of the Western. All Westerns have gunfights and riders on horseback; they are set in small, dusty towns west of the Mississippi; and the stories take place between the Civil War and the closing of the frontier at the end of the nineteenth century. There are similar stories set in colonial times, and there are stories set in contemporary times that resonate in the same way, but they are not "Westerns" as we normally think of them.

The classic Westerner is somebody who should have existed, more than he is a living, breathing person. A man of extraordinary qualities who comes into conflict with an increasingly settled society in which landowners, bankers, and politicians are remaking his world, he is willing to risk his life to defend the community, even if he must seek revenge to do it. If the question is, "Who is ultimately responsible for law, order, and morality?—a lone, superior man, or this early form of modern society—the Western answers, "The man, the gunman." In Westerns, always, "a man's got to do what a man's got to do."

It is an inherently elitist, undemocratic answer, because it assumes there is a single superior man, that he alone must decide, and that he must use force. The women who become important to him are either whores with hearts of gold or virgins. Ordinary women—the wives and mothers seen in the margins of the frame who provide a backdrop to the story—are irrelevant. By story's end, the man has brought justice with violence.

"Where the Westerner lives," says Robert Warshow in his classic essay, "it is always about 1870—not the real 1870, either, or the Real West."[6] It is a world of guns and horses and railroads, schoolmarms and whores, jailhouses and saloons, cattle and Indians. The railroad and the schoolmarm represent both the threat and promise of civilization.[7]

The Westerner is a man of principle who lives by that principle no matter what. He is, in Joan Mellen's words,

> tall, fair, muscular and straight-backed, an embodiment of courage and fortitude, selflessness and iron determination. . . . [He] . . . is sexually pure, if not innocent, and so is able to fight for justice unburdened by guilt, ambivalence or conflicting loyalties. . . . (He) is intelligent without being burdened by an Eastern education that would conflict with his reflexive ability to act without hesitation.[8]

In a gunfight or "walk down," he does not draw first, but he must draw not only if he is to save himself, but also if he is to be honorable. The woman in his life, who is likely to be from the East and need protecting, is against killing and finds it impossible to understand his need to face another man with a gun. When she asks him why he does what he does, he is inarticulate: It is "what he has to do." The only woman who understands him is the prostitute, a free woman who needs no protecting.[9] The Westerner will win his walk down. But in the end he will lose, because his very success in cleaning up the town will bring in new, civilizing influences that will make him and his gun irrelevant.[10]

The standard view of these Western tales is that they serve Americans as a kind of national saga. "Why else," ask Pilkington and Graham, "would a recent cover of *Esquire* magazine (March 1, 1978) present such a familiar icon from Western movies: a lawman dressed in formal-looking, dark pinstripes, striding alone down an empty street, his badge pinned on his breast, his face lined with stoic fortitude. The lawman was, of course, Gary Cooper; the movie, *High Noon*. Even Americans who had not seen the movie could identify the figure; it possesses the subliminal cognitive impact of myth."[11]

The problem with this view—that Westerns retell a myth about frontier settlement that has a strong hold on the popular imagination—is not that it is wrong about the significance of Westerns in the popular mind, but that it is too limiting, that it reduces them to folklore. The "secret" of the resonance of Westerns in American culture is not that they simplify into myth but that they complicate into a kind of proto-politics. That is, they combine two ways of viewing the world—the populist ideal and its opposite—just as American political thought has always done. Frank Capra was drawing on the same set of values in tension when he created his 1930s tales of homespun men of the people who turn out to be a part of a natural elite.

Westerns are "populist" because they favor the untamed West over the effete East, traditional values over modern institutions, freedom over conformity, violence over legal process, small business over big. They are always suspicious of large landowners, bankers, lawyers, and politicians. But they are also antipopulist because they stress, in classic American fashion, the supreme importance of individuals over organizations, and of a lone leader who, if necessary, will take the law into his own hands—though the Law must fail before he can act.

Critics of Westerns refuse to take them seriously because the genre emphasizes formulaic action over characterization, violence over understanding, male anarchy over female civilizing, Anglo-Saxons over ethnics, spectacular images over psychological development, and black-and-white moralizing over the shades of gray that mark serious drama.[12] In the critics' view, these films are inherently misogynist, racist, imperialist, and conservative.

For feminist critics, the Western is about the crisis of masculinity—and the centrality of women. Jane Tompkins offers a particularly eloquent summary of this view: Westerns, she says, "all describe the same man—a man in flight from the domestic constraints of Victorian culture, . . . at the center of an endlessly repeated drama of death, inarticulateness, emotional numbness in a genre whose pattern of violence never varies."[13] Women represent love and peace, and their role in Westerns is to articulate these values and then be ignored. But they must be there so that the men will be justified in acting violently to protect them.[14] It was to precisely this aspect of the genre that *High Noon* would speak so eloquently by "empowering" its women.

Whatever the ultimate usefulness of these criticisms, their analysis of the genre conventions of the Western goes far toward explaining both the genre's appeal and its importance. The "glorification of violence," for instance, makes it possible to play with both sides of yet another tension in American political culture: whether the (sometimes unreliable) government or the (extraordinary) individual should have the final say.

Despite its evident reliance on genre conventions and its willingness to employ both the populist–elitist and the state–individual conflicts, *High Noon* evoked an extraordinary amount of vitriol because it was almost instantly taken by lovers of Westerns to be an "anti-Western." The traditional Western that was so admired was uniquely burdened with a mythical weight that its defenders and enemies alike wished to see unchallenged as the source of both storytelling and meaning. The sin of *High Noon* was that it appeared to reject the Western's status as a holy relic, even as it borrowed its form and most of its conventions.

High Noon would be judged against a series of standards and found repeatedly wanting. In its basic form, the charge against it, especially from those who insisted that they respected its formal mastery, was that it represented a basic rejection of all that had made the Western dear to millions in its development over the previous half-century. They would be partly right: *High Noon* would uproot the genre's conventions to take it in a direction its fiercest defenders could neither envision nor tolerate.

Though the Western was nearly two decades old in 1916, its conventions were just beginning to be established when William S. Hart began making feature-length films around what had already become one of its defining conflicts, the struggle between the denizens of the bar and the churchgoing folk for the soul of the hero. Hart was one of several actors building on the seminal work of "Broncho Billy," the nom de six-gun of Gilbert Anderson. In hundreds of brief, two-reel Westerns between 1907 and 1917, "Broncho Billy" had employed nineteenth-century melodramatic conventions to depict "good badmen" who were shy with the ladies, fast with a gun, fearless in the face of evil, and daring on a horse. The good badman was always ripe for reformation "by religion or the love of a woman," though he had to first prove himself in a fistfight or a shoot-out. Whether he rode out of town or stayed to marry the girl, he would be a changed man.[15] Hart, who had starred on stage as "The Virginian," was determined to re-create cowboy life realistically, even as his plots relied on the same basic motifs.[16]

In *Hell's Hinges* (1916), the best-remembered film of his early screen career, Hart, following Anderson, anticipated the central role that institutions—the church and the bar—would come to play in Westerns, as a way to explore conflict between the respectables and ne'er-do-wells. Such a conflict would be useful to motivate what would come to be known as the "town-tamer" plot—though at this early stage, the audience's sympathies would still be with the church-people. Hart sought to make this new art form "respectable," and how better to do it than to follow his personal predilection and make modern Bible stories. But as writer and producer he had to adopt a straightforward strategy—the church stands for far more in a Western than in any other genre simply because it is the only obvious anchor for civilization in the Western.[17]

In *Hell's Hinges*, which brought all of his basic themes together, Hart anticipated the stark isolation of *High Noon*'s Hadleyville by setting his story in a town that seemed to be in the middle of a desert as barren as the lives of the townspeople.[18] As the purple prose of Hart's intertitle had it, Hell's Hinges is "a gun-fighting, man-killing devil's den of iniquity that scorched even the sun-parched soil on which it stood."

Hell's Hinges is run by saloon owner Silk Miller, who is described as "mingling the oily craftiness of a Mexican with the deadly treachery of a rattlesnake, no man's open enemy, and no man's friend." When a new pastor, the Reverend Henley, and his sister Faith arrive to minister to the town's few church-people, Miller determines to bring the naïve young man down. But Miller has not reckoned on Hart's gunman, Blaze Tracey. At the sight of Faith, Blaze is smitten— "I reckon God ain't wantin' me much, Ma'am, but when I look at you I feel I've been ridin' the wrong trail"—and determines to help the church-people. When Tracey leaves town briefly, Miller has one of his dance hall girls get the reverend drunk. When Blaze returns, he confronts and kills Miller and accidentally sets the town on fire. At the end, with the minister dead, the reformed good badman and the saintly young woman leave to start a new life together.

As with *High Noon*'s wedding, Hart's film opens with a solemn ceremony that should mark an end rather than a beginning—a newly minted minister delivering a sermon. And it closes, like the later film, with the hero and heroine departing the devastated town for the wilderness. It is the virginal heroine, the prime bearer of religious values, who attempts unsuccessfully to prevent conflict, and who in the process suffers the loss of something or someone dear to her. In *Hell's Hinges* "Faith" is the bearer of Christian belief and imagery, just as in *High Noon* the heroine is "Amy," which in French means "friend," the name Quakers give themselves.

The narration is accomplished through a fairly simple, one-dimensional structure. Because the hero undergoes virtually instantaneous (and, to modern eyes, quite crudely motivated) conversion, and because the villain owns the saloon, the conflict is between—and only between—the church-people and the bar-people.

Later Westerns, freed from religious strictures, would turn the one-dimensional conflict of *Hell's Hinges* on its head. John Ford, in *Stagecoach* (1939), would shift audience sympathies from the town's repressively puritanical Ladies' Law and Order League and the banker to "a prostitute, a drunken doctor, an escaped convict, a whiskey drummer, and a dubious gambler."[19] Regenerate outcasts would no longer enjoy Hart's instant salvation—nor would they need it.

High Noon would go a step further: There would be no sympathy for either group, sinners or church-people. The agent of civilization would be deserted by organized religion when the wilderness, in the form of the villains, attempts to reclaim its own. A civilization is shown to be rotten, and the villains are the least of it.[20]

By comparison to what came only a few years later, Hart's films, though effective in codifying the Western, were short and simple. By the mid-1920s, Hollywood was producing epics such as James Cruze's *The Covered Wagon* (1923) and John Ford's *The Iron Horse* (1924), and it would not be until the end of the decade that Westerns would return to the genre's well-established town-tamer theme with *The Virginian* (1929).

Director Victor Fleming's film was based on Owen Wister's 1902 novel about the Johnson County, Wyoming, cattlemen's war of the early 1890s, which would also inspire *Shane* (1953), *Heaven's Gate* (1980), and the television film *Johnson County War* (2002). It was in Fleming's film that the revenge plot, the second crucial element in the town-tamer Western after the struggle for the hero's soul, was fully codified.

The Virginian, a bashful Gary Cooper, is the foreman of a cattle ranch who falls for pretty Eastern schoolteacher Molly Wood (Mary Brian). When he catches his best friend, Steve, with a band of rustlers, he obeys the code of the West and hangs him. In the film, it is the pioneer woman Ma Taylor (Helen Ware), not the Virginian, as the genre might have it, or Judge Henry, as the novel has it, who defends the hanging and the "code" to a horrified Molly. When Ma tells her, "Somebody had to do it. He was in charge and it had to be done. That's our kind of law," Molly calls the hanging murder. Ma responds, "Crimes is ranked different in different countries, and out here stealing is about the meanest, lowest thing a man can do." When Molly protests that Steve was the Virginian's friend, Ma says, "It ain't a question of friends or enemies. It's a question of right and wrong. If we didn't hold a rope and six-shooter over them outlaws, you couldn't teach your school at all. Our lives would be worth nothing."[21]

Molly again calls it murder, and Ma replies, "Where you come from they have policemen and courts and jails to enforce the law. Here we got nothing, so when we have to, we do things our own way. Do you think it was easy for him to have to hang a friend? It was a durn sight harder for him to do it than for us to have to bear."[22]

The Virginian now wants vengeance on Trampas, who lured the foolish Steve into rustling and forced the Virginian to hang his best friend. Molly, who has agreed to marry the Virginian, threatens to leave him over this new threat of violence. She says, "We can go away." He responds, "I've got to stay. You think I want to do this?" She responds, "Think about our life together. If you do this, there will be no tomorrow for you and me." The Virginian faces Trampas in the streets of the town and kills him with Steve's gun. Molly acknowledges that he did what he had to do. Like Hart's "Blaze Tracey" before him, the Virginian marries Molly and rides away with her into the mountains.[23]

Through Ma Taylor's lecture and the hero's behavior, *The Virginian* summarized for all future Westerns the Code created by Broncho Billy, Hart, and others in the silent era: revenge and conscience, womanly submissiveness to masculine principle, and showdown "etiquette"—the hero does not draw first.[24] For many Western writers, these were the motifs central to understanding the Western, and therefore *The Virginian* not only preceded *High Noon*, it prefigured it in all important respects.[25] Only occasionally did someone notice that the tone of the two films and the meaning of the ending were completely different.[26] The available Mexican barmaid has become the steely Mexican businesswoman, the principled Judge Henry has become the frightened Judge Mettrick, and the face of the mature Gary Cooper conveys not only a physical but a psychic pain that is not there on the younger actor's face.[27] The Virginian, wherever he and Molly might end up, was fully integrated into this Western society, but Will Kane would leave it in disgust.

Despite the increasing naturalism of the Western, the genre began to fall out of favor with filmgoers the year after *The Virginian* was released, and it didn't fully recover for nearly a decade. Few Westerns were made during the depths of the Depression, when the studios and the audiences turned to gangster movies for gunplay. The few A-budget genre films produced, including Cecil B. De Mille's *The Plainsman*, were epics similar to the Ford and Cruze films of the mid-1920s. "Their themes," says Andrew Bergman, "revolved less around the individual moral dilemmas [and moral starkness] of a classic western like *The Virginian*, than around the growth of nationhood and justice."[28]

In the late 1930s, the Western made a gradual return to the screen until, in 1939, it seemed as if a flood had been unleashed. Though *Stagecoach* was only one of dozens of Westerns released that year— among the others were *Jesse James, Dodge City, Union Pacific,* and *Destry Rides Again*—John Ford's Western introduced a crucial change in the genre when it barely disguised its use of the frontier to indirectly comment on the present. It was, said one disgruntled critic years later, "the first Western to attempt social drama,"[29] by which he meant both an assault on the standard, socially acceptable stereotypes of the genre and the addition of psychological motivation.

In *Stagecoach*, a disparate group of characters depart in daylight from one morally parched Western town, travel though a wilderness threatened by the incomprehensible savage Geronimo, and arrive in darkness at another morally parched Western town. All arrive transformed, and they succeed against all obstacles because they "can overcome their differences to work together in civilized fellowship against the savagery."[30] These are less characters than social types, brought together to represent society in microcosm. The coach itself becomes the arena between the churchgoers and the outcasts, who were evicted from their previous lives by churchgoers.

Stagecoach was the most carefully structured, not to say stylized, Western of the first forty years of the genre, and the privileging of characters that would later be admired in Ford Westerns was heavily emphasized to make allegorical and plot points. The opening carefully established the various social positions of the characters, then moved them through a series of discrete "acts," as if in a stage play. There was the first section of trail, in which the stagecoach is left to its fate by the cavalry, the meal scene that favors John Wayne's escaped convict and Claire Trevor's prostitute, the second section of trail, the birth scene, the third section when the Indians attack, and the closing shoot-out in which the hero seeks revenge. It is in this last scene that the woman, who, as an ennobled whore, encompasses both "types" of the genre's women, worries about his safety but understands why he does what he does.

In its brief ninety minutes, *Stagecoach* manages both to rehearse the Western "code" and to offer spectacle—the landscape and the Indian attack. It is a kind of "summary" Western, but one which questions the easy distinction between the civilization of the town and the savagery of the wilderness.

Ford is not shy about communicating his purpose in *Stagecoach*. The central allegory, about "the bringing of civilization and fruitfulness to the savage wilderness," is treated bluntly.[31] Yet the images, far from being mythical, are shot as though they are documentary reality, as Tag Gallagher notes: "Low-angle, deep-focus shots of the offices and street of (the town they leave) seem to stress that we are there, that this is it; . . . the effect is like staring into a Matthew Brady photograph and imagining we are there."[32] In his "realistic" visual choices, Ford follows Hart and anticipates Zinnemann.

Stagecoach's social criticism is likewise both clear and unrestrained. Like Hart, Ford is a sentimentalist and traditionalist. Like Capra, he is a populist who "praised the little people and the fallible institutions that protected them, while he damned those who twisted the system to grab money and power for themselves."[33]

Thus while Warshow "considered *Stagecoach* an over-stylized archetype of the Western form," says Lenihan,

> where considerations of "landscape, the horses, the quiet men" dominate the story, unlike the social orientation of the deviant *High Noon,* . . . *Stagecoach* actually conveys as much social criticism as did *High Noon.* Ringo's departure from Lordsburg and "the blessings of civilization" at the film's conclusion are as much a condemnation of society's weaknesses as was Marshal Kane's departure from Hadleyville—a point that also appears to have escaped John Wayne when he criticized *High Noon's* denigration of America's heritage.
>
> Warshow's argument that *High Noon* lessened the stature of the western hero by submerging him in secondary characters would seem to apply better to *Stagecoach*, where the coach and passengers receive as much attention as the hero. In fact, Ringo does not appear in *Stagecoach* until well into the film, whereas the drama in *High Noon* revolves around Marshal Kane from beginning to end.[34]

Thus *Stagecoach* anticipates much that will later be spelled out in uncompromising detail in *High Noon*. The difference between the two seems to be not only the desperate cooperation between the disparate people on the coach but the ambivalence of the ending—a seemingly happy ending tacked on to a far from optimistic story.[35] Doc Boone's last line of dialogue about Ringo and Dallas being "spared the blessings of civilization" at least acknowledges there is a civilization, however troubled, to be left behind, though they must actually leave it to have hope of happiness.

If *Stagecoach* added an implied, then softened, confrontation with society to the long-standing themes of revenge and the struggle between church-people and bar-people, two other Westerns released in 1939, in the view of critic Richard Slotkin, began the struggle over the meaning of the "town-tamer" Western, the Hart specialty that would now begin to bear greater and greater symbolic weight.

Dodge City proposed the "progressive reform" vision, in which the hero defeats the criminals who cause injustice and thus empowers the decent folk who bring progress to the frontier. Like *Stagecoach*, Michael Curtiz's alternately jaunty, tragic, and heroic epic was an encyclopedic summary of the genre. A fictionalized retelling of Wyatt Earp's early career, *Dodge City* included the generic motifs of the train (and train robbery), stagecoach, cattle drive, saloon (complete with chanteuse and brawl), buffalo, wagon train, gundown, lynch mob, raging fire, and two sets of "respectables," the comically pompous women of the Pure Prairie League and the concerned professional men.

In Slotkin's view, Henry King's *Jesse James* answers the "progressive town-tamer" with an "outlaw" vision that locates "the source of injustice in the powerful institutions (railroads) that are also the agents of 'progress.' The sheriff who cleans up a town . . . is making it safe not so much for the ordinary 'decent folks' as for the big greedy concerns of capitalism. The outlaw represents a popular rebellion against those concerns but a rebellion that cannot win."[36]

But the film's vision is much more muddled than this summary would suggest. The opening title refers to the James brothers as "outlaws, for good or ill," suggesting the film wants to have it both ways, right up to the funeral at the end, when a valedictory refers to Jesse as an outlaw but one who wasn't altogether to blame and who frightened the establishment.

What was lacking in these films of the late 1930s was a tradition of social criticism that could tie the loner hero more completely to a hopeless situation—and a justification for doing so. Instead, the studio was relying on the tried and true formula of combining the populism that eviscerated any true politics by canceling out uncompromising views, a progressive idealism that defended the common man against unfeeling corporations and political machines, and a sentimental vision of free enterprise and a return to the land.[37]

Eventually, after a world war, a red scare, and a blacklist, these two models or visions, the "progressive town-tamer" and the "outlaw" critique of institutional oppression, would be combined in *High Noon*, which would shock precisely because it would shun compromise and undercut the simplicity of both models. In the films to follow, an unqualified "outlaw" vision would prevail, culminating in the desperately cynical vision of *McCabe and Mrs. Miller* (1971).

Four years after *Stagecoach* and the other films released in 1939 marked the triumphant return of the Western, William Wellman, who like Ford had begun in silent Westerns but had moved on to other genres, returned to Westerns with the grim *Ox-Bow Incident*. This was an indictment of mob rule and lynch law which, like *Stagecoach*, relied on character "types," and which the traditionalists Fenin and Everson, ignoring *Stagecoach*, *Jesse James*, and *Dodge City*, called the first of the "social" Westerns.[38]

The West is clearly a desert in Ox-Bow, too, rather than a garden. Like Hell's Hinges, "the town . . . is no more than a collection of ugly buildings—this place clearly does not stand for the civilizing process. The people are mean and brutal and the lynching is the most conclusive evidence for their qualities."[39] There is a conscience, an intelligence, in the form of Henry Fonda's sensitive cowboy, who belatedly tries to stop the hanging of three innocent men, but there is no hero. What leader the town does have, the sheriff, arrives too late, though he makes his influence felt immediately once he does. There is no ordinary villainy, only foolish, fearful men who scorn the legal system and arrogate life or death decisions to themselves.

After the lynching and the revelation that the victims were innocent, Fonda reads one condemned man's improbably eloquent letter to his wife, in which he talks about the rule of law and justice and links them to the conscience of humanity and to civilization itself. He is rebutting the frontier woman's code of the West in *The Virginian* and therefore the Western convention that justice must be assured by an individual hero.

The Ox-Bow Incident made it clear that individual villains were not required for injustice, that an entire town could be murderous even though none were as vicious as *High Noon*'s killers. *High Noon* would return to the same troubling notion of collective guilt in even subtler fashion by suggesting that a town could be murderous by inaction.

Stagecoach and *The Ox-Bow Incident* encouraged both a bleak picture of civilization and an allegorical approach to the reading of Westerns—a development not universally welcomed by film historians. Complains Jon Tuska, "There is a sharp divide between positive films before the war and bleak 'realism' after. . . . [For post-World War Two filmmakers, the Western] . . . was a vehicle for social protest, a platform for radical political ideas, a forum for special pleading, while the traditional hero increasingly became an object of ridicule."[40]

What presumably bothered admirers of more traditional Westerns was that filmmakers were using an essentially static genre to set contemporary social change in stark relief by contrasting its compromises, its corruptions, its sheer "grayness," to the black and white of the familiar Western hero who is upholding the code for people who, in the words of the crippled former marshal in *High Noon*, "really don't care."

With *My Darling Clementine* (1946), Ford returned to the Western after seven years in which his focus had been on the war—and quickly
showed that the underlying optimism of *Stagecoach* had not deserted
him. On the surface, *Clementine* is a revenge drama, though an unusually deliberate one: The killing of Wyatt Earp's youngest brother
by the Clantons eventually leads to the gunfight at the O.K. Corral,
but it takes a while. "Ford uses violence economically in [*Clementine*],"
says Alan Lovell, "building slowly to the final confrontation."[41]

When Earp, initially intent on revenge, becomes the Law, in the
form of the marshal of Tombstone, and is drawn into the life of the
town, the confrontation becomes a device that allows Ford to explore
what Lovell calls his recurrent theme: "the establishment of civilization in the virgin territory of the West. . . . Ford presents a picture of
Tombstone as the birthplace of the perfect American civilization
where the qualities necessary for survival in a hostile environment
like physical hardiness and practical intelligence combined with . . .
religion, law, manners, to create an ideal democratic social form."[42]

Clementine is classic Ford, artist of the familiar folk character. His
reliance on the same types, the same motifs, even the same actors, is
the art of sentimentalism and tradition.[43] What he is *not* concerned
with in his Westerns is historical accuracy, though those who decry
High Noon's historical inauthenticity either don't see Ford's careless-
ness with the facts or don't care. Earp grieves over the wooden grave
marker for his young brother James, whose death initiates the revenge plot. The marker has James dying in 1882—but the gunfight
occurred on October 26, 1881. Earp shoots a gun from Doc's hand in
a showdown—so accurately that Doc is not injured and can later operate on the wounded Linda Darnell.

Despite Ford's claim that Earp himself, a Hollywood hanger-on in
his later years, told him exactly what happened at the O.K. Corral,
the historical details are all wrong. The gunfight itself was quick and
deadly, and occurred near, but not in, the corral. The Clantons were
not alone against the Earps and Holliday. They had allies, including
the town sheriff, who is not a character in the film. And, except for
three Clanton allies, everyone, including Holliday, survived the brief
gunfight, rather than dying en masse, as in the film. Brother Morgan
(Ward Bond) guns the chief villain, Pa Clanton (Walter Brennan),
with three quick shots from the hip, even though Clanton is on a
horse some twenty to thirty yards away (and in actuality survived).
So much for historical accuracy—and the well-known inaccuracy of
the handgun. By comparison, *High Noon* is a model of restraint.

After *Clementine*, Ford and Howard Hawks both made allegorical commentaries on America's postwar role in the world—Ford with his cavalry trilogy [*Fort Apache* (1948), *She Wore a Yellow Ribbon* (1949), and *Rio Grande* (1950)], and Hawks with *Red River* (1948), although their philosophies—Ford, communitarian, Hawks, individualistic—would take them in starkly different directions. What they would keep, even as other Western filmmakers were leaving it behind, was their optimism, even if it was harder won, and the camaraderie of men banding together to do a job. Neither would seriously question their society, and so their Westerns would deviate sharply from the increasing expression of critical views in this most traditional of genres.

Hawks, who, along with Ford, would be celebrated for his Westerns more than all other filmmakers, ironically made very few, and did not actually "sign" a Western until 1948, just after the Red Scare and the blacklist hit Hollywood. It was handy at the time to assume that *Red River* was "just" a Western. Robert Sklar quotes a typical review of the time: "'When things get tough in Hollywood they start the horses galloping,' wrote Kyle Crichton, in the midst of the backlash from the blacklist, in his 1948 *Collier's* review of *Red River*. 'Nobody can yell 'propaganda' at a motion picture full of cows, horses, gunplay, brave women and daring men.' It became the central theme of *Red River* criticism, that here was a motion picture happily innocent of ideology."[44] And it has been a cardinal rule of Hawks criticism ever since to assume that he was not "about" ideology, at least of the kind that lent itself so readily to allegory, but about men working together and enjoying each other's company.

On the contrary, Sklar argues, *Red River*

> is a film about the issues of empire. . . . [It] is a film about cows, horses, gun play, brave women, daring men—and capitalism. . . . That the issues *Red River* raise of empire and markets were also central issues of American economic power and expansion after World War II should come as no surprise to anyone, except those film critics who prefer their masterpieces to be meaningless.[45]

In *Red River*, Hawks takes the standard ethnic stereotypes about Indians, Mexicans, and "carpetbaggers" as givens. But his too-individualistic hero, played by John Wayne, is in trouble, and his self-identity as the man who controls not only his but everyone else's identity is ultimately destroyed.[46] If he and his cattle business are to survive at all, he must compromise with the younger generation.[47] He must be "finally reintegrated into the group."[48]

Red River laid out the logic of capitalism and empire favorably, and the cavalry trilogy moved from (a limited) sympathy for the Indians toward the logic of unity in the face of a foreign confrontation. What remained to be developed as the Western moved toward a "showdown" with its own myth was unqualified sympathy for "The Other," the Indians, and a fully articulated version of what would come to be known as the psychological Western, toward which *Red River* and *Fort Apache*, with their troubled "commanders," pointed.

In 1950, Delmer Daves's *Broken Arrow* and Anthony Mann's *Devil's Doorway*, for the first time since the early silents, "showed Indians as sympathetic figures, victims of mistreatment and prejudice who were willing to make peace with whites."[49] Says Lenihan, "As a racial allegory *Broken Arrow* broke taboos about miscegenation: James Stewart plays a Civil War veteran who becomes a scout, goes to live with the Indians and marries an Indian (Debra Paget). He is subsequently ostracized and nearly lynched by white townspeople. Eventually he brokers a peace treaty between the United States Army and the Apache chief Cochise (Jeff Chandler), but not before a gunfight in which his wife is killed."[50]

Devil's Doorway, though fictional rather than being based on a true story as was *Broken Arrow*, seems more willing to confront the more typical state of white–Indian relations: It ends tragically, as an Indian (Robert Taylor) learns that not even heroic service to his country—he had won the Congressional Medal of Honor at the Battle of Gettysburg—can save him when the Wyoming legislature bars him from owning the land he has lived on all his life. First the townspeople, stirred up by rapacious lawyer Louis Calhern, and then the cavalry, come to take it away and send his people back to the reservation. The sense of betrayal is overwhelming. Revealingly, director Anthony Mann had just turned his attention from film noir to Westerns when he made *Devil's Doorway*. His "grim, dog-eat-dog view of the West"[51] would continue to be seen in such Westerns as *Winchester '73* (1950) and *Bend of the River* (1952)—both of which combined the new sociopsychological concerns with traditional Western motifs.[52]

"The point of [*Broken Arrow* and *Devil's Doorway*]," notes Lenihan, "was to redeem society, rather than individuals who were, like previous heroes, at odds with that society."[53] These films were suddenly politically acceptable because they answered communist charges of American racial prejudice.[54]

Also in 1950, Henry King directed *The Gunfighter*, starring Gregory Peck, which was widely seen as the first of the "psychological" or "adult" Westerns, as if *The Ox-Bow Incident, Fort Apache,* and *Red River* had never been made. *The Gunfighter* was the first Western whose theme was that the Westerner simply did not fit in anymore. He knew it, and the towns he lived in or passed through knew it.[55] The younger generation, so different from the one in *Red River,* was not the future; rather, it was useless—or even treacherous.[56]

The traditionalists were not amused by this development. Writing about *The Gunfighter,* Warshow commented:

> If the hero can be shown to be troubled, complex, fallible, even eccentric, or the villain given some psychological taint or, better, some evocative physical mannerism, to shade the colors of his villainy, that is all to the good. Indeed, that kind of variation is absolutely necessary to keep the type from becoming sterile; we do not want to see the same movie over and over again. But when the impulse toward realism is extended into a "reinterpretation" of the West as a developed society, drawing our eyes away from the hero if only to the extent of showing him as the one dominant figure in a complex social order, then the pattern is broken and the West itself begins to be uninteresting. If the "social problems" of the frontier are to be the movie's chief concern, there is no longer any point in re-examining these problems twenty times a year; they have been solved, and the people for whom they were once real are dead. Moreover, the hero himself, still the film's central figure, now tends to become its one unassimilable element, since he is the most "unreal."[57]

The film that inspired so much latter-day analysis was a brief (eighty-five minutes) story, set almost entirely in a small Western town, about an aging gunfighter trying to escape from his reputation, and returning to his past to visit his estranged schoolteacher wife and the young son whom he has never known. He is finally trapped by his reputation, and killed by a young punk.

The Gunfighter was ambivalent toward its hero, but it was also critical of the townspeople in a way that had not been seen since *The Ox-Bow Incident.* Even as the hero suffered from his disconnection from society, "the community [harbored] a vicarious thirst for violence while condemning the man of violence," says Lenihan. "For all of the loneliness, violence, and self-disgust that characterized [his] wasted life, he had at least acquired a dignity and integrity that distinguished him from the common citizenry."[58]

By 1952, the elements were in place for a single Western to employ all of the motifs that had been created during the previous forty-five years: bar-people versus church-people, revenge, the populist rejection of corrupting "civilization," the Westerner disconnected from an inexplicably changing world, the cowardice of the citizenry, and the tragic figure who was both the skilled town-tamer and the all too human man. All that was needed was to use these motifs, without compromise, in unexpected ways. This transformation, however, would also mark the death throes of the genre's traditional conventions. The standard explanations for this mid-century complication of the Western invoke the two classic evolutionary pressures affecting any art form, the internal and the external, which are not necessarily mutually exclusive.

Internal evolution occurs when the art form's practitioners can no longer take the conventions of its classic era, its golden age, seriously; those conventions seem naïve at best or stereotypical and destructive at worst. By 1948, in Thomas Schatz's words, the Western exhibited a "formal and thematic self-scrutiny. Such films as *Red River*, *I Shot Jesse James*, *The Gunfighter*, *Winchester '73*, *High Noon* and *The Naked Spur* indicate that the genre had begun to question its own conventions, especially regarding the social role and psychological make-up of the hero."[59] This is an inevitable process:

> Generally speaking, it seems that those features most often associated with narrative artistry—ambiguity, thematic complexity, irony, formal self-consciousness—rarely are evident in films produced earlier in a genre's development. They tend to work themselves into the formula . . . as it evolves. We are dealing here with the inherent artistry of the formula . . . as it grows and develops. . . . There is . . . a shift in emphasis from one cultural function (social, ritualistic) to another (formal, aesthetic).[60]

This internal evolution is partly a generational phenomenon, says Slotkin, with younger filmmakers, who had grown up with the genre anxious to move beyond familiar devices: "[One] might take a 'deeper' look into a mythic figure, emphasizing psychological analysis over 'action.' The 'psychological Western' . . . [appealed] to filmmakers and critics who sought to make the mature genre a vehicle for works of a 'literary' seriousness."[61]

The director of *High Noon* was inclined to agree; Fred Zinnemann, sounding almost dismissive, was happy to tell interviewers that his film was not a Western.[62] "The Western has become an art form in its own right, to the point where its conventions are as stylized as a ballet. It has it own laws; for example, the characters have to be rather primitive types, not subtle or complex personalities. Once you grasp the form, it is fairly easy to fit the whole thing together."[63] Of the widespread hostility among those who assumed the film was Foreman's political allegory, Zinnemann said, "The nervousness about subversion was perhaps not even political, but rather a subconscious worry that the classic myth of the fearless Western hero . . . was in danger of being subverted. The marshal was not fearless, he was scared; he was not a mythical figure—he was human."[64]

The traditionalists thought Zinnemann's European background made him the wrong man for Westerns—and because he couldn't make a real Western, he therefore had not made a real one.[65] *High Noon* was best understood, said many writers, as a remake of *The Virginian*, because it once again relied on a man intending to kill the hero, a fiancée who wants him to disarm and leave, and a final action governed by conscience.[66]

The alternative explanation for the evolution of the Western is that it was responding to external pressures—changes in society that influence the themes of films that hope to be meaningful to that society's moviegoers. For some historians, the connection was a close one, generating easily read allegory—if you ignored the difference between the forces that might produce allegory and the understanding of film *as* allegory. One simply decided either that the filmmakers were looking for themes, or that the influences were everywhere and unavoidable, and leaped to the presumably obvious conclusion. Stephen Tatum made such a leap when he asserted that in the 1950s

> the Western's previous emphases on a usable past, on national achievement, on the traditional virtues associated with heroic morality, and on group cooperation give way to other topical Cold War themes associated with the problem of returning war veterans, of racial conflicts, of disaffiliated youth, of defense technology and of subversive activity. . . . [The] triumph of civilization over savagery [becomes] the individual striving to retain his . . . integrity in the midst of a materialistic, conformist and complacent society.[67]

In responding to these pressures to produce allegory, the genre's basic story lines are drastically modified. The hero no longer simply

protects the townspeople from the villains; now the townspeople reject him even as he saves them.

Will Wright, in his *Sixguns and Society*, the most elaborate of the
"external evolution" arguments, claimed that *High Noon*, following
on *The Gunfighter*, was a "transitional" Western, meaning that its
story line, by inverting the classical plot of an outsider coming to the
aid of a town and then staying, encouraged the evolution of the
Western into a drama of professional gunfighters doing their jobs
and then moving on. Society is the enemy, and the ostensible villains
are there only to generate the action that fully reveals the extent of
society's evil.[68]

Both camps in the debate over genre evolution, the social change
exponents and those who detected the influence of filmmakers on
each other, were correct—up to a point. Both sources of influence
clearly changed the Western by weakening the hold of convention.
But these theorists of genre evolution were too anxious to fit movies
into their elaborate comparative and evolutionary schemes, instead
of looking closely at the films themselves. Analyzing Westerns
purely in terms of sociological themes and stylistic tropes is a reductionist enterprise: Neither explanation can predict what any particular Western will be *about*. The meaning of a Western ultimately
lies in that Western, not in its environment, and can be understood
only by formal analysis of the film itself.

Even on their own thematic rather than formal terms, however,
neither explanation, internal evolution or external evolution, allowed for an important possibility: that the Western broke apart on
the rock of social change into two distinct types, what might be
called the left-populist and the right-populist variants, rather than
simply evolving as a whole, and that a new generation of film artists
made use of that development.

In fact, the seeds of the genre "split" had been sown by 1939, as
the distinction between "progressive town-tamer" and "outlaw"
types suggests, even though the films produced then were severely
compromised by studio convention and politics. The studios, as we
have noted, were taking advantage of still-strong populist sentiment, that unique American ideology that pleased all sides and an-
gered no one.

John Ford and Howard Hawks were the "right-populists," trust-
ing in ordinary people finally to do the honorable thing, and privileging camaraderie over the larger community when there was ten-

sion between the two. They made important "pro-social" Westerns in the late 1940s from the perspective of this conservative side of populism, and they would continue to do so into the 1960s. The hero of *Red River* is tyrannical, but he is saved from himself by the love that was there all along. The hero of *My Darling Clementine* helps to build the town even as he takes his legalized revenge on villains, and the heroes of the cavalry trilogy find a meaningful life, despite the hardship of the frontier, in their military "family." Though their individual heroes might be troubled—and Ford would make a gesture at career's end toward the Indians he had always depicted as savages—neither Ford nor Hawks would ever make a film that was in any way critical of society as such.

But even before these films, the new, left-populist Western had begun to emerge. The first of these, *The Ox-Bow Incident*, made at the start of American involvement in World War II and released two years later, seemed to many a didactic Western, and its message-mongering at the end was clear, but it did far more than the somewhat artificial distinction between "progressive town-tamer" and "outlaw" to suggest that the evil could lie in a society of ordinary men. It would be called "antidemocratic"—as would, indeed, any film about a lynch mob, although why is not clear, since there seemed no question about the existence or evil of lynch mobs. It was a film with a conscience but without a hero, and its killers took action for what they conceived as moral reasons.

Other films—films influenced, as we will see, by the film noir trend of the postwar years—would emerge to reinforce this sense of betrayal by people who should be doing the right thing. Along the way, the compromised hero of *The Gunfighter* would face the hostility of the town before being gunned down from behind. But he would not be facing uncertainty by himself, even though the killer was part of the town.

Not until *High Noon* would a hero have to face a social abyss alone, without a single friend, or the posse to which the genre had always entitled its heroes.

High Noon is nothing if not a Western. As a town Western, it lacks some standard elements of the genre—cowboys, open range, "chases, cattle drives, wagon trains, campfires, coffee."[69] But the setting is familiar enough: a dusty Western village, a misguided Easterner, horses, a saloon, a church, gunplay, the honorable marshal who is not just a civil servant but a gunslinger. And at the center of the story is Gary Cooper, an icon of populist film visions since *The Virginian* and *Mr. Deeds Goes to Town.*

Yet many writers have felt free to say that *High Noon* is not a Western—some because they accepted the political allegory interpretation and decided that a Western cannot be an allegory with a real-world reference, a *roman à clef*—and some because it failed to "properly" employ the long-established narrative codes of the Western.

High Noon was released far along in the careers of the two directors most associated with the nostalgic, "right-populist" Western, Ford and Hawks, and of the two actors at the center of the genre, Wayne and Cooper. One important reason for the venom that Hawks and Wayne would direct at *High Noon* was their sense that their friend Cooper, symbol of the older Western, had been seduced into betraying it.

Traditionalists searching for a word to describe this new type of Western came up with "psychological," which seemed to refer to the new focus on carefully drawn characters—not always a strong point of the Western. "Psychological Western" really means that the horses and the gunplay are subordinated to fully realized characterizations and a powerful theme—in this case, betrayal under pressure by an entire society.

The influence of *High Noon* on Westerns up to the present has made it a target of those who defend the "classical" Western, the film that follows the rules. It is by far the most important film to question the sentimental conservatism of Ford and Hawks, and it turned the Western genre on its head in many ways, not least with its bitter vision of betrayal and its undermining of a genre dependent on landscapes, galloping horses, and instantly assembled posses. "[The] blending of documentary with genre conventions is what impressed critics about *High Noon*," says Louis Giannetti. "There are no sweeping vistas of open spaces and majestic natural monuments in this western, only plain cramped interiors, lackluster buildings, and white textureless skies."[70] Though it was not the first Western to subvert the conventions, it was by far the most influential. It is this influence that has made it a target of all those who defend what they consider the "classical" Western.

Some attacked it because they thought it violated the canons and also thought it politically subversive; others thought it violated the canons because it was made by a committee. What was happening was that *High Noon*, following on, and expanding on, developments in *The Ox-Bow Incident* and *The Gunfighter*, had created a sharp break in the genre. It had subverted the formula. There were now, unavoidably and permanently (right-populist) "nostalgic" Westerns and (left-populist) "progressive" ones that openly questioned traditional values in part by turning clichés to their own uses.

The action of *High Noon's* complex narrative structure takes place almost entirely in the town, which is seen as a kind of moral wilderness. This is not a particularly corrupt town; it is portrayed as typical of society.[71] But the marshal finds it impossible to assemble a posse. In fact, the film's plot could be summarized as: A marshal is unable to assemble a posse.

The rules of the genre and the "code" are violated from beginning to end. The story begins with the usual "happy ending"—the wedding of the central characters—and then everything falls apart. Its hero is openly afraid. His motives for staying and fighting are unclear, whether private conscience, fear, public obligation or pride, or some mixture. The middle-class church-people desert Kane, as do the working-class bar-people; the two groups are morally equivalent. The hero and the villain are each tied to both sides, but each is essentially alone. Most of the townspeople are afraid. The mayor worries about violence turning off investors. The retired marshal and the judge say the town isn't worth the effort to protect it. The denizens of the bar want the marshal out of the way because his strict law enforcement has discouraged the big spenders who prefer a wide-open town. The deputy is selfish and opportunistic. Thus, the real enemy is the town, not the gunmen, and the shoot-out, in which the marshal shoots from hiding or on the run, is almost an epilogue.

In the final and most telling inversion—of religion—the hero is saved by a wife committed to nonviolence who kills one gunmen and helps the hero kill another. The women undercut the stereotypical Western woman; in fact, by the end, they have become co-heroes of the tale. Amy is not just the virgin but is strong, determined, and gets her way in the end. Helen is not the prostitute but the businesswoman, the store owner who is connected to everyone and is caught in the middle.

Even the color of Kane's hat—black—is "wrong." It is almost as though Foreman and Zinnemann are working from a catalogue of Western clichés and upending every one.

Perhaps the greatest antagonism toward the film comes from chroniclers of the historical West, who concluded that it was an "anti-Western" that violated all the rules of the genre and displayed no knowledge of the real West. These criticisms about the historical accuracy of the "adult" Westerns are both technical and emotional.

The champions of technical accuracy tend to compare sound Westerns to the silents and generally find them wanting in authenticity of "landscape, clothing, actors and general historical detail."[72] In their overview of the Western, two of these "neorealists," Fenin and Everson, dismiss *High Noon*'s script as "inauthentic, too 'modern,' displaying little knowledge of the real conditions of the old West," and in his subsequent book Everson claims that historians of the real West "disclaim it, arguing that in essential details it is false and that the ballad is both artificial and anachronistic."[73] Another critic is dismayed with "Hadleyville, a town with no past—and no reason for existence, so far as we can see, completely outside of history, a whistle stop on a railroad that comes from nowhere and goes no further. There is no business in this town, not a hint of why it came to be here or even of why its inhabitants remain."[74] Fictional Western towns and their people, these critics are saying, must be firmly anchored in the historical West.

Several commentators pick out plot details that strike them as simply wrong, based on their own reading of history. One is incensed that such an experienced lawman as Kane doesn't pick up a shotgun during the climactic gunfight. (He considers using one early on, then puts it back in its rack.) Noting that John Wayne uses rifles and shotguns in *Rio Bravo*, the Hawks Western widely considered the traditionalists' answer to *High Noon*, Wayne Sarf says, "The Duke's brand of common sense appears even more admirable when compared with the idiocy of Marshal Will Kane . . . in *High Noon*, a totally phony, embarrassingly over-praised 'anti-western' drama." Sarf goes on,

> After almost ninety minutes of "running around like a wet chicken trying to get people to help him" [as Hawks had put it], and running up against his fellow citizens' unconvincingly presented moral cowardice, [Kane must face the killers single-handedly]. . . . His natural reaction is to meet them out in the open, armed with two measly six-guns, [unbelievable] . . . in a frightened, supposedly more "realistic" hero.[75]

What Sarf does not acknowledge, of course, is that Kane, barred by his badge from simply shot gunning the Miller gang, actually fights them not from "out in the open," but from behind or inside buildings.

Claims another commentator, "Coop, facing four men in a naked street under a remorseless sun, lets them make the first move."[76] The problem with this claim, of course, was that Kane has already informed us, in his speech in the church, that he has no choice about initiating action because the gang has done nothing wrong. In fact, he is "walking them down" as much as they are "walking him down"—he cannot be caught alone in his office—and he forces them into action by coming up behind them and challenging them. They must turn and draw simultaneously, giving him the advantage.

Indeed, if there is one single device with which *High Noon* marks its inversion of Western cliché, it is the marshal's total refusal to fight by the rules of the traditional Western. He kills the first man by catching the gang off guard from behind a building so that they cannot take a settled stance to shoot. He kills the second from behind a hayloft, after the man has shot wildly. His wife shoots the third man in the back while he is reloading and disables the fourth with her hands so that he cannot draw in time. We are as far removed from the traditional walk down as we can be.

A related critical approach was to attack *High Noon* for failing to understand the *spirit* of the West—that is, for being untrue to the heroism of real Westerners. Adams and Rainey protest that "the heritage of the Western and its traditional nobility is something that must not be allowed to be destroyed by irresponsible filmmakers who would have the nation believe that heroism, decency, individualism, patriotism and other admirable qualities never existed in the old West. They did."[77] And for Tuska, "setting this story in the Old West is irrelevant. It is a Western only incidentally. . . . *High Noon's* pastness is an example of intemperate escapism. Our ancestors had many imposing social problems, but cowardice and indecision [were] scarcely foremost among them."[78] He argues earlier that

> the concern [of Western stars and directors like Ford and Wayne] had never been to depict the west as it once was, but rather to interpret its spirit and give it new meaning. For them, the Western represented an enduring myth and they were part of a living tradition bound up in the articulation of that myth. Duke Wayne's objections to *High Noon* . . . came to this: rugged men of the frontier, men who had battled hostile

Indians and a harsh nature, who had scratched a living from barren land, clawed at rock to survive, would not cower as a group before (four) thugs. They would unite, as they had united in the past to make the land habitable, to build a town on dust, to drive their cattle a thousand miles to the railhead. The spirit of the West that *High Noon* depicted . . . may have been emotionally true for some in 1952, but not before that.[79]

For those who valued traditional Western storytelling, *High Noon's* genre reversal was a desecration. It seemed to mock the very idea of community—first privileging it over the camaraderie of earlier Westerns, and then turning it into desertion and betrayal: "*High Noon* . . . stands as a sort of line of demarcation between law man stories prior to it and law man stories after it," says Tuska.

> Before *High Noon*, town marshals were generally honest and capable, or dishonest, or just inept. When they were honest and capable, their heroics more often than not took on a quality of the superhuman. *High Noon* attacked this premise, showing a law man to be human and deeply troubled. . . . The ideology wishes to impress upon the viewer that a community, perfectly willing to hire a killer when the need exists, is also willing to go to any lengths to get rid of him once his job seems to be done. The law man's position in the community has no intrinsic value attached to it; rather it can become a source of community embarrassment.[80]

This genre reversal also undercut the effectiveness of Western storytelling. "The discovery of a 'social conscience' in the Western— and this applies . . . to films like *High Noon* . . . which dealt with the responsibility of the individual to the community—had one very definite effect on Westerns," say Fenin and Everson. "It slowed them down, badly, not only in their narration, but in their overall pacing. In the older Westerns, men acted; for better or for worse, wisely or stupidly, they acted. They didn't ponder, debate, subject their tortured souls to self-examination."[81]

To some critics, the most grievous sin committed by films like *High Noon* was that they imported alien ideas purely as a device, and a rather discreditable one at that. "Once it has been discovered," argues Warshow, "that the true theme of the Western movie is not the freedom and expansiveness of frontier life, but its limitations, its material bareness, . . . then even the landscape itself ceases to be quite the arena of free movement it once was, but becomes instead a great empty waste, cutting down more often than it exaggerates the stature of the horseman who rides across it."[82]

This was a broader argument than the anger over historical accuracy. The critics were saying that *High Noon*'s "social realism" removed it from the Western genre entirely. To Warshow, the marshal's encounter with the cowardly townspeople produced "social drama"

> of a very low order, incidentally, altogether unconvincing and displaying a vulgar anti-populism that has marred some other movies of Stanley Kramer's. But the falsity of the "social drama" is less important than the fact that it does not belong in the movie to begin with. *The technical problem was to make it necessary for the marshal to face his enemies alone; to explain why the other towns-people are not at his side is to raise a question which does not exist in the proper frame of the Western movie, where the hero is "naturally" alone. . . .* In addition, though the hero of *High Noon* proves himself a better man than all around him, the actual effect of this contrast is to lessen his stature: he becomes only a rejected man of virtue.[83]

Warshow is, in other words, angry that *High Noon* allows other people to figure in the hero's dilemma.

The critics, particularly the influential Warshow, were so anxious to condemn such an "alien" notion as "social realism," though, that they invariably misread the actual film. "Nearly everything that Warshow says about the emotion generated at the end of *High Noon* seems wrong to me," says Graham. "The marshal is not, for example, a 'rejected man of virtue' forced to leave the town; he chooses to leave the town." Film critic Andrew Sarris is wrong when he says that the final gunfight "'degenerates into a wasteful choreography of violent arabesques.'" We need a violent catharsis because "we have scarcely seen Cooper in action. . . . I daresay that no audience who ever watched *High Noon* was not moved by the final and quite long showdown. Violent arabesques are sometimes aesthetically and emotionally right."[84]

Warshow and the other critics simply assumed that *High Noon* was about a gunfight. The possibility that Westerns could be set in the West, just as other genres have settings, but not be *about* gunfights, or even the West *as* West, seemed unimaginable to these critics. And this is aside from the obvious fact that no two ideas of the West are likely to be the same. Westerns use their setting to explore a pure state of confrontation and community and individualism.

A second criticism by the traditionalists looking at larger questions than simple historical accuracy was that *High Noon*, along with several other Westerns, was substituting contemporary political commentary for the usual concerns of the genre. The plots of traditional Westerns, said Markfield,

> were as inexorable as a mathematical theorem. . . . Their very poverty, their absence of anything that was grandiose or irrelevant, enabled them to exist by the force of their own energies and inventiveness. . . . In comparison, the "new" Western has a strange, inauthentic quality, a pallid cast to its features. . . . It seems to be the product of men who have a basic contempt for the genre, who must disguise and distort it into a sickening parody that converts Custer's Last Stand into a lesson on race relations . . . It has a slick, high-powered realistic surface, an air of profound seriousness and maturity . . . Lurking in every frame is the cold, anesthetic hand of social constructiveness, stripping the Western of everything that was once true and pleasureful. . . . *Stagecoach* . . . was the first Western to attempt social drama. . . . Even a more traditional Western like *High Noon* suffers from the compulsion to sprinkle its action with pellet-like messages of high moral purpose.[85]

Andrew Sarris, in characterizing *High Noon* as a "liberal anti-Western," made a sweeping argument that combined several of these criticisms. The film, he said, was "a denial of the heroic premise of the Western and an application of anachronistic social principles to a milieu traditionally associated with anarchic individualism."[86] It used "the West as an allegorical device to denounce the East."[87] What Sarris was saying was that the real possibility for political commentary in the Hollywood studio film lay not in what was said, but what was implied. *High Noon* was simply too blunt, and therefore undermined its own chance of promoting its agenda.

A third criticism, building on the first two, alleged that *High Noon* and some of its contemporaries were attempting to create a new kind of Western, which sought social significance for the genre out of embarrassment with its conventions. Andre Bazin said *High Noon* is "ashamed to be just itself, and looks for some additional interest to justify its existence—an aesthetic, sociological, moral, psychological, political or erotic interest, in short some quality extrinsic to the genre and which is supposed to enrich it."[88] "Foreman," says Bazin, "treated the Western as a form in need of a content."[89]

British film critic Richard Combs tried to sum up the conflicting views:

> Is *High Noon* a classic Western, a realist Western, an ultimate Western, a watershed Western or an anti-Western? . . . What was once claimed as the film's realism, its documentary treatment of its subject, now looks like internal documentary, a record of the history of the Western genre itself. . . . To read the reviews of 1952 is to be struck by how little it was respected as a classic, realist or any other kind of Western; the tone is best summed up by one heading, "Western But Different." Most of the reviews begin with the sheepish acknowledgment that this is the Western as seen umpteen times before, but somewhat elevated, not by ambitious social allegory but by the classiness of its execution. . . . The continuing hostility to *High Noon* is based on a confusion as to whether it is intensifying the Western or importing something alien to it [i.e., Foreman's allegory].[90]

"Intensifying," yes. There was no doubt that *High Noon* had sacrificed the privileged moments that were so venerated in the nostalgic Westerns. But it was hardly "importing something alien." There had always been a "purpose" to Westerns, an underlying theme that ran like the main rail line through the genre, no matter what the specifics of the plot. *High Noon* was merely bringing that purpose front and center.

"The Western . . . is not so much true to the facts of American Western history," says James K. Folsom,

> as it is a mirror image of modern American life, in which the virtuous Westerner, representative of an older and different order, is contrasted with a morally inferior modern—and often Eastern—world. To say, as many critics have, that Westerns are "nostalgic," is to miss the point. They do not so much yearn for an older and simpler life as attempt to set up an alternate standard of values to the often shabby ones of modern finance capitalism. Whether these values are in fact "true" of Western life is relatively unimportant; they are "true" only insofar as they form a hypothetical, self-consistent set of values opposed to modern American life.[91]

These "opposed values" were a humanistic opposition to the growth of social bigness, of corporatism. It was the influence not only of the war but also of the Red Scare and a socially inspired film noir that split the genre right down the middle. Now there was not only the right-populist sensibility, which had always been there, but there was also the left-populist sensibility that motivated Foreman and Zinnemann, that refused to be sentimental, and that acknowledged the "mythic" status of the Westerner without assuming that he stood for anything but a symbolic ideal, an impossibility. The right-populist, or "Jeffersonian populist," view was celebratory, nostalgic, hopeful—but increasingly wary. The left-populist view had no illusions; it wished to call attention to the road not taken, and it avoided celebration, nostalgia, and hopefulness at all costs.

To realize their harsh, "left-populist" vision, Foreman and Zinnemann had to work within the confines of the Western even as they worked against generic expectations. Central to this effort was destroying the convention that made a bronze god of the hero—while still leaving him heroic in principle, even as that principle seemed more remote than ever.

"Zinnemann treated his Western hero," says Giannetti, "as thought he were a real human being, one who feels panic, fear and even some moments of cowardice. We're allowed to see his bruised and bloodied hands as he soothes them in a pan of water after a fistfight. He sweats profusely under the glare of the sun. He gets dirtier, more stooped and haggard as the urgency of his situation increases. Before entering the final shootout, he writes his last will and testament, unheroically assuming that he'll probably be killed since he's outnumbered and alone. After the violently unpredictable shootout, he gasps for breath and is hardly able to speak."[92]

Most destructive to the code of all was that this was a hero who could cry. "Critics who don't like the movie point to the lack of authenticity of the marshal's weakness," says Graham.

Cowboys didn't cry, they maintain. My facetious reply is, How do you know? My critical reply is: Kane breaks down . . . late in the movie, and then only after he has been deserted by his young Quaker bride, the judge who performed the marriage ceremony, the deputy marshal, a citizen-friend who hides behind his wife's lie to keep from seeing Kane, the former marshal, and a cross section of members of the two most powerful institutions in the town, the church and the saloon. To die for a town worth dying for is one thing; to die for a bunch of backbiting hypocrites is something else. Finally, of course, Kane is willing to die for himself, a commitment and risk that link him, critics notwithstanding, to the heroic tradition of classic Westerns.[93]

Ultimately, Foreman and Zinnemann had to create a real community that would be destroyed, even if only in a moral sense, by its own people. *This* town could not be the "backdrop" town of earlier Westerns in which only a handful of people had a stake in the events of the story, nor could it be the idealized community of the nostalgic Westerns because that—whatever the traditionalists might say—was fantasy. "Before *High Noon*," notes Graham, "townspeople were a 'lumpen' composed of sodbusters, shopkeepers, and other nondescript types. They set in high relief the mobility and superior skills of hero and villain, they talked about lynching prisoners and sometimes did, they filled up saloons, they rushed about in clots, and they were always there—in the background. *High Noon* brought them front and center; it was not a pretty sight."[94]

If Hart's milestone picture *Hell's Hinges* represents the beginning of the Western as it is widely known, that is, one in which the most basic elements of the genre are displayed, then *High Noon* marks an end point, because it suffuses a clear elemental structure with an enormous social-political burden by disrupting the genre rules. The classic Western grows between these milestones and then evolves into something quite different. *High Noon* represents the end of the traditional, sentimental, nostalgic Western—or at least, its rule over the genre.

With the demise of the conventional hero and the conventional town, the genre so closely tied to its conventions died, too. Nostalgic Westerns would survive in ever-more epic form for a decade and a half—as long as Ford and Hawks and their acolytes made them. But for the rest of the filmmakers, what would come after *High Noon* would be variations on its bitter theme—or parody.

NOTES

1. "Movie Chronicle: The Westerner," in *Focus on the Western,* ed. Jack Nachbar (Englewood Cliffs, N.J.: Prentice-Hall, 1974), 53.

2. *A Life in the Movies: An Autobiography* (New York: Scribner, 1992), 109.

3. Letter from Fred Zinnemann to Franklin Thomson Jr., January 15, 1954, who had attacked the ending in a term paper that he sent to Zinnemann. Courtesy Academy of Motion Picture Arts and Sciences Fairbanks Center for Motion Picture Study, Beverly Hills, California.

4. William T. Pilkington and Don Graham, *Western Movies* (Albuquerque: University of New Mexico Press, 1979), 5.

5. David Bordwell reviews this problem of the single-factor, overarching explanation in "Contemporary Film Studies and the Vicissitudes of Grand Theory," in *Post-Theory*, ed. David Bordwell and Noel Carroll (Madison: The University of Wisconsin, Press, 1996), 3–36.

6. Warshow, "Westerner," 141.

7. Joan Mellen, "The Western," in *Political Companion to American Film*, ed. Gary Crowdus (Chicago: Lakeview Press, 1994), 471.

8. Mellen, "Western," 469–70.

9. Warshow, "Westerner," 46, 48.

10. Mellen, "Western," 474, 475.

11. Pilkington and Graham, *Western Movies*, 1–2.

12. Lionel Godfrey, "A Heretic's View of Westerns," *Films and Filming* (June, 1967): 14–15; Leslie Fiedler, quoted in Douglas Pye, "The Collapse of Fantasy," in *The Book of Westerns*, ed. Ian Cameron and Douglas Pye (New York: Continuum, 1996), 14.

13. Jane Tompkins, *West of Everything* (New York: Oxford University Press, 1992), cited in Lee Clark Mitchell, *Westerns* (Chicago: University of Chicago Press, 1996), 11.

14. Tompkins, *West of Everything*, 41.

15. Peter Flynn, *The Silent Western as Mythmaker*, n.d., at www.imagesjournal.com/issue06/infocus/silentWesterns.htm (accessed December 12, 2002); William K. Everson, *The American Silent Film* (New York: Oxford University Press, 1978), 241.

16. Everson, *Silent Film*, 249; Peter Flynn, *Mythmaker*.

17. Jim Kitses, *Horizons West* (Bloomington: Indiana University Press, 1969), 21.

18. William Park, "The Losing of the West," *The Velvet Light Trap* 11 (Spring 1974): 3.

19. John G. Cawelti, *The Six-Gun Mystique Sequel* (Bowling Green, Ky.: Bowling Green State University Popular Press, 1999), 91.

20. Jeremy Byman, "Religion and Respectability in the Western: *Hell's Hinges* and *High Noon*," unpublished paper, New York University Department of Cinema Studies, January 1982.

21. From a screening of *The Virginian* (1929).

22. From a screening of *The Virginian* (1929).

23. From a screening of *The Virginian* (1929).

24. Richard Slotkin, *Gunfighter Nation* (New York: Atheneum, 1992), 183.

25. Larry Swindell, *The Last Hero* (Garden City, N.Y.: Doubleday, 1980), 293–94; Gilberto Perez, "Review of *Gunfighter Nation: The Myth of the Frontier in Twentieth-Century America* by Richard Slotkin (New York: Atheneum, 1993),"*The Nation*, October 25, 1993, 466–70.

26. Cawelti, *Six-Gun Mystique*, 95.

27. Mike Selig, *Cinema Texas Program Notes* (Department of Radio/ Television/Film, University of Texas at Austin, vol. 16, no. 2, February 28, 1979).

28. Andrew Bergman, *We're in the Money* (New York: Harper Torchbooks, 1971), 88–90.

29. Wallace Markfield, "The Inauthentic Western," *American Mercury* (September 1952): 84.

30. Gerald Mast, *Film, Cinema, Movie* (Chicago: University of Chicago Press, 1983), 136.

31. Bruce F. Kawin, *How Movies Work* (New York: Macmillan, 1987), 271.

32. Tag Gallagher, *John Ford* (Berkeley: University of California Press, 1986), 146–47.

33. Gerald Mast and Bruce Kawin, *A Short History of the Movies* (Boston: Allyn & Bacon, 1996), 271.

34. John H. Lenihan, *Showdown* (Urbana: University of Illinois Press, 1985), 22–23.

35. Tag Gallagher, "Shoot-Out at the Genre Corral: Problems in the 'Evolution' of the Western," in *Film Genre Reader II*, ed. Barry Grant (Austin: University of Texas Press, 1995), 255.

36. Perez, "Review," 468.

37. Peter Roffman and Jim Purdy, *The Hollywood Social Problem Film* (Bloomington: Indiana University Press, 1981), 64.

38. George K. Fenin and William K. Everson, *The Western* (New York: Orion Press, 1962), 251–52.

39. Alan Lovell, "The Western," in *Movies and Methods,* ed. Bill Nichols (Berkeley: University of California Press, 1976), 171.

40. Jon Tuska, *The Filming of the West* (New York: Doubleday, 1976), 62.

41. Lovell, "Western," 169–70.

42. Lovell, "Western," 169.

43. Not everyone admired Ford's broad-brush directing style: "Ford is too sentimental, too self-indulgent in his taste for buffoonery combined with anti-feminism (the other side of the sentimentality coin), and too visual, too concerned with *tableaux vivants* at the expense of dramatic tension." Lionel Godfrey, "A Heretic's View of Westerns," *Films and Filming* 13 (June 1967): 18.

44. Robert Sklar, "Empire to the West: *Red River,*" in *Howard Hawks: American Artist,* ed. Jim Hillier and Peter Wollen (London: British Film Institute, 1996), 152.

45. Sklar, "Empire," 153.

46. Pye, "Collapse of Fantasy," 20.

47. Don Graham, "*High Noon* (1952)," in *Western Movies*, ed. William T. Pilkington and Don Graham (Albuquerque: University of New Mexico Press, 1979), 51–62.

48. Selig, *Cinema Texas,* 6.

49. Richard Slotkin, "Gunsmoke and Mirrors," *Life* 16 (April 5, 1993); Fenin and Everson, *Western*, 282.

50. Lenihan, *Showdown*, 117.

51. William K. Everson, *The Hollywood Western* (New York: Citadel Press, 1992), 242.

52. Lovell, "Western," 173.

53. Lenihan, *Showdown*, 117.

54. Ironically, *Broken Arrow* was written by Albert Maltz of the Hollywood Ten and "fronted" by Michael Blankfort, who would himself be blacklisted. It was originally intended for director Joseph Losey before he, too, was blacklisted.

55. Thomas Schatz, *Hollywood Genres* (Philadelphia: Temple University Press, 1981), 58.

56. Graham, *High Noon*, 55–59.

57. Warshow, "Westerner,"157.

58. Lenihan, *Showdown*, 113.

59. Schatz, *Genres*, 40.

60. Schatz, *Genres*, 41.

61. Slotkin, *Gunfighter Nation*, 380–81.

62. Fred Zinnemann, interview, *American Film* 11 (January–February 1986): 62.

63. Gene D. Phillips, "Fred Zinnemann: An Interview," *Journal of Popular Film and Television* 7, no. 1 (1978): 60.

64. Zinnemann, *A Life*, 109.

65. Zinnemann was "never really comfortable with such essentially American subjects." Everson, *Western*, 240.

66. Larry Swindell, *The Last Hero* (Garden City, N.Y.: Doubleday, 1980), 293–94.

67. Stephen Tatum, "The Classic Westerner: Gary Cooper," in *Shooting Stars*, ed. Archie P. McDonald (Bloomington: Indiana University Press, 1987), 83.

68. Will Wright, *Sixguns & Society* (Berkeley: University of California Press, 1975), 75–77.

69. Cameron and Pye, *Book of Westerns*, 7.

70. Louis Giannetti, *Masters of the American Cinema* (Englewood Cliffs, N.J.: Prentice-Hall, 1981), 371.

71. Wright, *Sixguns*, 75–77.

72. Christopher Frayling, "The American Western and American Society," in *Cinema, Politics and Society in America,* ed. Philip Davies and Brian Neve (New York: St. Martin's Press, 1981), 137.

73. Everson, *Western*, 240.

74. John A. Barsness, "A Question of Standards," *Film Quarterly* 22 (Fall 1967), 34.

75. Wayne M. Sarf, *God Bless You, Buffalo Bill* (Rutherford, N.J.: Fairleigh Dickinson University Press, 1983), 83.

76. Stephen Hunter, "Movie Gunfighters Go Off Half-cocked When It Comes to Realism, Hollywood Shootouts Are Way Off Target," *Washington Post*, February 8, 1998, G1.

77. Lee Adams and Buck Rainey, *Shoot-Em-Ups* (New Rochelle, N.Y.: Arlington House, 1978), 596.

78. Jon Tuska, *The Filming of the West* (New York: Doubleday, 1976), 76.

79. Tuska, *Filming of the West*, 61–62. The writer is proud of his personal relationships with Wayne and Hawks.

80. Jon Tuska, *The American West In Film*. (Westport, Conn.: Greenwood Press, 1985), 37.

81. Fenin and Everson, *Western*, 42.

82. Warshow, "Westerner," 50.

83. Warshow, "Westerner," 53–54. My emphasis.

84. Graham, *"High Noon,"* 53.

85. Wallace Markfield, "The Inauthentic Western," in *American Mercury* 74 (September 1952): 83–86.

86. Phillip Drummond, *High Noon* (London: British Film Institute, 1997), 66.

87. Andrew Sarris, *Confessions of a Cultist* (New York: Simon & Schuster, 1971), 387.

88. Andre Bazin, "The Evolution of the Western," in *What Is Cinema: Volume II*, by Andre Bazin, ed. Hugh Gray (Berkeley: University of California Press, 1971), 150–51.

89. Bazin, "Evolution," 152.

90. Richard Combs, "Retrospective: *High Noon*," *Monthly Film Bulletin* 53 (June 1986): 186–87.

91. James K. Folsom, "'Western' Themes and Western Films," *Western American Literature* 2, no. 3 (Fall 1967): 197.

92. Giannetti, *Masters*, 362.

93. Graham, *"High Noon,"* 54.

94. Graham, *"High Noon,"* 54–55.

Chapter 8

High Noon and the End of the Western

> For the first time in movies, a community saw the hero not as a savior to be welcomed, but as a threat to be shunned.
>
> —Richard Schickel[1]

The most obvious measure of a film's lasting influence is how often filmmakers try to take advantage of its artistic achievement, its notoriety, or its financial success by remaking it, "updating" it, following it with a sequel or a variant—perhaps with a different ending—or recasting its plot and political perspective in a different setting.

What is less obvious, until much later when its influence is fully visible, is the film that renders its genre untenable, that casts it adrift, that eventually kills it off, except for the occasional one-shot made by a director or filmmaker who has the power to attract audiences not normally interested in such films. It is not difficult to locate such turning-point films: They are attacked by those who resist change, either by defending films that follow the tradition or by making films that use the tradition to harass the interloper from an "alternative" perspective.

Such was the power of *High Noon*. At the time of its release, most observers simply thought they were seeing a slightly different kind of Western. But the traditionalists, who knew the history of the Western, realized immediately that the genre was in danger of being remade, and they warned of the institutionalization of films with an implicit theme of social criticism. No less a figure than Andre Bazin, the leading figure in French film criticism of the 1950s and godfather of the auteurist movement, attacked *High Noon* and two other films of the early 1950s, *The Gunfighter* and *Shane*, ironically as "super-westerns." Writing at the same time, the American critic Robert Warshow dismissed these films as "anti-Westerns."

Many writers, angry at what they believed was the politicizing of a genre by filmmakers with no roots in or love for it, would propose other Westerns as viable alternatives, either as archetypes of the traditional Western that Bazin and Warshow so valued or as "dissenting" Westerns that implied criticism less of society in general than of the allegedly "liberal" social-realist mind-set behind the new film trend that *High Noon* epitomized. Whatever the virtue of these alternate films, as genre films began to be made less and less frequently, and as the masters of the classic Western—Hawks, Ford, and a handful of others—began to leave the field, the only question that remained was how many variants on *High Noon* could be created before the Western was reduced to a cottage industry.

Later critics, writing from a variety of perspectives, would dub *The Gunfighter*, *High Noon*, and *Shane* "professional," "gunslinger," "adult," "demythologizing," "transitional," or "liberal" Westerns. But whatever they called these films, these critics would invariably display a disturbing indifference to the subtle but important differences among them.

Most immediate among the transformations wrought by *High Noon* was its effect on the career of Gary Cooper. As one critic described his appearance in Anthony Mann's 1958 Western, *Man of the West*,

> what is especially revealing . . . is the expression on . . . Cooper's face as he performs his deadly duties. It is the characteristic Gary Cooper grimace—the same one he wears all the way through *High Noon*—a compound of pain, disgust and determination: pain at the horror of what he has to do, disgust at the venality of his fellow humans for forcing him to do it, and determination to do it anyway, despite his softer feelings.[2]

Long gone was the "boyishness" and "sweetness" that had characterized his Western roles up to that point.[3] The one exception, William Wyler's 1956 *Friendly Persuasion*, was the exception that proved the rule: It seemed to ask, "What if Will Kane had become a Quaker, like his new wife?"

Much more characteristic of the "new" Cooper was his disillusioned-idealist adventurer in the 1954 *Vera Cruz*. Indeed, in drama after drama in the 1950s, Cooper—frequently by his character's own, principled choice—would be the man at the end of his rope, sometimes literally. He faced an angry justice system in *The Court-Martial of Billy Mitchell* and *The Wreck of the Mary Deare* (1959), tried to escape a criminal past in *Man of the West* (1958), was branded a coward in *Springfield Rifle* (1952) and *They Came to Cordura* (1959), was suspected of murder by his wife in *The Naked Edge* (1961), and faced a lynching in *The Hanging Tree* (1959).

High Noon itself would be referred to in so many ways that it would sometimes seem to have provided the master plot for all its successors. It has been remade only once, in a disastrous 2000 television movie that pointlessly inflated Foreman's spare script and completely drained it of tension. It was the subject of a little-seen made-for-television sequel: *High Noon, Part II: The Return of Will Kane* (1980). The gunmen waiting at the depot were parodied in *Once Upon a Time in the West* (1968), and the church scene was famously lampooned in *Blazing Saddles* (1974). Coming as it did at the dawn of television, *High Noon* inspired dozens of self-conscious TV cowboys in what came to be known, after the initial marketing description of *High Noon*, as "adult Westerns."[4]

Because its stark plotline lent itself so readily to allegorical interpretations, it was eventually lumped with other Westerns as metaphors for one or another problem besetting America at home and abroad in the 1950s. Some saw it as a commentary on Korea, so it came to be known as a "Cold War Western," along with *Rio Grande* (1950), *Vera Cruz* (1954), and *The Magnificent Seven* (1960),[5] even though its story line had nothing to do with cross-border incursions.

High Noon had many uses other than as allegory. Its stark plot was easily transferred to other genres, most dramatically to outer space in *Outland* (1981), and clearly echoed in films such as *Taxi Driver* (1976) and the *Die Hard* films, with their contempt for the society in which the hero finds himself, and his sense of being abandoned to fight terrorists or criminals alone. It is said to have inspired foreign filmmakers, most notably Akira Kurosawa, whose *Yojimbo* (1961) is a tongue-in-cheek variant. *Yojimbo*, in turn, inspired *A Fistful of Dollars* (1964).

Perhaps it was that provenance that inspired the star of *A Fistful of Dollars*, Clint Eastwood, to revisit *High Noon* repeatedly both as actor and director. The connection is most obvious in *Dirty Harry* (1971), in which Eastwood's vigilante detective goes after a serial killer alone when his superiors abandon him. At the end, tri-umphant but disgusted, he throws his badge into a pond—in homage to Marshal Kane. And in *High Plains Drifter* (1973), a mysterious rider takes his revenge against a town for deserting its marshal, who had been whipped to death by three gunmen while the citizens hid.[6] Eastwood himself would explain that *High Plains Drifter* wonders what would have happened if Kane had been killed.[7]

Most important, the plot "spine" of *High Noon*—the lone, principled man facing danger who is deserted by fair-weather friends, ordinary citizens who turn out to be undependable, cynical, hypocritical, or venal—inspired dozens of 1950s Westerns. This "spine" was endlessly reinterpreted, giving rise to the vengeance, tragic misfit, community desertion, and professional variations well into the 1970s—though none quite captured the original's sheer bitterness.

Several of these films could also be read as Red Scare allegories (particularly *Johnny Guitar* in 1954, as we have seen), but instead were typically interpreted as criticisms of complacent, hypocritical, cowardly, and irresponsible communities, as if the trenchant observations of the social critics were clearly being felt.

Among the more obvious imitations, which together comprise a remarkable number of plot variants focused on injustice, lynch mobs, killers, and desertion, were *Silver Lode* (1954), in which John Payne desperately tries to clear himself of a murder charge before disbelieving townsfolk; *Three Hours to Kill* (1954), in which Dana Andrews is a stage driver unjustly accused of murder and embittered by a town that betrayed him; *The Fastest Gun Alive* (1955), a largely "indoor" Western like *High Noon* in which storekeeper Glenn Ford tries to persuade disbelieving townsfolk that he's a former fast gun, and then has to prove it; *Man Alone* (1955), in which Ray Milland is an innocent man on the run from a lynch mob; *Man with the Gun* (1955), in which Robert Mitchum rids the town of gunmen even as the citizens reject him; *Top Gun* (1955), in which gunfighter Sterling Hayden is cleared of murder and elected marshal; *At Gunpoint* (1955), in which storekeeper Fred MacMurray shoots a gang member and then has to face the man's friends without help; *Johnny Concho* (1956), in which cowardly Frank Sinatra must face two killers alone when the townspeople won't help him; *Tension at Table Rock* (1956), in which gunfighter Richard Egan is on the run for a murder committed in self-defense; *The Proud Ones* (1956), in which Robert Ryan is a disabled sheriff facing a showdown with outlaws; *Star in the Dust* (1956), in which sheriff John Agar must fight his own townsfolk; and *Last Train from Gun Hill* (1959), in which sheriff Kirk Douglas tries to arrest the man who murdered his Indian wife.

Even that most traditional of traditionalists, John Ford, couldn't quite escape the influence of *High Noon*. In *The Searchers* (1956), his first Western in five years and his first since *High Noon*, he turned John Wayne into a tortured hero. Ford's other post–*High Noon* Westerns would be equally as remote from his earlier films, though their pro-social sense would remain to the end.[8]

The most important 1950s films to respond to *High Noon* were those that effectively inverted the plot in some fashion—even as they retreated from its grimness: *Bad Day at Black Rock* (1955), *3:10 to Yuma* (1957), *The Tin Star* (1957), and *Warlock* (1959).

In *Bad Day at Black Rock* a modern Western town attempts to cover up a racist murder. One-armed Spencer Tracy steps off a train in 1945 in a Nevada hamlet and is instantly threatened by a menacing trio—Robert Ryan, Ernest Borgnine, and Lee Marvin—when they discover that he is trying to deliver a medal won by one of his fellow soldiers to the man's Nisei father. Tracy must take the killers on, with crucial help from the demoralized community he eventually rallies. Thus, the individual with a conscience comes as a complete stranger, faces killers who have buffaloed the town, and wins the support of frightened townsfolk. It is, in a sense, the situation in Hadleyville when Kane faces the Miller gang the first time; thus, it is the perfect inversion—and far more hopeful.

Two years later, *3:10 to Yuma* asks what would happen if farmer Van Heflin—a man with no obligation to risk his life but who needs the reward money to save his drought-stricken farm—took it upon himself to escort captured gang leader Glenn Ford to prison in the face of betrayal by his fellow townsmen and threats from Ford's gang. This film, which also relies, as the title suggests, on a looming deadline involving a train, is a particularly compromised variant. As John Lenihan puts it, during the climactic confrontation with the gang at the train station, Ford (improbably) helps Heflin to board the train, because he realizes that Heflin "could justifiably have killed him on several occasions, and he thus feels he must even the score."[9] And it ends with the lifesaving rain—very much unlike the physical as well as moral wasteland that is Hadleyville.

In *The Tin Star* (1957), the betrayal and the expert gunfighter hero devices are split and an element of racial prejudice added. Henry

Fonda is a former lawman, now a bounty hunter looking for a wanted killer, who finds himself in a town whose inexperienced young sheriff, Tony Perkins, is facing a murderous bully without help. The bitterness of *High Noon* has been entirely drained: Fonda, who feels no obligation to the town and expects nothing from it, helps Perkins take on the killer and establish himself, then rides off into the sunset with a widow and her half-Indian boy. Fonda's commitment is to individuals, not the society that treats them so shamefully—although that society will benefit from what he has done.[10]

Warlock (1959), as we have seen, can be interpreted as director Edward Dmytryk's elaborate rationale for becoming a friendly witness before HUAC. Henry Fonda is a gunman hired by a town to rid it of undesirables until he goes too far and they turn on him. The parallel, presumably, is to HUAC's "witch-hunters." Like Marlon Brando in *On the Waterfront* (1954), *Warlock*'s hero, Richard Widmark, keeps apart from his fellow gang members until he accepts the position of sheriff and finds himself caught in the middle.[11] In the most elaborate variant of all, the lawman is untrustworthy, and a gang member must rise above the situation to save the town. It is *Warlock*, rather than *Rio Bravo*, released the same year, that stands as the most complete rejection of *High Noon*.

The citations and homages continued into the 1960s. In *Firecreek* (1968), cautious James Stewart finally shoots it out with Henry Fonda's gang—and at least partially redeems the town.[12] *Death of a Gunfighter* (1969) takes the situation in *High Noon* to its logical extreme. It pits

> lawman [Richard] Widmark against the greed, hypocrisy and corruption of his own citizenry. As in *Warlock*, Widmark's relationship with the townsfolk is adversarial; here the reason is not an outlaw past but his mossback approach to law enforcement. To a town anticipating an economic bonanza at the dawn of the twentieth century, he is a civic embarrassment, compounded by his affair with the local madam . . . a black woman (Lena Horne). When Widmark marries her, it is as though Gary Cooper . . . had chosen Katy Jurado's worldly Mexican . . . rather than wed Grace Kelly's virginal Quaker. *Death of a Gunfighter*, with its long shots of the lawman alone on the street, purposely evokes *High Noon* and . . . develops [it] to its most treacherous conclusion: . . . the townsmen actually assassinate [Widmark] on the dusty Main Street.[13]

Far more than in the plot variants it inspired, which were numerous but rarely of much interest beyond their immediate story lines, *High Noon*'s importance to the future of the Western lay in its effect on the traditional Western, which, as we have seen, was not a type of plot but a philosophical stance toward the genre and society itself.

Many lovers of the classic Westerns were caught off guard and searched for a way to categorize and thereby dismiss this unwelcome phenomenon; thus, the wide adoption of the term "psychological Western" to explain this new breed of gunman who was both tragic and self-aware. The defenders of the traditional Western hastened to celebrate the very elements of the genre that had long dismayed critics: the emphasis on action, the two-dimensional characters, the avoidance of cliché-free, socially aware dialogue, and the simplistic, predictable plotting.

Andre Bazin with great sadness called *High Noon, The Gunfighter,* and *Shane* "super-westerns." Robert Warshow, too, saw some of the contemporary developments in the Western as a deviation from a purer essence. Warshow described the Western as

> an art form for connoisseurs, where the spectator derives his pleasure from the appreciation of minor variations within the working out of a pre-established order. One does not want too much novelty; it comes as a shock, for instance, when the hero is made to operate without a gun . . . and our uneasiness is allayed only when he is finally compelled to put his "pacifism" aside.[14]

The traditionalists fought against the new Western with a stream of reviews, articles, and books praising the films of those who held the faith against the mounting ambiguity and cynicism. The first to be lionized was Howard Hawks, an occasional director of Westerns whose *Rio Bravo* (1959) would come to be seen as the ultimate answer to the threat presented by *High Noon* and its fellow apostates.

The object of the most adoration, however, was Ford, who told "stories of moral education whose heroes learn the meaning of honor, courage, love and law (and often, how and when to fight)," said two historians. "*The Searchers* (1956) is typical in the way its lesson comes clear only at the end, with no sense of the formulaic or pat."[15]

But even *The Searcher*'s ambiguous "understanding" of a brutal white man was left behind in Ford's penultimate Westerns— *Sergeant Rutledge* (1960), in which the central character is a proud black soldier falsely accused of rape, and *The Man Who Shot Liberty Valance* (1962), which simultaneously celebrates and satirizes the West Ford had lovingly recreated for the previous forty-five years.

Even as Hawks and Ford were being singled out as the "masters" to whom purists could turn after the arrival of the "superwestern," another tradition, that of the "dissenting" or "termite" Western, was being developed by writers who would be linked to the auteurist school. These writers dismissed *High Noon* and related films not only for their presumed contempt for genre conventions but for their presumed political messages. Enemies of what they considered "dishonest" cinema, the critics described an alternate or "dissenting" Western that respected the genre's conventions even as it used them to subvert audience complaisance. Writing thirty years after the arrival of the "superwesterns," Richard Maltby provided the most elegant statement of this idea.

Following *Nation* critic Manny Farber's idea of the "underground" film,[16] Maltby celebrated Hollywood films that subverted not by proclaiming radical politics in their plots—which the studios and the Red Scare rendered exceedingly difficult in any case—or by reducing political questions to the purely personal, but by "working below the surface level of plot perception . . . [generating] a tension between plot event and its performance, which offers the audience a choice as to the level on which it wishes to read a the film."[17] He was referring to the claim that the seemingly uncritical Hollywood movies of the 1950s in fact revealed "ruptures" and "cracks" in American society through a "disconnect" between the plot and a social criticism inherent in the film style.

Filmmakers of the "liberal consensus" alleged to be dominant in Hollywood and represented by *High Noon* and *Shane* (1953) set out to destroy the Western, Maltby and his fellow critics argued, yet by insisting on their realism these "liberals" were as one-sided as before in demanding audience obeisance before their own standardized "types": the self-sacrificing hero, the maturing and learning hero, the professional hero. Echoing the more traditional Warshow, Maltby argued that "in all three types, the impulse to psychological realism in the central character did more than simply distance him from the supporting figures. As the fundamentalist man of integrity was revised into the liberal man of principle, his natural bonds to the small community he protected changed into moral obligations to a larger society and to abstract ethical beliefs."[18] The hero, Maltby claimed, was now vulnerable: "capable of some self-doubt, both about his physical capacity and his moral rectitude, which served to intensify his achievement when he was successful, reinforce his moral decision when he chose to make a stand, and provide grounds for sympathy when he failed."[19] The hero, in other words, had been modernized, and his self-concept was more important than his actions.

Standing against this rising tide of "liberalism" were Farber's "termite" directors, eating away at audience certitude and never guilty of waving banners. The French critics also noticed this handful of directors whose worldview—cynical and obsessed with violence—seemed very different from those who directed earlier Westerns. They saw classic heroism beginning to be replaced by a simple fight for survival in these films.[20] For their motifs and devices, many of these alternative films picked up on some of the themes common to recent Westerns such as generational conflicts and disturbed heroes, but shied away from political implications. They would be admired for how much they achieved, given the limitations of their sometimes contrived plotting, banal dialogue, wooden acting, and low-budget sets.

The principal names in the "dissenting" pantheon are Nicholas Ray, Joseph H. Lewis, Anthony Mann, Samuel Fuller, and Budd Boetticher—all of whom made a series of Westerns during the 1950s that were far more admired in retrospect than they were at the time[21]—partly because they "subverted" without ever violating the genre conventions, so that even traditionalists like Bazin could admire them.

The most mainstream of these "dissenters," not only in his approach to storytelling but in his access to major stars, was Anthony Mann, who, as noted earlier, had brought some of his experience with film noir to his Westerns. During the 1950s, he made eleven, including *Devil's Doorway* and *The Tin Star*, a latter-day Cooper Western, *Man of the West* (1958), and five with James Stewart: *Winchester '73* (1950), *Bend of the River* (1952), *The Naked Spur* (1953), *The Far Country* (1955), and *The Man from Laramie* (1955).

The last film, in particular, captivated Bazin, who used it as a cudgel with which to beat *High Noon*. "The richness of its script is of quite a different kind from that of the 'super-western' of which *High Noon* is an example. Here the initial elements remain rigorously pure. At the beginning Anthony Mann has nothing more at his disposal than the traditional themes and devices."[22] What intrigued those searching for subversion in the Mann/Stewart films in particular was that the star, edgy in a way he had never been before, always played a principled man who is severely tested, cannot rely on society and for the most part does not try to, and triumphs completely by his own effort. Society is secondary, and so the overtly political themes are eliminated.

Nicholas Ray made four Westerns during the 1950s, including one, *Johnny Guitar*, the film noted earlier as the most direct Red Scare allegory, which has acquired cult status. *Johnny Guitar* utterly confused reviewers; *The Hollywood Reporter* called it "one of the most confused and garrulous outdoor films to hit the screen in some time."[23] Featuring stylized sets and costumes and vibrant color, its hysterical scenes played like a Western opera sans the singing, and its subtext evoked sexual repression—in the form of a bizarre shootout between Joan Crawford and Mercedes McCambridge, both dressed in black and wearing holsters, and with Crawford in pants. As one filmwriter notes, while American reviewers ridiculed it, Europeans picked up on its adult fairy-tale quality. "Francois Truffaut proclaimed it 'the Beauty and the Beast of Westerns' and the film's cult following has grown considerably since its original release. . . . No where else in the Western genre will you find a film with such a hallucinatory quality, mixing melancholy lyricism, Freudian psychology, Greek tragedy, romantic melodrama, sexual hysteria and *film noir* elements in equal parts."[24]

But the fifties filmmakers who are most often said to represent this "dissenting" mode in the Western are Sam Fuller, Budd Boetticher, and Samuel H. Lewis, three directors whose reputations barely existed before they were resurrected by latter-day admirers.

Fuller, who made four Westerns during this period—*I Shot Jesse James* (1949), *The Baron of Arizona* (1950), *Run of the Arrow* (1957), and *Forty Guns* (1957)—is political, says Maltby, but not in the obvious ways. To Maltby and the other discoverers of "dissent," the word "political" had the narrowly cultural meaning of "undercutting smug liberalism" rather than promoting some public policy or coherent ideology. Fuller becomes the extreme anarchic individualist, who creates characters "at war with themselves"—caught "between love and revenge, between patriotism and the mercenary impulse," thus reflecting the complexities of the life around them. This—and Fuller's refusal to provide neat endings—is what is said to make his films political.[25] Violence is not simply a plot device in his movies; it is "a tool with which to attack the audience's comfortable complicity in their sentimental anaesthetization" by liberal cinema, which "holds its audience in contempt." Audiences are forced to see past the traditional generic forms, and thus "easy, sentimental readings are foreclosed."[26] This was a considerable didactic burden for any movie to bear, much less one on the bottom of a double feature.

Budd Boetticher was even more prolific: Between 1952 and 1960, he made no fewer than thirteen Westerns, including seven with Randolph Scott. Bazin admired Boetticher's B-Westerns, complaining that they were overlooked by critics who didn't take them seriously because they were not big-budget, ballyhooed epics like *Shane*, which he considered inferior. Of Boetticher's initial collaboration with Scott, he said, "The first wonder that strikes us in the case of *Seven Men from Now* (1956) has to do with the perfection of a scenario which achieves the tour de force of ceaselessly surprising us within the terms of a rigorously classical framework. No symbols, no philosophical backdrops, no psychological shading, nothing but ultraconventional characters in totally familiar occupations—but an extraordinarily ingenious mise-en-place and above all the constant inventiveness in relation to details capable of reviving the interest of the situations."[27] Boetticher did not, said another admirer, "inflate his material in the way Stevens did in *Shane,* or Zinnemann in *High Noon,* or Wyler in *The Big Country*—the three most overelaborated Westerns of the Fifties."[28]

Maltby thought the films of someone like Boetticher superior both to those of the social realists and those of the traditionalists. Boetticher and other "subversives," he said, "take advantage of the fact that the closed nature of the Western genre is well known, as opposed to the hidden closed-ness of the liberal cinema"[29]—"hidden" here meaning "disguising its manipulativeness." And while Ford drew his "conventional moral lessons," Boetticher's "rigid, ruthless adherence to generic conventions uses irony to turn the usual implications of the plot on their heads. Thus his villains may be sympathetic and his heroes' righteousness . . . absurd [as in *Comanche Station* (1960)]."[30]

That useful irony, however, could be undercut by bad plotting. Boetticher had intended *Decision at Sundown* (1957), his third collaboration with Scott, as his response to *High Noon*. It "spells out that film's message" about the need of the community to "take a stand against wrong-doing" but it turns into a story about infidelity.[31]

Joseph H. Lewis employed a frenziedly self-conscious style that was the farthest removed of any of these filmmakers from classical Hollywood compositions. His reputation rests primarily on his hysterical gangster film, *Gun Crazy* (1950). Like Mann he had made several films noir prior to his 1950s Westerns and brought some of that morally ambiguous sensibility to a genre in which right and wrong were supposedly clearer. He made four Westerns that were less than respectful of the genre conventions during the 1950s, including his own *High Noon* variant, *A Lawless Street* (1955), in which sheriff Randolph Scott tries to win the townspeople's support against the villains by pretending to be dead so they will realize how important he is to them. But then an old girlfriend, musical star Angela Lansbury, shows up, and the movie goes off on a tangent.

The most remarkable of Lewis's Westerns is his second commentary on *High Noon*, *Terror in a Texas Town* (1958), not least because it was written by Hollywood Ten blacklistee Dalton Trumbo under a pseudonym; the hero was played by unhappy "friendly witness" Sterling Hayden; and the improbably complex villain, a hired killer dressed in black with a right hand made of steel, was played by Ned Young, the blacklisted writer whose name would appear that same year on the credits of Stanley Kramer's *The Defiant Ones*.

Hayden plays a seaman who returns to visit his father, finds him murdered, and goes after the killer with a harpoon. In a scene that cites *High Noon* directly, the killer's now-ex-girlfriend asks a town meeting in a church for help—and the townsfolk immediately run out, unarmed, to help the hero. But the conventional tale of good versus bad is secondary: The tragedy seems to be the death of the troubled villain; it's almost as though the director, Lewis, was helping Young stick his finger in the eyes of the blacklisters.

The "dissenting" Westerns were long gone by the time they were "discovered"; they declined with the fall off of interest in Westerns generally in the 1960s. But the critics who favored them would rediscover subversion later in the Westerns—and Western-like *policiers*—of Sam Peckinpah and Clint Eastwood.

High Noon's emphasis on the weakness of the town—a weakness inseparable from villainy in a plot that introduced a greater sophistication about society to the individual good-versus-evil plot mechanisms of traditional Westerns—gave rise to yet another continuing argument about an "evolution" of the Western.

In his groundbreaking study *Six-Guns and Society*,[32] Will Wright used changes in the standard plots of the most popular Westerns to argue that *High Noon* was one of several "transitional" Westerns that prepared the way for a new, "professional" plot. The hero no longer is a stranger who is welcomed into his society. He is now an insider who is outside that society at the end—because he had to fight that society to survive. "There are still villains—particularly in *High Noon*—but they seem to provide only a source of action, not a real threat to anything recognized as 'good.'"[33]

In order to locate his "types," Wright, like other "structuralist" film analysts, stripped *High Noon* and the other movies he considered of whatever made them distinctive as films and focused exclusively on a plot line reduced to the bare bones of literary-critical "oppositions." He and others defined the distinction between the early 1950s "superwesterns" and their successors as that between "psychological" and "professional" Westerns—the latter an answer to the former.

As Thomas Schatz put it, "The psychological Western posed an implicit question: How could the morally upright, self-reliant Western hero continue to defend a repressive, cowardly, and thankless community without breaking down? The professional Western offered one of two responses, both of which were informed with the values of entrepreneurial capitalism as well as rugged individualism: either the Westerner becomes a paid lawman and develops an antagonistic rapport with the bureaucrats who hire him, or else he becomes an outlaw."[34] The point this "choice" missed was obviously that Will Kane thought he lived among friends.

Rio Bravo was considered the earliest and most important example of the professional Western, the response to the disturbing psychological Western. Whatever its intent, Howard Hawks's film borrowed from this professional gunfighter development without ever understanding what *High Noon* was about. *Rio Bravo*'s sole concern was "the honor and self-esteem of the few major characters,"[35] but even as it "replied" to *High Noon*, it had nothing to say to the earlier film because it had devised characters who were totally apart from their society.

Not every observer was thrilled by the arrival of the professional Western; some relied, as they had before, on external explanations, that is, ominous shifts in the larger society. Films, said Richard Slotkin, now reflected a social drift from populism toward hierarchy and expertise, and the pacifistic values associated with women were being definitively replaced by a male assumption that violence was the only way.[36] Despite the evidence of incessant imitation, Slotkin was not considering the possibility that a single film could have undercut the genre—and that no speculation about an elite's drift from populism was necessary.

Slotkin was guilty of other misreading, of the *post hoc, ergo propter hoc* variety. He insisted that *The Gunfighter, High Noon,* and *Shane* had given rise to the stylized gunfighter movie of the end of the decade, such as *No Name on the Bullet* (1959) and *Last of the Fast Guns* (1960).[37] But that was to assume that *High Noon* and the other films were, in fact, gunfighter movies, at least in the same sense of the term.

High Noon had, indeed, immediately been read as a "gunfighter" movie and lumped with *The Gunfighter* and *Shane,* as we've seen, even though in the former, the protagonist is a professional killer who has no ties to the town and is shot to death despite the best efforts of his old friend, the sheriff, and in the latter the protagonist has no ties to the community, saves the community from killers without asking for help, and is not rejected by the community but leaves because he knows he has no future there. Neither of the other two contain the implicit critique of the community that *High Noon* does, because the community is in no serious sense involved.

Though both *High Noon* and *The Gunfighter* are imbued with what Michael Coyne calls a "strong sense of inescapable tragedy" reflecting "a debt to noir movies of the late 1940s . . . which presented their protagonists—and, by extension, their audiences—with a profound consciousness of their own mortality,"[38] the two films are otherwise very different. *The Gunfighter*'s Johnny Ringo is trying to reestablish ties to someone in the town—his estranged wife. In *High Noon,* the gunman has had both the law and the town behind him—or so he thought. *The Gunfighter,* though, has been largely forgotten outside Hollywood, and it is *Shane* that has come to be linked with *High Noon* in the minds of reviewers and critics.

Shane is the tragic story of a "knight" who takes the side of the homesteaders in the Johnson County, Wyoming, war of the 1890s—as opposed to Cooper's knight in *The Virginian,* who sides with the ranchers in that same conflict. In *Shane* the lone gunman, who would give up guns if he could—every sharp noise rattles him—appears out of nowhere and is drawn into the life of a family of homesteaders. He is attracted to the farm wife and becomes a mentor to their young son. Eventually he must use his guns in their defense when they are threatened by ranchers who want their property for range-land.

The gunman has no history with these people, no reputation—he is what he is, and is therefore recognizable, and he connects out of loneliness. *Shane* is the classic Western situation, as is Wyler's *The Westerner* (1940), with Cooper. It is lumped together with the other two for reasons of chronology, budget, star power, and director—not because it is like either of them. "Where *High Noon* deliberately avoids mythic innuendo," notes one observer, "*Shane* as deliberately embraces it."[39]

There are obvious similarities to be sure, beginning with a faux re-alism going back to William S. Hart, and rigorous scripts. Shane and Kane are "reluctant gunfighters," the dialogue is laconic, and the cinematography is studied. The central theme is the need for com-munal resistance to evil, the community leaders' professions of af-fection for the hero are empty, the gunmen are seen more as a force of nature than as the central evil, and the moral leadership of busi-ness is regarded with skepticism. The problem of the immature male trying to grow up is central, a man insists on honor even unto death, and his wife accuses him of pridefulness.

But the failure of community is secondary in *Shane*, which is really about what happens when a gunman finds himself caught in a "ma-ture domestic dilemma," as Bob Sitton puts it. Shane is a sexual chal-lenge for a wife who wants to escape the life, and there's a boy. There's not the same sense here of the community failing the man—because he's an outsider.[40]

Shane does not challenge the traditional Western—it celebrates it, enshrining its devices and tropes for all time. It is, in the end, criti-cal of no one, other than the villains, who are traditional villains, ranching imperialists rather than vaguely sinister "people up North." Shane himself could not be farther removed from Kane's involvement in the life of his community and his horrified realiza-tion that it has betrayed him. Shane has merely realized his sepa-rateness from the community; Kane has dropped his star in the dust to indicate his disgust at the community that has failed him. "His last ride out of Hadleyville is in the wagon, accompanied by his wife, and not alone on his horse"—as though citing *Stagecoach* with-out so much as acknowledging what hopefulness that earlier film can manage.[41]

Even as *High Noon*'s influence in Hollywood and elsewhere continued to be felt in 1960s Westerns, the genre itself seemed to be withering away. "Up until the end of the '50s, a quarter of all Hollywood films were Westerns. After that, the figure fell at a staggering pace, dropping to an all-time low between 1979 and 1984 with a total of three."[42] The few Westerns that were made in the early 1960s all seemed to draw their inspiration from the "superwesterns'" tragic, even fatalistic vision. The heroes of *Ride the High Country, The Misfits*, and *Lonely Are the Brave* (all three, significantly, set at the turn of the century, when the frontier had closed, or in the present day) cannot connect to civilization, or at least the weak and self-centered civilization they know, something they finally realize or are shocked to learn. This was the epitaph of the left-populist Western—a weary resignation with the weakness of people and "a profound consciousness of [the gunmen's] own mortality."[43]

Even John Ford, in *The Man Who Shot Liberty Valance* (1962), finally tried to acknowledge that he had been dealing in Western mythology all the time with the famous order to "print the legend." But he couldn't quite leave the past behind. The doomed Westerner, John Wayne, is lionized even as James Stewart, the representative of modernity, admits he is a fraud—and as Ford presents Stewart's success as an inevitable evolution rather than a failure of society.

Ford and Hawks were still directing in unsubtle fashion as their careers faded out, while the other directors of Westerns in the early 1960s borrowed the *High Noon* model and underplayed. Philip French, in bizarrely describing the differences between Zinnemann and Ford as the difference between "Kennedy Westerns" and "Goldwater Westerns," was acknowledging the difference between "left-populist" and "right-populist" styles.[44] "The principal stylistic features of a typical Kennedy Western," he said, "might be defined thus: the overall treatment would be taut and fast-driving; its rhetoric would be elegant, ironic, laced with wit; pictorially the images would be carefully composed, bringing out the harsh challenge of the landscape; its moral tone would be sharp and penetrating; its mood would be cool with an underlying note of the absurd or tragic sense of life; the past would be rendered in a moderately realistic fashion, almost without regret, jut a token elegiacism. The overall style of the typical Goldwater Western would be slack and expansive; its rhetoric would be sententious, broadly humorous, woolly; its visual surface would involve a casual acceptance of the landscape; the moral tone would be generous but ultimately unforgiving, riding on a knife-edge between cruelty and sentimentality; its mood would be warmly nostalgic."[45] The hero in a "Kennedy Western," said French, was diffident, capable of change, professional, anguished over his failure, dealing with community stress, and wryly optimistic about the future. The hero in a "Goldwater Western" was resolute and his own man.[46] With the exception of the "wry optimism," this was the Gary Cooper of *High Noon,* in other words, versus the larger-than-life John Wayne in any of his Westerns.

By the late 1960s, the professional Western had evolved into something that would have been unrecognizable only a few years before, and not just because spaghetti-Western star Clint Eastwood had raised the body count to mythic proportions. The gunmen were either hired to do a job, with money their primary concern—though, as in *The Professionals* (1966), they were likely to experience betrayal—or they were sympathetic outlaws at the end of their tether at the end of the West, as in two surprisingly sentimental hits, *The Wild Bunch* (1969) and *Butch Cassidy and the Sundance Kid* (1969), who went out in a hail of bullets south of the border and inspired endless allegorical interpretations about political assassinations and the Vietnam War. By 1976, even John Wayne had been persuaded to portray a tragic Westerner—in his last film, *The Shootist*—though, characteristically, it ends on a note of triumph for Old West values even as the hero is dying.

But the legacy of *High Noon* was far from over, even as Westerns themselves had been reduced from an industry to a boutique business. Films as varied as *Welcome to Hard Times* (1967), *Firecreek* (1968), *Death of a Gunfighter* (1969), and *McCabe and Mrs. Miller* (1971) harked back to that now-iconic image of the lone, principled man abandoned. The difference was that there was nothing the least bit hopeful in these towns—and the lone hero was no Will Kane.[47]

This was the period when every movie was being called "revisionist"—as though the Western had not started changing almost two decades earlier. It was just that it was now possible for left-populists to leave allegory behind and comment explicitly on the alleged racism, sexism, and chauvinism of the classic Western.

One commentary on the time reveals just how far the left-populist/socially critical view had infiltrated the Western by the 1970s. Jim Hoberman describes a split between the "revisionist" films, such as Arthur Penn's *Little Big Man* (1970) and, by extension,

Bonnie and Clyde (1967) and Robert Altman's *McCabe and Mrs. Miller* (1971) and *Buffalo Bill and the Indians* (1976), on the one hand, and the inheritors of the traditional view, such as the John Wayne–Mark Rydell *The Cowboys* (1972) and Clint Eastwood's *High Plains Drifter* (1973) and *The Outlaw Josey Wales* (1976) on the other. The problem with this distinction is that even the conservatives had been profoundly affected by a sense of betrayal. As Slotkin notes, the post-Civil War *Josey Wales* "combines historical reconstruction with a response to a contemporary issue, the bitter aftermath of Vietnam. There is no mistaking the meaning of the film's final line, in which Josey forgives his last enemy: 'We all died a little in that damned war.'"[48]

The revisionist Western that most accurately reflected the evolution of the Western since *High Noon*, however, was *McCabe and Mrs. Miller*. Warren Beatty's "hero," a mysterious outsider who has set up a brothel, dies in the snow after killing three thugs hired by the mining company trying to take over his business. The townspeople are oblivious to his situation, and his madam, Julie Christie, lives in an opium-induced haze. There are no church-people to betray him directly, even as the irreligious townspeople put out a fire in the church. The industrial threat is made explicit, and killing all the bad guys does no good for either the town or the hero. Though *McCabe* is not film noir, some of that genre's sensibility is here, not least in its style, its "bleak, color-bleached effects and its take of a ruthless corporation extending its tentacles over all."[49] Both the heroic romance of *Hell's Hinges* and the bitterness of *High Noon* have drowned in cynicism as the battle of the traditional Western hero against modern capitalism has devolved into a battle between an amoral small entrepreneur and brutal big capitalism.

Even though Westerns would occasionally be produced for the next thirty years, in an important sense, *McCabe and Mrs. Miller* bookends the Western genre that had had its beginnings in William S. Hart's "realistic" dramas. Most Westerns after 1971 were barely visible among the competing science fiction and action genres, though two big star films, Kevin Costner's *Dances with Wolves* (1990) and Eastwood's *Unforgiven* (1992), would win Oscars and draw crowds—because, said the critics, they had re-imagined the genre for a new generation.

But one-shots couldn't save a genre that had gone as far as it could go. It didn't matter that many of the most recent films were the truest to history, as the critics of *High Noon* had demanded; the Western had never been about history. By the 1990s, all that was left was self-conscious citation, extravagance, star-vehicle, and parody.

The daring vision that was *High Noon* seemed long gone.

NOTES

1. *Gary Cooper: American Life and Legend* (1989 documentary copyright by and shown on Turner Classic Movies channel).

2. Jane Tompkins, Jane, *West of Everything* (New York: Oxford University Press, 1992), 219.

3. Schickel, *Gary Cooper.*

4. Michael Anderson, *Hollywood TV: The Studio System in the Fifties* (Austin: University of Texas Press, 1994), 203–5.

5. Richard Slotkin, "Gunsmoke and Mirrors," *Life* 16 (April 5, 1993).

6. Don Graham, "*High Noon* (1952)", in *Western Movies*, ed. William T. Pilkington and Don Graham (Albuquerque: University of New Mexico Press, 1979), 60–61; David Thomson, "The Winding Road of the Western Hero," *New York Times*, August 20, 2000, II-29.

7. Sam B. Girgus, *Hollywood Renaissance* (Cambridge: Cambridge University Press, 1998), 151.

8. Perhaps the only Western of the era that escaped the influence of *High Noon* was William Wyler's epic *The Big Country* (1958), in which Gregory Peck is a peaceable sea captain who conveys a message of utter disdain for guns and gunfighters and wins the day without ever using a gun in anger.

9. John H. Lenihan, *Showdown.* (Urbana: University of Illinois Press, 1985), 137.

10. Lenihan, *Showdown,* 123.

11. Michael Coyne, *The Crowded Prairie* (London: I.B. Tauris, 1997), 100–1.

12. Graham, "*High Noon* (1952)," 60–61.

13. Coyne, *Crowded Prairie,* 145–46.

14. Robert Warshow, "Movie Chronicle: The Westerner," in *Focus on the Western,* ed. Jack Nachbar (Englewood Cliffs, N.J.: Prentice-Hall, 1974), 156–57.

15. Gerald Mast and Bruce Kawin, *A Short History of the Movies* (Boston: Allyn & Bacon, 1996), 333.

16. Manny Farber, "Underground Films," in *Howard Hawks: American Artist,* ed. Jim Hillier and Peter Wollen (London: BFI Publishing, 1996), 35–45.

17. Richard Maltby, *Harmless Entertainment* (Metuchen, N.J.: Scarecrow Press, 1983), 140–41.

18. Maltby, *Harmless Entertainment,* 269–70.

19. Maltby, *Harmless Entertainment,* 272.

20. Alan Lovell, "The Western," in *Movies and Methods,* ed. Bill Nichols (Berkeley: University of California Press, 1976), 167.

21. It would be ungenerous to suggest that these largely unsung artists were discovered primarily to answer the old politician's warning, "You can't beat something with nothing."

22. Andre Bazin, "Beauty of a Western," in *Cahiers du Cinema: The 1950s,* ed. Jim Hillier (Cambridge: Harvard University Press, 1985), 166.

23. Reviewer "br," for the Turner Classic Movies website, at www.tcm .turner.com/ (accessed July 7, 2002).

24. "br."

25. Maltby, *Harmless Entertainment*, 301–3.

26. Maltby, *Harmless Entertainment*, 297–98.

27. Andre Bazin, "An Exemplary Western," in *Cahiers du Cinema: The 1950s*, ed. Jim Hillier (Cambridge: Harvard University Press, 1985), 170.

28. Richard Whitehall, "The Heroes Are Tired," *Film Quarterly* 21 (Winter 1966–1967): 14.

29. Maltby, *Harmless Entertainment*, 218–19.

30. Maltby, *Harmless Entertainment*, 141.

31. Bernard F. Dick, *The Merchant Prince of Poverty Row* (Lexington: The University Press of Kentucky, 1993), 163.

32. Will Wright, *Six-Guns and Society* (Berkeley: University of California Press, 1975).

33. Wright, *Six-Guns*, 75.

34. Thomas Schatz, "The Western," in *Handbook of American Film Genres*, ed. Wes Gehring (New York: Greenwood Press, 1988), 32.

35. Lenihan, *Showdown*, 125–26.

36. Richard Slotkin, *Gunfighter Nation* (New York: Atheneum, 1992), 402.

37. Slotkin, "Gunsmoke and Mirrors," 63.

38. Coyne, *Crowded Prairie*, 73.

39. Lee Clark Mitchell, *Westerns* (Chicago: University of Chicago Press, 1996), 194.

40. Drawn from Bob Sitton, "Refocusing the Western," review of *Shane* (London: British Film Institute, 1999) by Edward Countryman and Evonne von Heussen-Countryman, *Film-Philosophy* 4, no. 24 (October 2000): unpaginated, at www.film-philosophy.com/vol4-2000/n24sitton (accessed November 14, 2002).

41. Mike Selig, *Cinema Texas Program Notes* (Department of Radio/Television/Film, University of Texas at Austin, vol. 16, no. 2, February 28, 1979), 5–6.

42. Hal Hinson, "Life, Liberty and the Pursuit of Cows: How the Western Defines America's View of Itself," *Washington Post*, July 3, 1994, G1.

43. Coyne, *Crowded Prairie*, 73.

44. Philip French, *Westerns* (London: Secker & Warburg, 1977), 29.

45. French, *Westerns*, 29.

46. French, *Westerns*, 29–30.

47. Lenihan, *Showdown*, 163.

48. Richard Slotkin, "Gunsmoke and Mirrors," 67.

49. Joan Mellen, "The Western," in *Political Companion to American*, ed. Gary Crowdus (Chicago: Lakeview Press, 1994), 144.

The iconic image: Will Kane on his fruitless quest for help. (Courtesy of the Academy of Motion Picture Arts and Sciences.)

Gary Cooper, Fred Zinnemann, and Grace Kelly talk things over on the set during rehearsals. (Courtesy of the Academy of Motion Picture Arts and Sciences.)

How do you sell a movie that upends clichés? Apparently, with a publicity shot that couldn't be more misleading: At noon, Amy Kane is actually heading for the train. (Courtesy United Artists.)

A production still makes clear the gulf between the newlyweds. (Courtesy of the Academy of Motion Picture Arts and Sciences.)

Will Kane asks for help in church—and leaves humiliated. (Courtesy of the Academy of Motion Picture Arts and Sciences.)

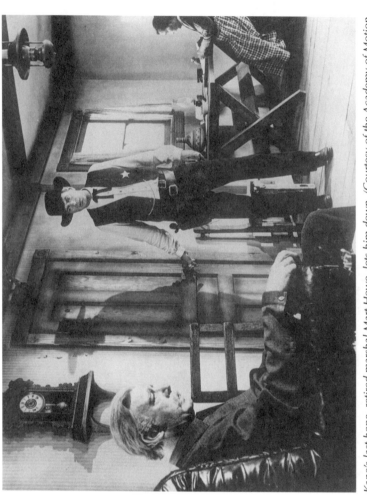

Kane's last hope, retired marshal Mart Howe, lets him down. (Courtesy of the Academy of Motion Picture Arts and Sciences.)

Out on the prairie, Will decides to take a stand. (Courtesy of the Academy of Motion Picture Arts and Sciences.)

Having sold her store, Helen Ramirez cuts her last tie, announcing her separation from a presumptuous Harvey Pell in no uncertain terms. (Courtesy of the Academy of Motion Picture Arts and Sciences.)

Part IV

AUTEURS, CRITICS, AND COLLABORATIVE FILMMAKING

Chapter 9

Auteurs and Westerns

One reason *High Noon* is despised by proponents of the auteur theory is that it seems effectively to demolish the theory.

—Larry Swindell[1]

When you're younger and hero-worshipping the people who make films . . . you put all the credit . . . on the directors. You realize as time goes by that film is full of collaborations, full of compromise, full of cheating.

—David Thomson[2]

Even as *High Noon* was angering lovers of the traditional Western and permanently changing the direction the genre would take, it was drawing fire from a new group of film theorists who admired the traditional Westerns less for their conformity to genre conventions than for their ability to inspire film artistry. The new theory was called "auteurism," from the French word for author, and it argued that movies should be seen as the creation of a single "author," or artist—the director. The auteurists, who search for signs of the director's personal "touch," and despise evidence of slick impersonality, claim that the "auteur"—who can be either the consciously planning artist or the moral structure he unconsciously imposes on his films—explains film artistry far better than social, formal, or generic analyses.

In the 1960s, the "auteur policy" developed by the French was sweeping through the American and British film criticism communities. *High Noon* became a particular target of auteurist critics when

they identified another Western, *Rio Bravo* (1959), as an important rejection of, and answer, to the earlier film. *Rio Bravo*'s director,
Howard Hawks, was especially important to the auteurist argument
because he was one of a handful of American directors the auteurists
were attempting to canonize as artists who controlled their films' visions, as opposed to the teamwork involved in the making of *High
Noon*.

In a 1968 book praising Hawks's cinema artistry, British auteurist
Robin Wood called *High Noon* a failed film, and in the process firmly
established it as the bête noire of the auteurist writers. Wood was not
the first to assail it from such a standpoint—it had been criticized in
similar terms by the reviewer for *The Nation* magazine, Manny Farber, at the time of its release—but Wood's attack was important because it underscored the auteurist credo—that the Zinnemann film
was a disaster and that it had inspired Hawks to make the film
widely considered by auteurists as his masterpiece.

In his book, Woods insisted that

the reputation of *High Noon*—it is still widely regarded as one of the
best Westerns, a film that confers dignity on a low genre by infusing
into it a seriousness of moral purpose—is very revealing, as regards
a current attitude to the Western and to film in general. . . . *High Noon*
. . . strikes me as the archetypal "Oscar" film, product of the combined talents of the archetypal "Oscar" director (Zinnemann), the archetypal "Oscar" writer (Carl Foreman), and the archetypal "Oscar"
producer (Stanley Kramer): three gentlemen whose work has been
characterized by those Good Intentions with which we understand
the road to hell to be paved. Mental intentions, not emotional or in-
tuitive intentions: intentions of the conscious, willing mind, not of
the whole man.

The film reeks of contrivance. Every sequence is constructed to lead
up to and make a simple moral point, character, action and dialogue
being painstakingly manipulated to this end. Nowhere is there that
sense of inner logic, of organic development, of the working-out of natural processes through the interaction of the characters, that one finds
in the best films of Hawks. This characteristic is not only in the script.
Zinnemann's direction, external and shallow, matches it perfectly. His
handling of the actors is almost uniformly abominable, cliché-gesture
following cliché-gesture (see, for instance, poor Thomas Mitchell,
whose Kid in *Only Angels Have Wings* is among the American cinema's
great supporting performances, in the church scene), just as cliché-
setup follows cliché-setup in the camera positioning.

Quite fundamental issues are involved here, including the question of what constitutes cliché. But in *High Noon* not a single character or situation is spontaneously-intuitively felt—everything is in the head, a painstaking application of carefully learned lessons. One could attack Carl Foreman's script for its contrivance but ultimately, to understand why *High Noon* is a bad film is to understand that the cinema is a director's art. There are situations, such as the scene between Katy Jurado and Lloyd Bridges where her contempt for him finally erupts after long suppression, which are perfectly valid emotionally, but which Zinnemann relentlessly turns into cliché-melodrama with his academically conceived jumps into close-up at the most obvious moments, his insistence on acting that is conventional in the worst sense (it isn't the actors' fault), the obviousness of gesture and expression exactly corresponding to the obviousness of the editing. . . .

One can . . . point to several obvious major inadequacies which are symptomatic of the quality of the film as a whole. . . . There is the entire church sequence, where the cliché-treatment both of the congregation en masse and of individuals reaches risible extremes. There is the handling of the Cooper–Kelly relationship. It is presumably of importance that the audience feel this as meaningful, that a sense of frustrated mutual needs and resulting tensions is communicated. Yet if we look at what Zinnemann actually offers us we find, apart from one or two tentative attempts at inwardness from Grace Kelly in the early stages of the film, nothing at all convincing. The wife remains a mere puppet, manipulated according to the requirements of the plot: no understanding of her reactions is communicated, beyond the explicit statement of her Quakerism, which is then merely taken for granted. Everything important, in fact, is taken for granted: Cooper's need for her, the importance of the marriage to him, is reduced to a bit of data, never felt as real. Someone, indeed, seems to have felt that there was something missing there, that the marriage theme needed a bit of artificial bolstering; hence the tiresome repetition on the soundtrack of the lines from the theme-song, "I'm not of afraid of death but Oh! what will I do if you leave me?"—the importance of the marriage is only there in the song, an explicit statement of the intentions that remain quite unrealized.

But most interesting of all, in relation to Hawks and *Rio Bravo*, is the motivation of the hero's actions. It is clear, I think, that for the Marshal, as for Hawks' heroes, the essential motivation is the preservation of self-respect—he goes back to face Frank Miller because a failure to do so would be, for him, a failure to live up to his own conception of manhood. One may reflect that this is a theme that lends itself readily to (could even be said to be implicit in) the Western genre. It is not its theme that makes *Rio Bravo* great, but the intensity and emotional maturity with which it is felt. The level on which the theme is handled in

High Noon can be, I think, fairly represented by the scene where Grace
Kelly confronts Katy Jurado and asks her why Cooper is determined to
stay. Cut to close-up of Jurado, who says, with heavy emphasis, "If you
don't know, I can't explain it to you." The reader who doesn't see what
I mean by cliché in terms of acting, editing, camera-position couldn't
do better than study that moment. The reputation of *High Noon*, rests,
in fact, on two things, both quite superficial in relation to what the film
actually is: its strict observation of the unities (which it never lets us
forget), and its "message." Its message is really its whole raison d'être.[3]

With its implicit definition of "cliché" as "that which Howard
Hawks avoided," Wood's analysis was a comprehensive inventory
of failure: *High Noon* was a contrived, manipulative "message film,"
of the sort admired by Oscar voters. No scene was ever allowed to
develop naturally; there was none of the intensity and emotional
maturity found in great films; the direction, script, and acting were
invariably hackneyed; and characters with motivations were replaced by puppets deployed to serve the message. It was hard to escape the feeling that Wood was piling on, like a basketball team running up the score against a hapless opponent.

Considering the vehemence with which the auteurists traditionally dismiss films with an apparent political agenda, such as *High
Noon*, and those who make them.[4] The irony involved in auteurism's
creation couldn't be greater. It was born of a politicized special
pleading in postwar France in reaction to the elegant literary adaptations of the period, the polarized politics of the war years, and the
limited opportunities for newcomers in the French film industry. It
was brought to America by young American writers reacting against
literary adaptations and films with political agendas, the polarized
politics of the postwar years, and the limited opportunities for newcomers in American film criticism.

Following their mentor, Andre Bazin, in the pages of the French
film journal *Cahiers du Cinema*, future New Wave filmmakers
François Truffaut, Jean-Luc Godard, and Jacques Rivette used their
newly created "la politique des auteurs" to champion French filmmakers who were rapidly slipping into obscurity or had been dismissed by the critics of the day as popular hacks. The *Cahiers* writers were struck by the emphasis in American films on deep-focus
photography and the long take—the exact opposite of the reigning
"politique" of "montage," or editing. It did not matter that Hitchcock, Ford, and Hawks had had limited control of casting, editing,

and writing, especially in their earlier films. In fact, argued the auteurists, their very strength as artists lay not in their power over plot or dialogue but over the films' "mise-en-scène," the camerawork and design that allowed a director to, as they said, "impose his personal vision."

By attacking the old-guard French filmmakers and praising a handful of critically ignored directors, the auteurists could build their reputations and open the way to making their own films. As their fame as "New Wave" directors grew in the early 1960s, so did the impact of their lists of artists and those dismissed as mere technicians.[5] Inevitably, this distinction led to attacks on American films not made by auteurs. *High Noon*, and other films made in its style, would be sent to the critical scrap heap by adherents of the new "theory" (actually, as the French title has it, "policy," suggesting an attack mode), even as more casual moviegoers and older critics like Bosley Crowther were praising them.

Fred Zinnemann was targeted for dismissal early on, not only because he was said to direct "impersonally," but because he was a "technician" who collaborated with a screenwriter, rather than controlling the final screenplay himself, as an artist would. In 1957, *Cahiers* writer and future director Jacques Rivette insisted that "the great American directors—Alfred Hitchcock and Anthony Mann—oversaw the general direction of the scriptwriting from the beginning, whereas the lesser directors—William Wyler and Fred Zinnemann . . . did not."[6] Reworking the script with the screenwriter, or making changes on the set, was not good enough.

Crowther's panegyric in the *New York Times*, published two years before the auteurists first formulated their policy in print, no doubt helped *High Noon* at the box-office, but his praise would also inspire the film's general condemnation by later film critics led by the *Village Voice* reviewer, Andrew Sarris. As the *Times*' lead reviewer between 1941 and 1968, Crowther was the most important figure in American film criticism. A pan from him could doom a documentary or foreign film. He had championed *Citizen Kane* when it had come under attack by Hearst, and he had opposed the blacklist, but in retrospect many of his judgments, such as his 1946 attack on Capra's *It's a Wonderful Life*, had come to seem foolish by the late 1950s. For many people inside and outside the film community, he was a stodgy writer who showed little interest in the formal aspects of film, and who all too easily confused thematic importance with cinematic greatness.[7] In other words, he was not merely a source of constant irritation for younger film writers, such as Sarris, who were soaking up all the foreign imports, he was an inviting target for writers who wanted to make a name for themselves and get noticed at journals in need of reviewers.

As a writer for the *Village Voice* in the late 1950s, Sarris had suffered what he would later consider a great embarrassment when he had followed the guidance of establishment critics in 1959 and put Stanley Kramer's *On the Beach* on his ten best list while leaving Hitchcock off. That deference to his elders would soon disappear. He spent 1961 in Paris immersing himself in film and soaking up the reigning orthodoxy of *la politique des auteurs*. Of that time, he has said, "André Bazin and the French critics, and the New Wave way of looking at American movies, that was one of the big influences, specific influences. So gradually my whole orientation changed. . . . I'm something of a Christian. What concerns me are issues like guilt and redemption. The dramatic progress to self-knowledge."[8]

Like Truffaut and the others at *Cahiers*, he understood the career-making possibilities of an attack theory. In Paris

> he realized that auteurism had been an unconscious means to an end, "that end being the common experience some of us shared . . . of being on the outside looking in, victims of failed career[s] seeking to justify the hours and hours of addictive gazing at the screen for some shred of insight into the human condition. . . . I was an English graduate at a time when colleges were beginning to admit the occasional art film into their curriculum, but it would never have occurred to me that one could think and write about American films with the same erudition or intensity as one brought to art films or literature or music, or that writing on movies could aspire to such eloquence."[9]

He came home determined to overthrow what he saw as a critical orthodoxy. Film critics who deferred to literature for their standards, he said, snobbishly subordinated "film to every other art."[10] Like the French auteurists whose Christian "Personalist" sensibility he shared, he would attack anything—"Marxists," "the Left," "the sociological critic"—that smacked of politics.[11] "The epiphanies he found 'in the mystical realm of mise-en-scène' were of individual redemption rather than class conflict."[12]

In 1962, *Film Culture* published two articles by Sarris, the first a draft of his seminal *The American Cinema*, which revolutionized American film criticism. In the first, Sarris suggested the director was the author of a film and visual style was the key to evaluation.[13] In the second[14] he "elevated" 106 American and seven foreign directors.[15]

The *Film Culture* articles essentially restated the *Cahiers* position. Instead of evaluating individual films by how well they dealt with important social questions, as Crowther and the other predominant social-realist critics did[16]—thereby encouraging comparisons to literature and plays and judgments about their "relevance"—the "auteurist" critic focused on a director's style, as displayed through his entire body of work.

In Sarris's version of "la politique," the "criterion of value" would not be the substantive concerns of the film but rather the distinguishable personality of the director. That is, "the way a film looks and moves should have some relationship to the way a director thinks and feels." That director, if he was to be considered an artist, would also have to demonstrate technical competence—"the ability to put a film together with some clarity and coherence"—and his films would have to exhibit an interior meaning, which is "extrapolated from the tension between a director's personality and his material."[17]

In his articles and weekly film criticism Sarris went on the attack against what he saw as an American "tradition of quality," the literary adaptations and social-problems dramas created by directors such as John Huston, William Wyler, Elia Kazan, and Fred Zinnemann. He insisted that movies should be analyzed *as* movies, not as illustrated books or filmed plays. Film art, he argued, was outside history, because it was created by individuals who rose above the conditions in which they found themselves. Artistic progress, artistic evolution, was an illusion. Editing was not the key to film art, as his predecessors supposed, but rather the mise-en-scène and the long take.[18]

Sarris wished to completely remove the judgment and analysis of film from the situation in which it was made. The great directors would resist the pressures of the studio, the script, and the stars and produce something profoundly personal—something that reflected, as the French would say, their very souls. The director's art, he insisted, was visible not in the dialogue or the editing, which were largely controlled by others, but in the mise-en-scène, the design of individual scenes in which all of the elements the director did control—the acting, the lighting, the movement of the camera and the actors, the shot length—could reveal his feelings about his characters.[19] The director could ignore or rework the script to some extent with the elements he did control.[20] Even if a producer brutally cut the resulting film, the director's art would emerge in individual scenes.[21]

One could judge that art only by considering the director's whole body of work, because the work of true artists possessed an inherent unity that emerged only on close analysis of his films.[22] An important corollary was that if a movie was to be not only coherent but interesting, there could be no true collaboration; a single sensibility would have to control it, and in almost every successful movie, that would be the director.

For many readers, Sarris's wholly new way of judging films and filmmakers came as a revelation. Before him there had been no intellectually supportable film theory in English. Films were being judged on a case by case basis, which is to say, a subconscious social and political esthetic—except for the conscious esthetic of the Marxist critics. Here was somebody saying that films could both be enjoyed as entertainment and admired as art—something presumably foreign to reigning critics like Crowther and James Agee, who "dismissed . . . popular Hollywood genre pictures that appealed to mass tastes."[23]

What had startled Sarris's readers had been his claim that the industrial conditions of the studio—pressure from studio heads and stars, genre conventions, the limits created by the screenplay—might actually create a useful "tension" in which real artists could do their best work, even as those same conditions limited "technicians" to mediocre work. That one redefinition of the critic's task turned film history on its head. Now it was vital to reexamine studio productions as potential works of art and to distinguish who had done what in individual movies, rather than consigning the entire production to a nebulous "collaboration."

Like the French, Sarris assembled lists of directors ranked by their importance in the development of film art. The evaluation was based on finding the directorial "personality" that underlay the films, then interpreting and evaluating them. In practice, this simultaneous evaluation and ranking created a certain circularity: The director must be an artist, an artist has a consistency of style and view, and thus where one finds such consistency, one finds an artistic director, an auteur. A film standing alone has, in this situation, little chance of being taken seriously.

Not only were certain Hollywood directors "rediscovered" and celebrated and others "discovered" in the first place, they were celebrated precisely because they could turn something as established as a genre to their own purposes. The auteur *was* the genre; it hardly mattered which one he was working in at the time.

Sarris insisted that it was misleading and pointless to call some films "art" and other films mere "entertainment." To do so merely encouraged invidious distinctions between American studio directors and European "art" film directors. Indeed, the same studio pressures that perversely encouraged the "auteur" also disguised the true nature of film. "Escapist" films such as a Ford Western, a Minnelli musical, or a Hitchcock thriller could be more socially aware and dramatic than an ostensibly serious drama.[24] Typically, Sarris made his point in a way sure to raise hackles: "Orson Welles makes many more mistakes than Fred Zinnemann ever could, and yet I wouldn't trade one shot from *Chimes at Midnight* for the entire oeuvre of Zinnemann."[25]

Certain corollaries inevitably followed from the auteur theory. Great films made by technicians, such as Michael Curtiz's *Casablanca* and Victor Fleming's *Gone with the Wind,* were happy accidents or really the work of a producer or someone else. The best that such a metteur-en-scène, or technician, could hope for would be to stumble on an imaginative screenwriter with whom he might make more than one good film.[26]

Great directors could make bad movies, but even in an auteur's worst films there were bound to be revealing, even fascinating elements. The genre films of, for example, John Ford, such as *They Were Expendable, Steamboat 'Round the Bend,* or *The Searchers,* "showed stylistic richness and thematic ambiguity that made them superior to the calculated artistry and social consciousness of Ford's 'serious' works, such as his 'Oscar caliber' movies *The Informer* and *The Grapes of Wrath.*"[27]

The Oscar was the kiss of death, for the films of auteur and technician alike—though those of the auteur's films most honored by Hollywood would still be found to have some redeeming artistic value. Directors whose films won Oscars—John Huston, David Lean, William Wyler, Delbert Mann, Fred Zinnemann, and Stanley Kramer, the social realists admired by Crowther—were consigned by Sarris to his "Less Than Meets the Eye" category, or worse. Kramer suffered the ultimate indignity of being assigned to "Miscellany."[28]

Even as the auteurists were dismissing critically admired directors, they were regularly discovering masterpieces that had been critically dismissed, thanks to a reanalysis in the light of the hitherto-unknown auteur's entire body of work. This triumphant revelation of treasures among films previously consigned to the scrap heap had a distinct disadvantage. It was too easy for auteurists to praise bad movies because of their directors. The reverse was true, too: Films made by critically dismissed *metteurs-en-scène* would have great difficulty being considered on their merits. What would happen if a director suddenly made a superb film after an undistinguished career? Would criticism degenerate into a "celebration of excellence"[29] for the anointed?

These and other concerns began to be raised almost as soon as Sarris's *Film Culture* articles appeared. In a hostile essay the same year,[30] Pauline Kael worried about the possibility of circular reasoning: The auteur would notice "themes" and "personality" either because he had to justify the time spent watching certain directors' movies over and over—or because he had a theory that needed examples. There would be a good deal of pressure, both esthetic and practical, to see these consistencies. And he would be likely to champion the old, in which he had found auteurist art, over the new.[31]

Elevating the director, she said, meant you didn't need to see the movie because you already knew whether the director made good movies or bad movies.[32] Using as an example a director she respected barely more than Sarris did, Kael complained that "for some unexplained reason those traveling in auteur circles believe that making [a] purse out of a sow's ear is an infinitely greater accomplishment than making a solid carrying case out of a good piece of leather (as, for example, a Zinnemann does with *From Here to Eternity* or *The Nun's Story*)."[33]

Over the years, other critics of the "distinguishable personality" criterion added their concerns. Said the film writer Richard Corliss, if the director's contribution, which involved working with other people, was harder to pin down than the screenwriter's, which was there on paper, that very fact made it easier for the auteurist to "infer reams and reams of metaphysical nuance. . . . Since the director allowed these filmic epiphanies to take place, who's to say he didn't make them happen?"[34]

And then there was the matter of just what it was about the director's vision that was being celebrated. Sarris had unintentionally contributed to the potential confusion by retaining the politique's overlapping definitions of "motifs" as themes and as stylistic devices. "Does Sarris mean," asked two film historians, in perhaps the most telling criticism of auteurist theory,

> that the "ultimate" glory is a director's imposition of "style" (e.g., the use of deep-focus photography) on a film's given "basic motifs" (e.g., domestic melodrama) or does he mean that the glory is the director's imposition of a "style' that elicits new "basic motifs" (e.g., the meaning of love) from that melodrama? If the latter, does Sarris realize that the same can be said of any artist (say, Shakespeare in *King Lear* or *Othello*)? If the former, does Sarris mean that a director whose films deal with trash stylishly is an artist worthy of our attention?[35]

Sarris, insisting that his ideas were tentative, confessed to being taken aback by the vehemence of his critics, but he was not deterred. In 1966, he helped found the National Society of Film Critics to offset the reviewers for the daily newspapers, "a stodgy crowd, unresponsive to new ways of making and seeing movies—this was, after all, the ascendant age of Bergman and Fellini, Truffaut and Godard—and generally exemplars of what [Sarris] . . . dubbed 'creeping Crowtherism,' after the hopeless Bosley."[36]

Sarris had another purpose—he wanted to develop a theory for academics. "Why rank directors at all?" he asked. "Why all the categories and lists and assorted drudgeries? One reason is to establish a system of priorities for the film student. Another is the absence of the most elementary academic tradition in cinema."[37]

In that he succeeded completely. "Sarris's influence in the '60s revolutionized film study and coincided with the growing number of film courses and monographs."[38] Despite the criticisms leveled at it, auteurism swept all before it, because it served so many interests—younger reviewers, revival house bookers, publishers, universities, the film industry. "Auteurism introduced new ways of seeing films; it abolished the distinction between art and entertainment; it elevated film studies to a legitimate area of scholarly concern; it legitimized the status of film as an art form. . . . Auteurism led to the rediscovery and revival of obscure American films in museums and art houses across the country, it resulted in new rankings of individual films within directorial careers, and it influenced what's considered to be the American film canon."[39]

By 1974, Sarris was triumphant. As he said, "Let us not forget that it was auteurism and not anti-auteurism that established the very existence of an artistically valid field of study."[40]

Though John Ford was lionized, by Sarris and others, as *the* auteur of the Western, it was Howard Hawks who came to personalize the auteur attack on *High Noon*. The director Jacques Rivette began the canonization of Hawks in the May 1953 issue of *Cahiers,* in which his review of *Monkey Business* declared, "The evidence on the screen is the proof of Hawks's genius: You only have to watch *Monkey Business* to know that it is a brilliant film." Eric Rohmer followed in the same journal a few months later, declaring Hawks "the greatest film-maker born in America, with the exception of Griffith." American critic Manny Farber began the elevation of Hawks among English-language critics, film writer Richard Roud put on a Hawks film festival in 1961, and in 1962, writer and future director Peter Bogdanovich conducted an important interview with him[41] and Andrew Sarris published an article entitled "The World of Howard Hawks."[42] British film theorist Peter Wollen would complete Hawks's elevation with a structural analysis of his films in his *Signs and Meaning in the Cinema* in 1969.

Hawks was an auteur in one obvious sense: He was unquestionably an independent-minded artist, going to great trouble to run his own show. "He chose the films he would work on, and worked on the scripts of all his films."[43] He

> maintained tight artistic control of his films, and was known to walk off the set when the studio or its producers interfered. Like many of the independent producers, Hawks viewed himself as a hit maker, creating films that pleased himself, but were designed to entertain the masses. He could not consider himself a success unless his tastes were in synchronization with the public. By carefully selecting his own projects, and methodically reworking them on the set, Hawks naturally gravitated toward a position where he could be his own boss.[44]

But he was never considered a director of Westerns; they merely served his—and the auteurist interpreters'—larger needs. Said Sarris, "That one can discern the same directorial signature over a wide variety of genres is proof of artistry. That one can still enjoy the genres for their own sake is proof of the artist's professional urge to entertain."[45]

Unlike Ford, who made Westerns to celebrate American history, Hawks made adventure films, some of which happened to be Westerns: *The Outlaw* (1943) (on which his work was uncredited), *Red River* (1948), *The Big Sky* (1952), *Rio Bravo* (1959), *El Dorado* (1967), and *Rio Lobo* (1970). But when he made them, in Bazin's view, he got them just right: "Howard Hawks . . . at the height of the vogue of the superwestern [such as *High Noon*] should be credited with having demonstrated [in *The Big Sky* that] it had always been possible to turn out a genuine Western based on the old dramatic and spectacle themes, without distracting our attention with some social thesis."[46]

Hawks celebrated a world of male camaraderie, courage, and triumph over adversity—a world that ought to exist even if it didn't. The characters are hard-boiled, the dialogue delivered so quickly that speeches overlap.[47] His heroes live apart from society, admit only the courageous—and then reluctantly—and are slow to trust others. "The group's only internal tensions come when one member lets the others down . . . and must redeem himself by some act of exceptional bravery. . . . The group members are bound together by rituals," such as singing songs prior to facing some deadly business.[48] Women are trouble, but there is hope for them. "Hawks decided early on that sexual attraction is always expressed through antagonism—a teasing, provoking, insulting badinage that he exploited in both his drama and his comedies."[49]

Hawks had no interest in realism; his goal was to entertain. He not only repeated devices and themes from film to film, but even from the beginning of a film to its end:

> He would slow down the whole production while everybody stood around, encouraging his collaborators to throw out ideas until he got a scene exactly the way he wanted it. He rarely stuck strictly to his script while shooting, always looking for ways of introducing a new element into familiar material, trying to improve material which had already passed the test of time.[50]

The action frequently referred to previous Hawks films, as if to urge the audience not to take what he was doing too seriously, and often stopped for privileged moments in which the characters would relax and in effect invite the audience to relax with them.[51]

The game-playing of characters within scenes makes clear that in a Hawks film the plot is less important than individual scenes. The plots, such as they are, can proceed at a leisurely pace. And they needn't be plausible.[52]

Rio Bravo, the standard of comparison the auteurists held up to *High Noon*, was the ultimate realization of Hawksian principles. Hawks said he made the film as a rejection of *High Noon*'s picture of a marshal's search for help against the killers. "I didn't like *High Noon*. I said 'it's phony.' Fellow's supposed to be good . . . with a gun. . . . He runs around like a wet chicken. . . . Eventually his Quaker wife saves his guts. . . . I said that's ridiculous. The man wasn't a professional."[53]

The right-populist Hawks objected to the picture of townspeople deserting the hero and decided to reverse the plot. Both Marshal Kane and the hero of *Rio Bravo*, John T. Chance, are professionals determined to do their job—Kane because he is loyal to his community, Chance out of loyalty to his job. But while Kane spends the whole film asking for help and in the end receives it only from an unexpected source, Chance never asks for help, often rejects it, and discovers he needs it in every crisis.

Chance is the sheriff of a tiny Texas border town that seems to have very few inhabitants—only those with speaking parts, an extreme version of the traditional Western's use of extras. It was an intentional contrast with *High Noon*, in which there are many townspeople who speak; all of them are "amateurs," in *Rio Bravo*'s terms.

Chance has to keep jailed killer Claude Akins from being rescued by his friends, who have the town surrounded. He gets help from ex-deputy Dean Martin, a drunk trying to reform,[54] crippled deputy Walter Brennan, dance hall girl Angie Dickinson, and fast gun Ricky Nelson.[55]

Chance, as incarnated by John Wayne's bemused, larger-than-life paterfamilias, offers lost souls a community and another chance. In one of the central scenes he refuses help from cattleman Ward Bond. "That's all you've got?"' asks Bond. "That's what I've got," says Wayne, declining amateurs, do-gooders, and sightseers, unlike Marshal Kane.[56] In another reference to the earlier film, Bond tries to loan Nelson, a baby-faced cowboy who wears two guns, but Nelson refuses at first; he'll "mind his own business."

Amid occasional outbursts of gunfire, this collection of oddballs slowly coalesces into a Hawksian mutual admiration society, as Hawks takes his time assembling his narrative: The movie runs nearly an hour longer than *High Noon* and is so loosely strung together that it encouraged speculation that Hawks made it up as he went along. He didn't, but as an admiring Peter Bogdanovich notes,

Rio Bravo was "an excuse to have a bunch of characters he was interested in in a pressure situation. . . .He was bored with plot and he eliminated the plot."[57]

Hawks was concerned with the logic of discrete scenes—the mise-en-scène, as the auteurists would say—not their relationship to other scenes. There's a good deal of comic relief in the form of a Mexican hotel keeper and his wife, and the inevitable Brennan. There are several bits of badinage between Wayne and Dickinson, the lone woman in the Hawks universe. And there's the famous songfest, with Martin and Nelson essentially stepping out of character and reminding the audience of their other careers as singers. "It's a kind of screwball oater (at least half-aware that the audience was beginning to laugh at the conventions)," concludes one observer.[58]

One wonders what these appreciative writers would have said had *Rio Bravo* been "unsigned," that is, had Hawks's involvement been unpublicized. Would they have recognized the hand of the master? They like to refer to it as a late peak in his career, but looked at simply as a Western, applying traditional dramatic standards of acting, writing, pacing, logic, and so on, it borders on parody. Even if we overlook the illogic of the villains' behavior as being irrelevant to a story whose real concern is the dynamics of friendship, *Rio Bravo* seems little more than an amiable farce. Compared to Hawks's own *Red River*, it is truly difficult to find anything admirable in it.

Rio Bravo amounted to a summary statement of the auteurist case against *High Noon*, a case that has continued undiminished since Manny Farber stated his version a half century ago, before *la politique* had even been enunciated. The shape of the attack on *High Noon* and on Fred Zinnemann was now clear. These were the ten commandments of the new faith:

1. High Noon *was a Message Movie.* Artists create films that abstract their characters from time and place, however specific their settings appear to be. *High Noon's* setting was stylized (thus its distinctive look—the bleached skies, the clocks, the converging railway lines), but its substance was conscience and community and betrayal, men and women—not having the "right stuff." It was an obvious political allegory and a "socially conscious" film, which auteurists find crude and pretentious.[59] Their themes are humanist and individual, not political

and collective. (Ironically, the theme of *High Noon*, of a lone man falling into a well of isolation and humiliation and then finding a way out through his own efforts, matches perfectly the religious and conservative philosophy underlying much auteurist thinking.)

2. *It was "liberal" cinema.* Ford stressed camaraderie within ancient institutions, Hawks within the small group—but Zinnemann deployed a handful of characters to comment on the individual in the entire, encompassing community. Hawks pulled back from his characters and was admired for his generosity toward them. As an auteur, he presented heroes who rise above sordid surroundings. *High Noon*, in contrast, is a remarkably bitter, downbeat work, filled with malice for a collection of human failures, even though its protagonist survives.

To the auteurists, all of this makes *High Noon* a work of "liberal" cinema, which converts large social issues into personal problems and thereby trivializes them. Liberal cinema is both dishonest and hypocritical, a fate avoided by both the committed cinema of the Left and the politically disinterested auteurist cinema.

3. *It failed to concentrate on mise-en-scène.* The auteur is devoted to the composition of scenes, whatever damage that might do to the film's continuity. His fealty to mise-en-scène places his films head and shoulders above a film such as *High Noon*, a triumph of editing, whatever else it is. Hawks sped up his films not through editing but by having his characters talk fast. Zinnemann's dismissal by the auteurists was part and parcel of their dismissal of montage, since editing was central to his esthetic.

4. *It was "impersonal."* Zinnemann treated his characters realistically and was considered slick, flat, falsely "objective." *High Noon* was filled with sharply defined performances, but his critics thought Zinnemann's direction "mechanical" rather than intimately involved with the actors. Auteurs, by contrast, create characters with "tics." Zinnemann's films are tightly plotted and leave no room for privileged moments of the sort that Hawks and Ford employed endlessly. In other words, plot overcomes performance, but for auteurs, as *Rio Bravo* suggests, performance is all. Zinnemann is at best a metteur-en-scène because he does not, like an auteur, make the film a unified reflection of his personality.

The seeming irony, given his concern with conscience, is that "thematically Fred Zinnemann has always been one of the most personal and consistent of Hollywood directors."[60] The irony is only apparent, say the auteurists; he hasn't been up to the tasks he's set himself. "Zinnemann's neutral style, with the stationary camera seemingly always at a safe middle distance, has not always been adequate to such interior subjects."[61] When Hawks sets his camera in the middle distance, he's forcing the audience to figure out subtle relationships. When Zinnemann does the same thing, he can't take the audience inside his characters' heads.

Zinnemann himself thought the argument about where he put his camera ridiculous. "The 'safe middle distance' is nonsense. It's just that I don't like to put people under a microscope and look at them as if they were like so many bugs. As to the auteur theory: It has always seemed to me to be little more than a gimmick, creating a completely arbitrary and pedantic set of rules by trying to put everyone's work into 'artistically correct' pigeonholes."[62]

Sarris famously consigned Zinnemann to the filmic outer darkness: His "neatness and decorum constitute his gravest artistic defects." *High Noon* revealed "the superficiality of Zinnemann's personal commitment. At its best, his direction is inoffensive; at its worst it is downright dull."[63] A film scholar put it rather differently: "There are few hammy performances in his movies, for above all, Zinnemann emphasizes naturalness. Instead of having the actors project out to the audience, the audience is allowed to tune in on them. We watch them behaving rather then performing. . . . [Sometimes] he simply asked his stars to behave as naturally as possible."[64]

5. *Zinnemann doesn't create a coherent body of work.* What is admirable about Hawks and the other auteurs is their construction of a "structure" throughout their work based on the repetition of "motifs," whether those were themes or stylistic tropes. They were, in a sense, always making movies about other movies—their own. The auteur theorists approvingly quoted Jean Renoir's famous dictum that the filmmaker is always trying to make the same film. *Rio Bravo*, for instance, was said to be a remake of Hawks's 1939 film *Only Angels Have Wings*. Zinnemann's failure was that his films stood alone in this sense; they did not quote each other.

6. *The conditions of* High Noon's *production gave the art no "tension" from which to emerge.* It was made by a small, independent company that thought it could make good, moneymaking films with fewer compromises of any kind. But the most important film artists were surviving and even thriving in the lion's den: Hollywood the factory was the ultimate test. (That Hawks had created a small independent company to make *Red River* presumably is not relevant.)

7. *It fails to recover the Real West. High Noon* is an unfortunate mixture of realism, stylization, and historical inaccuracy. Westerns might, like *Rio Bravo*, be abstracted from any specific history, but must follow what is known of the real West, and its style must be uniform.[65] The possibility that Westerns are not about the West but about a pure state of confrontation and community and individualism, and that everybody's idea of the West is different, is irrelevant.

8. *It has no story and therefore fails as an action picture.* In his original review Farber declared the film a "deftly fouled-up Western." Its dramatic action, he said, was limited to Cooper walking around. "The contrived result: A movie which does take you into every part of the town and features Cooper's beautiful rolling gait, but which reveals that someone spent too much time over the drawing board conceiving dramatic camera shots to cover up the lack of story."[66] To most critics, of course, this argument was the purest nonsense: *High Noon* had the most brilliantly structured plot that many of them could recall.

9. *It was too popular.* It was immediately hailed as a masterpiece by daily newspaper reviewers—a suspicious development, in that masterpieces are only located after the fact, in the filmmaker's entire body of work. That Zinnemann eventually won so many awards—two Oscars, seven Oscar nominations, four citations from the New York Film Critics Circle, and the D. W. Griffith Award for Lifetime Achievement—was reason enough to regard him as an "industry man"—a certified middlebrow hero.

10. *It was a collaboration. High Noon* is a film in which the director, the screenwriter, the producer, and the editor all played a major part. It was allegedly partly based on a short story, and the screenplay was written solely by a screenwriter. But auteur di-

rectors are intimately involved in the writing after the initial draft to shape the final film in the direction of their concerns. (As was Zinnemann.) The very idea of collaboration between director and screenwriter, or director and producer, is anathema.

To Zinnemann, the auteurists' conception of the director as elevated artist was a naïve oversimplification, but he disagreed with them that he had not had the film's controlling vision:

> In my day the film director was, ideally, the only man who had the central vision of a film. By that I mean he was the one person who, once he had a script to his liking, could really visualize what he was after, what kind of actors would be best for the action, how the picture should look, how it should sound, and what sort of pace it should have. And this would then be tested at a preview to see if the audience went along with it. After that, he had the right to re-cut or change the films. When it came out, it was that man's picture. . . . John Ford would not have a producer tell him how to shoot a picture, what kind of set-ups to use, or what kind of actors to use. Creatively, he was the locomotive. There were a number of us who worked like that. Granted, there were many others who weren't so fortunate. And that was based, I think, primarily on box-office and secondarily on the caliber and quality of the pictures. . . . The writer is certainly the author of the screenplay, the cameraman is the author of the photography. But all in all, the author of the *film* is the director, the only person who has the central, overall vision of it from beginning to end.[67]

As David Thomson, a latter-day apostle of auteurism, noted in acknowledging a kind of conversion experience: "When you're younger and hero-worshipping the people who make films . . . you put all the credit . . . on the directors. You realize as time goes by that film is full of collaborations, full of compromise, full of cheating."[68]

The attack on Zinnemann and on *High Noon* by the auteurists was so single-minded, so distinctly ideological, and so devoutly resistant to subtle but important distinctions that one could encounter these vastly overgeneralized theses, nailed to the door of the social-realist church, and all too easily leap to easy conclusions. Perhaps the problem for Hawks and the auteurists is simply that Zinnemann and Foreman create rounded characters who have no simple generic or mythic role to play. Perhaps *High Noon* was despised because the auteurists, anxious to promote their theory with forgotten or dismissed films, needed a target. Perhaps they accepted, however subconsciously, the notion that the popular could not be good: *High Noon* was far more successful at the box-office than most auteurist classics, including those of Hawks and Ford.

Using *Rio Bravo* as a bludgeon wasted the possibilities of the theory. Auteur analysis need not replace other approaches but could be used as a complementary approach: Could not "uniqueness of personality, brash individuality, persistence of obsession and originality [be] given an evaluative power [alongside] stylistic smoothness or social seriousness?"[69] If we accept the auteurist approach as the sole approach, we deny the possibility of comparison and interpretation within genres and between directors, a process that would allow the implications of the subject matter to stand out more clearly. This would better serve the cause of promoting admired directors than assuming a consistency of style and wit among the films of any one director. Auteurists would be freed from the need to find merit even in minor works, since they could be more easily ignored.

Occasionally one of the younger apostles is prepared to take a second look. "Revisiting some of Zinnemann's films from the perspective of 1997," said Robert Horton, "it must be said that Mr. Z's old, boring craftsmanship is looking better and better. I prefer the relaxed, warm humanity and humor of *Rio Bravo* to the brisk mechanics of *High Noon*, but the latter certainly has strong attributes: the surprisingly adult relationships, the eerily offbeat opening, the appreciation of Gary Cooper's thin-legged, very mortal vulnerability."[70]

But finding a few things to like is a minor concession. In the end, the auteurists felt free to dismiss *High Noon* because of its greatest failing in their eyes: Whoever provided its vision, it was clearly the work of a team.

If we look at the film-as-film, setting aside for the moment worries about the presence of a "personality" and refusing to dismiss collaboration as though by that fact alone a film must fail, we are left to ask a question that cannot be dismissed *a priori*: Who made *High Noon*? How was it that a film whose "authorial" provenance is so disputed could offer so coherent and bleak a vision of society? What was the relationship between the screenwriter's, the director's, and the producer/editor team's contributions? The screenwriter, Carl Foreman, maintained that the finished film is little different from the screenplay he submitted, but the director, Fred Zinnemann, made substantial changes to the script, and the producer, Stanley Kramer, and his editor claimed they were able to "save" the film only by making extensive changes, including adding the famous score and song.

One way to get at this question of "authorship" is to examine how the film was made, based on a detailed examination of the relationship between its short story source, the screenplay, the director's changes to the screenplay, and the final film.

NOTES

1. *The Last Hero* (Garden City, N.Y.: Doubleday, 1980), 292.

2. Quoted in Laura Miller, "Reel Lives," *Salon.com*, December 16, 2002.

3. Robin Wood, "Rio Bravo," in *Howard Hawks: American Artist*, ed. Jim Hillier and Peter Wollen (London: British Film Institute, 1996), 87–89. Originally published in Robin Wood, *Howard Hawks* (Garden City, N.Y.: Doubleday,1968). Emphasis added.

4. "If Stanley Kramer as a director categorized under 'Miscellany' had not existed, he would have had to have been invented as the most extreme example of thesis or message cinema. Unfortunately, he has been such an easy and willing target for so long that his very ineptness has become encrusted with tradition. He will never be a natural, but time has proved that he is not a fake." Andrew Sarris, *The American Cinema* (New York: Da Capo Press, 1996; reissue of 1985 revision), 260.

5. Dave Kehr, "Cahiers Back in the Day," *Film Comment* 37 (September–October 2001): 34.

6. Jacques Rivette, "Six Characters in Search of Auteurs," in *Cahiers du Cinema: The 1950s*, ed. Jim Hillier (Cambridge, Mass.: Harvard University Press, 1985), 387.

7. Film historian Gerald Peary, outlining his proposed documentary on the history of film criticism at his website, www.geraldpeary.com/filmproject/outline.html (accessed December 12, 2002).

8. David Walsh, "Andrew Sarris and American Filmmaking," review of Andrew Sarris, *"You Ain't Heard Nothin' Yet": The American Talking Film, History & Memory, 1927–1949.* (New York: Oxford University Press, 1998), *World Socialist Web Site*, at www.wsws.org (accessed June 6, 2000).

9. Molly Haskell, "Life with Andrew . . . and Film," in *Citizen Sarris, American Film Critic*, ed. Emanuel Levy (Lanham, Md.: Scarecrow Press, 2001), 16–17.

10. Andrew Sarris, *Confessions of a Cultist* (New York: Simon & Schuster, 1971), 14.

11. Walsh, "Sarris."

12. Haskell, "Andrew Sarris," 14–15.

13. Andrew Sarris, "Notes on the Auteur Theory," in *Film Theory and Criticism*, ed. Gerald Mast and Marshall Cohen (New York: Oxford University Press, 1979), 650–65. Also in this issue was Manny Farber's quasi-auteurist manifesto "White Elephant Art vs. Termite Art." "Elephant" films, he said, were "establishment," big budget, "bourgeois" films, such as *The Best Years of Our Lives*, and "termite" films were personal films that fit no establishment reviewer's notion of "quality." "The saddest thing in current films is watching the long-neglected action directors such as Raoul Walsh, Howard Hawks, William Wellman . . . and Anthony Mann fade away as the less talented De Sicas and Zinnemanns continue to fascinate the critics." Farber in Hillier and Wollen, *Howard Hawks*, 35. By way of illustration, he attacked Zinnemann's films in particular. *High Noon*, he said, offered nothing but "cross-eyed artistic views of a clock, silhouettes against a vaulting sky, legend-toned walking, a big song," reflecting "Zinnemann's glacéed picturemaking." Farber, "Underground Films," in Hillier and Wollen, *Howard Hawks*, 37.

14. Andrew Sarris, "The American Cinema," and "Directorial Chronology: 1915–1962," *Film Culture* (Spring 1963): 1–51, 52–68.

15. Emanuel Levy, "The Legacy of Auteurism," in Levy, *Citizen Sarris*, 78–79.

16. He attacked these critics, mocking them for their concern for movies that "deal Realistically with a Problem in Adult Terms." Sarris, "American Cinema," 21–22. "Throughout the sound era, the forest critic has been singling out the timely films and letting the timeless ones fall by the wayside. Unfortunately, nothing dates faster than timeliness." Sarris, "American Cinema," 24–25.

17. Sarris, "Notes on the Auteur Theory," 662–64.

18. James Naremore, "An ABC of Reading Andrew Sarris," in Levy, *Citizen Sarris*, 175–83.

19. "The Reviewer Re-Viewed: A Conversation between Andrew Sarris and Richard Schickel," *Directors Guild of America Magazine* (March, 2001),at www.dga.org. (accessed October 12, 2002). Also discussed in Levy, "Legacy of Auteurism."

20. David Bordwell, "Sarris and the Search for Style," in Levy, *Citizen Sarris*, 169.

21. Peter Wollen, from "Signs and Meaning in the Cinema: The Auteur Theory," in *Movies and Methods*, ed. Bill Nichols (Berkeley: University of California Press, 1976), 530–31. Sarris did the generally acknowledged artists who controlled their own projects no favor when he lumped them with the studio directors as equally important auteurs. "Sarris' insistence on the sheer value of a artist's triumphing over his material seems a mistake, even from Sarris' own point of view. This is a useful strategy for rescuing some Hollywood reputations, but it lays the wrong groundwork for demonstrat-

ing the merits of the directors that Sarris (and almost everyone else) most admires. Directors such as Lubitsch, Renoir, Chaplin, Welles, and Keaton in fact enjoyed a large measure of individual control over scripts, shooting and cutting. One does not, as Kael puts it, admire these directors for 'shoving bits of style up the crevasses of the plots.' In extending Truffaut's defense of the effective Hollywood studio director to cinema in general, Sarris has betrayed its limitations." Gerald Mast and Marshall Cohen, "The Film Artist," in Mast and Cohen, *Film Theory and Criticism,* 639.

22. He had accepted the director Jean Renoir's dictum that a director spends his life making one film.

23. John Belton, "Dear Mr. Sarris," in Levy, *Citizen Sarris,* 146.

24. Thomas Shatz, *Hollywood Genres* (Philadelphia: Temple University Press, 1981), 8.

25. Quoted in Levy, "Legacy of Auteurism," 87.

26. In "a true collaboration . . . the director influenced the scenario and the writer influenced the direction. Then there is the case of the 'short-term marriage made in heaven,' when a director and writer came together for a few years and the combination was sufficiently explosive for a few important films to come out of it. In cases like this . . . it is neither the writer nor the director but the combination of the two, plus a certain Zeitgeist into which they have momentarily been plugged, that creates the film." Richard Roud, "Introduction," in *Cinema: A Critical Dictionary,* ed. Richard Roud (New York: Viking, 1980), 10. Roud presumably was not thinking of Fred Zinnemann and Carl Foreman when he laid down this dictum.

27. Levy, "Legacy of Auteurism," 89.

28. "The categories were obviously heavily influenced by Sarris' disdain for Crowther and his ilk. . . . As much as Sarris wanted to canonize Samuel Fuller and Nicholas Ray, he needed to cauterize the work of directors laurelled by frontline movie reviewers. This made Crowther the hidden auteur of the 'Less Than Meets the Eye' category, a Hall of Shame that Wilder shares with, among others, John Huston, Elia Kazan, David Lean, and Joseph L. Mankiewicz. . . . The only thing the 'Less' directors had in common was praise from Crowther, and that, I suspect, sealed their fate." Richard Corliss, "Confessions of a Sarrisite," in Levy, *Citizen Sarris,* 134.

29. Levy, "Legacy of Auteurism," 82–83.

30. "Circles and Squares," reprinted in Mast and Cohen, *Film Theory and Criticism,* 666–79.

31. Pauline Kael, "Circles and Squares," in Mast and Cohen, *Film Theory and Criticism,* 668–69.

32. Kael, "Circles and Squares," 675.

33. Kael, "Circles and Squares," 678.

34. Richard Corliss, *Talking Pictures* (New York: Penguin, 1975), xx.

35. Mast and Cohen, "The Film Artist," 637–38.

36. Richard Schickel, "Advantage, Andy," in Levy, *Citizen Sarris,* 113.

37. Sarris, *American Cinema,* 27.

38. Richard Corliss, "The Hollywood Screenwriter," in Mast and Cohen, *Film Theory and Criticism,* 693.

39. Emanuel Levy, "Sarris' Magnum Opus," in Levy, *Citizan Sarris,* 51–52.

40. Andrew Sarris, "Preface," in Corliss, *Talking Pictures,* xii. Complete victory, was, however, temporary. "Auteurism was a connoisseurship that required a staggering knowledge of particular films. In an academic context, such knowledge could seem mere buffery, so auteur studies could not fully justify studying movies 'seriously.' An analysis of Hitchcock that purported to demonstrate a theory of signification or the unconscious was more worthy of academic attention than an analysis of recurring authorial motifs." David Bordwell, "Contemporary Film Studies and the Vicissitudes of Grand Theory," in *Post-Theory,* ed. David Bordwell and Noel Carroll (Madison: University of Wisconsin, Press, 1996), 19.

41. Reprinted in Hillier and Wollen, *Howard Hawks.* Rivette and Rohmer cited in same source, pp. 126 and 31.

42. *Films and Filming* (July and August 1962).

43. Sarris, *American Cinema,* 53.

44. J. A. Aberdeen, *Hollywood Renegades,* n.d., quoted at www.cobbles.com/ simpp_archive (accessed November 12, 2002).

45. Sarris, *American Cinema,* 57.

46. Andre Bazin, *What Is Cinema: Volume II,* ed. Hugh Gray (Berkeley: University of California Press, 1971), 154–55.

47. Raymond Durgnat, "Hawks Isn't Good Enough," *Film Comment* 13 (July–August 1977): 13.

48. Lee Russell, "Howard Hawks," in Hillier and Wollen, *Howard Hawks,* 83–86; Richard Combs, "The Choirmaster and the Slavedriver: Howard Hawks and *Land of the Pharaohs,*" *Film Comment* (July–August 1997): 48–49.

49. Combs, "Choirmaster and the Slavedriver," 47.

50. Peter Wollen, "Introduction," Hillier and Wollen, *Howard Hawks,* 2–3.

51. Combs, "Choirmaster and the Slavedriver," 48–49.

52. Richard Maltby, *Harmless Entertainment* (Metuchen, N.J.: Scarecrow Press, 1983), 86–88.

53. Quoted in Colin MacCabe, *Howard Hawks: American Artist,* British Film Institute documentary for the BBC, 1997.

54. Martin's shaking hands were parodied in *Blazing Saddles* (1973).

55. The design of *Rio Bravo* is closer to *High Noon* than it first appears, though the characters turn out to be opposites in practice: In *High Noon,* a boy and an old alcoholic offer their services, but Kane turns them down. In the end, he receives crucial help from a woman, as does Wayne.

56. David Thomson, "The Winding Road of the Western Hero," *New York Times,* August 20, 2000, II-29.

57. Peter Bogdanovich interview, in MacCabe, *Howard Hawks*.

58. Thomson, "Winding Road."

59. Tag Gallagher, *John Ford* (Berkeley: University of California Press, 1986), 402.

60. John Fitzpatrick, "Fred Zinnemann," in *American Directors*, ed. Jean-Pierre Coursodon with Pierre Sauvage (New York: McGraw-Hill, 1983), 178–79.

61. Fitzpatrick, "Zinnemann," 178–79.

62. Arthur Nolletti Jr., "Conversation with Fred Zinnemann," in *The Films of Fred Zinnemann*, ed. Arthur Nolletti Jr. (Albany: State University of New York Press, 1999), 13. Kramer agreed. "'I want to make it clear that I don't believe in the auteur theory. . . . Nor do I believe . . . that film is a director's medium. Film is a concert effort, it involves the work of a lot of people. The director just doesn't have that sort of overriding control, and he has to depend on the creative collaboration of writers, technicians, cameramen, actors—everybody connected with the picture. . . . In the days when I just produced films from 1948 to 1954 it was the producers who were the auteurs of the day." Kramer, quoted in Donald Spoto, *Stanley Kramer: Filmmaker* (New York: Putnam, 1978), 13–14.

63. Sarris, *American Cinema*, 168–69.

64. Louis Giannetti, *Masters of the American Cinema* (Englewood Cliffs, N.J.: Prentice-Hall, 1981), 369–70.

65. "*Stagecoach* is not truer than *High Noon*; both are versions of the past, one romantic and idealized, the other dark and constrictive." Don Graham, "*High Noon* (1952)," in *Western Movies*, ed. William T. Pilkington and Don Graham (Albuquerque: University of New Mexico Press, 1979), 53.

66. Manny Farber, Review of *High Noon*, *The Nation* 174 (April 26, 1952): 410. Farber's review, amazingly, appeared even before the notices in the trade press.

67. Nolletti, "Conversation," 11–12.

68. David Thomson, quoted in Laura Miller, "Reel Lives," *Salon.com*, December 16, 2002.

69. To paraphrase John Caughie, ed., *Theories of Authorship* (London: Routledge & Kegan Paul, 1981), 11.

70. Robert Horton, "Day of the Craftsman: Fred Zinnemann," *Film Comment* 33 (September–October 1997): 62.

Chapter 10

The Making of *High Noon*

> Which one of several individuals is most fully responsible for
> [*High Noon*] is a difficult matter to determine and nothing about
> which to quarrel. It could be Mr. Kramer, who got the picture
> made, and it could be scriptwriter Carl Foreman, who prepared
> the story for the screen. Certainly director Fred Zinnemann had a
> great deal to do with it and possibly Gary Cooper, as the star, had
> a hand in the job. An accurate apportionment of credits is not a
> matter of critical concern. What is important is that someone—or
> all of them together, we would say—has turned out a Western
> drama that is the best of its kind in several years.
>
> —Bosley Crowther[1]

The "accurate apportionment of credits" wasn't a crucial concern
outside the film industry in 1952 because what Hollywood produced wasn't considered art.[2] Everyone "knew" that movies were
made under the thumb of imperious producers. Directors, writers,
editors, cinematographers, and actors were so many hired hands.
The general glorification of directors as artists was still years away.

Crowther's speculation about who did what was artfully ingenu-
ous. Not only did he, along with a handful of other critics, consider
movies to be an art form, but he also knew Kramer and Foreman
from his visits to Hollywood. And, in all likelihood, he knew in a
general way how *High Noon* had come to be made, though he would
learn the details two weeks later from Foreman's letter.

Foreman, who would have reason to care deeply about the "accurate apportionment of credits," said that he had always wanted to

do a Western, but the inspiration for the Western he would eventually write came from an unexpected source. First and foremost, he would need something to say: "Some [writers] begin with character or incident; with me the theme has always been the essence. So the theme had to be one that was important to me emotionally and intellectually and otherwise."[3] That theme, he told another interviewer, was "the struggle of an individual against a society that for one reason or another is hostile. . . . There is a constant struggle going on between the individual and the mass."[4]

In his letter to Crowther, Foreman recalled that "the picture was born about four, perhaps five, years ago, while we were shooting *So This Is New York*. . . . Actually, it came into being simply as a technical idea of the *tour de force* type, the telling of a motion picture story in the exact time required for the events of the story itself."[5]

A suggestion for the theme that would run through this "tour de force" came out of the blue at about the same time. While Foreman was writing *Champion*, a United Nations representative tried to persuade Kramer to make a movie about the new international organization.[6] The theme would be "the necessity for free nations to align themselves in a common struggle."[7] It struck Foreman, for whom *Champion* was a metaphor for a corrupt society, that he could tell the story as an allegory about "a frontier town fighting for survival against marauding outlaws."[8] "The idea caught hold of me, and in about a week I had dashed off a four-page outline which, so far as plot is concerned, remains the basic plot of the completed film."[9]

He titled his movie *High Noon*. "The only thing of primary importance missing was the character of Helen Ramirez, the marshal's half-Mexican ex-mistress. . . . In this outline, the murderer has two cohorts rather than three, and they are both brothers of the released convict, here called Clyde Doyle. . . . The marshal's name is Will Tyler."[10]

At the time, Foreman had just finished writing the screenplay of *The Clay Pigeon* (1949) with its director, Richard Fleischer. By coincidence, the Foreman–Fleischer script dealt with the same subject as Zinnemann's *Act of Violence*, which was released the same year—an ex-serviceman accused of informing on his fellow prison camp inmates. As was his custom, Foreman was on the set every day, after making the long commute from the San Fernando Valley to the film's location with Fleischer. A neighbor and close friend, Fleischer had also directed *So This Is New York*.[11] According to Fleischer, Foreman suggested that they "'turn this time to account working (on) the idea of another film.' . . . So, driving up and down, we worked out

High Noon. I had (wanted) to direct it myself, but when it was time to start, I was no (longer) available."[12]

Foreman recalled telling the story first to Fleischer, and the director being

> tremendously enthusiastic. As you know, writers are lonely and insecure, and I needed that enthusiasm. A few days later, I told it to Stanley, who was also very enthusiastic and, of course, sympathetic to the United Nations angle. We decided that we would make it after *Champion*, and that, if possible, we would borrow Fleischer from RKO to direct it, in view of his feeling for it.[13]
>
> And then a strange thing happened. I had been telling the story to Rudy Sternad, our (art) director, and Sternad said that he had read something like it not too long before.[14] Disturbed, I instituted a search of *Saturday Evening Post* and *Colliers*—[Sternad] wasn't sure which—and, to my chagrin, ultimately found in [the December 6, 1947] *Colliers* a very good story by John Cunningham titled *The Tin Star*. It was a good story, and altho [sic] a very short one and not the same as *High Noon*, nevertheless there was a great similarity in the basic situation. Actually, Cunningham's central character was much closer to the Old Lawman (Lon Chaney) than to mine, but his ordeal was just about the same. As a matter of fact, the only dialogue I later retained from Cunningham's— I repeat, very good—story was some of that spoken by Chaney.[15]

In Cunningham's story, an aging, arthritic Montana marshal named Doane decides to face the four men who are coming back to town on the 4:10 train to kill him. The killers are led by a man named Jordan, whom Doane had sent to prison. Instead of getting married at the beginning of the narrative, as he does in Foreman's version, Doane is a widower. There are very few characters, no Helen Ramirez or justice of the peace. As Doane and his deputy await the Jordan gang, Toby, his deputy, says he will stay on as deputy only through the fight. In the gunfight, which rages through the town, Toby is wounded; Doane, who is also wounded, catches a bullet meant for Toby; and Toby kills the last of the gang. As Doane dies, Toby says he will take over Doane's job permanently.[16]

Foreman was shocked and "very unhappy" with the coincidence in the basic plots:

> I was certain-sure I'd had an original idea, but on the other hand, could I be really sure I hadn't read the Cunningham story and unconsciously plagiarized it? A problem. Finally, I felt there was no other way out but to purchase the Cunningham story if we were going to make the picture.

But when I took the matter up with Stanley, I was surprised and disappointed to discover that he had cooled on the project. One reason was that Hitchcock's picture, *Rope*, had since come out, using the time-for-time technique. There were other reasons, of course, and among them was the fact that Stanley had developed a desire to make *Cyrano.*[17]

We had by now reached a point in our development where more and more often decisions were being made unilaterally by Stanley, or pushed through by the force of his personality. So, in the end, we made *Cyrano* instead. It was a project I had great reservations about; without going into detail, I felt we were not equipped to do a good job on it. And I don't think we did.

But to get back. I still wanted to make *High Noon,* and if the company wasn't willing to risk the money, I was. I bought the film rights from Cunningham myself, after informing Stanley and George of my intention.[18]

According to Kramer, the purchase was a collaboration:

> We already had the title. . . . So when Carl Foreman suggested a rousing little Western thriller he'd read in a magazine we finally had the chance to use it! . . . . We had to buy the rights. . . . So Foreman went and bought it for us, because if I had negotiated the deal, we would have had to pay a whole lot more. As it was, Foreman got it for something ridiculous, like about $25,000.[19]

But the project was sidetracked repeatedly. *Champion* was an unexpected hit, and Foreman turned to writing *Home of the Brave* and *The Men*. "In my love for both the latter projects," said Foreman, "I didn't mind postponing *High Noon*. Meanwhile, I was thinking about it, and the story was taking shape and growing in my mind and in the notes I was making."[20] These projects were then followed by *Cyrano*, which Foreman also wrote.

Even as *High Noon* stalled, Kramer began publicizing its title and theme. The title was first used in publicity materials in March 1949, when Kramer used it to disguise the true purpose of *Home of the Brave.*[21] *Home of the Brave* could have been the title of the Western—if it had been used ironically.

"After (finishing) *Cyrano*," Foreman told Crowther,

> we held off production for several months, because of United Artists' shaky condition. . . .[22] It became apparent at once that I would not now be able to direct our next picture, as had been the plan. I would now have to become a full producer as well as an executive of a large com-

pany. And our great need now was product. We had to make seven pictures in our first year, six for Columbia and one for UA, still owed by
contract. We needed stories, lots of them.[23]

High Noon was finally scheduled for production in January 1951,
when Kramer needed the last picture to complete his contract with
United Artists.[24] Foreman immediately sold the story back to his
company so he could get his money back[25] and wrote "a fifteen-page
outline that sets up most of the characters and situations as we know
them."[26] He decided to use Cunningham's character names: The
marshal is Doane, the killer is Guy Jordan, and his gang consists of
his brother and two other men.[27]

The time of the story is intentionally vague—it could be anywhere
between 1870 and 1880—and the place is "Hadleyville," a small
town of about 400 somewhere in the New Mexico territory. At the
center of the story, Foreman notes, will be Will Doane, a man

> in his middle thirties. . . . He is direct, practical, not too articulate. His
> approach to the job of peace officer is matter-of-fact, unromantic. . . .
> He has enjoyed the prestige it has given him, and the knowledge that
> he is respected and liked by the townspeople. Now that he is being
> married, he is leaving the job and the town with some regret, but se-
> cure in the feeling that he is doing the sensible thing in moving to an-
> other town, where a general store should do good business. He is, cer-
> tainly, not an average man, but a very human one.[28]

His bride,

> Amy, is, . . . young, attractive, intelligent, strong-willed [and] deter-
> mined not to be a sheltered toy-wife but a full partner in her marriage,
> and it is she who has planned their future. More, Amy has strong emo-
> tional and intellectual convictions against any form of violence, be-
> cause her father and brothers were killed while taking part in vigilante
> action, and she has since embraced the Quaker faith. Marriage to
> Doane would have been unthinkable had he remained a peace officer.[29]

In his first full draft, dated March 19, 1951, Foreman's story
bluntly illustrated the fate of a town that doesn't back its marshal in
a showdown. Hadleyville is first seen as a ghost town. There is a
flashback to the Hadleyville of the story, and at the end the story returns to the deserted town.[30] By the third draft, dated July 30, Foreman would no longer assume he knew what would happen to

Hadleyville. Foreman was working on the second draft when he was subpoenaed in April, a month after HUAC had restarted its hearings and uncooperative witnesses were being blacklisted. He finished that draft on April 16, but then began another in which he changed the underlying allegory from the United Nations under attack to himself and his fellow Hollywood Leftists betrayed and under attack.

It would be his screenplay that would be filmed, but he would not direct it, as he had hoped. Fred Zinnemann, with whom he and Kramer had made *The Men*, loved the script for its exploration of individual conscience. Foreman would work with him as associate producer.[31]

"Of course, by now I had lived with *High Noon* so long that I finally felt equipped to direct it myself," Foreman told Crowther,

> but I sighed inwardly and said okay. Naturally, I've never regretted it. By this time, of course, my thinking about its basic stuff had undergone some changes. Hollywood had changed, too, since the time I'd written that four-page outline. As you, and a few others, have perceived, I began to draw inspiration from the contemporary scene, and if some of the characters have life it is because they are, of course, drawn from living models.[32]
>
> Anyway, Freddie and I went to work happily, but it soon became obvious that it wasn't going to be an easy picture to make. Almost from the start, it was apparent that *High Noon* was going to be an orphan, a ransom paid to UA, completely overshadowed by the really important Columbia product—in short, a B picture on the overall slate. As its producer I found myself short of just about everything—money, interest, manpower, facilities. Fred and I made our headquarters at the dirty but comfortable Motion Picture Centre, and I would go to my shiny new office on Gower Street two or three times a week for conferences with writers on my two other projects, *The Happy Time* and *Member of the Wedding*. Incidentally, it was very hard work, both physically and mentally, and I wouldn't care to do it again.[33]

According to Kramer, Gregory Peck was the initial choice to play the marshal, but he turned it down because it was too similar to his role in *The Gunfighter*.[34] Kramer and others have said that Marlon Brando, Montgomery Clift, and Charlton Heston were all considered, but declined for various reasons.[35] As it turned out, none of these actors could be seriously considered, because Kramer's most important investor, Bruce Church, a Salinas lettuce grower who had backed *The Men* and *Cyrano*,[36] would come up with the money only if Gary Cooper starred.

Of his motivation for taking the part, Cooper would say only that he jumped at the chance to play Will Doane because the movie represented what he had been taught—that law enforcement was everyone's job—by his father, a Montana Supreme Court Justice who had told him stories about sheriffs he had dealt with.[37]

Given the film's minuscule budget of $750,000, Cooper would have to agree to a cut in his usual price, from $275,000 to $100,000, plus a small percentage of the profits.[38] The general assumption was that Cooper agreed to the cut in exchange for a good script because his most recent films had not done well, either with critics or at the box-office.[39]

Cooper would be the first major star to experience Kramer's unusual financing methods, but he would not be the last. Kramer used only freelance actors. The big stars were asked to take a percentage in lieu of a large upfront payment, well-known supporting actors would shoot all their scenes back-to-back for a flat fee, and the cast would be "fleshed out" with unknowns.[40] The *High Noon* shoot would employ all three devices.

Kramer was not entirely happy with the star he'd been forced to hire. "He was not my favorite actor, my kind of actor. But Cooper belonged in *High Noon*. That part was made for him, that pebble-kicking, non-reacting, all-underneath kind of man who is tight-jawed and restrained."[41]

But Foreman was pleased: "His own character and integrity shone through the image he portrayed on the screen. . . . He was very likely the best film actor in the world. He had mastered the requirements of the camera better than anyone else I know."[42] Zinnemann also pronounced himself pleased.[43]

With the star's contract in place, there was little money, $35,000, for the rest of the cast. Five thousand dollars would go to the distinguished character actor Thomas Mitchell, an Oscar winner for *Stagecoach*, who had made a career of classics such as *Mr. Smith Goes to Washington, Gone with the Wind,* and *It's a Wonderful Life.* Mitchell, Lon Chaney, Harry Morgan, and Otto Kruger would work for a single week, shooting all their scenes back-to-back. Kramer's uncle, a talent agent, found Katy Jurado ("Helen Ramirez"), a Mexican actress who had had a supporting role in an American film, *The Bullfighter and the Lady* (1951).[44]

"Amy Fowler" was cast without a test. "The role was not demanding," Zinnemann would note. "We simply needed an attractive, virginal-looking and inhibited young actress, the typical Western heroine."[45] An agent showed around pictures of "twenty-two-year-old Grace Kelly, who had appeared in plays in New York and elsewhere and done TV shows and commercials. Kelly had appeared in only one feature film, *Fourteen Hours* (1951), playing a small role." Kramer met her in New York[46] and, after showing Zinnemann and Foreman a scene from the film, signed her.[47]

Zinnemann thought Kelly "was very, very wooden . . ., and her lack of experience and a sort of gauche behavior was to me very touching."[48] In his memoirs, Zinnemann notes, "She fitted the part admirably, perhaps because she was technically not quite ready for it, which made her rather tense and remote."[49] Kelly, though, was so unhappy with her performance that she went back to New York and asked her acting teacher for more lessons.[50]

While Foreman worked on the script and Kramer cast the film, the location team was scouting sites in northern California, near Yosemite Park. Columbia, an old gold-rush town, looked like a possibility for the main street of "Hadleyville." But, as Zinnemann discovered when he visited the town several months later on July 12, there was a problem —the trees on the main street, which had been bare in the winter, were now leafy, and would block the view. The only way to get around the problem was to "rent the standing Western street on Columbia Pictures' ranch in Burbank [the company's backlot] for the scenes involving the main street and some of the interiors—such as the marshal's office and the saloon—that looked directly out on the street."[51]

The town of Columbia would be used for other shots. As a postproduction press release noted, it was the source of "Hadleyville's" residential streets, the fire house and the back alleys that appear in the gunfight.[52] "A livery stable where the marshal and his deputy (Lloyd Bridges) brawl was found near Tuolumne City," reports Rudy Behlmer, "and an old church there was ideal for one (exterior) sequence. The Hadleyville railroad station could be re-created near the water tower at Warnerville" using an old wood-burning train that was regularly rented to movie companies.[53] A residence in Columbia with a picket fence and shrubbery would become Sam Fuller's house. A train car in what, in 1983, would become nearby Jamestown's Railtown 1897 State Historic Park would be used when Helen and Amy are seated on the train.[54]

During that July visit Zinnemann also settled on the one piece of straight railroad track long enough for the approach shots. It hadn't been his first choice. "The first image that (had) occurred to me was of the railroad tracks pointing straight to the horizon, the symbol for an enormous looming threat." He and Sternad looked at "tracks all over the Southwest." They couldn't afford the best they found, in New Mexico, because it was too far away.[55] Ironically, the film is set in the New Mexico territory.

All told, the press release noted, seven sites within thirty-five miles of Sonora were used over ten days. Every angle had to be storyboarded because the different sites had to match.[56]

There was another irony for Zinnemann. As he began to plan the "look" of his film, he realized that the switch to the backlot in the city had a "great advantage: the smog. It made the sky look blindingly white, just the way I wanted it as a backdrop, in contrast to the marshal's black clothes."[57]

The choice of a location represented a homecoming of sorts. Sonora had also been the location for two Cooper triumphs, *The Virginian* and *For Whom the Bell Tolls*.[58]

Even as he was choosing his locations, Zinnemann was visualizing his film: "From the time Stanley Kramer and Carl Foreman told me the outline of the story, I saw this film not as a comment on the American Western hero, but as an enormously important contemporary theme which happens to take place in a Western setting. For this reason, I resolved to shoot it in the style of a contemporary newsreel (if newsreels had existed at that time). The cameraman, Floyd Crosby, and I studied dozens of photographs of the 1860s, particularly the Civil War photographs of Matthew Brady."[59]

Zinnemann and Crosby, an Oscar-winner for the 1931 *Tabu*, settled on a high-contrast approach, which recaptured "the flat light, the grainy textures, the white sky (of Brady's classic photographs). . . . Our approach ran counter to the then fashionable style of Westerns—the pretty clouds in a filtered sky, the handsome, magnetic figure of the fearless young hero. Our hero, middle-aged, worried and very tired, was constantly moving against that white sky. This upset quite a few people and soon screams of anguish about the lousy quality of photography were heard. Floyd stood his ground and never wavered. No filters, no soft-focus lenses for the actors' close-ups. He didn't change an iota in his lighting; no spotlights, mostly just flat front light. It took a lot of courage on his part; . . . it was not I who was paying his salary."[60]

Crosby later told an interviewer, "We decided not to correct the skies . . ., to have hot skies because we thought it would give the feeling of heat. And the last thing we wanted to do was to make this little town look pretty or attractive or beautiful in any way. We wanted it to look like a crummy western town."[61]

In early August Cooper underwent a hernia operation, the first of four. He was in the hospital for a week.[62] To add to his woes, he "was still troubled by an ulcer, back problems and a hip ailment."[63]

Foreman's life away from the set had now grown so unpleasant since his subpoena that he almost welcomed the difficulties of making an "A" movie on a budget so tight "that the set designer had to keep using the same wallpaper for . . . wildly different sets."[64]

"We were being hampered on every side," he told Crowther,

> and it seemed to get worse as time went by. The production department, now headquartered at Columbia and disdainful of the little western, were slovenly and careless. Mistakes were made in the name of economy which later added costs to the picture, and so made the situation even more difficult. I was constantly fighting for more money, for the original budget was unrealistic, as was the schedule. It was like being back at a major studio again. Freddie's morale kept sinking; he couldn't understand what had happened to our operation, and I had to keep pretending that everything would turn out alright.[65]

Foreman turned in his final draft on July 30. It was time for Zinnemann, who was done scouting locations, to get involved:

> I finished the screenplay and Fred and I now began to spend nights as well as days together, going over the script line by line, action by action, shot by shot, scheming to make a good picture on little money and a too-short budget. But we worked together beautifully, even when we snarled and screamed at each other, because we were friends and we loved the story.[66]

Zinnemann was working once again in the style he favored, letting the writer produce a first draft—or in this case, a third—then shaping "it to whatever extent it needs to be reworked, before production if possible, but during the actual shooting if necessary."[67]

"Shaping" is the right word. Zinnemann's copy of the screenplay, in the Academy of Motion Picture Arts and Sciences Fairbanks Center for Motion Picture Study in Beverly Hills, is covered with his annotations, as well as some sketches, such as a diagram of Kane and

Harve in the marshal's office doorway. It is clear that he was involved in a major way in the direction the screenplay would take before shooting. That "final shooting script" of July 30 would go
through substantial changes wrought in those intense discussions
between Zinnemann and Foreman. If *High Noon* was "saved in the
editing," the editing process started long before the actual cutting
and pasting of pieces of film.

After only a week of discussion, Foreman revised thirty pages,
and there would be more revisions, dated August 17, August 24, August 29, and September 4—the latter the day before shooting began,
and after rehearsals had started. The collaborators would even look
back, if necessary. At one point—the scene in the marshal's office in
which Harve reveals to Kane his relationship with Helen—there is
the notation *"Revert to script of April 16."*

Zinnemann's script begins with a handwritten note: "Shot in 28
days." The shoot would follow the production schedule exactly: Six
days a week from September 5 to October 6, Sundays off, including
two days for travel.

At various points there are notes Zinneman has made for himself,
for the cinematographer, Floyd Crosby, and for the makeup artist,
Gustaf "Gus" Norin. Everywhere there are urgent suggestions for
changes in the visuals and the dialogue, which eventually show up
in the finished film: *"Dust and beards on riders." "Say something new
about riders in each shot." "Try to evoke Miller's terrifying effect."* The hotel clerk is *"malicious"*; he exhibits *"cold insolence."* There is a re-
minder to insert the *"business with trembling hands"* in the scene with
the drunk. Zinnemann orders dozens of close-ups, with exclamation
points—*"see badge*!!" *"clock!!!," "very close."* He inserts pendulum
shots.

Zinnemann would comment pointedly many times in later interviews that the clocks, which would be the subject of so much argument in the who-contributed-what debate that was to follow, "were
in the script . . ., an integral part from the beginning before I even
came on the script."[68]

His annotated script calls for minor changes in shots in order to
simplify: A follow-up scene is dropped:—*"We don't see Weaver and
Sam in store at safe in rear"*—because everything in the scene with Mr.
Weaver tells us we have no reason to doubt that Mrs. Ramirez's
business deal will go through. The fistfight now arrives without
elaboration: *"Kane simply walks into stable,"* instead of going from

front to back. Kane's "You think about a lot of things when you're tired" speech in the stable is drastically cut. He doesn't say "when people cross the street so they won't have to look at your face"—one of Foreman's signature political allegory lines. (The point has already been made on the street when the two men avoided him.) The "Don't shove me" speech is just two lines.

The opening ride into town is simplified—the little Mexican boy and the dog disappear; windows remain closed. Later, Zinnemann and Foreman will drop shots of shutters closing before the gunfight. The scene between the stationmaster and Amy no longer includes a reference to trains stopping. Helen, in acknowledging Kane's reason for not going, now says simply, "I know," instead of "I didn't think you would." Kane no longer hurls a chair through the saddlery window to distract Frank Miller in the final showdown, and Miller no longer fires off several wild shots while he holds Amy. Zinnemann has answered his own note: "*Should there be several shots from each man at this time or only one?*"

Most important, the first two scenes with Harvey and Helen, in which they talk about the gunmen, are cut, the first by the editor, the second by Zinnemann and Foreman. Zinnemann is clearly concerned with the relationship between Harvey and Helen. Note after note lays out the relationship visually: "*Helen only half responds;*" "*occasional tenderness, occasional maternal feeling, but she never takes him quite seriously—he feels it and is rankled.*"

In the scene that Zinnemann and Foreman cut, Harvey is smoking a cigar and Helen's hairdo has changed. "*(She) gives him (a) smile, (a) look while putting on earring.*" There is the implication of a just-previous sexual encounter. There is the same implication in Helen's reaction to Harvey's claim that Kane "was going mighty fast" as he drove out of town with Amy. Helen's initial amused reaction suggests she imagines he's referring to the Kanes' wedding night. "*She tweaks his ear and smiles.*" There are references to the "*mocking*" and "*teasing*" tone of Helen. But then his concern "*sinks in*"; that is, Helen realizes he's being serious. In a later scene, "*He has begun to bore her.*" Zinnemann worries, in the scene where Harvey finds her packing and kisses her abruptly, "*Does she slap him?*" She does—emphatically proclaiming both her disgust and her independence.

In the wedding scene, the judge now says: "Marshal, turn in your badge." There's a close-up of Will stalling with the badge before he says "You win." Added are close-ups of Amy and Howe saying that they can "see" Will in the store. New dialogue is given to Amy, Howe, and Fuller about staying versus going.

Always, Zinnemann and Foreman opt for simpler and less sexually charged dialogue and, where possible, add directions that will let visuals replace some of the dialogue. When Cooper takes out his watch on the prairie, Zinnemann notes, he is *"not looking at her."* Back at the office, Kane is *"only half-listening to her."* Amy's line "That's what makes it so stupid" is changed to "But don't you understand. That's exactly why we ought to go." *"Amy* (is) *not 'frantic' but 'angry.'"* Her speech about "you know there'll be trouble" is simplified. To Kane's claim that he understands her position as a Quaker, Amy no longer responds, "How do you know how I feel?" but rather, "Do you?" Zinnemann adds Amy's, "I won't be here when it's over." Amy no longer says, pleadingly, "You want me, Will, or you wouldn't have married me." Later, they drop Helen's remark to Kane "You're on your own," and her asking if he wants to kiss her.

Zinnemann and Foreman, in other words, have systematically removed overt sexual references between Kane and Amy, while adding them between Harvey and Helen—perhaps to underscore Amy's innocence and idealism, as well as to strengthen the chasm that has grown between the marshal and his former lover—and to give Harvey yet another reason to be angry. Zinnemann and Foreman evidently wish to make subtle points that will clarify character and strengthen the impact of the final scenes.

They want to avoid not only the obvious but the tendentious; often, the plot makes the points better than the dialogue could. Amy's "anti-gun" speech to Helen no longer justifies her position with the statement "because every other religion said it was all right for people to kill each other at least once in a while." The children's game, begun after they're sent out of the church, is drastically cut, until it is a simple tug of war—precisely paralleling what is happening in the church. Mrs. Fletcher—the woman who talks about not being able to walk safely down the streets before Kane cleaned up the town—is no longer chastised by a young woman as a hypocrite. Kibbee, the foolish man in the church scene, no longer says, "I don't hold with no killing on the Sabbath." Thus, we are spared the irony of Sunday killing. At the end of the film, Kane drops only his badge, not his guns and gunbelt.

If the story can be told with intervening scenes merely implied, Zinnemann and Foreman choose that course. The initial boom shot revealing both Kane and the gunmen is cut in favor of the single boom shot of Kane alone on the street. The first shoot-out, in which Ben Miller is killed, is greatly simplified; now there is simply a cut on Kane shooting Ben and the others vainly shooting at Kane as he retreats behind the building. We don't see Amy get off the train, only running away from the station and down the street. We never see her read Kane's will, only holding it crumpled and looking distraught. Harvey's pistols are on the wall within easy reach of Amy when Pierce stands a few feet away, because in the scene in which Harve quit, we saw him jamming his gun belt on a peg by the window. Connections are quietly, quickly made, never underlined.

Zinnemann writes dialogue on the spot: At the end of the church scene, Kane says "thanks"—ironically—to Henderson, and the gunmen are given obsequious dialogue at the train station to underline Frank Miller's status.

Zinnemann also creates a comic scene, one of several that give the lie to the oft-stated claim that the film is humorless. But the purpose is not a privileged or "human" moment, as in a Ford or Hawks film, but practical: to show that the back door, which Frank Miller will come through, is open. In the script version, "Kane takes a last look around the office" and goes out. In the film, he hears the drunk (Jack Elam) snore.

KANE: Hey, Charlie, you can go home now.

CHARLIE: Oh, thanks, Marshal. I sure appreciate it. I certainly do. (hesitates) You don't happen to know if the saloon's open, do you, Will?

KANE: I said, "Go home, Charlie."

CHARLIE: (abashed) Yes, sir.

(Kane lets him out the back door and then goes out the front.)

Zinnemann and Foreman add mordant touches, such as the barber's assistant hammering on the (unseen) coffins. The mordancy, and irony, carry over into crucial scenes: Mart Howe's comment on his career— "It's a rotten life"—becomes *"It's a great life."* Later, speaking of the citizenry's concern about law and order, his "Deep down they got no use for it." becomes *"Deep down, they don't care. They just don't care."*

And when Mart is speaking of Frank Miller, "When they didn't hang him, when they gave him that silly sentence" is changed to focus on Kane:

MART: "I was hoping you wouldn't come back."

KANE: "You know why I came back."

MART: "But not to commit suicide."

Except for the low-angle close-up of the bottle breaking on the tracks early on, Zinnemann reserves stylistic flourishes until the end.

The filmmakers, so concerned about dialogue and scene continuity, make only sparing references to music. The one exception comes when the women pass Kane in the buckboard and the filmmakers call for *"passionate and tender music."* If they have anticipated a bravura score or a linking ballad, they give no indication.

A week before rehearsals started, on August 17, Zinnemann, on his own, revised the fight sequence, trading the elaborate for the straightforward: *"High shot from Doane's p.o.v. Jordan throws the second lamp. Doane fires, break it in midair"* is cut. Even in the revision, before the editor becomes involved, some of the running and hiding is cut.

By this time, Zinnemann's depressed mood, which Foreman referred to in his letter to Crowther, begins to show up in his written remarks: When Kane is hiding in the loft, *"Colby is killed in a way which is at once extremely clever and not cowardly. This will be devised by either the producer or the writer."* When Kane mounts a horse in the stable to escape, there is this: *"Note: This sounds obscure, but you know what I mean. The producer or writer will clarify it in his own inimitable way. Anyhow, the horses exit."* And *"the final shots, including the young boy bringing the buckboard and the departure of Doane and Amy, will be supplied by the producer or the writer."*[69]

On the occasions when he stopped the rewriting with Zinnemann and the production planning long enough to go in to the production company offices, it seemed to Foreman that Kramer had abandoned the film.[70] He and Zinnemann would have to make the film alone. Zinnemann agrees: "[Kramer] was very little in evidence because he was busy making a picture at Columbia at the time: He was producing *Death of a Salesman*. Carl Foreman and I really made the picture by ourselves."[71]

Kramer's angry response to Foreman's characterization of the producer's involvement—or lack of it—inadvertently confirms Foreman's account of the shoot: "It was my production. The film was made simultaneously with my company's commitment to Columbia on *Death of a Salesman*. But I supervised the script and casting, selected the director, and controlled the editing and scoring of the production."[72]

Zinnemann was not interested in arguing the point as long as his own contribution was duly noted. "The entire picture is the result of a team effort," he told an interviewer, but "the visual concept . . . was entirely mine: Included in it are the railroad tracks stretching to the horizon, symbolizing the menace; the restless figure of the marshal moving about the town in his search for help; and the idea of letting the action slow down by degrees during the approach of the train by gradually increasing the camera's speed."[73]

Clocks do more than denote the passage of time. "Time, as exemplified by the clocks," notes Zinnemann, "(would move) more and more slowly and (become) larger and larger on the screen until a state of almost suspended animation is reached, just before the clock strikes the first bell of noon. To accomplish this we over-cranked the pendulums more and more so movement became almost dream-like in the end."[74]

Visually, *High Noon* is above all about the framing of specific shots and matching them to other carefully framed shots—such as the jump cut from the track to the church aisle—to increase the sheer oppressiveness, something that would have been difficult to accomplish if there had been major re-editing, as the post hoc argument had it.

This focus on framing begins with the first shot. "The credits were rolling, simple lettering over black-and-white images of the three (gunmen as). . . . Tex Ritter sings 'Do Not Forsake Me, Oh My Darlin'. The compositions of the riders and the landscape are very carefully framed, each shot bearing a sense of formal arrangement, the light and the dark of Floyd Crosby's cinematography altogether stark."[75]

And hanging over everything, invading every shot, would be that unrelenting sun and empty sky.

Whatever Zinnemann, Foreman, and Kramer might otherwise disagree about, on one thing they were in complete agreement. As with all of Kramer's films, there would be a rehearsal period—a week at the end of August, split between the Columbia ranch street set and the Motion Picture Centre, where many of the interior scenes were to be shot.[76]

"Everyone had thought that Cooper would not choose to take part in the rehearsals, since it was not in his agreement," Foreman told an interviewer.

> After a day or two of rehearsals, Cooper called the studio and asked why he had not been asked to participate. After that he was there every

day and apparently found stimulation in what was surely a new experience for him. During the rehearsal period, Katy Jurado was having difficulty pronouncing "Doane," the name of Cooper's character. To alleviate the problem the name was changed to Kane.[77]

No one seems to have recorded who proposed the change to "Kane," whether the director, the screenwriter or someone else. But it fit perfectly.

Finally Doane became Will Kane and Jordan became Frank Miller. Of the other three badmen, Colby's first name was changed to Jack and young Jordan became Ben Miller (Frank's brother); only Pierce's name was left unchanged.[78]

There would be a last-minute run-through just before a scene was shot. According to Crosby, Zinnemann would

> get the actors together . . . and he'd . . . rehearse the dialogue and get the thing going the way he wanted. Then he'd start to block out the scene to get the movements. Then I would come in and the rest of the crew, and would watch how the scene was blocked out. We'd get the marks for the actors, and whatever camera moves. We'd mark where he wanted the camera. He'd very often . . . lay it out through the [view]finder, if he had the camera moves. And then he'd turn the set over to me and we'd light it with the stand-ins.[79]

Production proved to be a nightmare. "The budget for the entire picture," Zinnemann noted, "was $750,000 [a figure remarkably close to its final "negative cost"—the expense of the film before print copies—which would total $786,600], based on a gruesome production schedule of twenty-eight days, which meant that we would have to shoot completely out of continuity."[80]

Filming began on September 5 at the Columbia Ranch, allowing Thomas Mitchell to do all of his scenes—the wedding and the church—in a week, according to his contract. The other "name" actors—Henry Morgan, Otto Kruger, and Lon Chaney—were similarly finished in a few days.

Closely following the shooting schedule, which is dated September 1, 1951, and lists Foreman as "producer," "the cast and crew started early every day . . . and worked late into the evening."[81] Zinnemann was not exaggerating the "out-of-continuity" nature of the shooting, extreme even by the standards of the industry, in which movies were rarely shot in scene order. The seeming "randomness"

of the shoot must have tested all the actors, as scenes far apart in the
final film were shot back-to-back.

Early in September, filming started at the Columbia Ranch with
the church scenes, the sequences in which a desperate Kane visits
Mart Howe and Sam Fuller at home, the courtroom scenes, most of
the scenes in the adjacent marshal's office, including the wedding,
and some street shots outside the marshal's office. The cameras went
back inside for the scene in the office in which Kane tries to explain
to Amy why he is staying. Then came the scenes in the barber shop
and all the scenes in the hotel lobby with the snide desk clerk (Howland Chamberlin, who would appear before HUAC five days later,
refuse to name names, and be blacklisted). In the following days
Zinnemann filmed Kane alone in his office, all of the bar scenes, the
bar exterior, Kane on the street being avoided by the two men, the
exterior of Mart's house, and the drunk accosting Kane.

Then came the day when Kane watched Helen and Amy's buckboard go by:

> We . . . over-cranked (for slow motion) the shot of the horses and
> wagon carrying the two women to the station, so that it almost floated
> by the marshal who was standing still, watching them disappear into
> the distance. The resolution of the sequence was a big close-up of the
> marshal with the camera on a boom receding into an enormous high
> long shot showing the entire village, empty of life, holding its breath,
> all windows and doors closed, not a soul, not even dogs to be seen,
> waiting for the impending gunfight.[82]

Zinnemann was asked later if the famous boom shot of Kane
alone on the street was unusual at the time. He replied,

> It's curious, but although it is a shot that technically would have been
> possible before, I don't remember ever having seen anyone do it that
> way. . . . The crane we used was an enormous monster which could be
> rented for the day.[83] Across the street George Stevens was shooting
> *Shane*, I think. We borrowed it from him for a day and it needed ten
> people to move it. Now you could do it with a zoom shot, but it would
> not be the same thing.[84]

Only now was the opening ride of the Miller gang within the
town shot, as well as Harvey watching Kane and Amy race out of
town, the walk-down to the gunfight, Amy running down the street
and seeing Ben Miller's body, and an insert of Kane writing his last
will and testament.

Two days before traveling to the northern California locations, Foreman told the assembled cast and crew that he had been subpoenaed by HUAC and would take the Fifth Amendment and be blacklisted. That day, Zinnemann shot the interiors of the gunfight at the stable: Colby rushing in, the fire, the frightened horses, Kane's escape on horseback, and Amy back-shooting Pierce and the finale from two angles.

Before shooting the finale, Foreman and Zinnemann had to make a critical decision: Could Will Kane possibly survive the shoot-out; after all, the marshal in Cunningham's story hadn't. Foreman finally decided that Kane had to survive. As he told Zinnemann, "'We're going to wear the audience out. If we're successful they're going to be completely identified with the marshal and they're going to want him to survive even though everybody in town is telling him to give in. If . . . he dies, what we'll be saying is that you just can't win, so give in. And I don't think we should do that because maybe he has a chance to survive.' . . . [Zinnemann] agreed, so we kept the happy ending."[85]

Zinnemann, who regarded *High Noon* as another of his commentaries on the individual in society rather than as a blacklist allegory, had a different reason for wanting Kane to survive. "The ending," he wrote a student two years later, "was arrived at not for purely commercial reasons. By far the most important reason for the gunfight and the happy ending was the fact that we wanted to do a Western in the strict, time-honored tradition. We wanted to see whether we could take the rigid classic form of the Western and give it new meaning."[86]

Monday, September 24, was the first travel day. Ninety actors and crew were flown to Modesto, then bused to Sonora.[87] It was also the day that Foreman appeared before the Committee and refused to name names.

Zinnemann welcomed the change of locale. "The location went well, despite the enormous pressures of budget and schedule. The northern Californian countryside was ravishingly beautiful; it was great to be in the open from dawn to dusk."[88]

The railroad scenes were the first to be shot, starting with the gunmen arriving at the station, then all the scenes involving the stationmaster, the long shots of the tracks, the train arriving, the train car interior, and the waiting gunmen.

Zinnemann was involved in the planning and execution of every shot[89]—a single-mindedness that almost got him and his cameraman killed when they lay on the tracks filming the train as it came into the station and it was unable to stop. Somehow, they managed to leap to the side as the engine roared past. "The camera was hopelessly beyond repair, but the magazine was OK. The film was developed and the shot is in the picture."[90]

The next day, September 27, the three riders were finally shot entering the town as the church bell tolls, as were the exterior-of-the-church scenes, the back alley parts of the gunfight, the exterior of the Fuller house, and the fireman polishing his truck. On September 28, the very first scene, the gunmen gathering outside of town, was shot, as well as Kane and Amy on the prairie in the buckboard.

The buckboard scene is crucial. The audience, as film historian Richard Griffith notes, is confused by the camera set-up—the abrupt reining of the horses, the jump to close-up—which is designed to capture Kane's own confusion. "We share the hero's feeling of not quite knowing what is happening, we have the sense, as he does, of a false solution being offered as a true one. From that moment we are not merely involved with the marshal: We sit in his seat, we see with his eyes, we are afflicted with his doubts and fears as he abandons any obvious course of action for one with unknown consequences."[91]

September 28 was also the first of three days given over to the only sequences that would never appear in the film in any form, except for a reference left in from the earlier bar scene. A second deputy (James Brown) is headed back to Hadleyville—he wants to get there in time for the wedding—with a prisoner (stunt man John Dayheim). They fight at a water hole and later stop at a stage station so the deputy can carry on with a Mexican girl (Roberta Haynes).

Foreman had written the scenes as "insurance" in case the scenes in town proved too claustrophobic. But the weather turned bad, making the shots difficult, and both Foreman and Zinnemann were relieved that what they had managed to shoot never had to be used.[92]

October 2 would bring more shots of the stable for use in the gunfight, as well as one of the shoot's major challenges, the fistfight between Kane and Harve. "Zinnemann recalled that Cooper's 'recurring hip problem . . . made it difficult for him to do the fight with Lloyd Bridges, but it didn't stop him from working very hard and very long hours under some trying conditions.'"[93] As Zinnemann himself notes, "He even volunteered to do the fistfight . . . without a stunt double."[94]

During the fight, Lloyd Bridges' son Beau was in the loft with several of the neighborhood children. When he laughed, he ruined the end of the fight, forcing a reshoot.[95] Shooting was also slowed when

Cooper flubbed his lines several times. He looked up at the children and said, "Must be all those chickens up there." Patricia Neal (who had shown up on the set and whom Cooper was driving around the countryside during breaks in a "shiny new Jaguar"[96]) caused a (further) delay in the filming when she picked up a squealing piglet and its mother rushed to the rescue, smashing equipment.[97]

With location shooting over, the company returned to Los Angeles on October 3. Over the next three days, back at Motion Picture Centre, all of the scenes in Helen's apartment were shot—Will and Helen, Helen and Harvey, Helen and Sam, Helen and Amy—as well as an unused shot of Harvey on his bed after the fistfight.

The hostility between Foreman and Kramer had by now grown so great that they were doing everything separately:

> I have to tell you, by this time the feeling had become so strong that the picture itself was the least popular aspect of the whole Kramer operation. Now he never came around at all, and while they did see the rushes, they saw them separately from us: By "us" I mean Freddie and myself. Stanley would see it with his editor, Harry Gerstad, and George. Freddie and I would see it with our editor, Elmo Williams. We were told Stanley just hated the rushes—nothing but rude remarks all the time. They didn't like what they saw and . . . Fred was a dope who couldn't direct and everything was going wrong—it was just no good.[98]

"The photography was questioned," Foreman told Crowther.

> There were remarks about slowness, dullness, too much under-playing. Somehow, altho [sic] everyone had read the script, nobody seemed to remember that the small pieces of mosaic they saw in the dailies were part of a carefully designed pattern, that suspense is often increased by retarding pace, that strong emotions need not be shrieked through a megaphone to be understood and felt. As was my custom, I was on the set from the first shot to the last, but I got the general reaction when any of the palace guard dropped by. Naturally, it depressed me a little, but I felt sure Fred and I knew what we were doing.[99]

The "mosaic" proved to be remarkably efficient in overcoming most of the limitations of a meager budget, but the inability to reshoot and the speed of production meant that it was easier for continuity errors, such as the reference in the bar to the second deputy, to creep in.

The most obvious is the problem of the loaded buckboard. When Helen and Amy board the train, the stationmaster (it was originally supposed to be Sam, but he is left back in town) is unloading Amy's bags from the buckboard. As the train is leaving, she is racing back to town. At the end, the boy drives up in the still-loaded buckboard. Then there were the telephone poles in the nearby Warner's lot, which are clearly visible in the top left of the high boom shot. Apparently only the editor, Elmo Williams, noticed them, but there was no way to correct the problem.

Other problems are less obvious—the "modern" zipper on the back of Grace Kelly's dress; the little girls who remain in the church scene after all the children are dismissed; Kane's collar, bloodstained after the stable fight, suddenly turning clean in the barber shop; the shadows cast by Kane and the gang at high noon; the second-story air conditioner in the back alley; and the sudden shift of gun from Kane's left hand to his right from one shot to the next.[100] Some of the gaffes are obvious; some require an eagle eye. None particularly detract.

For Gary Cooper, acting in *High Noon* was an extraordinary experience, both personally and professionally. His career was widely believed to be in decline, his health was fragile, he was separated from his wife, he was in the affair with Neal, and during filming he briefly became involved with Grace Kelly. (According to one biographer, he tried to persuade Neal that Zinnemann was having an affair with Kelly.)[101] Somehow, he gave the performance of his career.

The physically pained, ravaged look etched on his face was real. Not only had he undergone a hernia operation little more than two weeks before rehearsals, he had been out of the hospital only a week when he showed up on the set. He was also troubled by arthritis, back pain, and an ulcer that would require two operations, the first the following December.[102] To make things worse, he "threw his back out while rehearsing the wedding scene and lifting Grace Kelly onto a ledge."[103] But he soldiered on, working the same long hours as the other actors. "Not once were we delayed or held up by him for whatever reason," Zinnemann reported. "For most of the time he seemed to be in good health, and it was only two or three months after shooting had been completed that he became ill (with the duodenal ulcer). He did in fact look quite haggard and drawn, which was exactly what I wanted for the character."[104]

Zinnemann and Foreman both came to appreciate Cooper's ability to convey a sense of heroic resignation. Zinnemann was asking of Cooper what he asked of all his actors, a naturalism that was the opposite of theatrical projection. This emphasis on simple honesty was an especially apt choice for Cooper, who was frequently dismissed as an actor of narrow range.[105]

"A number of critics praised Cooper's acting-out of Will Kane's fear," a Cooper biographer reports, "especially the sad look in his eye. Zinnemann was surprised by this, as he didn't discuss the subject with Cooper and wasn't aware of the actor considering it as a guiding force, either."[106] Cooper had, said one critic, "an almost eerie ability to let a string of emotions bleed out of his face without seeming to move a muscle."[107]

Though his involvement between the end of casting and the beginning of the editing was minimal, Stanley Kramer remembered the making of *High Noon* as a personal trial. "We . . . had to fight everybody all during production and post-production. Everyone thought Cooper was too old to be playing a marshal. And no one had heard of Grace Kelly or Katy Jurado."[108]

For Carl Foreman, no longer involved with the film after the October 21 showdown with Kramer and aware of what was going on only from what friends were telling him, it was as though his baby was being raised by foster parents who were making up stories about his ability as a father. In the months after his departure, *High Noon* went through an agony of editing and re-editing, and the legend began to grow, aided by comments to the trade press from insiders, that it was saved in the editing room.

It was a claim that would make Foreman angry for decades after:

> Had I been in the country when the picture came out and took off, to the surprise and, in a way, to the chagrin of the Kramer Company, I can assure you that this very big lie would never have been allowed to be told and to grow. The truth is that Zinnemann and I were operating apart from the rest of the Kramer group, almost as an independent unit, and that neither Kramer nor anyone else around him had any use for the film from the beginning. . . . Having so little money made it necessary for Fred and me to work very closely together [Foreman as associate producer, a credit he would be denied later, as well as scriptwriter], which was a wonderful experience, despite the difficulties, and . . . Cooper and the . . . cast were heartwarmingly enthusiastic and cooperative.[109]

The editing, which would ultimately stretch over six months, began immediately. Zinnemann worked with a new editor at the Kramer Company, Elmo Williams, for the first week.[110] After that,

there is no agreement on who did what. "Kramer," said Zinnemann, "entered into the editing to a large extent afterwards but of
course there was not a foot of the picture re-shot or anything like
that."[111]

According to Foreman, "Fred's version followed the script
throughout. Stanley didn't like it, and took over. He cut it brutally,
almost it seemed with venom. Everyone agreed the version was bad.
He gave in, finally, and Elmo Williams took over and returned the
cut to Fred's original version."[112]

"What actually happened," said Foreman,

> was that when Kramer, who had fallen out with me over the blacklist,
> saw Fred's cut and recognized himself and his other partners in the
> roles of the townsfolk who let their friend down, he was furious and
> had to find some way of saving his dignity and image; the way he
> found was to "save" a disastrous film, and that is the credit that he and
> the editor, Elmo Williams, have falsely taken all these years. It's too
> bad Kramer wasn't able to "save" his next eleven films in the cutting
> room, and that Williams has never been able to "save" any of his own
> since he became a producer. . . . I did a seminar on *High Noon* . . . [113] and
> our group analyzed the film scene for scene, the screenplay against the
> final cut. With the exception of the two scenes [of the absent deputy] I
> mentioned before, it's remarkable how little fancy editing had to be
> done in comparison with practically any film ever made. True, there
> was a bit of messing about; they had to prove they made some contri-
> butions. But thank God they couldn't "save" the film too much, be-
> cause that's all the film there was, there wasn't any more, and no more
> was shot, not even an insert.[114]

Williams would describe the process quite differently, telling an
interviewer that Kramer was displeased with the first cut (that is,
Zinnemann's cut) and allowed Williams to work on it over a long
weekend. He focused on the central story, eliminating a scene with
Katy Jurado and Lloyd Bridges and trimming the confrontation between Grace Kelly and Jurado.[115]

In Kramer's telling, however, Williams's work is secondary to his
own contribution: "I was the one who did the final cut of this film—
I alone, and I stand by whatever flaws or virtues the film has to this
day."[116] Whoever gets the credit, Kramer, according to Williams, felt
better after seeing what his editor had done. To create the proper
mood, Williams had inserted the folk singer Burl Ives's "Riders in
the Sky" over the opening, a gesture that would prove enormously

important later, when Kramer was casting about for a song to tie the film together.

The legend of the editing has Williams inserting both the clocks and the close-ups of Cooper. The only way he could have done that was to follow the script and return some shots cut by Kramer, because, as Foreman noted, there was no reshooting. There was another problem. Williams's cuts were so extensive—twenty minutes' worth—that the film was now too short.[117] As Williams notes in a memo to Kramer,[118] over the months of trying out different possibilities, he had to "lift" and "put back" various "bits and pieces" of film because the rough cut left him with few options if they were to release a feature-length film. In retrospect, it is fortunate that Williams and Kramer eventually realized they had little room in which to maneuver.

At first, looking for a way to speed the action, Williams had drastically cut the post-wedding retirement scene by eliminating Jonas Henderson's attempt at humor and Kane's more sober concerns. In the following quotation comparing the July 30 script, Williams's memo to Kramer, and the transcript of the finished film, the cut-and-then-restored lines are in boldface, the permanent cuts in italics.

METTRICK: Well, one more ceremony, and Will's a free man. More or less . . . (he turns to Kane) Marshal, turn in your badge. . . .

(Laughing, smiling, the group has converged on Will and Amy at the desk. Kane understands Mettrick's reference, and his hand goes up to his badge, then falls away. Unconsciously, he stalls a little.)

KANE: I was hoping Harvey and Tobe'd be here . . . (he grins) A man ought to be able to make a final speech to his deputies. And here they don't even show up for his wedding.

METTRICK: They'll be along before you leave.

(Amy is watching Kane with quiet understanding.)

KANE: I guess so . . . (he reaches for his badge again, then stops) Tell the truth, I kind of hate to do this without your new marshal being here . . .

HENDERSON: (with mock solemnity) Will, Sam Fuller and Mart Howe and I are the entire board of selectman of this community. We are, also, your very good friends. And you've done such a fine job here, that I feel completely free to say, and the Judge will bear me out (he grins jovially for his punch line) that this town will be safe until tomorrow! . . .

(Kane joins in the general laughter. His eyes meet Amy's and when he speaks it is to her.)

KANE: (ruefully) You win. (to the others) But don't ever marry a Quaker. She'll have you running a store . . .

FULLER: Can't quite picture you doing that, Will . . .

AMY: (quietly) I can . . .

HOWE: (soberly) So can I. And a good thing, too.

AMY: (smiling at him) Thank you.

(Kane looks at Howe quizzically.)

KANE: You didn't talk that way when you were wearing a star. (He shakes his head with mock sadness. and then a wicked glint comes into his eyes.) All right, it's coming off, but I got to be paid first. (Swiftly he sweeps Amy off her feet and holds her aloft.)[119]

Minutes later, Kane is talking to the judge in the courtroom. Williams initially decided to cut the entire "civics" lesson, though he eventually returned it because, as he notes in his memo, he was afraid that without it, the scene would lose its "cumulate effect." Part of the problem, no doubt, was that while Mettrick was giving his little speech, he was packing up—and taking down the American flag.

METTRICK: (sharply) Are you forgetting I'm the man who passed sentence on Frank Miller?

Kane shakes his head numbly. Mettrick resumes his hurried packing.

METTRICK: You shouldn't have come back, Will. It was stupid . . .

KANE: I figured I had to. I figured I had to stay.

METTRICK: You figured wrong.

KANE: I can deputize a posse. Ten, twelve guns is all I'd need.

METTRICK: My intuition tells me otherwise.

KANE: Why?

Mettrick (looks up at the wall clock) It is seven minutes to eleven.

METTRICK: (bitterly) There's no time for a lesson in civics, my boy.

(On the wall behind the bench are an American flag of the period and a picture of Justice, with scales and blindfold. The Judge goes to them and starts to take down and fold up the flag. Almost helplessly, he begins to talk.)

METTRICK: (taking down the flag) In the fifth century B.C., the citizens of Athens—having suffered grievously under a tyrant—managed to depose and banish him. However, when he returned, after some years, with an army of mercenaries, these same citizens not only opened the gates for him, but stood by while he executed the members of the legal government. A similar thing took place about eight years ago in a town called Indian Falls. I escaped death only through the intercession of a lady of somewhat dubious reputation, and at the cost of a very handsome ring that once belonged to my mother. (He shrugs) Unfortunately, I have no more rings.

(He has neatly folded up the flag by now and has placed it in one of the saddlebags. He turns to the picture of Justice and takes it down.)

KANE: You're a judge—

METTRICK: I've been a judge many times in many towns. I hope to live to be a judge again.

KANE: (giving up) I can't tell you what to do . . .

METTRICK: (harshly) Why must you be such a fool! Have you forgotten what he is? Have you forgotten what he's done to people? Have you forgotten that he's crazy? (He points to the vacant chair near the defense table.) Don't you remember when he sat in that chair there and said—

CLOSE SHOT—Vacant chair

METTRICK'S VOICE (over): You'll never hang me! I'll be back! I'll kill you, Will Kane! I swear it. I'll kill you!

BACK TO SCENE. Kane and Mettrick stare at each other.

KANE: (after a pause) Yeah . . . I remember . . .

Williams considered cutting one of the scenes in the hotel lobby involving Amy and the "snide" clerk, then thought better of it, presumably because he realized that there was no other way to convey how some residents relished the thought of a "wide-open" town.

Williams contemplated major excisions in the scene in Kane's office in which he tries to explain why he's staying, and Amy says she will not wait to find out if she's to be a "wife or a widow." Williams did not indicate which lines he initially cut and then returned, other than a reference to the second deputy, but he eventually left all of them in—again, presumably, because this is the scene, together with the preceding one on the prairie, that lays out Kane's thinking.

Some material, however, was cut, put back, and then cut again, as with an early scene involving Harvey and Helen:

Helen's front room. Helen and Harvey are facing Sam.

HELEN: How could they pardon Frank? He was in for life.

SAM: (shrugging) He's out.

HARVEY: (a glint of triumph in his eyes) So that's why Kane ran away . . .

Helen looks at him, starts to say something, then stops. There is the off-screen clatter of hoofbeats in the streets. They turn to the window.

Williams wavered over many of the scenes—Kane and the drunk, Mr. Weaver being called from the church service, several shots of the gunmen at the depot, parts of various scenes involving Kane, Amy, and Helen, parts of scenes in the office. But two things presumably stayed his (and Kramer's) hand—not just ensuring a feature-length running time, but also the role of even seemingly inconsequential scenes, such as Jimmy the drunk and the teenage boy trying to persuade Kane to include them, in placing the fears of the church-people and the hostility of the bar-people in stark perspective.

But some material was, indeed, simply cut, including the first scene with Harve and Helen, in which Helen recognizes the gang as it rides into town.

And there is the brief moment when Kane seems to weigh suicide in his office:

Kane stares down at the gun. His hand turns the barrel upward, pointing toward his face. For an instant it almost seems as if he is weighing the benefits of a quick, more merciful self-inflicted death. He presses the trigger. The safety catch is on. It clicks harmlessly. He picks up the other gun in his left hand and works the trigger on it. Then, putting down both guns, he opens a drawer, takes out a box of bullets and stuffs bullets into his coat pockets.[120]

Several repetitive scenes are dropped, as when the bartender tells the men in the saloon, "Hit the bar, all of you! I'm settin' 'em up!," and one conversation between the stationmaster and the barber that emphasizes what we already know.

Perhaps the most dramatic cut comes in the final scene in Helen's apartment, as the women unburden themselves to each other. Foreman's script had had Amy explicitly referring to herself as a "feminist," and it had not been dropped during the script rewrites. Williams cut to the bone in this scene—not only to remove everything that was in any way peripheral to the central point of establishing "responsibility" for Kane, but also to eliminate an anachronistic reference to feminism and to avoid underlining each woman's motivation—Amy's Quaker beliefs, Helen's struggle for respect—already suggested in earlier scenes.

Helen's front room. Amy is still in the chair lost in her thoughts. Helen is standing at the window, looking down into the street.
HELEN: Where are you going when you leave town?
AMY: Home. St. Louis.

HELEN: *(turning to her) All that way alone?*

AMY: *That's the way I came. My family didn't want me to marry Will in the first place. I seem to make them unhappy no matter what I do. Back home they think I'm very strange. I'm a feminist. You know, women's-rights — things like that. (she looks up at Helen) Where will you go?*

Helen shrugs.

AMY: *Why are you going? Are you afraid of that man?*

HELEN: *Not afraid, no. There are very few men who cannot be managed, one way or another.*

They each think of Kane, and look at each other. Then Helen goes on.

HELEN: *I'm just tired. (she starts to pace)* I hate this town. I've always hated it. To be a Mexican woman in a town like this. *(she shakes her head) I married Ramirez when I was sixteen. He was fat and ugly, foolish. When he touched me I would feel sick. But he had money. When he died, I had money. I sold the saloon. I bought the biggest store in town. Nobody knew. I hired a big citizen to run it for me. Nobody knew that, either. Big citizens do many things for money. And all the fine ladies, who never saw me when they passed me on the street, they paid me their money and they never knew. I enjoyed it for a while. But now. . . . (She shrugs again)*

AMY: (after a pause) I understand.·

HELEN: You do? That's good. I don't understand you. (as Amy looks at her) No matter what you say, if Kane was my man, I'd never leave him like this. I'd get a gun—I'd fight.

AMY: *(deliberately) Why don't you?*

HELEN: He is not my man. He's yours.

She turns suddenly and goes to one of her bags, opens it quickly, rummages in it, comes up with a gun.

HELEN: *Here. Take this. You're his wife.*

AMY: *(sharply) No! If I did I'd be saying my whole life up to now was wrong!*

HELEN: *Right, wrong, what's the difference? He's your man.*

AMY: *(rising) Is he? What made him my man? A few words spoken by a judge? Does that make a marriage? There's too much wrong between us — it doesn't fit! Anyway, this is what he chose.*

There is an instant of complete silence, which is shattered suddenly by the distant but loud, hoarse scream of a train whistle. Involuntarily, both women react physically.

In the end, almost everything that had been cut, except two brief Helen–Harve scenes, the second deputy, and the longer version of the final Amy–Helen conversation, was returned to the film. As an essayist on Zinnemann's film would observe, "The rapid cross-cutting of the opening credits is typical of (Williams's) creative ingenuity, as also is his direct cutting of sound and image to eliminate all transitional devices such as wipes and fades. This helps to reinforce the classic simplicity of the story, underlining the Greek unities of time, place and action."[121]

And Williams did, in fact, make important contributions—the "messing about" that Foreman ridicules. The most important thing he did was to rearrange the continuity—that is, change the order of the scenes. The overall effect of these changes is to do exactly what Foreman sought—to increase suspense, as he said in his letter to Crowther, "by retarding pace."

The most important of these changes is to create an increasing sense of desertion by reordering the scenes in which Kane seeks help, to emphasize betrayal by those the marshal could most reasonably have expected to stand with him. The order, after the initial withdrawal of the judge and Harve, is now: the saloon, where his chances of help are slightest, then the cowardly Fuller, then the drunk—purely for its ironic value—then the church-people, and finally Mart, the old marshal, and his last hope. The following fistfight with Harve, who wants to justify his actions, simply reinforces our sense of Kane's desperation.

Sam, Helen's factotum, now finds Mr. Weaver in church, and Helen makes her deal with him before she talks to Kane, instead of after—and her deal-making is no longer intercut with Kane looking for help from Mart, the drunk, and Fuller. Thus, she has now cut her ties to the town before she sees Kane, and her reluctance to help him is reinforced—it is not just a matter of jealousy. She doesn't seem to be deserting him because she no longer does business while Kane desperately seeks help.

The impact of the growing hostility in the gang between Pierce and the childish Ben Miller is delayed when several related scenes—the "sweetened your disposition" scene, Ben's ride into town for liquor, his visit with the saloon habitués, and the shocking moment when he meets Kane outside the saloon—are all moved later in the film.

Amy and Helen now meet before Kane and Harve fight in the stable. Helen's planting of the idea in Amy's head, however resistant she is to it, that she must help Kane will now come earlier and thus have more time to develop.

The crosscutting during the church and stable scenes has been drastically reduced so that each can more effectively build to a climax. Several scenes have been moved later in the film to increase the sense of dread building on all sides: Amy's first indication, from the hotel clerk's "I wouldn't miss it for all the tea in China" speech, that Kane's position is far worse than she suspected; Kane's first, hopeful meeting with Baker (to which the revealing snore of the drunk has been added); the little boys playing "Bang, you're dead, Kane" now much later, immediately after the church scene, to provide ironic commentary.

The train whistle now comes after a series of montage shots of the principals frozen in place, rather than before, emphasizing that everyone is waiting for the marshal to meet his maker. "Montage musically slow. Time crawling to a standstill," Williams notes in a memo (on Kramer letterhead).[122] The whistle is now less a warning to Kane that he may be doomed than an admonition to take action. Zinnemann would eventually acknowledge the importance of Kramer's and Williams's editing, especially in this rapid-fire montage immediately preceding the train whistle at noon.[123]

"Once I started rearranging the continuity," Williams remembers, "the clocks kept jumping around in time—or, rather, out of it. I had to keep the audience from noticing. Since editors know that the eye follows gesture and brightness, I realized I was limited to shots with movement or light objects. I had to draw the audience's attention away from those clocks."[124]

Sometimes the clock problem was dealt with simply by cutting the clock shot. In the original script Herb Baker, the townsman who volunteers to help, looks at the clock during his first visit to the marshal's office. "It is seven after eleven," notes the script. In the finished film, he looks, but we don't see the clock, because his visit to the marshal now comes later than seven after eleven.

Williams's use of sound would be particularly important in the final montage. He notes in the memo to Kramer that he has inserted a muffled "sound effect of Kane sobbing."[125] As he told an interviewer: "What I wanted to do with the end was to play lonely, simple sound against the sudden, loud, staccato gunfire. So I have a fly buzzing around in the office, I have the scratch of Cooper's pen as he's writing his . . . will. . . . I have the ticking of the clock—single, isolated sounds, always with Cooper working and listening for the train."[126]

After his initial foray into the editing was less than successful, Kramer turned to the film's scoring, and it was here he would make perhaps his most important contribution, after the casting. In the earliest editor's cuts, the only music was the folk tune that Williams had inserted under the title credits. Kramer decided early on that the film lacked tension and needed a bravura score, and a song to comment on the dialogue sequences and propel the action during the gunfight.

For both song and score he turned to Dimitri Tiomkin, the Russian émigré composer he had worked with since the 1943 adaptation of W. Somerset Maugham's *The Moon and Sixpence*.[127] Tiomkin, notes a film music historian, "dealt in vivid melodies, exotic instrumentation and virtuoso fervor and is known for music which now has the thrust of a jet plane, now achieves pop status; quasi-Soviet realism one moment, then exotic orientalism of pre-Revolution Russian composers the next."[128]

Tiomkin had scored all of Kramer's films except *Death of a Salesman*. In recent years he had composed for several major Westerns, including *Duel in the Sun, Red River,* and *The Gunfighter* "because of his ability with a ballad-like melodic line underscored by soft and leisurely strings"[129] and because he employed a "virtually choreographic approach adopted to the showdown scenes."[130]

According to Behlmer, Kramer may have gotten the idea for a recurring ballad from a Tennessee Ernie Ford recording of the title song for the Randolph Scott Western *Man in the Saddle,* which was being completed at Columbia Studios while *High Noon* was being edited, or from the episode-linking ballad in the 1945 *A Walk in the Sun* (1945).[131]

At first, Kramer has said, Tiomkin balked at writing a song, protesting that he only did scores. But he was under contract, and Kramer insisted.[132] The producer didn't care for Tiomkin's early attempts and played him the Burl Ives tune that Williams had used.[133]

In his memoirs, Tiomkin tells the story rather differently: Not only does he not protest, he originates the ballad idea—and he and lyricist Ned Washington assemble the final song without further ado. "It would be a title song, featured throughout the film, a device relatively new then. The rule book says that in movies you can't have singing while there's dialogue; but I convinced Stanley Kramer that it might be a good idea to have the song sung, whistled and played by the orchestra all the way through. Now all I needed was a song. I had worked before on dramas of the cattle country and gold camps. I had studied the songs of the Texas range and the Mexican border and the traditional British tunes of the frontier, modified by the pioneer minstrels of the plains and mountains. A melody came to me." After hours of experimentation, he says, he came up with a workable melodic line.

"Now I needed a lyric. . . . I had to have something romantic, with a heart-throb. The trouble was that the pattern of the melody was far more complicated than a popular lyric writer was likely to have thrown at him. The usual form is a melodic line of eight bars, then another eight bars in more or less similar rhythm. But this tune ran into changing phrases and varying patterns. It would be hard to fit the notes with rhymes, and they'd have to be of the sticky sentimentality dear to the popular ear." Veteran lyricist Ned Washington came to his rescue. "I don't know what mental travail he went through, but in due time he came back with a lyric."[134]

In his memoirs Tiomkin says it was he who found the ballad's singer:

I chose Tex Ritter, who sang cowboy ballads in a low, husky voice, with a group of cowboy guitar players. . . . The way to do it was to have . . . Ritter come to my house and hear the song.

He arrived with his guitar players in full cowboy dress. I played and sang the song . . . The cowboys looked at each other. Never before had they heard a panhandle drawl with a Russian accent. Tex and his cowboys nearly fell off their chairs laughing, and Ned Washington doubled up with mirth at hearinig such a parody of his song. . . . Nevertheless, ... Ritter learned the song in fine style, and sang it with a simple, haunting quality. . . . "Do not forsake me" was there from beginning to end, sung, whistled, and played with instrumental variations.[135]

The song played an unexpected role in promoting the film when it became the first song in movie history to be released independently. After sitting through the previews that Kramer would find so depressing, Tiomkin bought the publication rights from the company. "Now I would see if I could make anything on the song on phonograph records. A flop song from a film fiasco didn't look very promising, but there was no harm trying."[136]

Tiomkin approached Capitol Records,

which had Ritter under contract, (but they) refused to let him cut a single for airplay. Tiomkin then approached Columbia Records, which had just signed Frankie Laine, and a deal was made. [In the four months between the release of the record and the film] the song . . . became a million-seller, and as a result, the film became a huge box office hit. Suddenly, every major motion picture had to have a title song, whether or not it was really called for.[137]

"The song was heard everywhere, in fact around the world," a delighted Tiomkin recalled. "I read in a newspaper that President Eisenhower liked it, and sent him a stack of records in German, Japanese, Hebrew, every important language except Russian."[138] But it would be Tex Ritter's, not Frankie Laine's, version that would be remembered.

If a country and western ballad as a signature tune wasn't entirely original, Tiomkin's use of it to provide the main thematic line of the surrounding score was. The composer had

> an unprecedentedly free hand (that) enabled him to break with Hollywood convention in three main respects:
>
> First, *High Noon* begins and ends pianissimo with a ballad-singer accompanied only by a guitar, accordion and drums. (This was contrary to the conventional blare of the orchestra.)
>
> Second, the idea of threading through a single tune, words and all, as an integral part of the dramatic underscore was unorthodox. . . . *High Noon* . . . is virtually monothematic; the tune is the source of practically every bar of the orchestral incidental music, thus a unique musico-dramatic unity. Tiomkin intuitively realized that the theatric idée fixe—the deadly approach of high noon—should be complemented and reinforced in the music.
>
> Third: Hollywood [practice] stipulated the use of the standard symphony orchestra in which the main expressive burden fell upon the strings. In *High Noon* Tiomkin dispenses with violins altogether, and the lower strings that remain—violas, cellos and double-basses—are totally subordinated to a wind, brass and piano-dominated sonority. The result is a darker, starker, de-glamorized quality of tone-color. The most elaborate orchestral treatment of the tune occurs at the film's climax, primarily in the montage of suspense which culminates in the arrival of high noon. . . . The clock's ticking is heard first as a throbbing pulse in harp and pizzicato strings, but grows gradually into a relentless hammering; the sequence is a kind of 'fantasia on one note.' Over this ostinato the full orchestra throws out a nerve-shattering development of the melodic phrase set in the ballad to the words "Oh to be torn 'twixt love and duty," the climax being reached with an ear-splitting blast from the whistle of the arriving train. The showdown sequence takes the theme to pieces in an eight minute tour-de-force of variation-cum-symphonic development, and puts it together again, momentously, only in the closing bars as the conflict is resolved.[139]

Once he had the score, Tiomkin had to fight for his vision. He wanted his music to be heard during the gunfight; Williams did not. Tiomkin and Williams took their disagreement to Kramer, who sided with his composer—much to Williams's dismay. "I still think the use of music hurt the effectiveness of the climax."[140]

But that continuity of scoring over the ending was actually the exception. "What is striking is how infrequently music is heard," Wolfgang Petersen told his *New York Times* interviewer. "Long sequences that today would be plastered with wall-to-wall music are allowed to play in silence or with some evocative ambient sound, like the ticking of a clock. Thus, when Tiomkin's score does emerge, it feels all the more powerful."[141]

The director was pleased with the result, according to film historian Richard Griffith. "Zinnemann says that Dimitri Tiomkin's score gave an emphasis and direction to the film's pace which no one had anticipated while shooting was in progress as well as emphasizing the mythical quality of the story."[142]

The legend of the saving of *High Noon* that would eventually emerge grew out of the last-minute editing that followed what Kramer, Tiomkin, and others described as disastrous previews. The first preview was actually a private showing that Harry Cohn, the head of Columbia Pictures, arranged for himself. According to Kramer, Cohn simply borrowed the film without his knowledge when he was out of town over the weekend. The following Monday morning Kramer confronted Cohn, who dismissed the "theft" and the film out of hand.[143] But Zinnemann says that Kramer was so worried he was thinking of selling Cohn the film's distribution rights—until Cohn actually saw it, without the music, and backed off.[144]

Kramer would always describe the first public preview, in Pomona, as a disaster. The audience began to laugh after the ballad welled up several times—and that was before it was heard several more times. His colleagues told him to drop the song.[145]

"The audience was given cards on which to mark its reaction," Tiomkin recalled, "and the verdict was unfavorable. Film experts agreed that the picture, music and all, was a flat failure. The producers hesitated to release the picture."[146] Kelly was thought to be dreadful.[147] After the preview, a columnist said, "half the picture was close-ups of Grace."[148] Kramer had Tiomkin eliminate several of the ballad reprises.[149] Williams also shortened the snatches of song that remained—the only other change before the second preview in Long Beach the following week. "All involved agreed that the second screening was also a disappointment."[150]

Zinnemann wasn't at either preview, but he thought he knew why audiences laughed: "This became one of the first, if not the first, song to be heard over the main title. Audiences used to the sound of full-blown studio orchestras at the start of a picture reacted rather nervously."[151]

Five decades after the previews, Zinnemann's son, Tim, attempted to set the record straight:

> I attended one of the disastrous previews . . . and can tell you that Columbia had no faith in the movie at that point, felt my father as a European did not understand Westerns and also felt that Gary Cooper was washed up as an actor. They did cut down the amount of music in the movie, but the film was released as my father made it. The clocks were storyboarded in his copy of the script (which is currently in the Academy Library in Hollywood), shot by him, and edited into the film as he originally intended. It was not until the film became a surprise success that everyone else connected with the project took credit for "saving it."[152]

The senior Zinnemann shared his son's view. "He (Kramer) told everyone *High Noon* was lousy till it was a smash—and then took credit for it."[153]

High Noon was screened for the trade press at the end of April, and the favorable reviews persuaded the newly reorganized United Artists to promote it energetically. The advertising "emphasized the suspense, the adult Western slant, the idea that this picture was different, unusual, and non-formulaic."[154] It went into general release on July 25, 1952, with the advertising catchline "Into Two Short Hours . . . Is Crowded the Action and Adventure . . . The Pulse-Pounding Thrills . . . The Loves and Hates . . . Of a lifetime . . . Gary Cooper at His Greatest . . . in the Outdoor Hit of the Year."[155]

It became the eighth-highest earner of the year, taking in $3.4 million—at the very least a success story if it had been distributed by one of the major studios, but a bonanza for a small independent working through a financially troubled distributor.

Writing to Bosley Crowther from London, Foreman shared his amazement:

> How Stanley and George [Glass] feel about the picture's reception so far, I have no way of knowing. However, I would venture the opinion that they are both rather surprised.

Fred and I used to talk about it, rather wistfully. He said it was the best script I'd ever written, and that it was a shame we were so loused up. Certainly, he came through brilliantly under probably the most trying conditions any director has had to work under, that I can think of. Incidentally, *High Noon* did very well here, both critically and at the box-office. Quite a hit. I'm so happy about the critical reaction to *High Noon*. And that audiences seem to like it, too. I understand from UA that it's broken house records, etc., and they're very pleased. But not as pleased as I am.[156]

High Noon had made Cooper number one at the box office for the first time. He could now command a percentage of the net plus $500,000 per picture. John Wayne had fallen to third, after being first in 1950 and 1951.[157]

Even as Kramer reorganized his company yet again, Zinnemann began to receive the first checks in a series of payments that would last five years. By July 1953, he had received more than $53,000. He was moved to comment in a letter: "What a wonderful business we are in when things go well."[158] If the money was good, his respect for the result was even better. "*High Noon* is the only (picture I made) that came out well from beginning to end."[159]

No amount of money or artistic success, though, seems to have been enough to entice him to work for Kramer again. He had begun *The Member of the Wedding*, his last picture for Kramer under his contract, in March 1952,[160] before *High Noon* had been released, and the *Member* shoot, too, was a less-than-happy experience—he noted that Kramer never visited that set, either.[161]

Rudy Sternad, the production designer, would stick with Kramer until Sternad's career ended in 1963. But none of the other principals—Foreman, Zinnemann, Crosby, Williams, or Tiomkin—would ever work for Kramer again.

In the end, even with Kramer's and Williams's "messing around," as Foreman put it, *High Noon* looked very much like the film that had grown in Foreman's mind, and not just in the time-for-time aspect, the running time of 84 minutes that was not much shorter than the story time of about 105 minutes.

The two teams—Foreman, Zinnemann, and Crosby, then Kramer, Williams, and Tiomkin—had had little to do with each other and yet they had "collaborated" on a classic. The process was about as far removed from the notion of the auteur as can be imagined.

NOTES

1. Review in *New York Times,* July 25, 1952.

2. It was critical *in* the industry, as two Hollywood insiders argue in their documentary about Carl Foreman's loss of his "associate producer" credit on *High Noon.* Lionel Chetwynd and Norman S. Powell, prods., *Darkness at* High Noon: *The Carl Foreman Papers* (PBS documentary, broadcast September 17, 2002).

3. Quoted in Rudy Behlmer, *Behind the Scenes* (Hollywood, Calif.: Samuel French, 1990), 269.

4. Penelope Houston and Kenneth Cavender, "Interview with Carl Foreman," *Sight and Sound* 27 (Summer 1958): 222. Despite the gunmen in *High Noon,* Foreman told Houston and Cavender, "There are no villains in my stuff: The 'heavy' is always the mass or the environment, never a personal 'heavy.' There are conflicts between individuals, but these conflicts will always be expressions of larger issues." 227.

5. Letter from Carl Foreman to Bosley Crowther, August 7, 1952, 1–2. Copyright © Carl Foreman Estate. Courtesy Eve Williams-Jones, widow of Carl Foreman.

6. Behlmer, *Behind the Scenes,* 269.

7. Malvin Wald, "Carl Foreman," *Dictionary of Literary Biography,* vol. 26, *American Screenwriters* (Detroit: Gale, 1984), 106.

8. Wald, "Foreman," 106, summarizing part of a Foreman lecture at the American Film Institute.

9. Foreman to Crowther, 1–2.

10. Behlmer, *Behind the Scenes,* 270.

11. Richard Fleischer, *The Clay Pigeon,* n.d., quoted at www.nettuno.it/mystfest/e/claypige.html (accessed September 27, 2002).

12. Fleischer.

13. Foreman to Crowther, 1–2.

14. Foreman to Crowther, 1–2. Others claim he heard the bad news from his agent. Wald, "Foreman," 106; Behlmer, *Behind the Scenes,* 270.

15. Foreman to Crowther, 1–2.

16. Summary from Behlmer, *Behind the Scenes,* 270; and Jim Hitt, *The American West from Fiction (1823–1976) into Film (1909–1986)* (Jefferson, N.C.: McFarland, 1990), 218.

17. After two other films in the pipeline, *Home of the Brave* and *The Men.*

18. Foreman to Crowther, 1–2.

19. Kramer, quoted in Donald Spoto, *Stanley Kramer: Filmmaker* (New York: Putnam, 1978), 99. As in other aspects of this story, it is Kramer's version that has been widely accepted: "Kramer bought *The Tin Star* for $25,000," according to Jeffrey Meyers, *Gary Cooper* (New York: Morrow, 1998), 239–40.

20. Foreman to Crowther, 1–2.

21. On Kramer's copy of the *Home of the Brave* screenplay, dated January 19, 1949, *High Noon,* the printed title, is crossed out and replaced by a hand-written *Home of the Brave.* University of California at Los Angeles Special Collections (hereinafter "Young Library").

22. Kramer was in negotiations with Columbia and buying Broadway plays.

23. Foreman to Crowther, 3.

24. Behlmer, *Behind the Scenes*, 270–71.

25. Foreman to Crowther, 3.

26. Behlmer, *Behind the Scenes*, 270–71.

27. Behlmer, *Behind the Scenes,* 271; Ed Andreychuk, *The Golden Corral* (Jefferson, N.C.: McFarland, 1997), 33.

28. From the July 30, 1951, version of the screenplay, reprinted in George P. Garrett, O. B. Harrison Jr., and Jane R. Gelfman, *Film Scripts Two* (New York: Meredith Corporation, 1971).

29. Garrett, Harrison, and Gelfman, *Film Scripts Two.*

30. Behlmer, *Behind the Scenes*, 279.

31. Behlmer, *Behind the Scenes*, 273.

32. Foreman to Crowther, 3.

33. Foreman to Crowther, 3–4.

34. James Robert Parish and Don E. Stanke, *The All-Americans* (New Rochelle, N.Y.: Arlington House, 1977), 46–47.

35. Stuart M. Kaminsky, *Coop* (New York: St. Martin's Press, 1980), 169.

36. Behlmer, *Behind the Scenes*, 273.

37. From www.research.umbc.edu/landon/Film%20Summaries/Summary_HighNoon. htm (accessed September 9, 2002); Kaminsky, *Coop*, 386; Mason Wiley and Damien Bona, *Inside Oscar* (New York: Ballantine, 1986), 222.

38. Hector Arce, *Gary Cooper* (New York: Morrow, 1979), 239. The $100,000 figure shows up prominently on the film's final accounting. Fairbanks Center for Motion Picture Study, Academy of Motion Picture Arts and Sciences, Beverly Hills (hereinafter "Fairbanks Center").

39. Behlmer, *Behind the Scenes*, 273–75.

40. Behlmer, *Behind the Scenes*, 273. Director Wolfgang Petersen commented on the quality of the cast: "It reminds you how important casting is, not just for the big roles but for everyone. There are a lot of great actors in this film, even in some of the smaller roles that appear only once or twice. Look, Lloyd Bridges is just great in [the] bar scene, and . . . the bartender, he's just perfect." Rick Lyman, "Watching Movies with Wolfgang Petersen; A Boy Shaped by 'High Noon,'" *New York Times*, March 30, 2001, E1.

41. Quoted in Meyers, *Cooper*, 239.

42. Quoted in Meyers, *Cooper*, 241.

43. Fred Zinnemann, *A Life in the Movies: An Autobiography* (New York: Scribner,1992), 99–100.

44. Behlmer, *Scenes*, 275.

45. Zinnemann, *A Life*, 99–100.

46. Behlmer, *Behind the Scenes*, 273–75.

47. Spoto, *Kramer*, 107; Behlmer, *Behind the Scenes*, 273–75.

48. Quoted in Meyers, *Cooper*, 242.

49. Zinnemann, *A Life*, 99–100.

50. Spoto, *Kramer*, 107. She should have been more patient. When Crowther summed up "The Year's Best" in December, he made a point of calling her work "outstanding." *New York Times*, December 28, 1952, II-1.

51. Behlmer, *Behind the Scenes*, 277.

52. Stanley Kramer papers, Young Library.

53. Behlmer, *Behind the Scenes*, 275. See Tinsley E. Yarbrough, "Those Great B-Western Locations," *Western Clippings*, "Special Limited Edition" (Albuquerque: Boyd Magers, Video West Inc.), 21–22.

54. "The Clock Strikes High Noon Again," *The Sacramento Bee*, undated article, 1993 (Fairbanks Center).

55. Zinnemann, *A Life*, 99–100, 101.

56. Stanley Kramer papers, Young Library.

57. Zinnemann, *A Life*, 101.

58. Meyers, *Cooper*, 239–40.

59. Zinnemann, quoted in Raymond Rohauer, *Fred Zinnemann* (Brochure for a Museum of Modern Art retrospective, 1957).

60. Zinnemann, *A Life*, 101–2.

61. Arce, *Cooper*, 244.

62. Kaminsky, *Coop*, 166; Meyers, *Cooper*, 272.

63. Stephen Tatum, "The Classic Westerner: Gary Cooper," in *Shooting Stars*, ed. Archie P. McDonald (Bloomington: Indiana University Press, 1987), 77.

64. Zinnemann, *A Life*, 101.

65. Foreman to Crowther, 4–5.

66. Foreman to Crowther, 5.

67. Louis Giannetti, *Masters of the American Cinema* (Englewood Cliffs, N.J.: Prentice-Hall, 1981), 367–68.

68. Zinnemann interview in Leonard Maltin, *The Making of* High Noon, (documentary included with fortieth anniversary video re-release of *High Noon*, 1992). Also in Chetwynd and Powell, *Darkness at* High Noon (script pages with clocks are clearly indicated).

69. All quotations are from the Zinnemann script in the Fairbanks Center.

70. Foreman to Crowther, 5. "Neither Kramer nor anyone around him had any use for the film from the beginning." Foreman, from 1979 interview in *American Film*, quoted in Kaminsky, *Coop*, 386.

71. Fred Zinnemann, "A Conflict of Conscience," *Films and Filming* 6 (December 1959): 34.

72. William R. Meyer, *The Making of the Great Westerns* (New Rochelle, N.Y.: Arlington House, 1979), 211–12.

73. Zinnemann in Spoto, *Kramer*, 104–5 .

74. Zinnemann, in a letter to Louis Giannetti, quoted in Behlmer, *Behind the Scenes*, 278–79.

75. Lyman, "Watching Movies," E1.

76. Meyers, *Cooper*, 239–40; Behlmer, *Behind the Scenes*, 277.

77. Foreman, quoted in Behlmer, *Behind the Scenes*, 277.

78. Andreychuk, *Golden Corral*, 33.

79. Quoted in Meyers, *Cooper*, 240.

80. Zinnemann, *A Life*, 99–100.

81. Meyers, *Cooper*, 239–40.

82. Quoted in "Fred Zinnemann: Sight and Sound Dossier," *Sight and Sound* (January 1996, Supplement): 12.

83. According to a *High Noon* publicity release, it was thirty-five feet high, had six wheels, took nine years to develop, and cost $45,000. Stanley Kramer papers, Young Library.

84. Brian Neve, "A Past Master of His Craft: An Interview with Fred Zinnemann, *Cineaste* 29 (Winter 1997): 15–19.

85. Behlmer, *Behind the Scenes*, 282.

86. Fred Zinnemann to Franklin Thomson Jr., January 15, 1954. Thomson, a student, had attacked the ending in a term paper that he sent to Zinnemann (Fairbanks Center).

87. From press release (Young Library).

88. Zinnemann, *A Life*, 106.

89. Behlmer, *Behind the Scenes*, 279.

90. Zinnemann, *A Life*, 102–6.

91. Richard Griffith, *Fred Zinnemann*. (The Museum of Modern Art Film Library), Pamphlet #1, n.d., 13 (Fairbanks Center).

92. Zinnemann, *A Life*, 106.

93. Kaminsky, *Coop*, 386.

94. Zinnemann, *A Life,* 99–100.

95. Lloyd Bridges in Maltin, *Making of* High Noon.

96. From a report in the *Sonora Union-Democrat*, June 19, 1992, quoting witnesses (Fairbanks Center).

97. "The Clock Strikes High Noon Again" (an article about Tuolumne County's forty-first anniversary of the shoot) (Fairbanks Center).

98. Foreman interviews, January 20–25, 1978, tapes 25–30, quoted in Chetwynd and Powell, *Darkness at* High Noon.

99. Foreman to Crowther, 6.

100. All these, and the other problems mentioned, were caught by the eagle eyes at www.nitpickers.com/movies/titles/2343.html (accessed August 24, 2002).

101. Meyers, *Cooper*, 231.

102. Meyers, *Cooper*, 272.

103. Meyers, *Cooper*, 241.

104. Kaminsky, *Coop*, 169.

105. Arthur Nolletti Jr. "Conversation with Fred Zinnemann," in *The Films of Fred Zinnemann*, ed. Arthur Nolletti Jr. (Albany: State University of New York Press, 1999), 11–36.

106. Meyers, *Cooper*, 212–13.

107. Brian Garfield, *Western Films* (New York: Rawson Associates, 1982), 45.

108. Quoted in Spoto, *Kramer*, 99.

109. "Foreman," *American Film*, 38. Elmo Williams agrees: "Kramer had no faith in *High Noon*. He even threatened to shelve it and take his name off it. But later on, because it became a big hit, he agreed to attach his name to it . . . naturally. In fact, until I talked to you today, I wasn't sure that Carl wasn't still on as the producer." Chetwynd and Powell, *Darkness at* High Noon.

110. Although Harry Gerstad, the Kramer Company "editorial supervisor," shared the Oscar with Williams, neither Foreman, Kramer, nor Williams has ever indicated that he was involved with the editing other than sitting through the rushes with Kramer.

111. Zinnemann, "Conscience," 34.

112. Foreman to Crowther, 10.

113. At Greystone, the American Film Institute Center for Advanced Film Studies in Los Angeles.

114. "Foreman," *American Film*, 38–39.

115. Behlmer, *Behind the Scenes*, 284–85.

116. Kramer in Spoto, *Kramer*, 103.

117. Behlmer, *Behind the Scenes*, 285.

118. Young Library.

119. Permanent cuts quoted from Garrett, Harrison, and Gelfman, *Film Scripts Two*.

120. Words in italics cut from original script.

121. John Howard Reid, "A Man for All Movies," *Films and Filming* (May 1967): 8.

122. Kramer papers, Young Library.

123. Griffith, *Zinnemann*, 13.

124. Quoted in Geraldine Fabrikant, "Grace on the Cutting Room Floor," *New Times*, March 18, 1977, 54.

125. Kramer papers, Young Library.

126. Meyers, *Cooper*, 249.

127. Tiomkin had scored the Capra unit's *Why We Fight* shorts and its *The Negro Soldier*.

128. Christopher Palmer, *Dimitri Tiomkin: A Portrait* (London: T. E. Books, 1984), 78–79.

129. Gerald Mast, *Film, Cinema, Movie* (Chicago: University of Chicago Press, 1983), 214.

130. Christopher Palmer, *The Composer in Hollywood* (London: Marion Boyars, 1990), 131.

131. Behlmer, *Behind the Scenes*, 285–86.

132. Meyer, *Great Westerns*, 215.

133. Spoto, *Kramer*, 103. The official title of the song is "The Ballad of High Noon."

134. Dimitri Tiomkin and Prosper Buranelli, *Please Don't Hate Me* (Garden City, N.Y.: Doubleday, 1959), 230.

135. Tiomkin, *Don't Hate Me*, 232–33.

136. Quoted in Behlmer, *Behind the Scenes*, 287.

137. *Video Hound's Soundtracks: Music from the Movies, Broadway, and Television*, ed. Didier C. Deutsch (Canton, Mich.: Visible Ink Press, 1997), xii.

138. Tiomkin, *Don't Hate Me*, 234.

139. Palmer, *Composer in Hollywood*, 142–43.

140. Quoted in Behlmer, *Behind the Scenes*, 286.

141. Lyman, "Watching Movies."

142. Griffith, *Zinnemann*, 13.

143. Spoto, *Kramer*, 103.

144. Zinnemann, *A Life*, 106–8; Behlmer, *Behind the Scenes*, 287. "Years later, when Cohn and I were doing *From Here to Eternity*, and had arguments and I wanted to torture him, I would say, 'Harry, you certainly made a mistake. You could have made five million dollars with that movie.' And he suffered. Poor Harry. It was a blow to his ego. He had a chance to make money and he passed it up." Zinnemann, *A Life*, 106–8.

145. Spoto, *Kramer*, 104.

146. Tiomkin, *Don't Hate Me*, 233.

147. Larry Swindell, *The Last Hero* (Garden City, N.Y.: Doubleday, 1980), 291.

148. Arce, *Cooper*, 247.

149. Spoto, *Kramer*, 104.

150. Behlmer, *Behind the Scenes*, 287.

151. Zinnemann, *A Life*, 108.

152. Tim Zinnemann to *Time Out*, London, May 14, 1997 (Fairbanks Center).

153. Michael Buckley, "Fred Zinnemann: An Interview," *Films in Review* 34 (January 1983): 34–35.

154. Behlmer, *Behind the Scenes*, 287–88.

155. *Box Office*, May 10, 1952. Kramer collection.

156. Foreman to Crowther, 10.

157. Arce, *Cooper*, 248. "Gary Cooper 'King' of the Box Office," *New York Times*, December 31, 1953, 11.

158. Zinnemann file, Fairbanks Center.

159. Zinnemann, "Conscience," 34. He has said that *Member of the Wedding* was his favorite even if it didn't quite work.

160. Fairbanks Center.

161. Buckley, "Zinnemann," 34–35.

Part V

THE FILM AS FILM

Chapter 11

A Citizen Named Kane

In retrospect, the greatest single piece of luck in the long and convoluted making of *High Noon* was the hiring of the actor who "made" *High Noon*. Gary Cooper's performance as the tortured Will Kane would become a touchstone of film acting, and not only for those who voted for Academy Awards. It was not simply a matter of being right for the part; it was the sheer timeliness—the extraordinary opportunity two contrarian filmmakers had been given to turn the Capra populist hero, which Cooper had embodied, to an unexpected use by his mere presence.

Even before he had been Longfellow Deeds, Cooper had been that other rural hero, the Western star, since *The Virginian* in 1929. Long before he appeared in William Wyler's 1940 *The Westerner*, Cooper evoked the image of the "Westerner" in the mind of the public, whether the film actually was a Western or not, because he was, even in big-city roles, the epitome of the stalwart small-town boy. Whether it was as *The Plainsman* (1936) or the hero of the previous year's *Lives of a Bengal Lancer*, he was a Westerner in values and manner, if not in locale. He would remain the Westerner until *Man of the West* (1958) and *The Hanging Tree* (1959)—nearly his last films.

Though most of his films were not Westerns—he made twenty in the third of a century between *The Winning of Barbara Worth* in 1926 and *The Hanging Tree*—he would, along with John Wayne, come to be thought of as the epitome of the cowboy hero as the sound Western developed its characteristic conventions, saw them blossom, and then turn on themselves. When *High Noon* was released, *Life* magazine noted that in *The Virginian*, "Cooper took the archetypal cowboy character established by Owen Wister . . . and gave it his own embellishments. By some trick of nature he managed to look both shy and sheepish, fierce and valiant, and occasionally, in a quiet way, almost kittenish. . . . [Now, in *High Noon*,] at times he has a nobility of bearing that is genuinely Lincolnesque."[1]

Like all stars, he carried iconographical baggage: People expected him to be the hero. Almost by accident, since his casting had been something of an afterthought, Kramer, Foreman, and Zinnemann had been able to take advantage of Cooper's unique position in the public eye, both as star persona and as conservative. "In the public's mind, the star personified both the social idealism of Capra's *Mr. Deeds* and *John Doe* and the laconic, fearless Westerner of *The Virginian* and *The Plainsman*. Much of the impact of *High Noon* results from the humiliation its hero/star must endure. Audiences are genuinely shocked—and moved—by Cooper's profound vulnerability."[2]

The filmmakers needed the exact opposite of John Wayne. "Cooper was the quiet American—strong and resolute, capable of doubt, incapable of cruelty. It was the gentleness that set him apart from actors such as John Wayne and James Stewart, who could be aggressively harsh. In contrast to them, Cooper was solitary and shy, with a terrible anxiety at the heart of his personality."[3]

They also needed the exact opposite of the early Cooper. Will Kane could not project a superhuman confidence, but neither could he be a boy. He must be world-weary, profoundly aware of his own mortality, and yet obviously at home in his body and master of his profession. In the earlier Westerns he had operated within the confines of the Code and the conventions, and *High Noon* was "cracking" both.

High Noon is a summary of the Cooper screen persona, the epitome of the "brave but modest" man[4] who is ill at ease in unfamiliar settings. Except for the passing boyishness of the wedding scene—his one happy moment in the film—he is grave, his face drawn, the early mannerisms suppressed, the role underplayed, with the eyes and the mouth revealing all. The ravages of time disturb the audience, who remember him from his youthful heroism, and make them receptive to his anguish and his fear.

It seems fated that Cooper would be directed in *High Noon* by Fred Zinnemann, an "actor's director" who encouraged his performers to underplay their roles. Zinnemann had already made a career out of movies about "crises of conscience," with protagonists who are "intelligent, proud, . . . articulate, [and] slow to act, yet finally aroused to pursue a defiant course which sometimes leads to defeat. . . . Most of the protagonists are reluctant loners, men and women who long to be part of a larger social unit yet are unable in the end to pay the price—a yielding of personal identity."[5]

The Zinnemann hero must, above all, be true to himself and his duty—once he decides what that duty is. "Inevitably Zinnemann's heroes are figures apart, for they cannot fulfill themselves as cogs in a wheel; even if they are married they must resolve their problems themselves. The intense isolation of Zinnemann's characters was embodied in its most quintessential form in *High Noon*."[6]

Zinnemann was regularly described as a "social-realist" director, one who brought a restrained, documentary-like style to the telling of strongly plotted, politically themed stories that avoided sentiment and rarely strayed into the comic—and thus he was in every respect the opposite of Capra, Ford, and Hawks. If camaraderie and traditional institutions were the ne plus ultra for Ford and Hawks, Zinnemann's focus was always on something larger—the community from which that lone individual felt cut off. Zinnemann, as those who decried *High Noon* were only too eager to point out, was a foreigner who had worked his way up in the film industry after emigrating from his native Austria. He had worked briefly with the documentarian Robert Flaherty, whom he always claimed as his mentor,[7] and had made a film in Mexico called *The Wave* (1935), before moving to MGM, in 1937, to direct shorts. He would say that this experience "proved to be invaluable training when the time came for shooting complicated, jigsaw puzzle pictures like *High Noon*, in twenty-eight days."[8] He learned to tell a story quickly and economically, and there would be little time for relaxed moments.[9]

The first feature that allowed him to pursue the themes for which he would always be known was *The Seventh Cross* (1944), a film that *High Noon* would echo—and reject—in important ways. Spencer Tracy plays a political prisoner who escapes a concentration camp in prewar Germany and is heartened to find that while some of his countrymen will betray him to the pursuing Nazis, many others will help him despite the danger they face. Zinnemann said that it foreshadowed *High Noon*,[10] but there is a crucial difference—Will Kane will not find his faith in humanity similarly restored.

Zinnemann would make two more notable pictures before his MGM contract ended. He employed a semidocumentary style and nonprofessional actors in supporting roles in *The Search*, the story of an American soldier helping a boy find the mother from whom he has been separated in the confusion of war.[11] And he made a film noir called *Act of Violence* (1949), which, like *High Noon*, is about a man seeking revenge and also about a man's difficult relationship with his townspeople. But here the genial protagonist is the "villain," and the bitter man seeking revenge is the victim. Though he would make only two more films in the semidocumentary style— *The Men* (1950) and *Teresa* (1951), which was concerned with the problems of an American soldier and his Italian war bride— Zinnemann would now move into Stanley Kramer's world of independent production, finding there a connection between that style of economical filmmaking and his own concern for unsentimental stories that were "grounded in real, lived human experience" and imagery free of "elaborate visual or technical gimmickry."[12]

With the technical preparation provided by his documentary shorts and the thematic preparation of *The Seventh Cross* and *Act of Violence*, he was ready to make *High Noon*. But his social-realist style, his European background, his association with Kramer, his political commitment, and most important, the way in which he would shoot *High Noon*, would all make him a target of the critics of committed filmmaking.

If *High Noon* is in one sense the story of a failed community, it is also the story of what it means to "grow up," to be mature—which is to say, to be able to have what Zinnemann would call a "crisis of conscience." Kane, of course, is the one mature citizen in Hadleyville (though not necessarily the only smart one—the judge and the mayor in particular are wily, and pragmatists by their own lights). Kane is doing what a man has to do, and besides, running is no good. He is an altruist—but one very much grounded in the realities of his world. His repeated comment, "It seems to me I've got to stay," represents both his sense of obligation—after all, by doing his duty as marshal he "caused" the trouble that is now coming back to haunt both him and the town—and his well-founded fear, not simply his moral choice.

Kane's choices are in fact far more complicated than they appear, both on their own terms and in the terms of the elaborate tale that Foreman and Zinnemann are telling. For one thing, by refusing to leave when he is expected to, and when the people he thought were his friends want him to, Kane is put in an anomalous position—he becomes a defender who is no longer wanted, a rebellious lawman.[13] The standard assumption is that Foreman wrote the screenplay this way either to provide protective cover for a leftist assault on the "vital center" or to take ironic advantage of Gary Cooper's well-known anticommunism and his appearance in King Vidor's earlier adaptation of conservative ideologue Ayn Rand's celebration of selfish individualism, *The Fountainhead* (1949). But Foreman got the original inspiration for his screenplay in 1948—either on his own or from Cunningham's short story—and Cooper was hired only after the screenplay was well along in the writing.

The reason the rebel against the townspeople is the lawman is quite simple—the story of desertion doesn't work otherwise; private citizens aren't "abandoned" in the same sense. The irony, ultimately, is not Cooper's presence; it is that the townspeople "fear for their 'safety and security' should the lawman remain among them."[14]

The lawman is not only a "rebel," he is a kind of internal exile, because he will discover that his once-exalted position counts for nothing. "That nothing in Hadleyville 'is really important' [as the judge tells Kane] makes Kane's decision to stay an existential one, done for its own sake in a moral vacuum."[15] It's not a vacuum to Kane, but perhaps to us. Kane "really cannot appreciate how the crisis before him will turn into one not of mind, intelligence and the will to act, but of faith," observes Sam Girgus.

> He will be left entirely alone and be brought to the extremes of despair and anguish as he comes to realize that his effort does not seem to mean anything to anyone but himself. Believing that he acts for everyone, he finds himself alone. Looking for validation from the townspeople, he grows aware of his total disagreement with them. Expecting to gain legitimacy for his efforts through their approval, he becomes the object of their ridicule and the cause of their embarrassment. No longer certain as to how to measure or know the truth, he finally has to act totally upon faith in himself.[16]

The best that can be said of the church-people's feeling toward him, as Harvey tells Will in the stable, is "nobody wants to see you get killed." It is undoubtedly true, and a perfect measure of his transformation into an embarrassment.

Kane is in a kind of limbo—an extraordinary limbo that is rarely so thoroughly elaborated in movies. The threat to his life has been thrust on him completely out of the blue. Having turned in his badge, he is no longer marshal but a private citizen. His replacement is expected the next day. But he and everyone around him still *see* him as marshal. He has married and expects to begin a new life in a new place and a new occupation, as a storekeeper. He is trying to leave town on his own terms rather than being forced out or threatened with violence then or later. His marriage seems to have ended before it has begun. With his wife leaving him and the townspeople abandoning him, he is in effect homeless. (We never do see him at home.) He quickly learns he is alone, but he doesn't know he is until he calls on the help of his friends. Even though he is the object of revenge rather than the revenge-seeker, he will still learn in the course of doing what he thinks is right that he is not, and may never have been, truly a part of the community, which is not as hostile to the revenge-seekers as he thought.

As a man whose life has revolved around protecting the community, he is caught between two powerful but conflicting messages: the threat to the community generally and women in particular, as against the advantage to the community in general from Northern investment and to the yahoos looking for good times. The problem is that he and the others can only guess at the nature of the threat (other than to him) and of the promise.

He has almost no time until the train arrives; it is almost as though he is suspended in time. His life becomes totally structured by the clocks he constantly checks. Between the tolling of the church bell and the blast of the train whistle, he must move quickly around town to raise a posse, warn a potential target of the killers, arm himself, and encounter endless rejection.

As his world contracts, so, too, does his former position in the town—a position he learns too late was built on sand. He is humiliated by the cowboys in the bar, by old allies, by the church-people. He hears his coffin being built in back of the barber shop, he is lied to by his friend's wife, he runs into kids shouting "Bang, you're dead, Kane," he watches his new wife and his old lover ride past him out of town, he writes his will.[17] No wonder he is reduced to tears.

In light of all this suffering, why does Will Kane do what he does? In fact, his decision to stay and fight is not quite the "crisis of conscience" its director and many others have called it. It is both ambiguously motivated and overdetermined; that is to say, it's not obvious on reflection that he must stay, as he says, but at the same time he gives too many reasons and no very clear ones for facing the killers.[18]

As he and Amy are being rushed onto their wagon for the ride out of town, he says only, "I think I ought to stay." When he stops the wagon on the prairie a few minutes later, he exclaims in exasperation, "This is crazy. I haven't even got any guns." A moment later he says "They're making me run. I've never run from anybody before." It's not clear if he's referring to the Miller gang or to his erstwhile friends, but it is his first clear statement of a reason, and it is obviously pride—and some frustration—that is motivating him. "The . . . song," says Philip French, "tells us that he must 'be brave and . . . face a man who hates me or lie a coward . . . in my grave.'" It's not duty that concerns him first, despite that word in the song's next stanza. He doesn't want to be remembered as a coward.[19]

That scene on the prairie is fraught—not only with Will's internal struggle, but with our effort to read it. It is the beginning of a disturbing process in which Kane will ricochet from self-interested friend to self-interested friend, find that he is not in control, stumble, and frequently—or so it appears—rationalize what he is doing.

Notes Jennifer Lawrence in a contrarian, feminist analysis,

> We . . . accept without question the value of 'facing the enemy,' even when there is clearly no real need to do so. Will, in turning the horse around, has determined to create a conflict, and perhaps our response to such an action should mirror Amy's: "Well, I don't understand any of this." Will, however, has "no time to explain." . . . He makes up the rules, it seems, as he goes along, rationalizing his actions after the fact. There is never an appeal to the safety and well-being of others, and rightly so, for Will's presence in Hadleyville is the element that will ultimately lead to the violence. . . . What is clear from Will's grim face and serious demeanor throughout the film is that he does not want to stay in Hadleyville. What is not clear, then, is why he stays. Despite Will's lack of ability to explain reasons for his actions, and his seeming lack of clear vision, he forces Amy, in his first hour or two of their marriage, to return to Hadleyville with him, wait while he engages in life-threatening activity, and finally abandon a highly important moral/religious belief.[20]

Actually, Kane will hold on to both manhood and wife because she has (however briefly) "suspended" her beliefs in extremis—though there's no actual reason to suppose she has given up her Quaker ideals permanently.

A few minutes later, back in the office, Kane adds three more reasons—that the new marshal "won't be here till tomorrow. Seems to me I've got to stay. Anyway, I'm the same man—with or without this [star]"—a summary judgment of his character and of his view of his role. And a moment later, "They'll just come after us. Four of them, and we'd be all alone on the prairie." When she accuses him of pridefulness, he replies, "I'm not trying to be a hero! If you think I like this, you're crazy!" And then, realizing how harsh he sounds, he tries a new tack: "Look, Amy. This is my town. I've got friends here. I'll swear in a bunch of special deputies. With a posse behind me, maybe there won't even be any trouble."

Minutes later he tells the judge, "I figured I had to [come back]. I figured I had to stay." The judge tells him to leave—and then, by packing up and leaving, underscores what Will had told Amy about always having to run. The judge is not a coward,[21] but he's also not a gunman—and he knows perfectly well what is likely to happen.

Along with all his other justifications, Will is trying to hold on to his social ties. "Will's decision to return isn't just a matter of personal courage, or fighting, rather than running, but is also an attempt to reclaim his social membership within a community," observes Stephen Prince. "By going back, Kane chooses to make the social space of the town the arena for his fight rather than become a man without a society. He chooses fraternity over isolation, and it is the narrative irony which entails that the community will not honor the choice he has made."[22]

Many writers, noting Will's focus on his obligation, have trouble figuring out why he would stick around to help such undeserving people. But his decision to help is made long before they desert him. That is the first choice: He is torn between a specific promise to his wife—to give up his guns and leave for a peaceful life—and a career-long sense of obligation. It is only after the people, one by one for their own reasons, abandon him, that the choice becomes more complicated. Now it is his life *and* his wife he is immediately at risk of losing. Some of the reasons he gave Amy have been stripped away, and only the unarticulated—because inarticulate—obligation remains.

Kane's choice is thus "overdetermined," which is to say, he has no choice. This is an important point to the film's critics, who feel suffocated by a plot they consider manipulative. But the critics must misread the film to make their points. Richard Maltby, who has mounted perhaps the most sustained criticism of the film from an auteurist point of view, notes that Kane never smiles—as if anyone could in the midst of a nightmare—and claims that the marshal's seriousness substitutes for a discussion of his "moral dilemma."

Maltby insists, incorrectly, that "not only is there not a single joke in the film, there is no light relief of any kind"—not true, as the scenes of the drunk being released from jail and the children delightedly "escaping" church prove. Finally, says Maltby, the plot points Kane in only one direction—his duty. This is true but reductionist: One must ignore the depth of characterization that permits, for example, his anguished indecision in the stable over saddling the horse and leaving.[23]

Even the song, whether originally intended as such, points to the complexity of a story that moves in a single direction because it is psychologically credible: The song pleads, "'Do not forsake me, O my darling.' Who, we ask, is doing the forsaking? Amy? Will? The town? Like the film, the seemingly simple ballad implies far more than it says."[24]

For instance, what is the now ex-marshal's position in the town? It is not obvious. In walking grimly out of the church, Kane has abandoned the preferences of the church-people, the town's decision makers, and is operating on his own moral sense *and* his reading of his perilous situation. Slotkin says he has become a "vigilante, a private man assuming the power of the law without submitting himself to the democratic process."[25] But that cannot be right: Vigilantes act outside the law and in the temporary absence of legitimate peace officers. Kane is not taking the law into his own hands as an ordinary private citizen would be doing, he's protecting himself in the absence of a peace officer.

Slotkin insists that Kane is no different from the Virginian, or the white-sheeted clansmen of Griffith's *The Birth of a Nation*, or the cavalry men of Ford's trilogy—who all behave as though defending civilization may mean ignoring democratic procedure:

> Kane's ultimate appeal is to the authority of "character" and his "manhood"—the same "red-blooded" principles to which Judge Henry and the Virginian appealed in justifying the lynching of rustlers. Kane is the only man with knowledge, skill and power enough to defeat Miller; and his conscience . . . holds that . . . possession of the power to act entails an absolute responsibility to act, whether or not the action is legal or acceptable to the public. . . . Kane forthrightly asserts the need for pre-emptive violence to prevent atrocities which he (apparently alone) believes are certain to follow Miller's return.[26]

But this is to make of Kane a more arrogant and self-conscious man than he is; he is simply trying to do right by his lights.

Kane's honesty makes his situation worse. He always tells the truth, even when the truth undermines his efforts. He could have told Herb Baker, the one townsman who offered to help, that others had already joined the posse; he could have said he would persuade the town fathers to give Harve the marshal's job. He could even have let the drunk and the teenager pack guns. But he wouldn't—he wouldn't put incompetents at risk, he wouldn't understate the dangers, he wouldn't "buy" Harve's help.[27] He is the last honest man, the man who never veers an inch from the straight and narrow.

Some writers think that the sheer fact that Kane and Miller shared a lover must mean that there is a "dark side" to Kane, that he has a "savage character" that has been repressed. The hint of Kane's savage character, says Slotkin, "is there in the name 'Will Kane,' which combines the suggestion of 'will' as the drive to power with a homonym of the Bible's first murderer."[28] As Cooper biographer Jeffrey Meyers puts it, "The hero's first name suggests his will to defy his wife, face his enemies and defeat them. Kane (the biblical murderer) suggests the dark side of his character: His old affair with Helen . . . , the men he'd killed while enforcing the law, his capability for violence."[29]

But this is to impose a willful misreading, when there are others that make more sense. Notes a legal scholar about the name "Kane": "If Hadleyville has become dependent on Kane for its support—as suggested by the homonym of his last name [cane]—Kane may be an adequate lawman and still fail as a founder. If he made the town safe for the women and children, he made it too safe for the men. And in doing so he did not make it safe enough for anyone."[30]

It is obviously true, in one sense, that that first name "Will" refers to his determination; it also refers to the "last will and testament" he leaves the townspeople. But, like "Kane," "Will" has another, larger meaning. The appropriateness of the hero's name is suggested by an understanding of *High Noon* as an illustration of Kantian ethical theory, which insists that it is a person's intention, or "will," that makes an action moral. As philosopher Gerald Kreyche summarizes Kantian theory, "Only the will can be called good, absolutely, and only when the will acts in conformity with duty will it be good. Hence, one should act so that one's act could be the way each human should act in that situation. This, in effect, is the famous categorical imperative," otherwise known as the Golden Rule.[31] Whoever changed the name of the marshal from Doane to Kane on the set that day in August 1951, was clever—or cleverer than he knew—because the names taken together perfectly describe the film's view of the man, not as a killer, but as a man who must do the right thing, who would be his brother's keeper, the cane on which others lean. As Nichols puts it, Kane stays because he must, because "courage is an end, not simply a means. When Helen Ramirez tells Kane she knows he cannot leave, it is possible she understands the point as well."[32]

Kane didn't simply decide to be brave, decide to do the right thing; he had to realize, as the situation developed, that his options were closing down or completely chimerical. Whatever its auteurist enemies may say, *High Noon*'s screenplay is not about eliminating all choices but one, it is about a man discovering he has no choice if he is to be true to himself.

The key word is "discovering." *High Noon* is about a journey, not a destination. It is about "selfhood, individualism, and dignity. These can be summed up in one word—autonomy." Autonomous people serve ends or goals; they do not manipulate others. That is why Kane cannot lie.[33] In the language of the mass society theorists, it means being free to think for yourself rather than being "other-directed," or looking to what others think you ought to do. As Kreyche notes, rule-following can be risky. "Because he viewed others as members of the kingdom of ends [in Kantian terms], he refused to arrest the three gunslingers waiting for Miller, even though the townspeople were ready enough to have him do so. He recognized their rights as much as his own, explaining 'I didn't have anything to arrest them for, Mr. Trumbull. They haven't done anything. There's no law against them sitting on a bench at the depot.'"[34]

Kane, says Kreyche, "refused the services of the boy who wanted to stand up with him, as well as the offer of the drunk. Kane saw that neither was motivated by duty; the boy wanted excitement and recognition of his coming to be a man—the drunk wanted to restore a false sense of courage and a feeling that he still could be something worthwhile." Kane would not "use" them. Even little things point to his character. After the fight with Harve in the barn, "Kane got cleaned up by the barber. The barber told Kane, 'No charge,' but Kane gave him the money anyway. Duty this time took the form of . . . giving to the other his rightful due. (If Kane was going out of life, like Socrates, he wanted no debts.)"[35] It was also, of course, a contemptuous acknowledgment that the barber expected to make money off his death with those coffins in the back.

Looked at this way, even Kane's most famous act—the one that got Kramer et al. in trouble with John Wayne and the MPA—takes on a different meaning. "Kane's final act in the movie is one of contempt, throwing his badge into the dust," concludes Kreyche. "But the act is as much a condemnation of himself as it is of the townspeople. He is angry that he misread them."[36]

As painful as all of this is, it is necessary if Kane is to become autonomous. Discovering how alienated he is from the community, says Sam Girgus, "constitutes his real awakening to his own existence as an individual with a self-determined identity. He undergoes a midlife transformation and becomes his own man, a rebel-hero, as demonstrated by his final rejection of the town. Intuitively, Wayne and Hawks reacted to this implication behind 'Coop's' rebellious act of discarding the badge into the street."[37]

High Noon is in the end a kind of existential detective story, in which Kane and Helen are the only ones who know the initial rules, the starting point. Thus Kane tells Harvey and Helen tells Amy that if they don't know, they can't explain it to them. You understand or you don't. It's just that Kane doesn't realize at the beginning how little he knows.

"*High Noon* is a movie," says Mary Nichols,

> in which people ask questions that are left unanswered. In particular, they ask unanswered questions about Kane, whom the movie presents as something of an enigma. When Harvey asks Kane why he will not help him become the next marshal in exchange for his support against Miller, Kane answers only that 'if you don't know, it's no use me telling you.' When Kane announces to Amy he is returning, she does not understand. But even after he tells her about Miller, Amy still does not understand his decision. Just as Harvey suspects that Kane is angry about him and Helen Ramirez, Amy suspects that Kane is staying because of Helen. They are as mistaken as Mart, who although he has been a lawman all his life, thinks that someone staying under such circumstances must want to commit suicide. By the end of the movie, even Kane himself does not seem certain of what moves him, for he admits to Harvey, perhaps in a moment of weakness, that he himself doesn't know why he can't leave.[38]

To be autonomous, one must be mature. *High Noon* is overwhelmingly concerned with maturity and what it takes to be a man— though the question is asked in more, and more complicated, ways than in traditional Westerns, where it is never articulated more clearly than, "a man's got to do what a man's got to do." It's really a matter of reaching a certain point of understanding, rather than a question of being macho, or reacting to one's hormones, or being violent. The language here is deceptive, because it seems, over and over, to be about "growing up," about being a "man." Kane is not simply some "masculine" principle, or the agent of "gun law"; he is the agent of law itself in a situation where there is no one else around to enforce, it and the gun is unavoidable.

The characters in *High Noon* are obsessed with this problem of "growing up," of the relations between the generations.[39] Will is a father figure by virtue of his age compared to Amy, and his position vis-à-vis Harvey. (In the original script, Will and Amy were much closer in age.) This contrast between youth and mature middle age is ever-present in the conflict between Kane and the youthful Harve and between Kane and the even younger Amy. It governs the relationship between Helen and Amy, who may be only a few years apart in age but have experienced the world in vastly different ways. The older, obviously mature characters are constantly asking the younger ones when they'll grow up. Pierce chides Ben Miller for his childish behavior, Helen irritates Harve with her talk of his immaturity, and Kane suggests that Harve was passed over for the marshal's job because of his behavior.[40]

Will negotiates with father figures who fail him—the judge who presided over the marriage is the ultimate frontier realist who is now fleeing; the old marshal is a cynic based on his own experience; the mayor is looking out for the town with an eye to its industrial future, not its prairie past.

In a sense, Will fails as a father figure: The age difference is particularly crucial to an understanding of Will's tormented relationship with Harve Pell. Viewing their fistfight through the lens of traditional Western coding, Jane Tomkins notes that "Gary Cooper . . . has to slug it out at length with a man half his age before facing Frank Miller and his gang. . . . The physical punishment heroes take is not incidental to their role; it is constitutive of it. Prolonged and deliberate laceration of the flesh, endured without complaint, is a *sine qua non* of masculine achievement. It indicates the control the man can exercise over his body and his feelings."[41]

But the real importance of the fistfight is less as a proof of Kane's superiority before the gunfight than as a struggle with a younger man who represents the self Kane might have been, the "other-directed," immature, jealous man who fails. Harve is the man who cannot grow up, who can't look beyond his own self-interest.

Helen doesn't make the situation any easier. Late in the story she says to the callow deputy, "I'm going to tell you something about you and your friend Kane. You're a nice looking boy. You have big wide shoulders. But he is a man. . . . It takes more than big wide shoulders to make a man, Harvey. And you've got a long way to go. . . . You know something? I don't think you'll ever make it."[42] Because she has been a lover to both, the remark seems to be as much about a sexual relationship as about maturity. And this from a woman whose breakup with Kane remains completely unexplained.

Harve is jealous in every way. Says Lee Clark Mitchell, he is an "ambitious deputy, who harbors growing resentment at Kane's refusal to be a mentor. Harvey first interprets this stance as a paternal judgment that he is 'too young',' but Kane's intransigence turns the conflict into an Oedipal struggle, as Harvey now suspects that his affair with Kane's ex-lover lies at the heart of the matter."[43] Actually, Kane has been Harve's mentor for quite some time, we gather. Whatever lessons were offered, by word or by deed, obviously didn't take. Harve has no self-confidence, despite his braggadocio (some of which was left out of the revised script), because he is a man whose abilities must be confirmed by others for him to believe in them himself.[44] Harve has no choice; he must assault Kane, "thereby destroying the father figure."[45]

Kane has experienced endless betrayal. But his nightmare is far from unique in American film. We have been misled by the time of day: Though his story takes place during the blaze of noon, it was inspired by the moral darkness of noir.

NOTES

1. "'Highpockets' Cooper in *High Noon*," *Life Magazine* 34 (August 25, 1952): 79.

2. Louis Giannetti, *Masters of the American Cinema* (Englewood Cliffs, N.J.: Prentice-Hall, 1981), 369–70.

3. Scott Eyman, review of *Gary Cooper Off Camera* (New York: Harry N. Abrams, 1999), by Maria Cooper Janis, *Palm Beach Post*, October 26, 1999, 1D.

4. Stuart M. Kaminsky, *Coop* (New York: St. Martin's Press, 1980), 162.

5. Giannetti, *Masters*, 364–65.

6. Alan Stanbrook, "A Man for All Movies, the Films of Fred Zinnemann, part II," *Films and Filming* 13 (June 1967): 11.

7. Fred Zinnemann, *A Life in the Movies: An Autobiography* (New York: Scribner, 1992), 25–26.

8. Zinnemann, *A Life*, 42.

9. Giannetti, *Masters*, 357.

10. Zinnemann, *A Life*, 50.

11. John Fitzpatrick, "Fred Zinnemann," in *American Directors, Volume II*, ed. Jean-Pierre Coursodon with Pierre Sauvage (New York: McGraw-Hill, 1983), 379.

12. Stephen Prince, "Historical Perspective and the Realist Aesthetic in *High Noon* (1952)," in *The Films of Fred Zinnemann*, ed. Arthur Nolletti Jr. (Albany: State University of New York Press, 1999), 81.

13. Stephen J. Whitfield, *The Culture of the Cold War* (Baltimore: Johns Hopkins University Press, 1996), 147; Nora Sayre, *Running Time* (New York: Dial Press, 1982), 176.

14. Whitfield, *Culture*, 147.

15. Bruce F. Kawin, *How Movies Work* (New York: Macmillan, 1987), 508.

16. Sam B. Girgus, *Hollywood Renaissance* (Cambridge: Cambridge University Press, 1998), 148.

17. Girgus, *Hollywood*, 151.

18. Mike Selig, *Cinema Texas Program Notes* (Department of Radio/Television/Film, University of Texas at Austin, vol. 16, no. 2, February 28, 1979), 6; Jennifer A. Lawrence, "If I Only Had the Nerve: A Feminist Critique of *High Noon*" (paper presented to the Popular Culture Association, Philadelphia, Pennsylvania, April 15, 1995), 1.

19. Philip French, *Westerns* (London: Secker & Warburg, 1977), 101–2.

20. Lawrence, "If Only I Had the Nerve," 3.

21. Mary P. Nichols, "Law and the American Western: *High Noon*," *The Legal Studies Forum* 22, no. 4 (1998): 595.

22. Prince, "Realist Aesthetic," 86–88.

23. Richard Maltby, *Harmless Entertainment* (Metuchen, N.J.: Scarecrow Press, 1983), 273. Maltby sees only an endlessly reinforcing façade—"Cooper's scenes of doubt reinforce his heroic status, because he makes the right decision"—rather than a decision that might actually be made.

24. Nichols, "Law," 603.

25. Richard Slotkin, *Gunfighter Nation* (New York: Atheneum, 1992), 394.

26. Slotkin, *Gunfighter Nation*, 394.

27. This is the script's most direct reference to Foreman's own troubles; he had said the same thing to his wife when he was subpoenaed.

28. Slotkin, *Gunfighter Nation*, 394.

29. Jeffrey Meyers, *Gary Cooper* (New York: Morrow, 1998), 243.

30. Nichols, "Law," 604.

31. Gerald Kreyche, "*High Noon*—A Paradigm of Kant's Moral Philosophy," *Teaching Philosophy* 11, no. 3 (September 1988): 223. Kreyche also notes that ethics and religion are the same to Kant—posing a problem for the church-people, if Will is the only truly ethical man among them.

32. Nichols, "Law," 597.

33. Kreyche, "Paradigm," 224.

34. Kreyche, "Paradigm," 226.

35. Kreyche, "Paradigm," 228.

36. Kreyche, "Paradigm," 227.

37. Girgus, *Hollywood*, 150–51.

38. Nichols, "Law," 596–97.

39. Don Graham, "*High Noon* (1952)," in William T. Pilkington and Don Graham, *Western Movies* (Albuquerque: University of New Mexico Press, 1979), 55.

40. Donald Spoto, *Stanley Kramer: Filmmaker* (New York: Putnam, 1978), 106–7.

41. Jane Tompkins, *West of Everything* (New York: Oxford University Press, 1992), 105.

42. Shots, Screenplay of *High Noon*, in *Film Scripts Two*, ed. George P. Garrett, O. B. Harrison Jr., and Jane R. Gelfman (New York: Meredith Corporation, 1971), 177–82.

43. Lee Clark Mitchell, *Westerns* (Chicago: University of Chicago Press, 1996), 200.

44. Mitchell, *Westerns*, 218.

45. Mitchell, *Westerns*, 179–80.

Chapter 12

Noir at High

Cooper enters a long and desolate night of the soul as the heat gathers, his fellow citizens scatter, and it grows dark, dark, dark amid the blaze of noon.

—Sheila Johnston[1]

The great film puts the genre and the culture into question, permanently altering both by means of its defiance of meaning and its simultaneous search for a true meaning.

—Dudley Andrew[2]

High Noon was attacked for its Western revisionism and for sneaking contemporary politics into a genre picture. The Left saw it as an undemocratic privileging of a superior individual, the Right imagined an attack on capitalism, and everyone assumed it was an assault on "the people."

It became the bête noire of the auteurists and others who despaired of Hollywood conformity. It seemed to them the perfect example of a trend they saw taking over studio filmmaking in the wake of the Red Scare and the blacklist—the mix of psychologically acute characterization, tightly written scripts, documentary-like photography, and political commitment they called, contemptuously, "liberal filmmaking."

They were blaming the victims. *High Noon* was no doubt a product of its times, but it reflected a change brought about by the only filmmakers in the late 1940s who were able to deal in political issues at a time when anything not flag waving was forbidden. These were the makers of film noir, which, together with social realism, inspired the variants—film gris and the noir-inflected Western—that would in turn inspire *High Noon*.

After all the concern about Red Scare allegories, subversion of genre, metteur-en-scène cliché, and questions of conscience and masculinity, *High Noon* must finally be understood outside the traditional categories, because it fits none and is reduced by being included among them. Will Kane is far more than the straw man "liberal" figure; he is the anguished, ethical man seeking an authentic life. If other films seemed drained of political spunk by the terrors of the time, *High Noon* never lost sight of its goal.

That is why it has come under such sustained attack from those who consider themselves the enemies of "bourgeois art." The worldwide admiration it has inspired over half a century has made it a target too big to ignore.

It was the Kramer connection that would ultimately evoke the most contemptuous of the analyses, the ones mounted by auteurists. The auteurist critique is remarkable for its ability to conflate Fred Zinnemann and Carl Foreman with Stanley Kramer, films made in the depths of the Red Scare with films made at the end of the decade, subtle films like *High Noon* with routine genre pieces—and films like *Champion*, made by filmmakers learning the ropes, with films that revealed mastery.

To mount their attack the critics had worked both forward—from the pulled punches of *Home of the Brave*—and backward, from Kramer's big, personal projects—*The Defiant Ones*, *On the Beach*, *Inherit the Wind*, and *Judgment at Nuremberg*—that won him praise from newspaper reviewers for dealing with "important" issues. The auteurists despised these films as message-mongering, destructive of good filmic principles, and many then looked to the one film he had had the least to do with—*High Noon*—and found the same "unfilmic" approach at work there.

Their ability to note the larger context in which *High Noon* was produced and then ignore its real implications was both astounding and depressing. Liberalism, they said, began as a defense against the Red Scare but soon became the controlling point of view in Hollywood—one that was embarrassed to admit that it controlled. That *High Noon* had resorted to indirection, like the other films of the period, because it was not safe to be explicit, and that it had been created by artists with a powerful vision, was, to the auteurists, irrelevant. That *High Noon* might reflect only Kramer's general themes, but not his directorial approach—because he was barely involved its making—was not a consideration.

The principal charge against *High Noon* has always been that it is manipulative, pretending to deal with important issues but in fact being paternalistic, draining all that is "political" from the film by turning every issue into a personal problem in which politics are kept vague, studio censorship is implicitly justified, heroes are righteous, character determines everything, the plot is one-directional, and the complexities of the real world are ignored.[3]

The particular importance of *High Noon* to the auteurists is that it is the central document in this reorientation toward the spurious that is supposed to have happened in the wake of the Red Scare. "Social Realism survived rightwing attempts to stifle it by compromising," claims Richard Maltby. After the 1947 Waldorf Statement creating the blacklist,

> liberals accepted the imperatives of loyalty to the industry. In turn, it accommodated their consciences. When in [1953] Gary Cooper, archetype of the populist consensus and HUAC friendly witness, won the Best Actor Academy Award for *High Noon*, Hollywood's liberal compromise was institutionalized . . . largely [securing] for itself the conventional structures of American cinematic narrative, and [recasting] them in its own image, to its own ends.[4]

This liberal "social realism," said the critics, substituted character for action and masochism and inarticulateness for the masculine certainty of John Wayne.[5] Everything was seen through the protagonist's viewpoint, even to the point of shooting him in close-up or through windows to reinforce the emotional connection of the audience. The new hero was "passive, defensive, [emotionally vulnerable, and] unwilling to or unable to take the initiative himself but prepared and capable of committing himself to action in defense of a principle, and, if necessary, of sacrificing himself to it." This hero connected with the audience emotionally, rather than through what he actually did, as Wayne's action heroes had.[6] The point was to remove any idea the audience might have that the hero has a choice. "The characters around Cooper serve to provide excuse for his self-explanation; importantly, their discussions avoid or misinterpret the real motive for his actions, which is left to be tacitly understood by the audience and, finally, by Grace Kelly."[7] Kane, in this reductionist view, is the pure liberal hero, a flawed-if-noble man who must in some way be defeated in a world that is otherwise deterministic.

To hold this view required ignoring the obvious—that all plots are designed to go in one direction, even if they seem as free and easy as Hawks made them look. But it also dismisses the sophistication of the characters as nothing more than a device to undercut action—as though movies in general, and Westerns in particular, must always rely on two-dimensional characters and breezy one-liners for their charm.

Far more important, the auteurist attack ascribes a power to the social-realist filmmakers they did not have—not to mention insisting that they were doing something different from what had always been done. To say that the liberal view dominated Hollywood moviemaking[8] is to seriously misrepresent the position these politically committed filmmakers found themselves in, their response to their situation, and their ultimate effect on American film. What Maltby sees as a liberal conquest of Hollywood narrative would be more accurately characterized, after the evisceration of the Left, as the modification of the standard-issue "social problem" film, in which larger social explanations are replaced by individual criminal action, with an overlay of the new method acting from Broadway and its attendant psychological approach to characterization.

As Roffman and Purdy note, the movies continued to deal with issues in the semineutered style that had ruled since the arrival of sound and the Production Code two decades earlier:

> Matters of race, juvenile delinquency, prison conditions, political corruption, and big business were dramatized throughout the fifties as conflicts between shysters and liberal redeemers, between victims and victimizers. . . . There was no need for HUAC to control politics in movies since the politics were already inoffensive. Still, the number of these films did decline and, more importantly, the dramatic urgency characteristic of the genre throughout the thirties and forties was for the most part lacking in the fifties. If this cannot be traced directly to HUAC, it can be traced to a new cultural temper of which HUAC was an ingredient. McCarthyism signaled the end of the era of social idealism that had so permeated the Depression and postwar years and had given the problem film genre its vitality.[9]

"Institutionalization" is, thus, hardly the word to describe the approach of those filmmakers who had barely survived. And these are people whose pointed dialogue, plotting, and characterization had always been subject to the "neutering" hand of the studios. It was just that now, self-censorship replaced the heavy hand of the studios' official censors, the Breen Office.[10]

If the Left was going to continue to make movies with what might be loosely described as a Left point of view, they would have to rely increasingly on independent filmmaking and allegorical content. What they did was to cast about for a seemingly safe way to talk about American society, and what they found was an established form that had never had an explicit political content—film noir. Here was a "genre" that seemed at the very least apolitical and was usually characterized as cynical about politics—a common confusion of the attitudes of the characters with those of the filmmakers.

The studios had been making these bleak visions of urban corruption and betrayal since the early 1940s. American studios had invented film noir, but it wouldn't be recognized for what it was until the same French critics who discovered American auteurs toiling away in the studio vineyards also discovered "dark films."

What better place than a studio "B" film, intended for the lower end of a double feature in urban movie theaters, for "idiosyncratic" artists buried in the bowels of the machine to do their "subversive" thing, undermining "generic conventions."[11] Precisely because these films were low status even in their own studios, "the creative workers enjoyed more autonomy from the front office, pressure groups, and—arguably—the Breen Office." In other words, those who made politically keyed noirs—and some did not—flew under the political radar, so long as their political commentary was not explicit. And because their makers had a relatively free hand, they could explore serious issues.[12]

However stylized and generalized, film noir attempted to capture the audience's sense of social disruption and increasing government involvement in their lives during and after a hot war that quickly gave way to a cold one internationally and, after the unity of the war, the return of ideological conflict and competing group interests at home.

Early noir, before the end of the war, focused on criminal behavior. After the war, the "lighting grew darker, characters more corrupt, themes more fatalistic, and the tone more hopeless. By 1949, American movies were in the throes of their deepest and most creative funk. Never before had films dared to take such a harsh uncomplimentary look at American life, and they would not dare to do so again for twenty years."[13] The recurrent themes involved "the corrosive power of money," oppressive class distinctions, and an absence of a sense of community[14] in films with titles such as *Force of Evil* (1948), *The Dark Past* (1948), *Caught* (1949), *Cry of the City* (1948), *Act of Violence* (1949), and *They Live by Night* (1949).[15]

The noir protagonist is an ordinary man trying desperately to find out why his once-familiar life has turned into a nightmare in which he is assaulted by his enemies, some of them psychopaths, and betrayed by his friends. His world is a labyrinth—often conveyed by elaborate plot twists and flashbacks—from which he struggles to escape. He "must uncover a secret, expose a lie or a conspiracy, and no one is safe from suspicion," summarizes Joan Mellen. "It is always urgent to move swiftly because the plot revolves around matters of life and death."[16]

"So labyrinthine and deep-rooted is the corruption of the community in most *films noirs*," notes Mellen, "that it is beyond the power of any individual to redress it,"[17] and the women, while sometimes totally supportive of the hero, are mostly evil. At some point the hero is filled with an existential bitterness, resigning himself to his own destruction. "Once the story has been told, nothing changes, and no one is better off."[18]

The classic noir takes place at night; scenes are underlit, with light and dark contrasts (chiaroscuro), shadows and silhouettes, unusual camera angles or lenses underscoring the unexpected and the dangerous.[19] It is shot in black and white, despite the increasing availability of inexpensive color photography, because black and white can seem more realistic even as it is being stylized.[20]

The threat to the hero is often conveyed by the framing alone, rather than by physical action.[21] He is constantly being framed by objects—clocks, mirrors, banisters, windows—almost as if he were being impaled. "Directors working with *noir* stories," says Foster Hirsch,

> avoid openness and horizontality; the sense of space, the feeling for landscape that distinguish a Ford Western or a Griffith epic have no place within the *noir* frame. . . . In *noir*, narrative continuity is typically achieved through tight cutting rather than a roving camera. Even tracking shots are used to create tension rather than the smooth, loose, flowing quality that such movement often imparts. Close-ups abound, creating a sense of claustrophobia. . . . The high angle overhead shot, the most unheroic of perspectives, a visual signal of impending doom, may be the most frequently used camera placement in *noir*.[22]

Noir was a welcome alternative for what remained of the Hollywood Left. As James Naremore notes,

> most of the 1940s directors subsequently associated with the form—
> including Orson Welles, John Huston, Edward Dmytryk, Jules Dassin,
> Joseph Losey, Robert Rossen, Abraham Polonsky, and Nicholas Ray—
> were members of Hollywood's committed leftwing community. . . .
> The credits for *noir* screenplays usually included such names as Albert
> Maltz, Howard Koch, Waldo Salt, and Dalton Trumbo, all of whom
> were eventually blacklisted.[23]

In the late 1940s these and others on the Left had been forced to rely on a generalized allegory that could only hint at social problems. The "racism" of *Storm Warning* (1951), starring those two fixtures of the MPA, Ronald Reagan and Ginger Rogers, involved the lynching of whites by whites. Fascism took the form of prison guards in *Brute Force* (1947), gangsters in *Key Largo* (1948), and politicians in *All the King's Men* (1949). Anti-Semites were psychopaths (*Crossfire*, 1947), rapacious capitalism was overshadowed by Christmas and angels in *It's a Wonderful Life* (1946) and by melodrama in *The Strange Love of Martha Ivers* (1946),[24] and the Bomb was overshadowed by fantasy in *The Boy with Green Hair* (1948). The Red Scare itself was represented by a screenwriter (Humphrey Bogart) being blacklisted not for his politics but for his drinking in *In a Lonely Place* (1950)[25] and by comedy in *People Will Talk* (1951), which "included subtle references both to McCarthy and to the dispute in the Screen Directors Guild . . . over loyalty oaths."[26]

If the overarching vision of *High Noon* is broadly inspired by film noir, its specific incarnation is more in the style of noir's socially committed cousin, film gris, or "gray film." "*Film gris*," according to Tom Andersen, who originated the term, "may be distinguished from the earlier *film noir* by its greater psychological and social realism. . . . These films are often drab and depressing and almost always photographed in black and white."[27] The focus in these films, which draw on the conventions of film noir, is on a greater psychological and social realism—on the material, rather than the psychological, torment of the protagonist.[28] "The unreality of the American dream is a constant theme in *film gris*."[29] These films are at the other end of the spectrum of noir from the cynical, even misanthropic efforts of a Billy Wilder.[30]

Few films actually qualify as film gris—Andersen counts a mere thirteen, all made between the two sets of HUAC hearings in 1947 and 1951—and most were directed by men whose careers were destroyed or damaged by the blacklist: Robert Rossen, Abraham Polonsky, Jules Dassin, Joseph Losey, Cy Endfield, and John Berry. The survivors were Nicholas Ray, John Huston, and Michael Curtiz.

Gris films are unrelievedly bleak tales (frequently filled with cautious references to HUAC) of desperate criminals, lynchings, racial hysteria, destructive capitalism, greed, and betrayed idealists: Jules Dassin's *Thieves' Highway* (1949) and *Night and the City* (1950), Nicholas Ray's *They Live by Night* (1949) and *Knock on Any Door* (1949), Joseph Losey's *The Lawless* (1950) and *The Prowler* (1951), John Huston's *We Were Strangers* (1949) and *The Asphalt Jungle* (1950), Cy Endfield's *The Sound of Fury* (1951), Michael Curtiz's *The Breaking Point* (1950), John Berry's *He Ran All the Way* (1951), Robert Rossen's *Body and Soul* (1947), and Abraham Polonsky's *Force of Evil* (1948)—the last four of which featured the definitive film gris star, John Garfield.

Of all these directors and films, those with the greatest influence in Hollywood were either written or directed by Abraham Polonsky, who left Paramount for the new Enterprise Studio to write Rossen's *Body and Soul* and then to write and direct *Force of Evil*. Polonsky's scripts were unapologetic anti-capitalist allegories, in which an all-powerful system—Polonsky referred to it as "finance capital"—is represented in the first film by corrupt boxing promoters and in the second by gangsters who murder a small-time numbers racket operator (that is, a small-time capitalist). In the boxing film, director Rossen preferred an ending in which John Garfield, winner of a match he was supposed to throw, is murdered by the gangsters. But Polonsky's more upbeat version—in which Garfield tells the villains, "What are you going to do, kill me? Everybody dies."—was used because it completed the story of the character's "spiritual growth and his romantic return to his roots" in the neighborhood.[31]

Financed, in the ironic logic of filmdom, by Bank of America, and located firmly "within the gangster genre, which hid the film's social critique, *Force of Evil* drew an explicit parallel between corruption and racketeering, and the 'normal' operation of American business."[32] It turned traditional Hollywood "political" films, in which apparent institutional problems like capitalism turned out to be merely gangsterism, on their head, by following the awakening of a mob lawyer, John Garfield, after his idealistic numbers racketeer brother is murdered by the mob. There is "a kind of moral awakening on the part of [Garfield's character, Joe Morse], rather than any 'solution' to a problem. . . . Polonsky does suggest, through his central character, how the fetters of the system can be broken by self-knowledge."[33]

"Part of Abraham Polonsky's strength [in *Force of Evil* and *Body and Soul*] is in his criticism of capitalism through character study rather than polemics," note Roffman and Purdy. "While there are still social victims and victimizers, all the people in a Polonsky film are the product of their society. In effect there is no distinction between society and individual since social values are what makes up the individual. The struggle between the two thus becomes a personal one, full of complexities. No one remains uncontaminated by the American emphasis on success and getting the good things out of life at any cost."[34] It is in this sense that *High Noon*, following the lead of *Force of Evil* in turning depoliticizing themes around, treats "friendly witnesses" allegorically as Kane's fair-weather friends and HUAC as the Miller gang.

Polonsky emerges as the crucial revisioning force between the mentor, Capra, and the students, Foreman, Kramer, and their successors:

> In its fusion of psychology and social commentary, *Force of Evil* is a precursor of the political cinema which would emerge in the sixties. Like Capra, Polonsky presents a cohesive vision of the relationship between individual behavior and political values. But Polonsky does not yearn for a more humane populist past. Instead, he argues for the need to assert humanity, no matter how futile the gesture, against the urban, economic corruption of the present. His conclusion may not be as emotionally inspiring as Capra's but it is certainly intellectually tougher. His is a guarded optimism that the . . . Morses will make their stand no matter what the price.[35]

By the 1950s the second direct influence on *High Noon*, the noir-inflected Western, was well established, and many noirs, including *High Sierra, Kiss of Death*, and *The Asphalt Jungle*, were beginning to be remade as Westerns[36]—though not by future blacklistees.

The Westerner and the film noir detective had always found themselves in similar plots involving an outsider who rectifies injustice and then discovers he is still an outsider. But the Westerner had never faced a society in the early stages of decay—at least, not until the 1950s—which was the familiar lot of the noir detective. Now the Western hero was swimming against the tide.[37]

The noir Western began in 1947 with *Pursued* and *Blood on the Moon*, two films Robert Mitchum made almost simultaneously with his classic noir *Out of the Past*,[38] and relying on the same motifs: betrayal, pessimism, cynicism—a general sense of a world spinning out of control. "*Pursued* was a commercially successful blend of fatalistic melodrama, laden with dark psychological undercurrents, in a Western setting. . . . In an increasingly complex world, . . . Western . . . heroes were now most likely haunted, obsessed, arrogant or doomed."[39] Three years later, in the tragic *The Gunfighter*, director Henry King "creates a constrained, shadowy world by tightly framing his exterior shots and placing much of his action inside, where the soft interior lighting will naturally play down any sense of the magnificent scenery outside."[40]

The earliest noir-inflected Westerns also included *Yellow Sky* (1948), *Red River* (1948), *Station West* (1948), *Whispering Smith* (1949), *Ramrod* (1951), and *Rawhide* (1951). It was during this early phase that Anthony Mann abruptly switched from making films noir such as *Raw Deal* (1948) and *Side Street* (1950) to making noir Westerns, including *The Furies* (1950) and his five films with James Stewart. Mann was supposed to have disliked *High Noon* intensely,[41] and the irony was that in moving from film noir to the Western, Mann had carried with him the conventions of noir—producing Westerns that reflected a world much like that of *High Noon*.[42]

By the time Foreman came to write *High Noon* and Zinnemann to direct it, each had had some experience with films noir beyond watching colleagues make them—either directly, as in the case of Zinnemann, or on its fringes, as in the case of Foreman, but they were by now making films in a climate in which they had little room to maneuver.

As Buhle and Wagner say of Foreman's script for the "marginally noir"[43] *Champion* (1949):

> The unwilling boxer who becomes a brute . . . begins throwing punches to help his crippled brother, but thanks to his rise to celebrity and wealth is soon beyond salvation himself. . . . This *No Exit* conclusion to years of seemingly successful struggle or the seemingly courageous adventure becomes a general condition of a certain kind of later forties

film. Whenever the protagonist tries 'to escape a condition of life in which [he and the heroine] no longer believe,' a 'helplessness' overwhelms them.[44]

That same year—not long after the 1947 HUAC hearings—Zinnemann had made his one true noir, *Act of Violence,* which in some ways thematically prefigures *High Noon,* and, at eighty-two minutes, runs virtually the same length. Written by Robert L. Richardson, who would be blacklisted about the same time as Foreman, it is also about a man seeking revenge.

In the film loner Robert Ryan, made lame by the war, stalks Van Heflin, loving husband, respected citizen, and successful California builder, who is hiding a guilty secret—that, in return for extra food, he had informed on his fellow wartime prison camp inmates when they were planning a breakout. Like Grace Kelly, Heflin's pretty young blonde wife Janet Leigh is just trying to understand what is going on. "When the boosterish Heflin confesses bitterly to his wife, 'I was an informer!' he also casts considerable light on contemporary Hollywood."[45] As in *High Noon,* we slowly learn the truth as Ryan circles his prey. Attempting to escape in the shadowy back streets of Los Angeles, the once jaunty and upbeat Heflin nearly falls to pieces as he descends into the noir nightmare world of a prostitute and a hit man before returning home for a showdown—at a railroad station.

Foreman, Kramer, and Zinnemann knew film noir, and they knew what the politically committed artists at Enterprise such as Polonsky had tried to do. It was left to them to use what others had created in a totally new way.

Film noir, film gris, social realism, noir-inflected Western—*High Noon* is all of these—indeed it almost plays as a noir allegory designed to deflect the criticism heaped on its predecessor, *Force of Evil.* It hardly matters that the action takes place not in the shadows of night but under the noonday sun. This is an "urban" Western; only two scenes take place outside the town: the opening, when the gang gathers, and Kane and Amy leaving on the buckboard. It is filmed in the noir style—expressionist, hard-boiled, dark, pessimistic, bitter, its look intentionally harsh and unfiltered. There are no clouds in the sky, and no one smiles, except at the wedding scene, when the danger is unknown.[46]

Like a noir hero, Will Kane is "unknowingly investigating the rot at the heart of Hadleyville"[47] as he tries to escape a past that has caught up with him. Indeed, one could construct the plot of *High*

Noon out of noir titles: *Out of the Past, Appointment with Danger, Abandoned, Fear, In a Lonely Place, I Walk Alone, The Other Woman, The Killers, Cornered, Desperate, Act of Violence, Suddenly, Hollow Triumph.*[48] In everything—dialogue, mise-en-scène, editing—it is spare, in the noir style—except that it rigorously avoids that approach's visual extremes.

The screenplay, even before Foreman and Zinnemann began the rewrite, was remarkable for its ability to convey far more than is actually happening at any moment. An early reviewer picked up on the design immediately:

> Without a single flashback and with almost no explanatory [dialogue], the background of the action unfolds clearly to the viewer. Somehow, by an indirection sharper than A,B,C direct statement, you know just when you need to know, and what each character means in terms of the story. . . . As a storytelling job *High Noon* bears comparison to a giant mosaic, perfectly clear when you stand away and look at it from the proper distance, immensely and painstakingly complicated when you come to consider the craft with which it was put together.[49]

The *story* of *High Noon* extends over at least five years (not counting Kane's arrival) and the marshal's destruction of the Miller gang with the aid of "six top guns," his involvement with Helen Ramirez, their breakup, and his involvement with Amy Fowler. Within minutes the *plot*, coming at the very end of the story, puts in question all the existing relationships built up over the years—indeed, turns them upside down.

"What is disconcerting about *High Noon*," say Richard Combs, "is the way its starkly compressed and stylized storyline goes with a psychological realism that simultaneously diffuses and complicates the plot."[50] Critics complained about the stripped down screenplay because there was no room for the filigrees—the "human moments"—of other films. But that very spareness allowed for the maximum play of ideas. "Every situation and almost every line of dialogue of *High Noon* are charged with metaphorical meaning."[51]

"The reactions of the inhabitants are minutely particularized," notes Stanbrook—the Mexican woman crossing herself, "the fear of the [fireman], who backs away as the camera tracks past, and the contented smiles of the men in the saloon. A sudden tilt up by the marshal's sign and the first line of dialogue ('You in a hurry?') discloses the purpose of the ride into town—to murder the marshal.

The scene is intercut with the wedding scene between the marshal and the Quaker girl in the judge's office so that in one short scene the exposition has been deftly dispatched."[52]

Much is never revealed. We neither know (nor care) how Kane did his work as marshal, what led to Miller being sentenced to death, how Amy's father and brother came to be killed, how Amy came to Hadleyville, how Will and Amy fell in love, or how Will's and Helen's relationship ended. At any one time little of the "action" that auteurists so admire is occurring, and much is being implied.[53] Kane is both constantly engaged with others and simultaneously totally isolated from them.[54] The movie is held together by this one man walking around town and the one-on-one conversations at the end of each walk. The villains have very little to say—Lee Van Cleef's "Jack Colby" has no dialogue at all—but every word conveys something important about them: their focus, their childishness, their impatience, their penchant for trouble. There are a half-dozen story lines in various stages of progress—Kane and Frank Miller, Kane and Amy, Helen and Harvey, Helen and Kane, Kane and the townspeople. When the final montage begins after Will writes his will and the camera moves quickly from anxious face to anxious face, we know all we need to know about these people because in a moment of great tension they have revealed their inner selves.[55]

The themes are often understated visually, from the symbols: the badge as sign of office and symbol of disgust; the flag coming down from the wall;[56] the depot and tracks; Amy in white, Helen in black.[57] Zinnemann exteriorizes the film's inner drama in the visual design: Kane's black clothes, the white cloudless sky, the low angles,[58] the sweat rolling off the marshal and the piano player in the saloon.[59] Without unnecessary exposition, realizations come suddenly: The marshal's gun hangs on the wall next to the window Amy looks out of. From in front, we hear a gunshot and see the killer fall forward. Amy is framed in the window behind him, the gun still in her hand—we had not known she had seen it.[60]

Glances rather than words become the key to relationships: "When Kane's deputy kisses her, Helen turns away in boredom. In a later scene, when she decides to sell the saloon on generous terms, her partner explains 'You know, my wife . . .' and Helen immediately freezes in resentment of the implied antipathy of the town matrons."[61]

If the themes are understated, the cutting is anything but. Famously, there is the "track towards the chair in which Miller had vowed vengeance, followed by a cut to the depot as the train pulls in. The movements of the camera and the train are in head-on collision, symbolizing the conflict about to be played out."[62] Collisions are a favorite device. "Kane nearly collides with Ben Miller leaving the saloon; . . . boys playing sheriff and outlaw collide with him, yelling 'Bang, bang, Kane, you're dead.'"[63]

In making his argument for the manipulativeness of *High Noon*, Maltby had defined it as a "static" film, because it is shot from fixed camera positions and rarely uses medium shots, relying instead almost exclusively on long shots, whether of groups of people or of railway tracks, or on close-ups of individuals or clocks. And when we *do* see two people in a shot, they are separated along the vertical axis, as if to underline their psychological separation. To Maltby, this is constrictive; medium shots permit interaction and fluid relationships, and Zinnemann's design doesn't permit that.[64]

Maltby's description is accurate, even if his approach is reductive. In movies based on the noir design, heroes don't enjoy "interaction and fluid relationships." "Unlike most realists," observes Giannetti,

> Zinnemann's techniques emphasize closed forms, with many claustrophobic medium and close shots and tightly framed compositions which permit little freedom of movement. The edges of his frame are often sealed off, and the ceilings are oppressively low, visually reinforcing the sense of confinement. . . . Zinnemann also uses many anticipatory setups, suggesting fatality, for the camera seems to be waiting for the protagonist to enter a preordained visual design. . . . The director's famous lengthy takes . . . are unnerving precisely because Zinnemann refuses to dissipate the tension by cutting to a variety of shots.[65]

"The director's feel for the correct camera position is infallible," says Stanbrook.

> A high angle shot as Kane enters and leaves the church meeting accentuates the timidity of the congregation and Kane's isolation. But Zinnemann really comes into his own in the precise geography of the closing gunfight. As Kane walks toward the camera, a ninety-degree pan reveals Miller and his men advancing down the side street. Similarly, when Kane takes shelter in the hay loft, the camera is placed in the roof beside the aperture so that we can see the respective positions of Kane and the gunman stalking him far below at all times.[66]

It is the trapping of the characters in those verticals that underlines the movie's sense of hopelessness so powerfully. Zinnemann relies heavily on

> borders imaged explicitly in windows—with people moving toward them or away from them, catching themselves gazing through them. Staring through the saloon's plate glass, Harvey resentfully watches a Kane he can neither emulate nor defeat . . .; later, Amy indignantly scrutinizes a Kane who gains in integrity through a window's stark outline. . . . Kane [peers] through a fragmented window frame just before his wife is wrenched through a door and across the street. . . . Amy [walks] out of her marriage by walking through Judge Mettrick's door, reversed in her later decisive return to her husband's office when she hears the sound of shots . . .; Harvey proudly [makes] his "final" exit from Helen; the judge [leaves] town with his office door wide open. Later, Harvey adolescently tries to stop Kane from entering his office, while Amy strides through the hotel's wide doors into Helen's room. . . . Countless other occasions are marked by dramatically closed doors: of Sam walking into church, followed by Kane asking for help; of Kane blocked at the Fuller's front door by Mildred, his friend's wife, then forced to exit through a picket gate; of Kane repeatedly entering and leaving his marshal's office . . ., or of his elaborate release of the town drunk, Charley . . ., from a jail cell, then from the office; of Kane climbing stairs to Helen's room, re-entering her life, only to turn away; and of walking to the livery stable where Harvey Pell attacks him, then heading to the barber shop to recover; of his constant retreat through other doors in the vain search for aid. Throughout, Zinnemann maintains an unusually low camera angle, forcing the viewer to look up to Kane through windows or doors.[67]

The clocks are never far from our minds, as they are never far from the minds of the characters. Their effect is both to ratchet up the excitement and to add the most disorientingly noir effect in the film. "The film's race against time, its compressed, over-driven narrative," notes Combs, "creates a strangely hallucinatory air with great fluctuations in the sense of time and reality."[68]

The clocks plus the shoot-out amount to 105 minutes of story time, compared to the 84 minutes of screen time. But the "real time effect" disguises the sometimes inadvertent effect of the editing. Alan Stanbrook, Richard Combs, and Bruce Kawin have paid extremely close attention to those crawling clock hands. "The assumption that real time and film time follow an identical course would be quite inaccurate," notes Stanbrook.

Clocks are strategically placed throughout the film—in the court room, in the marshal's office, at the railroad depot—but the hands on the clock faces have little connection with those on the cinema clock as the film unrolls. Time is often artificially prolonged: in two scenes between Lloyd Bridges and Katy Jurado, separated by ten minutes of real time, the clock in her room has advanced by only a few minutes. Time elapses very much faster early in the film, so that the subsequent slowing down increases the tension in the moments before the train arrives. Fifteen minutes on the cinema clock absorb thirty minutes of screen time and there is a constant sense of time running out at an accelerated rate.[69]

Will and Amy's race out of town and back takes only five minutes according to the film clocks. After a slow start—judging, again, by the clocks—"the film's on-screen time tends to move ahead much more quickly than its actual running time," says Combs. "It takes only some four minutes of screen time to get between Judge Mettrick leaving at 10:47 and Kane's first arguing with Harve at 11:03. Harvey is seen in the saloon at 11:10 after Kane warns Helen at 11:15. The two clocks in the bar read 11:20 as Kane enters and 11:20 as he leaves."[70]

"In Katy Jurado's room there are two clocks so that from every camera angle we are aware of the time and when Kane comes down the stairs after leaving her, the hotel clerk is standing in the well moving the hands on the grandfather clock forward," notes Stanbrook. "After the initial rapid consumption of time, reflecting Kane's panic at the thought of Miller's return, the pace eases, seventy minutes of film time taking fifty-five on the clock. The chronometric and psychological measurements of time are still out of alignment but a brake has been applied. Immediately before noon the process is dramatically reversed and three minutes of the story are spun out for five of real time, building up a powerful atmosphere of tension."[71]

Kawin notes that Amy's and Helen's "conversation takes place at 11:43 A.M., and from then until noon, story and discourse time are in sync; seventeen projection minutes later, the clocks in the film are at noon."[72]

"Finally," concludes Stanbrook, "the closing stages of the story (taking place after noon) are compressed into the last fifteen minutes, whereas in reality they would have occupied double this time, giving a concentrated impression of rapid and violent action."[73] "Once the train arrives, the careful monitoring of story time stops entirely," observes Kawin, "as if the characters had entered the 'mythical' time of the Western as they stepped into their archetypal roles."[74]

High Noon was a film noir and a Western, but it was more than the sum of its parts, and that was never more true than in its presentation of its women. The film carefully confused the stereotypical presentation of Western women, turning them into the exact opposite of the clichéd images they initially convey. In their meeting, Katy Jurado's Helen wears black and Grace Kelly's Amy wears white—symbolism that intentionally misleads. What are actually opposed here are experience and innocence, rather than good and evil or sexual experience and virginity. Amy, the genre's "white, blonde, Anglo-Saxon . . . bringer of civilization"[75] will be strong twice, first leaving her husband out of principle and then saving him out of love.

High Noon also confused the stereotypical presentation of the noir woman. Unlike the Western, noir had transformed the postwar image of women. To be more assertive at home and at work in real life was to be a sexually voracious femme fatale on screen. But the picture was ambiguous, because the femme fatale's intelligence and power had made her attractive. If in the cynical noirs such as Billy Wilder's *Double Indemnity* women were "cold and frustrated and greedy and ambitious and vicious and selfish and cruel and mean and nasty"[76]—not to mention cold-blooded killers—the Left-written noirs tended to have strong, dependable women, such as Lilli Palmer's girlfriend and Anne Revere's mother in *Body and Soul*.[77]

Just as it inverted the image of the woman in the Western, or at least made much more of her than she had ever been, *High Noon* inverted the traditional film noir woman: This, indeed, was the "new woman" who was not seen through the funhouse mirror, but who asserted "herself in ways that her culture had not previously encouraged"[78] going well "beyond the social constructed roles of daughter, wife and mother."[79]

Zinnemann, the "social realist," took women seriously at a time when most directors did not—and when the women in Howard Hawks's movies had to prove themselves worthy of acceptance by men. Zinnemann women were "intelligent and serious" and never "adorable. . . . The female characters . . . are as courageous and principled as the males and are often more perceptive. They seldom define themselves in terms of a man."[80]

In important ways, *High Noon* is about more than Will Kane's struggle to work his way through the labyrinth; it offers no fewer than three points of view, three protagonists. The centrality of the woman has been routinely missed because the action revolves around Will, and he is on screen far more. But it is the women who by their words and their very presence add a moral point of view. Will Kane, Amy Fowler Kane, and Helen Ramirez are all protagonists in the sense that we see them in scenes without the other two, and in the sense that they are all on a quest: Will to answer to his heroic pride, Amy to uncover the meaning of Will's actions, Helen to separate herself as a woman and as a citizen from the corruption of the town. Kane and Amy and Helen are, in effect, three people in search of the truth about themselves—perhaps three aspects of the whole person. Amy spends the movie trying to find out the meaning of it all, even as Will tries desperately to find out how these unexpected developments apply to him, and Helen acts on her complete knowledge to save herself. In this sense, the betrayals and the shoot-out become not the subject but the context.

The difference is that Will is able to have it all—obey his conscience and still keep his marriage—while the women must sacrifice. Amy must relinquish her principled rejection of violence—at least temporarily—and Helen must give up a profitable store, source of her sense of both security and self-worth, and flee.[81]

Like the women in a Hawks film, Amy and Helen are outsiders, but they will not be "judged" in the film's terms simply by their ability to be accepted. They are outsiders not just because they are women, but because they are a pacifist Quaker and a Mexican—the ultimate outsiders in an Anglo town in the post-Civil War West—and they are the only ones to question the deadly dynamic of revenge, the only ones to voice the unexpressed truths about death and self-deception.[82]

Amy struggles to comprehend the bizarre events around her. "I don't understand any of this," she says plaintively, and it's not obvious that she ever does "understand," at least in the way we are meant to. "She argues aggressively with her partner, rather than listening passively, yet she does not adopt the mother role of guidance and temperance."[83] Initially she seems as inflexible as Will does, and at least as conscience-stricken as he—the only other person in town who is.[84] When she kills a killer, Amy is hidden in the marshal's office. She does not have to disclose herself, so the choice to shoot Pierce is all the more wrenching.[85]

The traditional view of Amy pulling the trigger is that she has embraced her new husband's values and therefore has surrendered her integrity,[86] that "the conflict has so transformed her that she now recognizes the necessity of violence and the limits of what a wife can ask."[87] A slightly more generous view is that "Amy realizes that her love for her husband outweighs all other considerations. . . . Unlike Molly in *The Virginian*, Amy does not passively accept her lover's values; she actively integrates them into her life and assumes the traditional male values of courage and duty." By comparison, in *Rio Bravo*, John Wayne still dominates Angie Dickinson at the end.[88]

The alternative view—which grants the plot a human logic, rather than simply a commercial or a political one—is that Will is acting ethically, that he has been as honest as he can with Amy, that he has asked her to stay after trying, inarticulately, to explain that he has no choice by his own lights. The most useful way to see Amy's return, and her help for Will, is not that she has subordinated her own beliefs to his, accepting the "way of the West," but that this persistent woman has realized—once she sees what danger he is in and that she can help—that she has no choice if she is to save her husband and her new marriage.

Amy, whom Helen has lectured on the subject of standing by one's man, is struggling with her views, unlike the other two. She holds to her pacifism but then faces the existential moment of choice when, sitting on the train, she hears the gunshot. Moments later she is reading the will (reading Will?). She does not abandon her Quaker views in that instant; she acts instinctively, out of love. In a sense, shooting the gunman affirms the commitment she made in the marriage ceremony—though she would not agree that that is what happened. At the end she recommits to her marriage. She had taken her vows, but now she must live by those vows, including "till death do us part." She has not accepted a "need" to kill; rather, she has acted out of emotion, in the most extreme situation imaginable, to save her husband, and now she knows they will live her way.[89]

Amy, at least, had a precedent in characters such as Molly, the virginal Eastern schoolteacher in *The Virginian*. But Helen—the sultry beauty in the low-cut gown who takes her lovers and her business deals to suit herself—is one of a kind, a worldly woman. Despite being serially shared by three men, she is not only her own woman but is able to overcome her bitterness and treat her ex-lover's new wife with compassion.[90]

Helen, in a sense, unites the various groups of the story. She was both Miller's mistress and Kane's lover, and she is now Harv's; she is the silent partner in a store with one of the church-people; her name is on the saloon.

Unlike her genre predecessors, Helen is seductive but does not seduce[91] (though, as we've seen, in the original cut of the film, her sexuality was more forthrightly displayed). Her Anglo silent business partner, Mr. Weaver, acknowledges her character by saying that her price was more than fair and that he appreciates that she never made public their business relationship because it would have embarrassed him.

Helen's response on hearing Amy's heartrending tale of her brother's and father's deaths "is to bond with her and to explain why she must leave: 'I hate this town, I've always hated it. To be a Mexican woman in a town like this . . .' The women do not overcome their differences, but they bond and wait together for the killing to end."[92] Yet Helen's concern for Amy doesn't prevent her from asking "What kind of woman are you? How can you leave him like this?"

Helen is a particularly complex character, wearily voicing a woman's anger at her mistreatment by men, whether by the immature Harve, the marshal who left her, or the crazed killer returning to town. When she "explains to Harvey why she must leave, Helen . . . restates her revulsion to male violence and power over her body: 'I'm all alone in the world . . . I have to make a living . . . and as for you . . . I don't like anybody to put his hands on me unless I want him to and I don't like you to, anymore.'"[93] But she also distinguishes between men of principle and all the others—and she is obviously a sexually sophisticated woman whom the inexperienced Amy initially finds threatening.

One reason for the emphasis on the women is that Zinnemann not only takes individual women characters seriously, he wishes to seriously examine what the return of brutal men like the Miller gang might mean for the women of the town. Much of the dialogue, from the woman in church recalling when "a decent woman couldn't walk down the street in broad daylight" to Harve's warning Helen about what Miller might do to her, to Ben Miller's ogling of Amy and his theft of the bonnet, points to the coming threat.

The bonnet-snatching scene represents the second time the childish Ben Miller has been asked if he can't wait (the other came at the beginning, when he reared his horse at the "Marshal" sign when the gang first entered the town). This scene thus does triple duty, not only reinforcing the sexual threat and playing out the implications of Ben's earlier impatience, but also warning Kane, who is just around the corner.

Both Millers are associated with brutal sex. Ben's lustful impulse leads to the death of the gang. Frank's involvement with Helen both drives her away and helps Kane make up his mind to stay, and his use of Amy as a shield gets him killed when the woman he is brutalizing turns on him, literally.[94] In this final shoot-out, we rely on Amy's perspective as much as we do Will's. She is, at last, living up to her name: Before she was Amy Kane she was Amy "Fowler"—as in one who shoots wild creatures with a gun.

In the end, Kane is the hero determined to tie himself to domesticity; he can proceed with his marriage only after eliminating a challenge to his life and his honor that might interfere with it. Amy has her man; Helen will go on to prosper in some safer town. It is as much the women's victory as the man's.

But we don't know what is going to happen to this town after Will and Amy and Helen leave. It's quite possible that it will go on as before, since it no longer appears to be under any threat. If the people up North can be persuaded that the gunfight was the last act of a personal drama, and all the principals are either dead or gone, there's every reason to believe that that hoped-for investment will come.

That is where the structuring anger, the bitterness, of *High Noon* is most keenly felt—the idea that nothing will change. Except, that is, for Will Kane, who has been "liberated"[95] by a shocking discovery—that he is free of the venality that he had unknowingly been surrounded by. That he, like the kids and the jailhouse drunk, is free, though in his case it is from the obligations of manhood, of older Westerns, of duty, of conscience. He has discarded his badge and found his authentic self, which requires a continuing duty to himself and his wife but not to those who betrayed him.

In the end, the bitterest fact of all is that everyone had his reasons, everyone did what he felt he had to do. It is this bitterness that the design of *High Noon* is most concerned to convey. It's all so very modern—so un-Western.

If the characters' survival is victory enough in the film, "triumph" is not too strong a word to describe what Stanley Kramer, Carl Foreman,

Fred Zinnemann, and their colleagues have wrought. *High Noon* is Kramer's not-quite-accidental triumph of independent filmmaking; it is Foreman's HUAC allegory; it is Zinnemann's crisis of conscience tale; it is the remaking and the end of the Western; it is that auteurist nightmare, the artistic collaboration; it is the existential, ethical drama; it is the convergence of the film noir, the film gris, and the social-realist traditions.

Where existential angst meets Kantian ethics, there stands Will Kane. Where the dark of noir night meets the showdown of conscience at high noon, the marshal watches his world crumble and a new one open to him.

Kane does not "win" simply because he kills the killers. He does not win simply because he survives. He does not lose a town—because it was never his town. And he does not lose his friends—because they were never his friends.

Kane's story is an allegory, but it is more than allegory—though it is not realistic. He is too perfect; he is our ideal—the noblest hero in the history of American film.

Will Kane survives a nightmare under the noonday sun and becomes, finally, his own man—not simply the man of principle he had always been, but the man who has chosen to be free after the scales have lifted from his eyes. And that is why we have never forgotten him.

NOTES

1. *"High Noon,"* in *The Time Out Film Guide,* ed. Tom Milne (London, Penguin, 1989), 261.

2. *Concepts in Film Theory* (Oxford: Oxford University Press, 1985), 171.

3. Richard Maltby, *Harmless Entertainment* (Metuchen, N.J.: Scarecrow Press, 1983), 266–72, 274–75, 283, 287–88.

4. Maltby, *Harmless Entertainment,* 258.

5. Maltby, *Harmless Entertainment,* 272.

6. Maltby, *Harmless Entertainment,* 258, 261.

7. Maltby, *Harmless Entertainment,* 274. Kelly, of course, never does understand; she acts from other motives. It is Katy Jurado who understands.

8. Maltby, *Harmless Entertainment,* 258.

9. Peter Roffman and Jim Purdy, *The Hollywood Social Problem Film* (Bloomington: Indiana University Press, 1981), 296–97.

10. James Naremore, *More Than Night* (Berkeley: University of California Press, 1998), 106.

11. Foster Hirsch, *The Dark Side of the Screen: Film Noir* (New York: Da Capo, 1983), 9.

12. Brian Neve, *Film and Politics in America: A Social Tradition* (London: Routledge, 199), 147.

13. Paul Schrader, "Notes on Film Noir," in *Film Genre Reader II,* ed. Barry Grant (Austin: University of Texas Press, 1995), 212.

14. Philip Kemp, "From the Nightmare Factory," *Sight and Sound* 55 (Fall 1986): 269.

15. Rebecca House Stankowski, "Night of the Soul: American Film Noir," *Studies in Popular Culture* 9, no. 1 (1986): 61–83, at library.calumet.purdue.edu/nitesoul.htm (accessed July 17, 2002).

16. Joan Mellen, "Film Noir," in *Political Companion to American Film,* ed. Gary Crowdus (Chicago: Lakeview Press, 1994), 139.

17. Mellen, "Film Noir," 138.

18. Mellen, "Film Noir," 140.

19. Mellen, "Film Noir," 139.

20. Naremore, *More Than Night*, 172.

21. Schrader, "Film Noir," 219–21.

22. Hirsch, *Dark Side*, 89–90.

23. Naremore, *More Than Night*, 103–4.

24. The latter nevertheless was cited by the MPA as containing "'sizable doses of Communist propaganda.'" Neve, *Film and Politics*, 140.

25. Naremore, *More Than Night*, 127; Neve, *Film and Politics*, 184.

26. Neve, *Film and Politics*, 182

27. Thom Andersen, "Red Hollywood," in *Literature and the Visual Arts in Contemporary Society,* ed. Suzanne Ferguson and Barbara Groseclose (Columbus: Ohio State University Press, 1985), 183–84.

28. George Lipsitz, *Rainbow at Midnigh.* (Urbana: University of Illinois Press, 1994), 287–89.

29. Andersen, "Red Hollywood," 186–87.

30. Naremore, *More Than Night*, 124–25.

31. Neve, *Film and Politics*, 132–33.

32. Neve, *Film and Politics*, 132–33.

33. Neve, *Film and Politics*, 134–35. Friendly witness Elia Kazan's *On the Waterfront* would reverse the perspective of *Force of Evil*: The gangsters are now metaphorical communists, not capitalists.

34. Roffman and Purdy, *Social Problem Film*, 273.

35. Roffman and Purdy, *Social Problem Film*, 278.

36. William K. Everson, *The Hollywood Western* (New York: Citadel Press, 1992), 216.

37. Edward Recchia, "Film Noir and the Western," *The Centennial Review* 4, no. 3 (Fall 1996): 602–3.

38. Recchia, "Film Noir," 604.

39. Michael Coyne, *The Crowded Prairie* (London: I.B. Tauris, 1997), 48.

40. Recchia, "Film Noir," 608–9.

41. John Fitzpatrick, "Fred Zinnemann," in *American Directors*, ed. Jean-Pierre Coursodon, with Pierre Sauvage (New York: McGraw-Hill, 1983), 380.

42. Phil Hardy, *The Western* (New York: Morrow, 1983), xii.

43. Hirsch, *Dark Side*, 164.

44. Paul Buhle and Dave Wagner, *Radical Hollywood* (New York: New Press, 2002), 326.

45. Buhle and Wagner, *Radical Hollywood*, 337.

46. Thomas Shatz, *Hollywood Genres* (Philadelphia: Temple University Press, 1981), 112.

47. Mellen, "Film Noir," 140.

48. Titles from Alain Silver and Elizabeth Ward, eds., *Film Noir: An Encyclopedic Reference to the American Style* (Woodstock, N.Y.: Overlook Press, 1979), passim.

49. Al Hine, review of *High Noon*, *Holiday* 12 (September 1952): 27. The reviewer had unknowingly used Foreman's own term for the process.

50. Richard Combs, "Retrospective: *High Noon*," *Monthly Film Bulletin* 53 (June 1986): 187.

51. Adam Garbicz and Jacek Klinowski, *Cinema: The Magic Vehicle, Volume Two* (New York: Schocken Books, 1983), 112.

52. Alan Stanbrook, "A Man for All Movies, the Films of Fred Zinnemann, part II," *Films and Filming* 13 (June 1967): 12.

53. Donald Spoto, *Stanley Kramer: Filmmaker* (New York: Putnam, 1978), 100.

54. Sam B. Girgus, *Hollywood Renaissance* (Cambridge: Cambridge University Press, 1998), 141.

55. Rick Lyman, "Stanley Kramer, Filmmaker with Social Bent, Dies at 87," *New York Times*, February 21, 2001, A:1.

56. "There are certain ironic things you like to do for your own pleasure, and some people catch them and others don't—like the judge in *High Noon*, who talks about compromise and at the same time is folding the American flag and sticking it in his pocket." Fred Zinnemann, quoted in Arthur Nolletti Jr., "Conversation with Fred Zinnemann," in *The Films of Fred Zinnemann*, ed. Arthur Nolletti Jr. (Albany: State University of New York Press, 1999), 18.

57. Stanbrook, "Man for All Movies," 12.

58. Stephen Prince, "Historical Perspective and the Realist Aesthetic in *High Noon* (1952)," in *The Films of Fred Zinnemann*, ed. Arthur Nolletti Jr. (Albany: State University of New York Press, 1999), 84–85.

59. Rick Lyman, "Watching Movies with Wolfgang Petersen; A Boy Shaped by 'High Noon,'" *New York Times*, March 30, 2001, E1.

60. Lyman, "Watching Movies," E1.

61. Stanbrook, "Man for All Movies," 12.

62. Stanbrook, "Man for All Movies," 12.

63. Lee Clark Mitchell, *Westerns* (Chicago: University of Chicago Press, 1996), 214.

64. Maltby, *Harmless Entertainment*, 273–74.

65. Louis Giannetti, *Masters of the American Cinema* (Englewood Cliffs, N.J.: Prentice-Hall, 1981), 366.

66. Stanbrook, "Man for All Movies," 12.

67. Mitchell, *Westerns*, 212–13.

68. Combs, "Retrospective: *High Noon*," 187.

69. Stanbrook, "Man for All Movies," 11–12.

70. Combs, "Retrospective: *High Noon*," 188.

71. Stanbrook, "Man for All Movies," 11–12.

72. Bruce F. Kawin, *How Movies Work* (New York: Macmillan, 1987), 507.

73. Stanbrook, "Man for All Movies," 11–12.

74. Kawin, *How Movies Work*, 507.

75. Joanna E. Rapf, "Myth, Ideology and Feminism in *High Noon*," *Journal of Popular Culture* 23, no. 4 (Spring 1990): 79.

76. Molly Haskell, *From Reverence to Rape: The Treatment of Women in the Movies* (New York: Henry Holt, 1974), 189.

77. Buhle and Wagner, *Radical Hollywood*, 351.

78. Hirsch, *Dark Side*, 20.

79. Rapf, "Myth," 79.

80. Giannetti, *Masters*, 370.

81. Rapf, "Myth," 78.

82. Gwendolyn Foster, "The Women in *High Noon* (1952): A Metanarrative of Difference," in *The Films of Fred Zinnemann*, ed. Arthur Nolletti Jr. (Albany: tate University of New York Press, 1999), 95.

83. Foster, "Women in *High Noon*," 93–4.

84. Kawin, *How Movies Work*, 509–10.

85. Kawin, *How Movies Work*, 510.

86. Kawin, *How Movies Work*, 506–7.

87. Cheyney Ryan, "Print the Legend" in *Legal Reeling*, ed. John Denvir (Urbana: University of Illinois Press, 1996), 33–34.

88. Cheryl J. Foote, "Changing Images of Women in the Western Film," *Journal of the West* 21 (October 1983): 69.

89. Gerald Kreyche, "*High Noon*—A Paradigm of Kant's Moral Philosophy," *Teaching Philosophy* 11, no. 3 (September 1988): 227; Rapf, "Myth," 78. One argument puts Amy in the driver's seat throughout: "Amy Fowler (Grace Kelly) is having her new husband, Marshall Will Kane (Cooper), quit his career, leave his town, leave his friends, marry outside his church, and open a store of her choosing (wearing, perhaps, an apron?). Does Will Kane take on the villains at noon as a final gasp of masculine protest, as a declaration of independence from his wife's control?" John Mulholland, High Noon, *A Look Forward*, n.d., at http://www.coopandpapa.com/modalive/highnoonprogram.htm (accessed July 7, 2003).

90. Rapf, "Myth," 78. "A similar quartet of figures—gunfighter, gambler, Mexican woman, Christian woman from the East—set the terms of the

moral drama in Hart's *Hell's Hinges* (1915); but Hart's turn-of-the-century morality insists on the (racial) purity of Blaze Tracey's sexual inclinations. The foursome of marshal, gambler, Mexican woman, and virginal Anglo maiden also forms the central group in . . . *My Darling Clementine* (1946)." Richard Slotkin, *Gunfighter Nation* (New York: Atheneum, 1992), 394.

91. Foster, "Women in *High Noon*," 96–97.
92. Foster, "Women in *High Noon*," 96–97.
93. Foster, "Women in *High Noon*," 98–99.
94. Foster, "Women in *High Noon*," 99–100.
95. Girgus, *Hollywood*, 150–51.

Bibliography

Aberdeen, J. A. *Hollywood Renegades: The Society of Independent Motion Picture Producers.* Los Angeles: Cobblestone Entertainment, 2000. Quoted at http://www.cobbles.com/simpp_archive (accessed November 12, 2002).

Adams, Lee, and Buck Rainey. *Shoot-Em-Ups.* New Rochelle, N.Y.: Arlington House, 1978.

Alpert, Hollis. "The Postwar Generation: Movies." *Saturday Review* 36 (March 14, 1953): 16–17, 62–63.

———. "Something Worth Fighting For." *Saturday Review* 46 (December 28, 1963): 16–18.

Andersen, Thom. "Red Hollywood." In *Literature and the Visual Arts in Contemporary Society,* edited by Suzanne Ferguson and Barbara Groseclose, 141–96. Columbus: Ohio State University Press, 1985.

Anderson, Michael. *Hollywood TV: The Studio System in the Fifties.* Austin: University of Texas Press, 1994.

Andrew, Dudley. *Concepts in Film Theory.* Oxford: Oxford University Press, 1985.

Andreychuk, Ed. *The Golden Corral.* Jefferson, N.C.: McFarland, 1997.

Arce, Hector. *Gary Cooper.* New York: Morrow, 1979.

Balio, Tino. *United Artists: The Company That Changed the Film Industry.* Madison: University of Wisconsin Press, 1987.

Barsness, John A. "A Question of Standards." *Film Quarterly* 22 (Fall 1967): 32–37.

Bazin, Andre. "Beauty of a Western." In *Cahiers du Cinema: The 1950s,* edited by in Jim Hillier, 165–68. Cambridge: Harvard University Press, 1985.

———. "An Exemplary Western." In *Cahiers du Cinema: The 1950s,* edited by in Jim Hillier, 169–74. Cambridge: Harvard University Press, 1985.

———. "The Evolution of the Western." In Andre Bazin, *What Is Cinema: Volume II,* edited by Hugh Gray, 149–57. Berkeley: University of California Press, 1971.

Behlmer, Rudy. *Behind the Scenes*. Hollywood, Calif.: Samuel French, 1990.

Belton, John. "Dear Mr. Sarris." In *Citizen Sarris, American Film Critic*, edited by Emanuel Levy, 145–49. Lanham, Md.: Scarecrow Press, 2001.

Bentley, Eric. *Thirty Years of Treason*. New York: Viking, 1971.

Bergman, Andrew. *We're in the Money*. New York: Harper Torchbooks, 1971.

Biskind, Peter. *Seeing Is Believing*. New York: Pantheon, 1983.

Bordwell, David. "Contemporary Film Studies and the Vicissitudes of Grand Theory." In *Post-Theory*, edited by David Bordwell and Noel Carroll, 3–36. Madison: University of Wisconsin, Press, 1996.

———. "Historical Poetics of Cinema." In *The Cinematic Text: Methods and Approaches*, edited by R. Barton Palmer, 369–98. New York: AMS Press, 1989.

———. "Sarris and the Search for Style," In *Citizen Sarris, American Film Critic*, edited by Emanuel Levy, 165–73. Lanham, Md.: Scarecrow Press, 2001.

Bowers, Lynn. "'High Noon' Superb Film," *Los Angeles Examiner*, August 14, 1952. Page not listed. Archived in the Academy of Motion Picture Arts and Sciences Margaret Herrick Library, Beverly Hills, California.

Brown, Peter. "Blacklist: The Black Tale of Turmoil in Filmdom." *Los Angeles Times*, Sunday Calendar Section, February 1, 1981, 5.

Brown, Peter H., and Jim Pinkston. *Oscar Dearest*. New York: Harper & Row, 1987.

Buckley, Michael. "Fred Zinnemann: An Interview." *Films in Review* 34 (January 1983): 25–40.

Buhle, Paul, and Dave Wagner. *Radical Hollywood*. New York: New Press, 2002.

Buscombe, Edward, ed. *The BFI Companion to the Western*. New York: Atheneum, 1988.

"Bush Gives *High Noon* Poster to Koizumi." *Japan Today,* September 26, 2001, at www.japantoday.com/gidx/news86548.html (accessed July 16, 2002).

Byman, Jeremy. "Religion and Respectability in the Western: *Hell's Hinges* and *High Noon*." Unpublished paper, New York University Department of Cinema Studies, January 1982.

Capra, Frank. *The Name Above The Title*. New York: Macmillan, 1971.

Carroll, Harrison. "'High Noon" Is Top Suspense," *Los Angeles Herald-Express*, August 14, 1952. Page not given. Clipping archived in the Academy of Motion Picture Arts and Sciences Margaret Herrick Library, Beverly Hills, California.

Carroll, Noel. "Prospects For Film Theory: A Personal Assessment." In *Post-Theory*, edited by David Bordwell and Noel Carroll, 37–66. Madison: University of Wisconsin Press, 1996.

Caughie, John, ed. *Theories of Authorship*. London: Routledge & Kegan Paul, 1981.

Caute, David. *The Great Fear*. New York: Simon & Schuster, 1978.

———. *Joseph Losey*. New York: Oxford University Press, 1994.

Cawelti, John G. *The Six-Gun Mystique Sequel.* Bowling Green, Ky.: Bowling Green State University Popular Press, 1999.

CBS television, *60 Minutes II,* December 19, 2000, at www.cbsnews.com/stories/2000/12/19/60II/main258362.shtml (accessed November 5, 2002).

Ceplair, Larry. "The Communist Party in Hollywood." In *Political Companion to American Film,* edited by Gary Crowdus, 66–70. Chicago: Lakeview Press, 1994.

———. "The Hollywood Blacklist." In *Political Companion to American Film,* edited by Gary Crowdus, 193–99. Chicago: Lakeview Press, 1994.

Ceplair, Larry and Steven Englund. *The Inquisition in Hollywood.* Berkeley: University of California Press, 1983.

Champlin, Charles. "It's Been a Life of Pride, Passion—and Defiance." *Los Angeles Times,* September 20, 1997. Archived in the Academy of Motion Picture Arts and Sciences Margaret Herrick Library, Beverly Hills, California.

Chetwynd, Lionel, and Norman S. Powell, prods . . . *Darkness at High Noon: The Carl Foreman Papers.* PBS documentary, broadcast September 17, 2002.

Cogley, John. *Report on Blacklisting I : The Movies.* New York: Fund for the Republic, 1956.

Combs, Richard. "The Choirmaster and the Slavedriver: Howard Hawks and *Land of the Pharaohs.*" *Film Comment* 33 (July–August 1997): 42–48.

———. "Retrospective: *High Noon.*" *Monthly Film Bulletin* 53 (June 1986): 186–88.

Corliss, Richard. "Confessions of a Sarrisite." In *Citizen Sarris, American Film Critic,* edited by Emanuel Levy, 129–37. Lanham, Md.: Scarecrow Press, 2001.

———. "The Hollywood Screenwriter." In *Film Theory and Criticism,* edited by Gerald Mast and Marshall Cohen, 692–701. New York: Oxford University Press, 1979.

———. "Still Talking." *Film Comment* 28 (November–December 1992): 11–19.

———. *Talking Pictures.* New York: Penguin, 1975.

Coyne, Michael. *The Crowded Prairie.* London: I. B. Tauris, 1997.

Crowther, Bosley. Review of *High Noon. New York Times,* July 25, 1952. Copyright © New York Times Company, 1952. Reprinted with permission.

Cunningham, John M . . . "The Tin Star." In *A Century of Great Western Stories,* edited by John Jakes, 35–48. New York: Forge, 2000.

Deutsch, Didier, ed. *Video Hound's Soundtracks: Music from the Movies, Broadway, and Television.* Canton, Mich.: Visible Ink Press, 1997.

"Dialogue on Film: Carl Foreman." *American Film* 4 (April 1979): 35–46.

Dick, Bernard F. *The Merchant Prince of Poverty Row.* Lexington: University Press of Kentucky, 1993.

Dirks, Tim. *Greatest Films,* n.d., at www.filmsite.org (accessed July15, 2002)

Dixon, Wheeler Winston. "*Act of Violence* and the Early Films of Fred Zinnemann." *Film Criticism* 18 (Spring–Fall 1994): 30–45.

Drummond, Phillip. *High Noon*. London: British Film Institute, 1997.

Durgnat, Raymond. "Hawks Isn't Good Enough." *Film Comment* 13 (July–August 1977): 8–19.

Eder, Bruce. *All Movie Guide,* n.d., at movies.yahoo.com (accessed March 13, 2002).

Eells, George. *Hedda and Louella*. New York: Putnam, 1972.

Everson, William K. *The American Silent Film*. New York: Oxford University Press, 1978.

———. *The Hollywood Western*. New York: Citadel Press, 1992.

Eyman, Scott. "The Blacklist in Hollywood: A Look Back—50 Years Later." *Palm Beach Post*, October 19, 1997, 1J.

———. Review of *Gary Cooper Off Camera* (New York: Harry N. Abrams, 1999), by Maria Cooper Janis. *Palm Beach Post*, October 26, 1999, 1D.

Fabrikant, Geraldine. "Grace on the Cutting Room Floor." *New Times* 7 (March 18, 1977): 53–58.

Farber, Manny. Review of *High Noon*. *The Nation* 174 (April 26, 1952): 410.

———. "Underground Films." In *Howard Hawks: American Artist*, edited by Jim Hillier and Peter Wollen, 35–45. London: BFI Publishing, 1996.

———. "White Elephant Art vs. Termite Art," *Film Culture* 27 (Winter 1962–1963): 9–13.

Fenin, George K., and William K. Everson. *The Western*. New York: Orion Press, 1962.

Ferrer, Jose. "Cyrano and Others" (Interview). *Films and Filming* 8 (July 1962): 13–14, 45.

Fitzpatrick, John. "Fred Zinnemann." In *American Directors, Volume II,* edited by Jean-Pierre Coursodon with Pierre Sauvage, 378–86. New York: McGraw-Hill, 1983.

Fleischer, Richard, quoted online at www.nettuno.it/mystfest/e/claypige.html (accessed September 27, 2002).

Flynn, Peter. *The Silent Western As Mythmaker,* n.d., at www.imagesjournal.com/issue06/infocus/silentWesterns.htm (accessed December 12, 2002).

Folkart, Burt A., "*High Noon* Writer Carl Foreman, Ex-film Exile, Dies." *Los Angeles Times*, June 27, 1984, Part 2, 3.

Folsom, James K. "'Western' Themes and Western Films." *Western American Literature* 2, no. 3 (Fall 1967): 193–203.

Foote, Cheryl J. "Changing Images of Women in the Western Film," *Journal of the West* 21 (October 1983): 64–71.

Foreman, Amanda, and Jonathan Foreman. "Our Dad Was No Commie." *New Statesman* 128 (March 26, 1999): 20–22

Foreman, Carl. Carl Foreman Interviews. January 20–25, 1978, tapes 25–30. Quoted in Lionel Chetwynd and Norman S. Powell, prods. *Darkness at High Noon*. PBS documentary, broadcast September 17, 2002.

———. Letter to Bosley Crowther, August 7, 1952. Copyright © Carl Foreman Estate. Courtesy Eve Williams-Jones, widow of Carl Foreman.

Foster, Gwendolyn. "The Women in *High Noon* (1952): A Metanarrative of Difference." In *The Films of Fred Zinnemann,* edited by Arthur Nolletti Jr., 93–102. Albany: State University of New York Press, 1999.

Frayling, Christopher. "The American Western and American Society." In *Cinema, Politics and Society in America,* edited by Philip Davies and Brian Neve, 136–62. New York: St. Martin's Press, 1981.

"Fred Zinnemann." *Current Biography.* Volume 14. New York: H.W. Wilson, 1983.

French, Philip. *Westerns.* London: Secker & Warburg, 1977.

Furhammar, Leif, and Folke Isaksson. *Politics and Film.* New York: Praeger, 1971.

F. Y. I. CBS television broadcast, February 14, 1960, transcript in the Stanley Kramer collection, Young Special Collections, University of California at Los Angeles.

Gabler, Neal. *An Empire of Their Own.* New York: Doubleday Anchor, 1988.

Gallagher, Tag. *John Ford.* Berkeley: University of California Press, 1986.

———. "Shoot-Out at the Genre Corral: Problems in the 'Evolution' of the Western." In *Film Genre Reader II,* edited by Barry Grant, 246–60. Austin: University of Texas Press, 1995.

Garbicz, Adam, and Jacek Klinowski. *Cinema: The Magic Vehicle, Volume Two.* New York: Schocken Books, 1983.

Garfield, Brian. *Western Films.* New York: Rawson Associates, 1982.

Garrett, George P., O. B. Harrison Jr., and Jane R. Gelfman. *Film Scripts Two.* New York: Meredith Corporation, 1971.

Giannetti, Louis. *Masters of the American Cinema.* Englewood Cliffs, N.J.: Prentice-Hall, 1981.

Girgus, Sam B. *Hollywood Renaissance.* Cambridge: Cambridge University Press, 1998.

Godfrey, Lionel. "A Heretic's View of Westerns." *Films and Filming* 13 (June 1967): 14–20.

Goodman, Walter. *The Committee.* New York: Farrar, Straus & Giroux, 1968.

Graham, Don. "*High Noon* (1952)." In *Western Movies,* edited by William T. Pilkington and Don Graham, 51–62. Albuquerque: University of New Mexico Press, 1979.

Griffith, Richard. *Fred Zinnemann.* New York: Museum of Modern Art, 1958.

———. "High Noon Wins Praise From Eastern Critics," *Los Angeles Times,* August 5, 1952, III-6. Archived in the Academy of Motion Picture Arts and Sciences Margaret Herrick Library, Beverly Hills, California.

Guernsey, Otis L., Jr. "Oscar's Getting Stodgy." *New York Herald Tribune,* March 29, 1953. Archived in the Academy of Motion Picture Arts and Sciences Margaret Herrick Library, Beverly Hills, California.

Hardy, Phil. *The Western.* New York: Morrow, 1983.

Haskell, Molly. *From Reverence to Rape: The Treatment of Women in the Movies.* New York: Henry Holt, 1974.

———. "Life with Andrew . . . and Film." in *Citizen Sarris, American Film Critic*, edited by Emanuel Levy, 11–22. Lanham, Md.: Scarecrow Press, 2001.

Hatch, Robert L., "Gary Cooper a Tragic Hero," *The Reporter*, September 16, 1952. Quoted in Stanley Hochman. *American Film Directors*. New York: Frederick Ungar, 1974, 38.

High Noon, discussed by "br," n.d., on the Turner Classic Movies website, at www.turnerclassicmovies. com (accessed July 7, 2002).

"'Highpockets' Cooper in *High Noon*." *Life Magazine* 34 (August 25, 1952): 73–79.

Hilliard, Gloria. "Variety a Hallmark of Lloyd Bridges' Career." *CNN.com*, March 11, 1998.

Hillier, Jim and Peter Wollen. *Howard Hawks: American Artist*. London: British Film Institute, 1996.

Hine, Al. Review of *High Noon*. *Holiday* 12 (September 1952): 24–27.

Hinson, Hal. "Life, Liberty and the Pursuit of Cows: How the Western Defines America's View of Itself." *Washington Post*, July 3, 1994, G1.

Hirsch, Foster. *The Dark Side of the Screen: Film Noir*. New York: Da Capo, 1983.

Hitt, Jim. *The American West from Fiction (1823–1976) into Film (1909–1986)*. Jefferson, N.C.: McFarland, 1990.

Holden, Anthony. *Behind the Oscar*. New York: Plume, 1993.

Horton, Robert, "Day of the Craftsman: Fred Zinnemann." *Film Comment* 33 (September–October 1997): 59–67.

Houston, Penelope. "Kramer and Company." *Sight and Sound* 21 (July–September 1952): 20–23, 48.

Houston, Penelope, and Kenneth Cavender. "Interview with Carl Foreman." *Sight and Sound* 27 (Summer 1958): 220–23, 264.

Hunter, Stephen, "At AFI, 'High Noon" Once More Reaches Its Zenith," The Washington Post, May 30, 2001, c. 03

———, "Movie Gunfighters Go Off Half-cocked When It Comes to Realism, Hollywood Shootouts Are Way Off Target." *Washington Post*, February 8, 1998: G1.

———. "No Escaping Politics in Movies." *Baltimore Sun*, August 23, 1992, 1L.

James, Caryn. "The Day Gary Cooper Didn't Walk Down Main Street." *New York Times*, August 18, 2000, E28.

Jarvie, Ian. *Philosophy of the Film*. New York: Routledge & Kegan Paul, 1987.

Johnston, Sheila. In *The Time Out Film Guide*, edited by Tom Milne, 261. London: Penguin, 1989.

Jones, Dorothy. "Communism and the Movies: A Study of Film Content." In *Report on Blacklisting I : The Movies*, edited by John Cogley, 196–233. New York: Fund for the Republic, 1956.

Kael, Pauline. "Circles and Squares." In *Film Theory and Criticism*, edited by Gerald Mast and Marshall Cohen, 666–79. New York: Oxford University Press, 1979.

———. *Kiss Kiss Bang Bang*. New York: Bantam, 1969.

Kaminsky, Stuart M. *Coop*. New York: St. Martin's Press, 1980.

Kanfer, Stefan. *A Journal of the Plague Years*. New York: Atheneum, 1973.

Kawin, Bruce F. *How Movies Work*. New York: Macmillan, 1987.

Kehr, Dave. "Cahiers Back in the Day." *Film Comment* 37 (September–October 2001): 30–34.

Kemp, Philip. "From the Nightmare Factory." *Sight and Sound* 55 (Fall 1986): 266–70.

King, Susan. "*High Noon* Showdown." *Los Angeles Times*, April 11, 2002, F58.

Kitses, Jim. *Horizons West*. Bloomington: Indiana University Press, 1969.

Kramer, Stanley, "The Independent Producer." *Films in Review* 2 (March 1951): 1–4, 47.

Kreyche, Gerald. "*High Noon*—A Paradigm of Kant's Moral Philosophy." *Teaching Philosophy* 11, no. 3 (September 1988): 216–28.

Landon, Phil, Department of English, University of Maryland, Baltimore County, homepage: www.research.umbc.edu/landon/Film%20Summaries/Summary_HighNoon.htm (accessed September 9, 2002).

Lawrence, Jennifer A. "If I Only Had the Nerve: A Feminist Critique of High Noon." Paper presented to the Popular Culture Association, Philadelphia, Pennsylvania, April 15, 1995.

Lenihan, John H. "Classics and Social Commentary: Post-war Westerns, 1946–60." *Journal of the West* 21 (October 1983): 34–42.

Lenihan, John H. *Showdown*. Urbana: University of Illinois Press, 1985.

Levy, Emanuel. "The Legacy of Auteurism." In *Citizen Sarris, American Film Critic*, edited by Emanuel Levy, 77–90. Lanham, Md.: Scarecrow Press, 2001.

———. "Sarris's Magnum Opus." *Citizen Sarris, American Film Critic*, edited by Emanuel Levy, 49–52. Lanham, Md.: Scarecrow Press, 2001.

Lipsitz, George. *Rainbow at Midnight*. Urbana: University of Illinois Press, 1994.

Lorence, James. "Cold War Hollywood: Militant Labor and the Rise of Anticommunism." In *The Suppression of* Salt of the Earth. Albuquerque: University of New Mexico Press, 1999. At www.unmpress.com/book/suppression.html (accessed November 9, 2001).

Los Angeles Times, October 30, 1951 to April 11, 2002.

Lovell, Alan. "The Western." In *Movies and Methods*, edited by Bill Nichols, 164–75. Berkeley: University of California Press, 1976.

Lyman, Rick. "Stanley Kramer, Filmmaker with Social Bent, Dies at 87." *New York Times*, February 21, 2001, A:1.

———. "Watching Movies with Wolfgang Petersen; A Boy Shaped by *High Noon*." *New York Times*, March 30, 2001, E1.

MacCabe, Colin, and Paula Jalfon, prods. *Howard Hawks: American Artist*. Documentary, British Film Institute, 1997. Broadcast on American Movie Classics channel, November 10, 2002.

McClay, Howard, "High Noon," *Los Angeles Daily News*, July 29, 1952 (Fairbanks Center).

Maltby, Richard. "A Better Sense of History." In *The Book of Westerns*, edited by Ian Cameron and Douglas Pye, 34–49. New York: Continuum, 1996.

———. *Domesticity and Paranoia: Postwar Hollywood and American Culture*. Flinders University, Australia, n.d., at www. ehlt.flinders.edu.Au/screen /SCRN3001lectures/Introduction/SCREEN3001FirstpageFrame1.htm (accessed September 27, 2002).

———. "Film Noir: The Politics of the Maladjusted Text." *Journal of American Studies* 18 (1984): 49–71.

———. *Harmless Entertainment*. Metuchen, N.J.: Scarecrow Press, 1983.

———. "Made For Each Other: The Melodrama of Hollywood and the House Committee on Un-American Activities, 1947." In *Cinema, Politics and Society in America* edited by Philip Davies and Brian Neve, 76–96. New York: St. Martin's Press, 1981.

Maltin, Leonard. *The Making of High Noon*. Documentary included with fortieth anniversary video re-release of *High Noon*, 1992.

Markfield, Wallace. "The Inauthentic Western." *American Mercury* 74 (September 1952): 82–86.

Mast, Gerald. *Film, Cinema, Movie*. Chicago: University of Chicago Press, 1983.

Mast, Gerald and Marshall Cohen. "The Film Artist: Introduction." In *Film Theory and Criticism*, edited by Gerald Mast and Marshall Cohen, 637–41. New York: Oxford University Press, 1979.

Mast, Gerald and Bruce Kawin. *A Short History of the Movies*. Boston: Allyn & Bacon, 1996.

May, Lary. "Movie Star Politics: The Screen Actors' Guild, Cultural Conversion, and the Hollywood Red Scare." In *Recasting America*, edited by Lary May, 125–53. Chicago: University of Chicago Press, 1989.

McBride, Joseph. *Frank Capra: The Catastrophe of Success*. New York: Simon & Schuster, 1992.

McGilligan, Patrick. "John Berry, Man of Principle." *Film Comment* 31 (May–June 1995): 46–58.

Mellen, Joan. "Film Noir." In *Political Companion to American Film*, edited by Gary Crowdus, 137–44. Chicago: Lakeview Press, 1994

———. "The Western." In *Political Companion to American Film*, edited by Gary Crowdus, 469–75. Chicago: Lakeview Press, 1994.

Meyer, William R. *The Making of the Great Westerns*. New Rochelle, N.Y.: Arlington House, Publishers, 1979.

Meyers, Jeffrey. *Gary Cooper*. New York: Morrow, 1998.

Miller, Laura. "Reel Lives." *Salon.com*, December 16, 2002.

Mitchell, Lee Clark. *Westerns*. Chicago: University of Chicago Press, 1996.

Mulholland, John. High Noon, *A Look Forward*, n.d., at http://www. coopandpapa.com/modalive/highnoonprogram.htm (accessed July 7, 2003).

Naremore, James. "An ABC of Reading Andrew Sarris." *Citizen Sarris, American Film Critic,* edited by Emanuel Levy, 175–83. Lanham, Md.: Scarecrow Press, 2001.

———. *More Than Night.* Berkeley: University of California Press, 1998.

Navasky, Victor. *Naming Names.* New York: Viking, 1980.

Neve, Brian. *Film and Politics in America: A Social Tradition.* London: Routledge, 1992.

———. "A Past Master of His Craft: An Interview with Fred Zinnemann." *Cineaste* 29 (Winter 1997): 15–19.

New York Times, March 19, 1951 to March 30, 2002.

Newsweek 30 (September 15, 1947): 13.

Nichols, Bill, ed. Movies and Methods. Berkeley: University of California Press, 1976.

Nichols, Mary P. "Law and the American Western: High Noon." *The Legal Studies Forum* 22, no. 4 (1998): 591–605.

Nitpickers website, Nitpickers.com/movies/titles/2343.html (accessed August 24, 2002).

Nolletti, Arthur, Jr. "Conversation with Fred Zinnemann." In *The Films of Fred Zinnemann,* edited by Arthur Nolletti Jr., 11–36. Albany: State University of New York Press, 1999.

Obits web site, Obits.com/ bridgeslloyd.html (accessed March 3, 2002).

O'Neill, William L. *A Better World.* New York: Simon & Schuster, 1982.

Pacific Film Archives website, www.bampfa.berkeley.edu/cgibin/ifetch?PFA_Filmnotes+74565919630+F (accessed December 15, 2002).

Palmer, Christopher. *The Composer in Hollywood.* London: Marion Boyars, 1990.

———. *Dimitri Tiomkin: A Portrait.* London: T. E. Books, 1984.

———. "Tiomkin." *Sight and Sound* 55 (Spring 1986): 78–79.

Parish, James Robert, and Don E. Stanke. *The All-Americans.* New Rochelle, N.Y.: Arlington House, 1977.

Park, William. "The Losing of the West." *The Light Trap* 11 (Spring 1974): 2–5.

Peary, Gerald, at www.geraldpeary.com./filmproject/outline.html (accessed December 12, 2002).

Pells, Richard. *The Liberal Mind in a Conservative Age.* New York: Harper & Row, 1985.

———. *Not Like Us.* New York: Basic, 1997.

Perez, Gilberto. Review of *Gunfighter Nation: The Myth of the Frontier in Twentieth-Century America* by Richard Slotkin (New York: Atheneum, 1993). *The Nation* (October 25, 1993): 466–70.

Phillips, Gene D. "Fred Zinnemann: An Interview." *Journal of Popular Film and Television* 7,/ no. 1 (1978): 56–66.

Prince, Stephen. "Historical Perspective and the Realist Aesthetic in *High Noon* (1952)." In *The Films of Fred Zinnemann,* edited by Arthur Nolletti Jr., 79–92. Albany: State University of New York Press, 1999.

Pumphrey, Martin. "Why Do Cowboys Wear Hats in the Bath." In *The Book of Westerns*, edited by Ian Cameron and Douglas Pye, 50–62. New York: Continuum, 1996.

Pye, Douglas. "The Collapse of Fantasy." In *The Book of Westerns*, edited by Ian Cameron and Douglas Pye, 167–73. New York: Continuum, 1996.

———. "Introduction: Criticism and the Western." In *The Book of Westerns*, edited by Ian Cameron and Douglas Pye, 9–21. New York: Continuum, 1996.

Rand, Ayn. *Film Guide for Americans.* Los Angeles: Motion Picture Alliance for the Preservation of American Ideals, 1950. At Michigan State University website, http://digital.lib.msu.edu/onlinecolls/display.cfm?TtleNo=168&FT=gif&I=001 (accessed December 12, 2002).

Rapf, Joanna E. "Myth, Ideology and Feminism in *High Noon*." *Journal of Popular Culture* 23, no. 4 (Spring 1990): 75–80.

Recchia, Edward. "Film Noir and the Western." *The Centennial Review* 4, no. 3 (Fall 1996): 601–14.

Redelings, Lowell K., "'High Noon' A Suspenseful Western Film," *Hollywood Citizen-News*, August 14, 1952 (Fairbanks Center).

———, "The Hollywood Scene," *Hollywood Citizen-News*, August 19, 1952 (Fairbanks Center).

Reeves, Richard. "The Last Angry Men." *Esquire* 89 (March 1, 1978): 41–48.

Reid, John Howard. "A Man for All Movies." *Films and Filming* 13 (May 1967): 4–11.

"The Reviewer Re-Viewed: A Conversation Between Andrew Sarris and Richard Schickel." *Directors Guild of America Magazine* (March 2001), at www.dga.org (accessed October 12, 2002).

Richards, Jeffrey. "Frank Capra and the Cinema of Populism." In *Movies and Methods*, edited by Bill Nichols, 65–77. Berkeley: University of California Press, 1976.

Rivette, Jacques. "Six Characters in Search of Auteurs." In *Cahiers du Cinema: The 1950s*, edited by Jim Hillier, 31–46. Cambridge: Harvard University Press, 1985.

Roffman, Peter, and Jim Purdy. *The Hollywood Social Problem Film.* Bloomington: Indiana University Press, 1981.

Roffman, Peter, and Beverly Simpson. "Stanley Kramer." In *Political Companion to American Film,* edited by Gary Crowdus, 235–36. Chicago: Lakeview Press, 1994.

Rogin, Michael Paul. *The Intellectuals and McCarthy: The Radical Specter.* Cambridge, Mass.: MIT Press, 1967.

———. *Ronald Reagan: The Movie.* Berkeley: University of California Press, 1987.

Rohauer, Raymond. *Fred Zinnemann.* Brochure for a Museum of Modern Art retrospective, 1957.

Roud, Richard. "Introduction." In *Cinema: A Critical Dictionary*, edited by Richard Roud, 1–20. New York: Viking, 1980.

Ryan, Cheyney. "Print the Legend." In *Legal Reeling*, edited by John Denvir, 23–43. Urbana: University of Illinois Press, 1996.

Sanders, Terry, and Freida Lee Mock. *Word into Image: Portraits of American Screenwriters: Carl Foreman*. Video production. Santa Monica, Calif.: American Film Foundation, 1981.

Sarf, Wayne M. *God Bless You, Buffalo Bill*. Rutherford, N.J.: Fairleigh Dickinson University Press, 1983.

Sarris. Andrew. *The American Cinema*. New York: Da Capo, 1996 (reissue of 1985 revision).

———. "Notes on the Auteur Theory in 1962." In *Film Theory and Methods*, edited by Gerald Mast and Marshall Cohen, 650–65. New York: Oxford University Press, 1979.

———. "Preface." In *Talking Pictures*, edited by Richard Corliss, xi–xv. New York: Penguin, 1975.

———. *Confessions of a Cultist*. New York: Simon & Schuster, 1971.

Sayre, Nora. *Running Time*. New York: Dial Press, 1982.

Schatz, Thomas. *Hollywood Genres*. Philadelphia: Temple University Press, 1981.

———. "The Western." In *Handbook of American Film Genres*, edited by Wes Gehring, 25–46. New York: Greenwood, 1988.

Schein, Harry. "The Olympian Cowboy"(translated from the Swedish by Ida M. Alcock). *American Scholar* (Summer 1955): 309–20. Quoted in Philip French. *Westerns*. London: Secker & Warburg, 1977.

Scheuer, Philip K., "Gary Hits Target on Stroke of Noon," *Los Angeles Times*, August 14, 1952, III-8. Archived in the Academy of Motion Picture Arts and Sciences Margaret Herrick Library, Beverly Hills, California.

Schickel, Richard. "Advantage, Andy." In *Citizen Sarris, American Film Critic*, edited by Emanuel Levy, 111–22. Lanham, Md.: Scarecrow Press, 2001.

———. *Gary Cooper*. London: Pavilion Books, 1985.

———. *Gary Cooper: American Life and Legend*. Documentary copyrighted by and shown on Turner Classic Movies channel, 1991.

Schrader, Paul. "Notes on Film Noir." In *Film Genre Reader II*, edited by Barry Grant, 213–26. Austin: University of Texas Press, 1995.

Schwartz, Nancy Lynn. *The Hollywood Writers' War*. New York: Alfred A Knopf, 1982.

Scotchie, Joe. "Peter King's Lonely Vote." *Long Island Business News*, January 1, 1999, at LongIsland.com (accessed August 13, 2002).

Selig, Mike. *Cinema Texas Program Notes*. Department of Radio/Television/Film, University of Texas at Austin, vol. 16, no. 2, February 28, 1979, 1–8.

Shepard, Richard F. "'Duke,' an American Hero." *New York Times*, June 12, 1979.

Silver, Alain and Elizabeth Ward, eds. *Film Noir: An Encyclopedic Reference to the American Style*. Woodstock, N.Y.: Overlook Press, 1979.

Sitton, Bob, "Refocusing the Western," review of Edward Countryman and Evonne von Heussen-Countryman, *Shane* (London: British Film Institute, 1999), *Film-Philosophy* 4, no. 24 (October 2000), at http://www.film-philosophy.com/vol4-2000/n24sitton (accessed November 14, 2002).

Sklar, Robert. "Empire to the West: Red River." In *Howard Hawks*, edited by Jim Hillier and Peter Wollen, 152–62. London: British Film Institute, 1996.

———. *Movie-Made America*. New York: Vintage Books, 1975.

Slotkin, Richard. *Gunfighter Nation*. New York: Atheneum, 1992.

———. "Gunsmoke and Mirrors." *Life* 16 (April 5, 1993): 60–68.

Spoto, Donald. *Stanley Kramer: Filmmaker*. New York: Putnam, 1978.

Stanbrook, Alan. "A Man For All Movies, the Films of Fred Zinnemann, part II." *Films and Filming* 13 (June 1967): 11–15.

Stankowski, Rebecca House. "Night of the Soul: American Film Noir." *Studies in Popular Culture* 9, no. 1 (1986): 61–83, at http://library.calumet.purdue.edu/nitesoul.htm (July 17, 2002).

"Stanley Kramer." In *Current Biography*, Vol. 12. New York: H.W. Wilson, 1983.

Stempel, Tom. *FrameWork*. New York: Continuum, 1991.

Swindell, Larry. *The Last Hero*. Garden City, N.Y.: Doubleday, 1980.

Tatum, Stephen. "The Classic Westerner: Gary Cooper." In *Shooting Stars*, edited by Archie P. McDonald, 60–86. Bloomington: Indiana University Press, 1987.

Thomas, Bob. *King Cohn*. New York: Putnam, 1967.

Thompson, Kristin. *Breaking the Glass Armor*. Princeton, N.J.: Princeton University Press, 1988.

Thomson, David. "The Winding Road of the Western Hero." *New York Times*, August 20, 2000, Sec. 2-29.

Tiomkin, Dimitri, and Prosper Buranelli. *Please Don't Hate Me*. Garden City, N.Y.: Doubleday, 1959.

Tompkins, Jane. *West of Everything*. New York: Oxford University Press, 1992.

Tuska, Jon. *The American West in Film*. Westport, Conn.: Greenwood, 1985.

———. *The Filming of the West*. New York: Doubleday, 1976.

Twain, Mark, "The Man That Corrupted Hadleyburg: And Other Essays and Stories," New York: Harper, 1903.

United States Congress. *Annual Report of the Committee on Un-American Activities for the Year 1952*. Excerpted in *Film Culture* (Fall–Winter 1970): 77–78.

United States Congress, 82nd Congress, 1st Session. Hearings Before the Committee on Un-American Activities. "Communist Infiltration of Hollywood Motion Picture Industry—Part 5." Testimony of Carl Foreman. September 24, 1951, 1753–71.

Variety, September 19, 1951, to December 8, 1965.

Wald, Malvin. "Carl Foreman." In *Dictionary of Literary Biography*, Volume 26, *American Screenwriters*, 104–9. Detroit: Gale, 1984.

Walsh, David. "Andrew Sarris and American Filmmaking," review of *"You Ain't Heard Nothin' Yet": The American Talking Film, History & Memory, 1927–1949,* by Andrew Sarris. *World Socialist Web Site,* July 1, 1998, at http://www.wsws.org/arts/1998/july1998/sarr-j01.shtml (accessed June 6, 2000).

———. "Why Was Stanley Kramer So Unfashionable at the Time of His Death?" *World Socialist Web site,* February 28, 2001, http://www.wsws.org/articles/2001/feb2001/kram-f26.shtml (accessed February 28, 2002).

Warshow, Robert. "Movie Chronicle: the Westerner." In *Focus on the Western,* edited by Jack Nachbar,. 45–56. Englewood Cliffs, N.J.: Prentice-Hall, 1974.

Wayne, John. Interview in *Playboy* 18 (May 1971): 75–92.

Whitehall, Richard. "The Heroes Are Tired." *Film Quarterly* 21 (Winter 1966–1967): 12–24.

Whitfield, Stephen J. *The Culture of the Cold War.* Baltimore: Johns Hopkins University Press, 1996.

Wiley, Mason, and Damien Bona. *Inside Oscar.* New York: Ballantine, 1986.

Williams, Gordon. *The Queen Bee and the Stork Club, or Hedda Hopper's Hollywood,* n.d., at www.sonic.net/~doretk/ArchiveARCHIVE/1's%20of%20a%20Kind/HeddaHopper.html (accessed August 17, 2002).

Wills, Garry. *Reagan's America.* Garden City, N.Y.: Doubleday, 1987.

Wollen, Peter. "Signs and Meaning in the Cinema: The Auteur Theory." In *Movies and Methods,* edited by Bill Nichols, 529–42. Berkeley: University of California Press, 1976.

Wood, Robin. "Rio Bravo." In *Howard Hawks: American Artist,* edited by Jim Hillier and Peter Wollen, 87–102. London: British Film Institute, 1996.

Wright, Will. *Sixguns & Society.* Berkeley: University of California Press, 1975.

Yacowar, Maurice. "Cyrano de H.U.A.C." *Journal of Popular Film* 5 (January 1976): 68–75.

Yarbrough, Tinsley E. "Those Great B-Western Locations." *Western Clippings,* Special Limited Edition. Albuquerque: Boyd Magers, n.d.

Zinnemann, Fred. "A Conflict of Conscience" (Interview). *Films and Filming* 6 (December 1959): 7, 34.

———. Interview. *American Film* 11 (January–February 1986): 12–13, 62, 66–67.

———. *A Life in the Movies: An Autobiography.* New York: Scribner, 1992.

Zinnemann, Tim. Letter to *Time Out,* London, May 14, 1997.

Zolotow, Maurice. *Shooting Star.* New York: Simon & Schuster, 1974.

Index

About the Author

Jeremy Byman, who has a Ph.D. in political science and M.A. in cinema studies, has taught political science and film courses at several colleges and universities. He was the film reviewer for an arts and entertainment weekly for nineteen years. This is his seventh book.

LIBRARY
ST. LOUIS COMMUNITY COLLEGE
AT FLORISSANT VALLEY